English

English

Meaning and Culture

A<small>NNA</small> W<small>IERZBICKA</small>

OXFORD
UNIVERSITY PRESS

2006

OXFORD
UNIVERSITY PRESS

Oxford University Press, Inc., publishes works that further
Oxford University's objective of excellence
in research, scholarship, and education.

Oxford   New York
Auckland   Cape Town   Dar es Salaam   Hong Kong   Karachi
Kuala Lumpur   Madrid   Melbourne   Mexico City   Nairobi
New Delhi   Shanghai   Taipei   Toronto

With offices in
Argentina   Austria   Brazil   Chile   Czech Republic   France   Greece
Guatemala   Hungary   Italy   Japan   Poland   Portugal   Singapore
South Korea   Switzerland   Thailand   Turkey   Ukraine   Vietnam

Copyright © 2006 by Oxford University Press, Inc.

Published by Oxford University Press, Inc.
198 Madison Avenue, New York, New York 10016

www.oup.com

Oxford is a registered trademark of Oxford University Press.

Library of Congress Cataloging-in-Publication Data
Wierzbicka, Anna.
English : meaning and culture/Anna Wierzbicka.
p. cm.
Includes bibliographical references and index.
ISBN-13 978-0-19-517474-8; 978-0-19-517475-5 (pbk.)
ISBN 0-19-517474-7; 0-19-517475-5 (pbk.)
1. English language—Semantics.   2. Great Britain—Civilization.
3. English-speaking countries—Civilization.
4. English language—Foreign countries.
5. Language and languages—Philosophy.   I. Title.
PE1585.W53 2006
420.1'43—dc22   2005047789

Cover Art: Thomas Gainsborough, Mr and Mrs Andrews. Courtesy of National Art Gallery, London.
Bought with contributions from the Pilgrim Trust, the National Art Collections Fund, Associated
Television Ltd, and Mr and Mrs W.W. Spooner, 1960.

9 8 7 6 5 4 3 2 1

Printed in the United States of America
on Acid-free paper

Acknowledgments

I would like to express my gratitude, and acknowledge my debt, to Cliff Goddard, who read successive drafts of all the chapters and provided invaluable feedback. Many semantic analyses presented in the book incorporate his ideas. His help was indispensable.

The Australian Research Council funded the research assistance without which I would not have been able to complete this project. I am very grateful both to the ARC and to several research assistants, who provided (at different times) not only invaluable practical and technical help, but also extremely helpful ideas, comments, and suggestions. They were: Anna Brotherson, Laura Daniliuc, Anna Gladkova, Brigid Maher, Elisabeth Mayer, Donna Toulmin, Jock Wong, and Kyung Joo Yoon. In the last phase of the work on the project, I also had the benefit of wide-ranging research support and many discussions with my research associate, Ian Langford. Anna Gladkova undertook the onerous task of preparing the index.

I had the opportunity to discuss many of the analyses presented in this book at my Seminar on Semantics at the Australian National University. I want to thank the participants for their ideas and also for their enthusiasm, which was for me a great source of encouragement and joy.

Two persons particularly closely involved in the thinking behind this project were my daughters, Mary Besemeres and Clare Besemeres, who over the years spent hundreds of hours discussing with me, and arguing about, the meaning of quintessentially English words like *right* and *wrong*, *reasonable* and *unreasonable*, or *fair* and *unfair* (without equivalents in my native Polish) and of Anglo values and assumptions associated with them. My husband John read the whole manuscript and suggested innumerable rephrasings aimed at making my English prose sound a little more 'Anglo' ('reasonable' and 'dispassionate') than it otherwise might have done.

For helpful discussions on particular topics, I would like to thank James Franklin, James Grieve, Douglas Porpora, Arie Verhagen, and Zhengdao Ye.

I am particularly indebted to my editor at Oxford University Press, Peter Ohlin, whose suggestions and advice on this, as on earlier projects, have been invaluable.

Two chapters of the book (2 and 6) are partially based on papers published earlier. They are "Right and wrong: From philosophy to everyday discourse" (*Discourse Studies* 4(2): 225–252) and "English causative constructions in an ethnosyntactic perspective: Focusing on LET" (In Nick Enfield, ed., *Ethnosyntax*. Oxford: Oxford University Press, 2002, 162–203).

Contents

PART I

MEANING, HISTORY, AND CULTURE

Chapter 1

English as a Cultural Universe

1.1. English—the Most Widely Used Language in the World

Few would now disagree with the view expressed in Quirk et al.'s (1985, 2) *Comprehensive Grammar of the English Language* that "English is the world's most important language." It is certainly the world's most widely used language. As David Crystal noted more than a decade ago in his *Encyclopedic Dictionary of Language and Languages* (1992, 121), it is spoken "by a large and ever-increasing number of people—800,000,000 by a conservative estimate, 1,500,000,000 by a liberal estimate. . . . It has official status in over 60 countries. Estimates also suggest that at least 150 million people use English fluently as a foreign language, and three or four times this number with some degree of competence. . . . English is also the language of international air traffic control, and the chief language of world publishing, science and technology." Crystal's more recent estimates are even higher (Crystal 2001, 2003a, 2003b). In the words of the Indian American linguist Braj Kachru (1997, 69), "the hunger for learning the language—with whatever degree of competence—is simply insatiable."

Given the rapidly expanding role of English in the contemporary world, it is hardly surprising that numerous books concerned with different aspects of English, both scholarly and pedagogical, are published every year. And yet there is one striking gap in this literature: although many books have been and are being published that link the Japanese language with Japanese culture or Chinese language with Chinese culture, hardly any recent books explore the links between the English language and Anglo culture.

There are, no doubt, many reasons for this weakness within the huge literature dealing with English. I believe one of them is that in recent times considerable opposition has developed in the English-speaking world to the notion of "a culture," that is, "culture in the singular," an opposition linked with fears of 'essentialism' and 'stereotyping'.

3

Although the notion of 'Japanese culture' may be frowned on, it does not usually evoke a reaction as suspicious, or even hostile, as the notion of 'Anglo culture.' No doubt this is partly because the Japanese language is spoken mostly in one region, whereas English is widely spoken in many different parts of the world. The question "to whom does this language belong?" posed recently (with respect to German) by the German Arab writer of Moroccan origin, Abdellatif Belfellah (1996), raises more problems in the case of English than, for example, in the case of Japanese (or indeed German), and it reverberates throughout the literature on English and 'Englishes' (e.g., Hayhow and Parker 1994; Widdowson 1994). The very fact that the use of English is so widespread, and that its role in the modern world is so all-embracing, means that trying to link it with any particular culture or way of living, thinking, or feeling seems all the more problematic.

From the point of view of people in the postcolonial world, for whom the local variety of English is often their native language or the main language used outside the domestic sphere, discussions of the links between English and Anglo culture may even seem offensive or at least insensitive. From the point of view of "Anglo Celtic" speakers of English—in Britain, the United States, and elsewhere—discussions of possible links between English and Anglo culture may also seem to be best avoided. Quirk et al. (1985, 16), for example, emphasize the "cultural neutrality" of English:

> English, which we have referred to as a lingua franca, is pre-eminently the most international of languages. Though the mention of the language may at once remind us of England, on the one hand, or cause association with the might of the United States on the other, it carries less implication of political or cultural specificity than any other living tongue.

The authors do not deny the English language any cultural underpinning altogether:

> But the cultural neutrality of English must not be pressed too far. The literal or metaphorical use of such expressions as *case law* throughout the English-speaking world reflects a common heritage in our legal system; and allusions to or quotations from Shakespeare, the Authorized Version, Gray's *Elegy*, Mark Twain, a sea shanty, a Negro spiritual or a Beatles song—wittingly or not—testify similarly to a shared culture. The Continent means "continental Europe" as readily in America and even Australia and New Zealand as it does in Britain. At other times, English equally reflects the independent and distinct culture of one or the other of the English-speaking communities. (Quirk et al. 1985, 16)

If English, which "may remind us of England," nonetheless "equally reflects" the culture of numerous other communities, then the notion of a "shared culture" would seem to require some further discussion. But the subject is not mentioned again in that book. Crystal's (2003b) influential recent books on the subject do not dwell on the issue of language and culture either. For example, his *Cambridge Encyclopedia of the English Language* (2003a), after noting that "English is now the dominant or official language in over 75 territories" (rather than 60, as in Crystal 1992), goes on to comment: "With over 60 political and cultural histories to consider, it is difficult to find safe generalizations about the range of social functions with which English has come to be identified. General statements about the structure of the language are somewhat easier to make" (Crystal 2003a, 106).

Clearly, if it is difficult to find "safe generalizations" about the social functions of English, the same applies to its cultural underpinnings, which are not discussed in the *Cambridge Encyclopedia of the English Language* any further.

It is understandable that more than sixty cultural histories can't be all discussed at length in a one-volume encyclopedia. But the question still suggests itself: what about the "shared culture" mentioned, for example, by Quirk et al.'s A *Comprehensive Grammar of the English Language* (1985)? The founder of modern general linguistics, Wilhelm von Humboldt, affirmed that "there resides in every language a characteristic world-view . . . every language contains the whole conceptual fabric and mode of presentation of a portion of mankind" (1988, 60). Although Humboldt's language may now seem dated, twentieth-century "language-and-culture" studies have not undermined this view—quite the contrary. Should we now modify Humboldt to say "every language but English"? Because English, unlike other languages, is "neutral"—a purely functional international language free from the baggage of any particular history and tradition? Or perhaps because English is so diversified that while sixty or more different traditions may be reflected in it there isn't any one tradition that provides some sort of shared "conceptual fabric" (in Humboldt's sense)?

With the growing importance of English in the contemporary world, there is an increasing urgency to the question of whether there is an irreconcilable conflict between, on the one hand, the view that English is shared by people belonging to many different cultural traditions and, on the other, the notion that English itself—like any other language—is likely to have certain cultural assumptions and values embedded in it.

The position taken in this book is that while there are many "Englishes" around the world (all of them worthy of recognition, appreciation, and study), there is also an "Anglo" English—an English of the "inner circle" (Kachru 1985, 1992), including "the traditional bases of English, where it is the primary language: . . . the USA, UK, Ireland, Canada, Australia and New Zealand" (Crystal 2003b, 60) and that this Anglo English is not a cultural tabula rasa.

1.2. English and Englishes

As the provocative title of Tom McArthur's *The English Languages* (1998) indicates, the word *English* (in the singular) and the phrase *the English language* have for many commentators become problematic. With the expansion of English worldwide came its diversification, and so many different varieties of English are now used in the world that the propriety of the term *English* itself is increasingly called into question.

For millions of "ordinary people," however, especially those who have their hearts set on learning "English" or having their children learn "English," the news that according to some language professionals "English" does not exist any more is unlikely to be of much interest. On the other hand, the notion that there are many varieties of English and that in some contexts it may be appropriate to use the term "English" with a modifier can be relevant outside academic circles. The distinction between, for example, "British English" and "American English" is widely accepted as useful.[1]

It is also recognized that some other language varieties are sufficiently close to British English and American English to be perceived as "varieties of English" and yet are more different from British English and American English than these two are from one another—for example, Indian English, Nigerian English, and Singapore English.

Braj Kachru's (1985) proposed distinction between the "inner circle" and the "outer circle" of English has been widely accepted in the literature as pertinent and helpful. In accordance with this distinction, we can say that, for example, Australian English—different as it is in many ways from both British and American English— belongs nonetheless to the inner circle, whereas, for example, Singapore English belongs to the outer one.

Differences between different "varieties of English" have often been adduced in the literature as an argument against linking the concept of "English" with that of "culture": how can English be an expression of culture (so the argument goes) if it is used in so many different societies and if there are so many different "Englishes"? As I have argued for decades, however, the fact that there are many varieties of English, linked with different societies and different cultural traditions, supports rather than undermines the Humboldtian view of language as an expression of culture.

For example, the unique character of Australian English, consistent with the unique aspects of Australian culture, illustrates the closeness of the links that exist between the language spoken by a given community and its distinctive way of living and thinking (i.e., its culture). At the same time, the fact that Australian English shares a great deal with British English—more so than it does, for example, with Singapore English—reflects the common cultural heritage of Britain and Australia.

I have been studying Australian English as an expression of Australian culture for more than two decades (Wierzbicka 1984, 1986a, 1991, 1992, 1997, 2002a, 2003a, 2003b). I have also studied (on a much more modest scale) Singapore English as an expression of Singapore culture (Wierzbicka 2003c; Besemeres and Wierzbicka 2003; for a much more extensive study, see Wong 2004a, 2004b, 2005). In both cases, a contrastive perspective is of paramount importance: it is illuminating to compare Australian English with British English and to compare Singapore English with Anglo English.

Kachru's concept of the inner circle reflects his interest in distinguishing the "new Englishes" (such as Indian English and Singapore English) from the older varieties. My own interest in identifying aspects of the shared cultural core of the older varieties makes the term "Anglo English" more appropriate than the contrastive term "English(es) of the inner circle" (not to mention cryptonyms like ENL, from "English as a native language," which are problematic for a variety of reasons, as well as technical and cryptic).

In essence, however, "Anglo English" studied in this book corresponds to Kachru's "English of the inner circle." Although Anglo English, too, is an abstraction, it is in my view a concept that captures an important historical and cultural reality. It goes without saying that Anglo English is neither homogeneous nor unchanging, and the fact that, for example, Australian English differs in many ways from British English makes this abundantly clear. At the same time, to adequately characterize Englishes of the outer circle such as Singapore English and to fully understand them as expressions of local cultures, it is eminently useful to be able to compare and contrast them with Anglo English.

In a sense, this book is, primarily, about Anglo English, both as an expression and as a vital aspect of Anglo culture.[2] The phrase "Anglo culture" is even more controversial these days than "the English language" (not to mention "Anglo English," which is hardly used at all): to speak of Anglo culture is to run the risk of being accused of essentialism, imperialism, even racism. But the attacks on the notion of culture in general, and Anglo culture in particular, are little more than academic *Schöngeisterei*. As I wrote a decade ago, arguing against anthropologists Wolf and Wallerstein, "while cultures are not immutable essences, with clearly drawn boundaries, to reduce us all as cultural beings to members of myriad groups—cross-cutting, overlapping, and ever evolving, means to overlook the central reality. . . . no one is more acutely aware of this reality than a bilingual who lives his or her life in two languages and cultures" (Wierzbicka 1997, 18; see also 2005a, 2005b).

The concept of Anglo culture is potentially particularly useful to millions of immigrants to Anglophone countries like Britain, the United States, and Australia. To deny the validity of this concept means to deny the immigrants culture training, which is essential to their social advancement. The same applies to Anglo English, which is an essential part of Anglo culture.

Western scholars who are more focused on ideology than on the realities of the immigrant condition have sometimes claimed that immigrants to English-speaking countries do not need (Anglo) English and are not interested in acquiring it. For example, Claire Kramsch (1998, 26) asserts that "immigrant language learners are increasingly disinclined to . . . buy into the values and beliefs that underpin native speaker language use in their respective communities." Kramsch supports her view on this point with a quote from the French semiotician Julia Kristeva (1988, 10): "The absorption of foreignness proposed by our societies turns out to be inacceptable [*sic*] for modern day individuals, who cherish their national and ethnic identity and their intrinsically subjective, irreducible difference."

As an immigrant myself, I can testify that such high-minded theoretical views do not match the reality of my own life. Much as I cherish my national and ethnic identity (not to mention my personal "irreducible difference"), during my thirty odd years of living in Australia I have had to absorb a good deal of "foreignness" (that is, in my case, "Angloness" and also "Anglo-Australianness") into my ways of speaking, thinking, and acting. In particular, I have had to learn to use words like *fair, reasonable*, and *presumably* (not to mention *privacy*)—and not just words, but the ideas and the cultural scripts associated with them. Autobiographical testimonies by other immigrants to English-speaking countries are more consistent with my experience than with Kristeva's theorizing (e.g., Chow 1999; Danquah 2000; Besemeres and Wierzbicka, to appear).

1.3. An Illustration: Words, Scripts, and Human Lives

I will illustrate both the shared cultural content of Anglo English and its heterogeneity with two examples from Australian English. In a book-length essay entitled "Made in England: Australia's British Inheritance," the eminent Australian writer David Malouf (2003) emphasizes distinct features of Australian English such as "boldness and colour," which "arise for the most part from a strong sense of humour and larrikin sense of play, qualities we might trace back to the cockney and criminal world of the convicts" (p. 49). At the same time, Malouf (who is himself of part-English, part-Lebanese background) stresses "'kindred' ties and feelings" linking Australians with all those who share the same habits of mind fostered and transmitted by the English language and often alien to people "outside the magic circle of Anglo-Saxon thinking" (p. 61). It is a circle characterized by "an ethos in which terms like 'fair play,' 'sportsmanship,' 'team spirit' are meant to be translated out of the narrow world of schoolboy rivalry and endeavour into the world of action and affairs; not as metaphors but as practical forms of behaviour" (p. 60). It is fascinating to see how often the untranslatable English word *fair* (see chapter 5) recurs in Malouf's discussions of "Australia's British inheritance" (as when he talks, for example, about Australia's bonds "with people with whom we have a special relationship in which we are trusted to 'play fair', and to speak fair too," p. 61).

The concept of 'fairness', "made in England" but elaborated in Australia and given a special role in expressions like *fair dinkum* and *a fair go* (see OED 1989; AND 1988), is a good example of both the cultural continuity and cultural change evidenced by Australian English.

A concept that illustrates innovation rather than continuity in Australian English and culture is that of 'dobbing'. *Dob*, defined by the *Oxford English Dictionary* (1989) as "to betray, to inform against," is described by it as "Australian slang," but as I argued in earlier work, this description is misleading: "in Australia, *dob in* is not slang . . . , it is simply part of common everyday language, a word which is (still) in general use and which is clearly one of the key words in Australian English" (Wierzbicka 1997, 212).

I have examined the meaning and the cultural significance of the verb *dob* and the noun *dobber* in a number of earlier publications (see Wierzbicka 1984, 1986a, 1991, 1992, 1997). Here, I will restrict myself to pointing out that the salient presence of these words in Australian English is linked with a powerful "cultural script": "it is bad to *dob*, it is bad to be a *dobber*" (i.e., to "dob" on one's "mates")—a script that probably has its roots, at least partly, in the solidarity of convicts vis-à-vis the authorities in the early period of Australia's history.

The value of the traditional taboo against dobbing is now contested in public discussion in Australia,[3] but the concept remains salient in everyday thinking and continues to influence people's behavior, as the following recent quotes illustrate:

> A lot of kids who are bullied to say that "you just don't dob."
> (Queensland Government 2002)
> The Australian attitude of "don't dob in a mate" prevails within the
> adolescent subculture thus reducing the possibility that older teens will
> disclose those that bully. (Betlem 2001)
> Dob in a dumper. (Butler 2003)

The continued relevance of the concept of 'dobbing' in people's (including immigrants') lives is illustrated by the following testimony of a Chinese immigrant in Australia:

The other day at the dinner table, I asked my 6 year-old boy, who is attending kindergarten, what he had learned in school. He happily told me that they learned how to deal with bullies. My son used his five fingers of his right hand and said: "First, talk friendly, second, talk firmly, third, ignore, fourth, walk away, and . . ." Before he finished, my nephew, who is a 18 year-old Chinese boy, said: "Report to the teacher." My son burst into tears and said: "No, not report to the teacher. I don't like the word 'report.' It doesn't sound nice." From my son's reaction to the word "report" I can see that the concept of "report" is different from my Chinese nephew to my half-Chinese half-Australian Australian-born son. For a Chinese the word "report" is just to tell something to somebody, but "report" to an Australian kid in this context is not just to tell somebody something. It is "dobbing in," which is a big offence, not at all encouraged in Australian culture. This incident reminds me of another situation in China. If you ask a primary school student the question "What do you do if someone in school bullies you or does a bad thing to you?" 90% of the answers will be "Go to report to the teacher." "Talk friendly, but firmly, ignore and walk away" are not part of the main attitude in dealing with bullies in China. "Dobbing in" in China is not as offensive as in Australia. (Wang 2005)

Neither language nor culture stands still, but in every period there are certain shared understandings and shared cultural norms that find their expression in a community's ways of speaking. Words, with their meanings, provide evidence of the reality of such shared understandings. Anglo English words like *fair* and *fairness* are constitutive of Anglo culture, and distinctively Australian words like *dob* and *dobber*, of Australian culture. Neither expressions like *English*, *Anglo English*, and *Australian English* nor those like *Anglo culture* and *Australian culture* stand for any unchanging monolithic realities with sharp boundaries. They stand for certain constructs, but these constructs are not fictions, and they have an impact on people's lives.

1.4. "Anglo English" as a Historical Formation

In the recent second edition of his *English as a Global Language* (2003b), in which he notes "an increasingly public recognition of the global position of English" (p. ix) and the "continued spread of a global lingua franca" (p. x), Crystal continues, nonetheless, to use the singular: English, not Englishes (unlike, for example, McArthur 1998, whose book bears the provocative title *The English Languages*). He also endorses the Humboldtian view of languages: "Language is the repository of the history of a people. It is its identity." If all the different varieties of English don't have an identifiable shared cultural core, this book argues that the historically shaped Anglo English does have such a core. And arguably, it is this Anglo English that provides a point of reference for all the other Englishes, one without which the notion of Englishes would not make sense either.

Despite the apparent reticence on this subject prevailing in many centers of English studies in Britain and in America, in places like Hong Kong, Singapore, India, and Africa, far away from the historical moorings of Anglo culture, it is often felt keenly that the cultural dimensions of the English language do need to be addressed.

For example, David Parker, professor of English at the Chinese University of Hong Kong, in his inaugural lecture (in 2001) unequivocally rejected the view that English is somehow culturally neutral and warned of the dangers of ethnocentrism inherent in such a view:

> Western modernity has a long history of discursively constructing itself, using vo- cabularies largely derived from the Enlightenment, as the template for the future of mankind. This is why it is so important to understand Western modernity not as a universal destiny but *as a particular historical formation*, with its own multifiliated traditions, and not least the vocabularies of disengaged rationality and universal- ism that are internal to these traditions. These, as we all know, can be precise and necessary instruments for the sciences, law or administration, but to use them rather than be used *by* them requires an understanding of their history, as part of the "tra- ditionary content" handed down through the English language. (Parker 2001, 10)

In his defense of a cultural approach to the teaching of English, Parker draws on E. D. Hirsch's (1987) concept of "cultural literacy" and on the support given to this concept by the eminent African American sociologist and historian, Orlando Patterson: "Patterson says that it is a fatal error to see the demands of cultural literacy in terms of one dominant sector of society imposing its culture and values on the rest. . . . Those who achieve only a narrow functional literacy are . . . condemned to the lower-paid positions . . . the more powerful people, those at the tops of organizations, will increas- ingly be those who have achieved cultural literacy" (Parker 2001, 3).

It is interesting that Patterson passionately embraces two views that many others tend to see as incompatible: that "the English language no longer belongs to any single group or nation" and that "cultural literacy" in Hirsch's sense — that is, the cultural heritage mediated through the English language — should be seen as something rele- vant and potentially valuable to *all* groups of speakers of English.

Parker characterizes the focus of his lecture as "the roots and trunk of English rather than its branches" (2001, 7, a metaphor used earlier in Kachru 1995); and he elaborates the image by likening English to the banyan tree:

> The key feature of this tree for me is the fact that it has aerial roots. They symbol- ize the fact that historically newer forms of English, taking root in different cul- tural soil, sooner or later begin to nourish the whole tree. The whole tree is global: the new roots reach out in all directions. But after a while, most of the roots, old and new, begin to entangle and fuse — which may be an emblem of the language in the globalized future.

This book, too, seeks to focus more on the roots and the trunk of English than its branches, while at the same time seeing the whole tree as a kind of banyan tree. It gives special attention to those Anglo concepts which are both particularly impor- tant and invisible to insiders, in keeping with the insight of the philosopher Hans-Georg Gadamer (on whom Parker also draws) that often "concepts which we use automatically contain a wealth of history" (Gadamer 1975, 11).

As I will try to show in this book, everyday English words like *right* and *wrong, facts, evidence, reasonable, fair, exactly, precisely,* and *really* (among many others) are important instances of words that are "used automatically" and yet contain "a wealth of history" and pass on a great deal of cultural heritage. Words of this kind may be invisible to native speakers, who simply take them for granted and assume that they must have their equivalents in other languages. By analyzing such "invisible" words, their history, and their current use, including the conversational routines and discourse patterns associated with them, I will try to show from a linguistic point of view the extent to which (as Parker puts it) "cultural knowledge constitutes a shared social space" (Parker 2001, 4), handed down through, and embedded in, the English language itself.

Gadamer writes that "if we are not to accept language automatically, but to strive for a reasoned historical understanding, we must face a whole host of questions of verbal and conceptual history" (1975, 11). This book tries to face such questions of "verbal and conceptual history," seeking to explore English as a vehicle of culture(s) and, in particular, to explore the links between aspects of English and aspects of Anglo culture.

Given the spread and the diversity of English in the modern world, it is important to study various local Englishes as vehicles of local cultures—for example, Singapore English in Singapore or Indian English in India (see chapter 9). It is also important to study these local Englishes through local literatures—and to recognize and explore the new cultural impulses brought to English literature worldwide through the work of cross-cultural writers (such as Maxine Hong Kingston, V. S. Naipaul, Rohinton Mistry, Jhumpa Lahiri, Chinua Achebe, and Ahdaf Soueif).

But the very notion of a "cross-cultural writer" implies that there *are* some cultures to begin with, obviously not discrete, unchanging, and homogeneous but nonetheless real enough to make a person feel bicultural—as many contemporary writers in Britain, America, and elsewhere testify that they do (Besemeres 1998, 2002; Pavlenko 2001). The testimony of immigrants to English-speaking countries (e.g., Chow 1999; Danquah 2000; Besemeres and Wierzbicka, to appear) shows with particular clarity how important it is for them to study English in its cultural context and not in a cultural vacuum, if cultural misunderstandings are not to mar their linguistic and social progress.

1.5. The Tendency to Mistake "Anglo English" for the Human Norm

It has been fashionable in linguistics in the last few decades to speak of "universals of politeness" and of universal "principles of conversation" (e.g., Grice 1975; Leech 1983; Brown and Levinson 1987; for discussion, see Wierzbicka 2003a; Goddard and Wierzbicka 2004; Goddard 2004). But these putative universals (usually stated in a technical English and thus untranslatable into most other languages) are unlikely to be of much help in cross-cultural encounters, where people of different backgrounds need to learn, above all, in what ways their cultural worlds differ, not what they have in common. Immigrants to Britain, America, or Australia need to learn, for example, to understand the meaning of unfamiliar conversational routines and to grasp the cultural values and assumptions reflected in them. Similarly, it is useful for Anglo speakers of English—especially in countries with a large influx of immigrants—to become aware of the cultural underpinnings of their own conversational routines and of the key concepts that they themselves live by.

In fact, many of the putative universals of politeness put forward in the literature have been shown to be simply a reflection of Anglo cultural norms. In particular
(as I argued in Wierzbicka 1985, 1991/2003a; see also Matsumoto 1988), the "freedom from imposition," which Brown and Levinson (1978, 66) saw as one of the most
important guiding principles of human interaction, is in fact an Anglo cultural value,
and the avoidance of "flat imperative sentences," which Searle (1975, 69) attributed
to the "ordinary [human] conversational requirements of politeness," does not reflect "universal principles of politeness" but, rather, expresses special concerns of
modern Anglo culture (see chapter 2).

In a recent book of popular anthropology, the author suggests that the ancient
Greek injunction "know thyself" is no longer apposite; what we need to do, rather, is
to learn to "know others." But in fact, one can't learn to know others without learning to know oneself at the same time. As Humboldt put it in a famous passage, "every
language draws about the people that possess it a circle whence it is possible to exit
only by stepping over at once into the circle of another one" (Humboldt 1988, 60).
By stepping over the boundaries of one's first language, one can look at that language
from outside and then become aware of the thick web of assumptions and values embedded in it; conversely, one cannot fully appreciate the assumptions and values embedded in a "foreign" or second language without having become aware of those
embedded in one's first language. This applies also to Anglo speakers of English.

In the novel *The Return of Ansel Gibbs* by the American writer Frederick
Buechner (1957, 14), the protagonist's daughter, Anne, driving with her father and a
friend through East Harlem, notices the sign (in Spanish) "Pronto Viene Jesus Cristo,"
which she takes to mean "Jesus Christ come quickly," and she is struck by "how rude
it sounds." The friend disagrees: "*Pronto* isn't rude in Spanish. . . . It just means quick."
But the girl is not convinced: "'Come quick, Jesus Christ' then, do you like that?"
What Anne Gibbs fails to realize is not only that "Pronto viene" doesn't mean "come
quick" (but rather, "is coming soon") but also that the literal equivalent of "come
quick" doesn't sound rude in Spanish and, more generally, that "come quick" is more
likely to sound rude in Anglo English than its literal equivalent would sound in most
other languages (including many "new Englishes," such as Singapore English; see
Wong 2004a)—presumably because of the Anglo cultural emphasis on "personal
autonomy" and on "not telling others what to do" (see chapter 2; see also Wierzbicka
1985, 1991, 2003a, in press a). To learn effectively about Spanish ways of speaking,
people like Anne Gibbs need to become aware of their own unconscious assumptions and values and learn not to take them for granted as simply "normal" and
"human." At the same time, immigrants of non-Anglo background need to learn about
Anglo values and assumptions and about speech practices associated with them.

The literature on language and society often dismisses popular perceptions of
differences in ways of speaking prevailing in different cultures as "stereotyping."
Sometimes it even prides itself on its own inability to match these perceptions with
any "solid" analytical findings. For example, Miller, having set out to study misunderstandings in Japanese-American workplace interaction, finds that "contrary to
many folklinguistic theories about the respective languages, the discourse strategies
most commonly used when giving negative assessments in English and Japanese are
quite similar" (Miller 2000, 251). The author scoffs at "folk theory and popular stereo-

types [that] would lead us to blame Clint Eastwood-style Americans who blast their way through every conversation, or compromising ambiguous Japanese who produce a trail of uncertainty in their wakes" (Miller 2000, 253). She does not deny that misunderstandings occur and that they can be due to a "mismatch in cultural assumptions," but rather than seeking to replace "folk theory and popular stereotypes" with more precise generalizations about such mismatches, she seems to reject any need for generalizations in favor of examining "the tiny crevices of talk" — apparently on a case-by-case basis. "It is here, in the finely-tuned traces of everyday talk, that recurring misinterpretations and patterned misunderstandings arise and, eventually, assume the guise of grand characterizations of entire populations and ethnic groups" (Miller 2000, 253).

But surely a failure to come up with firm generalizations is anything but a virtue — whether from a theoretical or from a practical point of view. The generalizations that "ordinary speakers" come up with in their "folk theory and popular stereotypes" based on their cross-cultural experiences are no doubt often simplistic, but it should be the task of scholars to offer better generalizations, rather than abandoning the search for tenable generalizations altogether. And if our analytical tools are such that using them does not lead to any tangible results, then perhaps we should look for better analytical tools rather than dismissing "ordinary people's" perceptions as "groundless stereotyping."

The challenge is to find better ways to articulate the truth about different ways of speaking that ordinary speakers are often intuitively aware of, to separate the wheat of perception and experience from the chaff of prejudice, and to find ways of formulating generalizations that can be stated in a coherent theoretical framework and supported by hard linguistic evidence.

To say, for example, that Singapore English is an expression of Singapore culture is an abbreviated and simplified way of speaking, given that both Singapore English and Singapore culture are abstractions standing for complex and nondiscrete realities. As argued persuasively by Wong (2005), however, these abstractions are useful and revealing. The same applies to Anglo English and Anglo culture.

1.6. The Cultural Underpinnings of (Anglo) English

Countless recent publications have titles including expressions like "global English," "international English," "world English," "standard English," and "English as a lingua franca." To the best of my knowledge, however, there are no recent publications devoted to Anglo English, let alone using this expression in their titles. Yet it is precisely this Anglo English, with the Anglo cultural heritage embedded in it, that in the postcolonial and increasingly global world continues to provide a basis for talking about English in the singular.

Nothing is more revealing of the cultural underpinnings of, say, Singapore English (see Wong 2005) or Sri Lankan English (see Parakrama 1995; Fernando 1989) than a comparison of these new Englishes with the older Anglo English and its own cultural underpinnings. Needless to say, Anglo English does not stand still, and the ever-increasing penetration of new Englishes into the language of "English literature" is one obvious factor contributing to its transformation. Nonetheless, Anglo English has a sufficient measure of stability to be perceived by millions of people, on all continents, as an extremely important reality. In particular, immigrants to countries like Britain, the United States, Canada, and Australia are usually interested in "the English language" (rather than "the English languages"), and it is "the English language" that most of them feel they need to study if they are not to remain socially disadvantaged for the rest of their lives (see chapter 2).

According to Braj Kachru (1995, 1), "the concept of world Englishes demands . . . a distinction between English as a medium and English as a repertoire of cultural pluralism: one refers to the form of English, and the other to its function, its content." Kachru elaborates: "What we share as members of the international English-speaking community is the medium, that is, the vehicle for the transmission of the English language. The medium per se, however, has no constraints on what message—cultural or social—we transmit through it. And English is a paradigm example of medium in this sense" (Kachru 1995, 1).

From the point of view of world Englishes, such a distinction between English as a global medium—a "global and cross-cultural code of communication"—and Englishes as vehicles of local cultures may be useful. From the point of view of Anglo English, however, it is more problematic, for Anglo English is not a culturally neutral or culture-free medium but a cultural world of its own.

According to Kachru, it is its function as a "medium" that "has given English an unprecedented status as a global and cross-cultural code of communication" and has made it a "universal language, a language with no national or regional frontiers" (Kachru 1995, 2). The fact is, however, that in the present-day world it is Anglo English that remains the touchstone and guarantor of English-based global communication. (I do not mean here phonology but above all vocabulary and discourse patterns associated with it.) The idea advanced, for example, by Quirk (1981) (see also Stein 1979) that international English can take the form of a culturally neutral "nuclear English" and thus be divorced from the historically shaped and culture-bound (Anglo) English is in my view totally unrealistic. To see this, it is enough to consult international trade agreements such as that concluded recently between the ASEAN countries of South East Asia and the People's Republic of China (Agreement 2002), where an exceedingly Anglo English is used to ensure full reciprocal comprehensibility with legally binding consequences on both sides. (For further discussion, see chapter 9.)

The whole issue of the relationship between English as a global lingua franca and English as used in what Kachru (1985, 1992) calls the countries of the inner circle is the subject of a wide-ranging controversy, especially in educational circles concerned with the teaching of English.

One of the key questions is this: should "English as a foreign language" (EFL) try to take as its model the "native" varieties widely used in countries like Britain and the United States, or should it rather distance itself from them? According to some, "the native speaker is dead" (Paikeday 1985), and the whole notion of native speaker is "an outdated myth" (Kramsch 1998, 23). Accordingly, "instead of a pedagogy oriented toward the native speaker . . . , we may want to devise a pedagogy oriented toward the intercultural speaker." Others—especially many of those at the receiving end of progressive culture-free pedagogy—disagree. To quote the Chinese scholar Ming Li from Suzhou University in China: "The neglect of cultural factors in foreign language teaching in China in the past years was responsible for the poor performance of Chinese students in their interaction or contact with foreigners" (Li 2004, 231). The editors of the book in which Ming Li's paper was published, Kwok-kan Tam and Timothy Weiss (2004), make a more general observation:

> Recent trends in postcolonialism and the advocacy for the nativization of English, which have led to the localization of English language teaching by minimizing its Western cultural contents, run counter to the Chinese desire . . . of being globalized. In China there is a strong tendency to go against the trend of nativization by reinstating the cultural component in English language teaching. (Tam and Weiss 2004, vii)

I will return to the question of English teaching in the era of globalization in chapter 9. Here, let me adduce only one more quote on the subject, which is particularly apposite to the issue of links between language, culture, and history:

> If English is learned simply as a lingua franca—i.e. if the teaching of EFL is not firmly rooted in the cultural context of native speakers—there is a danger that it will become unidiomatic, and that EFL speakers may wrongly come to regard unidiomatic echoes of their own mother tongue as the "natural" (and therefore universally understood) mode of expression in English.
>
> With the evolution of a multiplicity of culturally autonomous Englishes, Standard English maintained as an instrument of cross-cultural communication will only be effective at the level of communicative competence to the extent that it is based on shared cultural assumptions. English has evolved as the result of a historical process, and the history of the language is an inescapable factor influencing its use even as a lingua franca. For this reason it seems inevitable that those shared cultural assumptions, to be reflected in the teaching of pragmatics in EFL, should derive from the cultural contexts of Standard English in its two most influential varieties. (Preisler 1999, 265–266)

In a telling commentary on the Anglo basis of English as an international language, the Sri Lankan linguist Thiru Kandiah (educated in Sri Lanka and Britain) has written:

> Community is created through communication, in a discourse which uses linguistic patterns and discursive conventions whose nature and manner of use are agreed on or authorized by those who go to make up the community. Indeed, it is by virtue of such agreement or shared authorization that these people emerge as a community. What induces such agreement or sharing is that it is just these patterns and conventions that construct for them the model of reality that makes sense to them, the structures of knowledge and so on that maintain it, the precise kinds of meaning that they need to convey, and so on. Not to know and control these patterns and conventions is to remain outside of the community they define, to be characterized as an "other" who has neither the entitlement nor the ability to participate actively in it. (Kandiah 1995, xxxi)

Full participation in worldwide communication in science, international law, trade, business, aviation, and many other domains requires access to a shared medium of communication, and this medium requires not only shared forms but also shared meanings. As things stand now, key Anglo English concepts such as 'fair', 'reasonable', 'evidence', 'impartial', 'bias', 'commitment', 'compromise', 'opportunity', 'efficiency', 'presumably', and 'alleged' are among the linguistic tools that create and define a worldwide Anglophone community of discourse (in Kandiah's sense) across a wide range of domains.

This book argues that the cultural semantics of such concepts and of the discourse patterns associated with them require careful and systematic study and that a study of this kind requires a suitable methodology.

1.7. A Framework for Studying and Describing Meaning

The subtitle of this book combines two words, both central to this book's approach to English: *meaning* and *culture*. So far, I have focused mainly on culture. Now I will turn more specifically to meaning, which in fact, as I will try to show throughout this book, is a key to understanding culture.

There are good reasons to think that even if all the ideological and political obstacles that stand in the way of exploring English from a cultural perspective were to be removed, it would still not be possible to explore English in this way—at least not effectively and in depth—without a semantic perspective.

Throughout the second half of the twentieth century, the study of English was dominated by the Chomskyan approach and thus was conducted "within a framework that understands linguistics to be a part of psychology, ultimately human biology" (Chomsky 1987, 1). In effect, for half a century the dominant (generativist) approach to the study of English was totally blind to culture. Focused on syntax and preoccupied with formalisms, it was also inimical to the study of meaning. This book, which studies English as a historically shaped semantic and cultural universe, radically breaks with that tradition.

There *are*, of course, books that include both *English* and *meaning* in their titles, and one would expect less opposition on a priori grounds to looking at English from a semantic perspective than to looking at it from a cultural perspective. But to explore English in depth from a semantic perspective, one needs a well-grounded semantic theory and an effective methodology. In most recent books on English that in principle are not hostile to semantic considerations, such a theoretical and methodological foundation is lacking. As a result, if they do discuss the meaning of English words, expressions, or constructions, they usually do so on an ad hoc basis. This can also be valuable, but it is not enough for a systematic and precise investigation of meanings, changes in meaning, and differences in meaning. Without such a systematic and methodologically informed investigation of meaning, it is not possible to investigate, in a rigorous way, the cultural underpinnings of English key words, pragmatized expressions, salient discourse patterns, and so on.

This book is based on the semantic theory (to be described shortly) whose name comes from the initials of the name of its main tool: the natural semantic metalanguage (NSM). This theory, whose main ideas were first presented in English in my 1972 book, *Semantic Primitives*, has since been developed in collaboration with my colleague Cliff Goddard and with valuable input from other colleagues (see, in particular, Wierzbicka

1996c; Goddard, ed., 1997; Goddard 1998; Goddard and Wierzbicka, eds., 1994, 2002). It has also been extensively tested in practice, through empirical study of a large number of diverse languages, and is now supported by a large body of semantic descriptions of aspects of many languages, carried out within the NSM framework.

The NSM approach to linguistic description is based on two fundamental assumptions: first, that every language has an irreducible core in terms of which the speakers can understand all complex thoughts and utterances and, second, that the irreducible cores of all natural languages match, so that we can speak, in effect, of the irreducible core of all languages, reflecting in turn the irreducible core of human thought.

As Leibniz argued eloquently three centuries ago, not everything can be explained. At some point, all explanations must come to an end, for a *regressus ad infinitum* explains nothing. Some things must be self-explanatory (intuitively clear), or we could never understand anything. The explanatory power of any explanation depends, therefore, on the intuitive clarity of the indefinable conceptual primes that constitute its ultimate foundation.

A natural language is a powerful system in which very complex and diverse meanings can be formulated and conveyed to other people. The NSM theory of language assumes that the intelligibility of all such meanings depends on the existence of a basic set of conceptual primes that are intuitively clear (and presumably innate) and do not require any explanations and that constitute the bedrock of human communication and cognition. Cross-linguistic empirical work undertaken within the NSM framework suggests that there are some sixty universal conceptual primes. They are set out in Table 1.1.

The first hypothesis, then, is that all languages have lexical exponents for each of the sixty or so conceptual primes (words, bound morphemes, or fixed expressions). The second, concomitant, hypothesis is that in all languages conceptual primes can enter into the same combinations. Of course, the word order and the morphosyntactic trappings may differ from language to language, but the hypothesis is that the elements, their combinations, and their meaning will be the same (see Goddard and Wierzbicka, eds., 2002). This means that just as we can have a rudimentary universal lexicon of indefinable concepts, we can also have a rudimentary universal grammar of such concepts. And if we have a minilexicon and a minigrammar, then we can have a minilanguage—a minilanguage carved out of natural languages that can be used for the description and comparison of languages, in their lexicon and grammar, and also in their discourse practices: in short, a "natural semantic metalanguage" (NSM).

Since this metalanguage is carved out of natural language (any natural language), the semantic explications and scripts constructed in it are intuitively meaningful and have psychological reality. Consequently, unlike semantic formulae based on various artificial formalisms, NSM formulae are open to verification (they can be tested against native speakers' intuitions). Being based on the shared core of all languages, the natural semantic metalanguage can serve as a "cultural notation" for the comparison of cultural values, assumptions, norms, and ways of speaking across the boundaries between societies, communities, subcultures, and epochs.

The authors of a relatively recent article entitled "Culture as an Explanatory Variable," Bond, Žegarac, and Spencer-Oatley (2000, 48), state that when they

TABLE 1.1 Table of semantic primes—English version

Substantives	I, YOU, SOMEONE/PERSON, SOMETHING/THING, PEOPLE, BODY
Relational substantives	KIND, PART
Determiners	THIS, THE SAME, OTHER/ELSE
Quantifiers	ONE, TWO, SOME, ALL, MUCH/MANY
Evaluators	GOOD, BAD
Descriptors	BIG, SMALL
Mental/experiential predicates	THINK, KNOW, WANT, FEEL, SEE, HEAR
Speech	SAY, WORDS, TRUE
Actions, events, movement	DO, HAPPEN, MOVE
Existence and possession	THERE IS/EXIST, HAVE
Life and death	LIVE, DIE
Time	WHEN/TIME, NOW, BEFORE, AFTER, A LONG TIME, A SHORT TIME, FOR SOME TIME, MOMENT
Space	WHERE/PLACE, BE (SOMEWHERE), HERE, ABOVE, BELOW, FAR, NEAR, SIDE, INSIDE, TOUCHING
Logical concepts	NOT, MAYBE, CAN, BECAUSE, IF
Augmentor, intensifier	VERY, MORE
Similarity	LIKE (AS, HOW)

• Primes exist as the meanings of lexical units (not at the level of lexemes).

• Exponents of primes may be words, bound morphemes, or phrasemes.

• They can be formally, i.e., morphologically, complex.

• They can have different morphosyntactic properties, including word-class, in different languages.

• They can have combinatorial variants (allolexes).

• Each prime has well-specified syntactic (combinatorial) properties.

After Goddard and Wierzbicka 2002.

attempted to study "differences in communication across cultures" they found in the literature "a patchwork quilt of unrelated studies, focusing on a myriad speech forms and their associated non-verbal behaviours . . . when these studies invoked culture to explain results, they made opportunistic and speculative forays into the available literature." The authors concluded that there was no "emerging paradigm or paradigms (Kuhn 1962) that could help guide future research in this topic area, so important for our twenty first century" (p. 48).

With one proviso, the NSM framework and the theory of cultural scripts based on it (see chapter 2) are proposed as just such a paradigm. The proviso has to do with the idea of "measuring cultures," which Bond and his colleagues include in their vision of what is to be done. They ask "whether more promising ways to conceptualize and measure cultures, especially when studying speech behaviour, can be found by bringing together concepts from different disciplines (including social psychology, pragmatics, linguistics, the psychology of culture)" (p. 98).

Although statistical evidence *is* used in this book, among other kinds of evidence, the theory on which the book relies offers a framework for *conceptualizing* cultures, not for *measuring* cultures. As such, however, it does provide a paradigm that I believe could guide future research into "differences in communication across cultures," including different cultures associated with different varieties of English.

In particular, as this book seeks to demonstrate, the new paradigm based on the natural semantic metalanguage makes it possible to explore in depth the cultural meanings that are embedded in Anglo English and that in the twenty-first century continue to inform the use of English in the world at large.

Thus, this book seeks to launch a new, meaning-based approach to the study of the English language. Its aim is to investigate English as a historically shaped universe of meaning and to reveal English's cultural underpinnings and their implications for the modern world.

Chapter 2

Anglo Cultural Scripts Seen through Middle Eastern Eyes

2.1. Linguistics and Intercultural Communication

"The fate of the Earth depends on cross-cultural communication." Deborah Tannen's (1986, 30) words represent no doubt only a partial truth, but it is an important part. In our increasingly "global" world, successful cross-cultural communication is essential for nations, ethnic and social groups, and individuals.

In a book entitled *Becoming Intercultural*, the Korean American scholar Young Yun Kim (2001, 1) writes: "Millions of people change homes each year, crossing cultural boundaries. Immigrants and refugees resettle in search of new lives. . . . In this increasingly integrated world, cross-cultural adaptation is a central and defining theme." "Cross-cultural adaptation" is particularly relevant to immigrants and refugees, but the need for cross-cultural understanding extends further. In modern multiethnic societies, newcomers need to learn to communicate with those already there, but those already there need, for their part, to learn to communicate with the newcomers. In a world that has become a global village, even those living in their traditional homelands need to develop some cross-cultural understanding to be able to cope with the larger world confronting them in a variety of ways.

Language has been defined, traditionally, as a tool for communication, and linguistics as the study of language. In practice, the dominant linguistic paradigm of the second half of the twentieth century had very little to do with human communication and even less, with problems of cross-cultural communication. Fortunately, in the last quarter of the century, linguistics "greened" (Harris 1993), and the sterile, formalistic approaches of generative grammar have been supplemented, if not supplanted, by approaches more concerned with meaning, culture, and people than with formalisms. Nonetheless, as far as the theory and practice of cross-cultural communication are concerned, the contribution that linguistics has made so far is still limited, and there is certainly room for much more. Arguably, progress in this domain has been hampered not only by the legacy of Chomskyan linguistics and its various offshoots but also by certain ideological pressures.

The literature on intercultural communication (including what Kim 2001 calls cross-cultural "adaptation," "competence," and "fitness") often refers to cultural learning, but it seldom tries to spell out, concretely, what it is that must be learned. To take the example of immigrants starting a new life in English-speaking countries like the United States, Britain, or Australia, the need for cultural learning and "cultural transformation" is often referred to in the literature, but attempts are seldom made to identify the Anglo cultural patterns of which the immigrants should be made aware. And if one does dare try to identify some such patterns, one risks being accused of stereotyping, as well as essentialism and sometimes even racism. The so-called new ethnicity movement, which started in the United States in the 1970s, was inimical to the idea of there being any Anglo or Anglo American culture at all. In his book *The Rise of the Unmeltable Ethnics*, published in 1972, one theorist of this movement, Michael Novak, wrote:

> There is no such thing as *homo Americanus*. There is no single culture here. We do not, in fact, have a culture at all — at least, not a highly developed one, whose symbols, images, and ideals all of us work out of and constantly mind afresh; such "common culture" as even intellectuals have is more an ideal aspired to than a task accomplished. (Novak 1972, 18, quoted in Kim 2001, 24)

The new ideology of "cultural pluralism" celebrates the notion of many diverse cultures coexisting in one country (such as the United States) and at the same time plays down the role of Anglo culture among those diverse cultures; indeed, it often questions the viability of such a notion. The English language tends to be presented as a purely functional means of communication, not associated with any cultural patterns or values. Immigrants need to learn English but do not need to learn any Anglo cultural patterns or Anglo ways of speaking — first, because there are no such identifiable patterns and, second, because even if there were, teaching them would be somehow undemocratic and reactionary. The tone of the following passage in Kim's *Becoming Intercultural* is characteristic in this respect:

> In many ethnically diverse societies, the cultural patterns widely regarded as standard are mainly those of the dominant culture. In the United States, for example, the standard cultural patterns are mainly those of Anglo-Americans. Although acquiring minority cultural patterns is a part of the overall adaptation process of newcomers, the most forceful pressure to conform generally comes from the dominant group. (Kim 2001, 51)

In this atmosphere, trying to teach immigrants some Anglo cultural patterns could easily smack of exerting undue pressure on them to "conform" and of supporting and trying to perpetuate the "hegemony" of the "dominant group." In fact, even trying to identify any Anglo cultural patterns could be taken as showing that one was unaware of variation within English and of the diversity of values, ways of thinking, and discourse patterns reflected in English speech.

In my view, there are at least two important considerations arguing against such a position. First, it denies the subjective experience of immigrants to English-speaking countries, who often discover the reality of Anglo ways of speaking the hard way, by at first painfully clashing with them and then learning increasingly to avoid the clashes and attendant pain (see Hoffman 1989; Besemeres 1998, 2002). Second, it goes against the vital interests of the immigrants, who need to acquire cultural as well as purely linguistic competence in English to be able to function successfully in the society and pursue their life goals as effectively as possible. To deny the validity of the notion of Anglo cultural patterns or Anglo ways of speaking is to place the values of political correctness above the interests of socially disadvantaged individuals and groups.

For example, in Australia there are courses of "English in academic context" for "international students," there are various cultural induction courses run by migrant resource centers, and there are counseling services for both students and migrants. What should those who offer such courses and services tell newcomers about Anglo culture? To simply deny its existence—in the name of diversity, variation, and change—is certainly an option, but one whose usefulness is limited. Talking about the value of tolerance might be more useful, because "tolerance" (with its roots in the ideal of "toleration," advanced three centuries ago by John Locke and other British thinkers) *is* a key Anglo value. But first, tolerance (and the whole family of values related to it) needs to be related to concrete speech practices (e.g., how to use and how not to use the bare imperative), and second, there are other Anglo values, also reflected in specific speech practices, that are important for successful social interaction and interpersonal communication in English-speaking countries. These speech practices need to be described and made sense of.

It should be the task of linguistics to provide models both theoretically viable and practically useful—that is, models seeking not only to explain in the abstract how cross-cultural communication and adaptation occur but also to provide practical tools that could be implemented in cross-cultural education. I believe such a model is provided by the theory of cultural scripts, whose usefulness has already been demonstrated in many descriptive studies carried out within the NSM framework.[1]

2.2. The Theory of Cultural Scripts

The way we speak reflects the way we think. Not necessarily at the individual level—a skilled speaker can conceal his or her way of thinking behind carefully chosen words and phrases. At the social level, however, ways of speaking do reflect ways of thinking, in particular, as Franz Boas (1911) emphasized nearly a century ago, ways of thinking of which the speakers are not fully conscious. They reveal, and provide evidence for, *patterns* of thought.

Ways of thinking that are widely shared in a society become enshrined in ways of speaking. Ways of speaking change as the underlying ways of thinking change. There can be a lag between the two, but as one can see by studying ways of speaking at the times of revolutions and other dramatic social transformations, ways of speaking can change very quickly, too, in response to changes in prevailing attitudes. Of course, cultures are not "bounded, coherent, timeless systems of meaning" (Strauss and Quinn 1997, 3). At the same time, however:

> Our experiences in our own and other societies keep reminding us that some understandings are widely shared among members of a social group, surprisingly

resistant to change in the thinking of individuals, broadly applicable across different contexts of their lives, powerfully motivating sources of their action, and remarkably stable over succeeding generations. (Strauss and Quinn 1997, 3)

Common expressions and common speech routines involving those expressions are particularly revealing of social attitudes. The German philosopher Hans-Georg Gadamer put it well when he said in his *Philosophical Hermeneutics*:

> Common expressions are not simply the dead remains of linguistic usage that have become figurative. They are, at the same time, the heritage of a common spirit and if we only understand rightly and penetrate their covert richness of meaning, they can make this common spirit perceivable again. (Gadamer 1976, 72)

To penetrate this "covert richness of meaning," we need an adequate methodology. I believe that such a methodology is available in the natural semantic metalanguage (NSM) theory of semantics and in the theory of cultural scripts that is its offshoot. As discussed in chapter 1, the key idea of NSM semantics is that all meanings can be adequately portrayed in empirically established universal human concepts, with their universal grammar. The key idea of the theory of cultural scripts is that widely shared and widely known ways of thinking can be identified in terms of the same empirically established universal human concepts, with their universal grammar. (See in particular Wierzbicka 1994a, 1994b, 1994c, 1996a, 1996b; Goddard 1997, 2000a; Goddard and Wierzbicka, eds., 2004, in press.)

In the last few decades, cross-cultural investigations of ways of speaking have often been conceived in terms of an "ethnography of speaking" (Hymes 1962). This perspective provided a very healthy and necessary corrective to the one-sided search for a universal "logic of conversation" and for "universals of politeness" (see Wierzbicka 2003a). The theory of cultural scripts, however, proposes that we go still further and complement the ethnography of speaking with an ethnography of thinking, and it offers a framework within which such an ethnography of thinking can be meaningfully and methodically pursued.

I do not see the ethnography of thinking as an alternative to the ethnography of speaking or, more generally, to the "ethnography of social practices." On the contrary, I believe that we discover shared ways of thinking by studying ways of doing things, including ways of speaking, and further that the study of social practices, including linguistic practices, is best seen not as a goal in itself but rather as a path to understanding a society's attitudes and values. The theory of cultural scripts represents a cognitive approach to culture and society, and it offers a methodology that allows us to explore thinking, speaking, and doing in a unified framework.[2]

The theory of cultural scripts combines an interest in the uniqueness and particularity of cultures with a recognition and affirmation of human universals, and it rejects the widespread perception that, as Sandall (2000, 19) put it, "The enemy of the particular, the local, the idiosyncratic, the cultural is the universal, and the universal is always Bad News."

In the semantic theory of which the theory of cultural scripts is an offshoot, the universal is good news, and it is the universal — in the form of universal human concepts and their universal grammar—that gives us the tools for unlocking the secrets of the particular. Every human being, and every human group, is a blend of the universal and the particular. The theory of cultural scripts is based on the assumption that we need to understand people (both individuals and social groups) in their particularity, but that we can understand them best in terms of what is shared, and that one thing that is shared is a set of universal human concepts with their universal grammar. (See Wierzbicka 1996b; Goddard 1998; Goddard and Wierzbicka, eds., 2002.)

As discussed in a number of earlier publications, the theory of cultural scripts differs from other attempts to describe and compare cultures in at least four major respects.

First, it describes cultural norms and values from within rather than from outside. Thus, the researcher does not bring to the description of a culture external conceptual categories such as 'individualism', 'collectivism', 'rationalism', 'high context', and 'low context', as is usually done in the literature (e.g., Hall 1976; Hofstede 1980; Schwartz 1994). Rather, norms and values are always identified from within—that is, from the point of view of those people who are the bearers of the postulated norms and values (and in their own language). This means that there is no common grid, no set list of categories invented by the researcher and then "applied" to various human groups. Instead, norms and values are always identified from the perspective of a given culture and presented in simple (nontechnical) formulae that are unique to that particular culture. Comparing different norms and values does not mean, in this approach, assigning different numerical scores to the *same* norms and values (e.g., 'individualism', 'collectivism', and so on). Rather, it means identifying norms and values that are unique to a given human group and tradition. At the same time, these unique norms and values are presented in a way that makes it possible to compare them: not through identical labels applied across the board but through identical building blocks out of which the different formulae are built.

This is the second major difference between the cultural script approach and all other approaches: the generalizations proposed are formulated in terms of a universal set of concepts, found in a wordlike form in all languages. Thus, although no set of universal labels is introduced or relied on by the researcher, a set of universal concepts, which are actually found in all languages, is utilized and capitalized on. As a result, the proposed formulae are both unique and comparable: each is qualitatively different from all others, and yet each constitutes a configuration of the same elements—nonarbitrary, universal, and universally understandable.

The third distinctive feature of the cultural script approach is that it is practical: it can be used in language teaching, cross-cultural education, and intercultural communication. For example, when Hofstede (1980) asserts that cultures differ in their degree of 'masculinity', degree of 'collectivism', or degree of 'uncertainty avoidance', or when E. T. Hall (1976) compares cultures as 'high context' and 'low context', such generalizations can hardly help a language learner or an immigrant. By contrast, cultural scripts formulated in simple and universal human concepts are intuitively intelligible and can be immediately practically useful. For example, an immigrant to the United States, Britain, or Australia can be introduced to the following cultural script:

[people think like this:]
when I want someone to do something
I can't say to this person: "you have to do it because I want you to do it"

This script can later be refined and expanded, and its implications for acceptable and unacceptable ways of speaking can be explored in detail, but even in this basic form it is likely to be useful. The concomitant negative script would also be useful to the newcomer:

[people think like this:]
when I don't want someone to do something
I can't say to this person: "you can't do it because I don't want you to do it"

The fourth distinctive feature of the cultural script approach is that it relies on hard linguistic evidence. In books where a culture's "dominant cultural patterns" and "value orientations" are described in terms of "individualism," "conformity," "mutability," or "low context," descriptions of this kind are usually not required to be supported by specific linguistic facts. In the cultural script approach, however, all generalizations must be so supported. For example, the two Anglo scripts formulated above are justified with reference to conversational routines such as "could you / would you do X?" (the so-called whimperatives), used instead of a bare imperative ("do X!"), which developed late in modern English and were not used, for example, in Shakespeare's language (see Brown and Gilman 1989), or the semantics of speech act verbs like *to suggest* (that someone do something), (for detailed discussion from a cross-cultural perspective, see Wierzbicka 1985, 1991/2003a, 1996a, in press a; see also section 2.7).

In this chapter I focus, in particular, on Anglo cultural scripts, approaching them from the point of view of the subjective experience of immigrants to English-speaking countries—specifically, Middle Eastern immigrants. Throughout the chapter, I quote from the testimony of one well-placed witness: Abraham Rihbany, an early-twentieth-century immigrant from Syria to America and a "migrant" from Arabic to English (in the sense of Besemeres 1998, 2002). My analysis of Anglo cultural scripts is based on linguistic evidence, not on the personal testimony of one particular immigrant, and I analyze Anglo cultural scripts as such, not Middle Eastern perceptions of these scripts. But the phenomenological perspective provided by one person's cross-cultural experience enriches, I think, an analysis based on objective linguistic evidence and adds to it a human dimension, which can be lost sight of in what is often called "linguistic science."

2.3. The Anglo Ideal of "Accuracy" and the Practice of "Understatement"

Abraham Rihbany, the author of a 1920 book entitled *The Syrian Christ* (an attempt at explaining some aspects of the Gospels by placing them in their cultural context), emigrated from Syria to the United States as a young man. Having lived for many years in America, he became acutely aware of many differences between Anglo American and "Syrian" (Middle Eastern) ways of speaking and between the cultural values reflected in them. On a visit to his homeland, he realized that over the years he had become bicultural: he still understood the Syrian cultural scripts, but in his own speech, he tended to follow the Anglo scripts. (Rihbany uses the term *Syrian* in the older sense of the word, modeled on the Arabic *Sham*, which, as Hopwood (1988, 1) says, is the name "for the region in the eastern Mediterranean between Egypt and Turkey.")[3] Thus, Rihbany wrote:

> While on a visit to Syria, after having spent several years in the West, I was very strongly impressed by the decidedly sharp contrast between the Syrian and the Anglo-Saxon modes of thought. The years had worked many changes in me, and I had become addicted to the more compact phraseology of the Western social code.
>
> In welcoming me to his house, an old friend of mine spoke with impressive cheerfulness as follows: "You have extremely honoured me by coming into my abode [*menzel*]. I am not worthy of it. This house is yours; you can burn it if you wish. My children are also at your disposal; I would sacrifice them all for your pleasure. What a blessed day this is, now that the light of your countenance has shone upon us"; and so forth, and so on.
>
> I understood my friend fully and most agreeably, although it was not easy for me to translate his words to my American wife without causing her to be greatly alarmed at the possibility that the house would be set on fire and the children slain for our pleasure. What my friend really meant in his effusive welcome was no more or less than what gracious host means when he says, "I am delighted to see you, please make yourself at home." (Rihbany 1920, 89)

In this passage, trying to analyze his experience, Rihbany links Anglo culture with the use of "compact phraseology" and the Syrian culture with "effusiveness." The term *effusiveness* (and also *impetuosity*) appears again in the following passage:

> The Oriental's impetuosity and effusiveness make his imprecatory prayers, especially to the "unaccustomed ears" of Englishmen, blood-curdling. And I confess that on my last visit to Syria, my countrymen's (and especially my countrywomen's) bursts of pious wrath jarred heavily upon me. In his oral bombardment of his enemy the Oriental hurls such missiles as, "May God burn the bones of your fathers"; "May God exterminate you from the earth"; "May God cut off your supply of bread (*yakta rizkak*)"; "May you have nothing but the ground for a bed and the sky for covering"; "May your children be orphaned and your wife widowed"; and similar expressions. (Rihbany 1920, 65)

Rihbany explains that to understand such outbursts, it is essential to realize that the speakers do not mean what they say and that Anglo norms differ from Middle Eastern norms concerning saying what one means: "It is unpleasant to an Anglo-Saxon to note how many things an Oriental says, but does not mean. And it is distressing to an Oriental to note how many things the Anglo-Saxon means, but does not say" (p. 77). In addition to compactness, conciseness, and brevity as putative Anglo values, Rihbany often speaks of the Anglo value of accuracy—from a Syrian cultural point of view, not a positive, but an irritant:

> To an unreconstructed Syrian the brevity, yea, even curtness, of an Englishman or an American, seems to sap life of its pleasures and to place a disproportionate value on time. For the Oriental, the primary value of time must not be computed

in terms of business and money, but in terms of sociability and good fellowship. Poetry, and not prosaic accuracy, must be the dominant feature of speech. (Rihbany 1920, 77)

Explaining, and defending, the value of *in*accuracy in Middle Eastern speech (in contrast to prosaic, pedantic, pedestrian and dull accuracy), Rihbany writes:

> There is much more of intellectual inaccuracy than of moral delinquency in the Easterner's speech. His misstatements are more often the result of indifference than the deliberate purpose to deceive. . . . He sees no essential difference between nine o'clock and half after nine, or whether a conversation took place on the housetop or in the house. The main thing is to know the substance of what happened, with as many of the supporting details as may be conveniently remembered. A case may be overstated or understated, not necessarily for the purpose of deceiving, but to impress the hearer with the significance or the insignificance of it. If a sleeper who had been expected to rise at sunrise should oversleep and need to be awakened, say half an hour or an hour later than the appointed time, he is then aroused with the call, "Arise, it is noon already—*qûm sar edh-hir.*" Of a strong man it is said, "He can split the earth—*yekkid elaridh.*" The Syrians suffer from no misunderstanding in such cases. They *discern* one another's meaning. (Rihbany 1920, 77–78)

Although Rihbany says in this passage that "a case may be overstated or understated," in fact in both cases he means an exaggeration: for example, saying *all* when one means *many* or saying *none* when one means *few*. In his experience, from an Anglo point of view, to say *all* when one means *many* or to say *none* when one means *few* is a sin, whereas from a Syrian point of view, it is a virtue.

Rihbany himself often speaks in this connection of "exaggeration" as a feature of what he calls "Oriental speech" and as something that Anglo culture, with its emphasis on accuracy, abhors: "Just as the Oriental loves to flavour his food strongly and to dress in bright colours, so is he fond of metaphor, exaggeration, and positiveness in speech. To him mild accuracy is weakness." Rihbany links Anglo culture's taste for 'accuracy' and distaste for 'exaggeration' with the value of "correctness." For example, he writes:

> Again, let me say that an Oriental expects to be judged chiefly by what he means and not by what he says. As a rule, the Oriental is not altogether unaware of the fact that, as regards the letter, his statements are often sadly lacking in correctness. But I venture to say that when a person who is conversing with me knows that I know that what he is saying is not exactly true, I may not like his manner of speech, yet I cannot justly call him a liar. (Rihbany 1920, 88)

It is interesting to note the use of the word *sadly* in this passage: "Oriental statements" are said to be "sadly lacking in correctness." The word *sadly* reflects here, of course, an Anglo perspective: as Rihbany emphasizes again and again, from a Syrian point of view, there is nothing sad or inappropriate about such absence of literal correctness and accuracy—quite the contrary.

What exactly does the Anglo ideal of accuracy, as intuited in Rihbany's bilingual and bicultural experience, really mean? Drawing on Goddard's (2004a) insights into the semantics of figurative language, I suggest that it means, in essence, a match between what a person wants to say with some words, and what these words actually say: ideally, the words as such should bear exactly the meaning that the person wants to convey with these words.

But this is only a first approximation. First of all, if accepted as it is stated, the script just sketched would rule out metaphorical language: a metaphor implies, as Goddard puts it, that the words themselves do not mean what the speaker wants to say with these words. Because the ideal of accuracy is not incompatible with the use of metaphors, this script should be revised, in the first instance, along the following lines: the words that a person says should say *no more and no less* than what this person wants to convey with these words; if they are metaphorical, they can say "something else," but if they are not metaphorical, they should say "no more and no less" than what the speaker wants to say.

If, however, the cultural ideal in question is aimed, primarily, at avoiding exaggeration, then the primary concern is that the words as such should *not say more* than the person wants to say with these words. It is not so much a question of "no more and no less" as of "no more." If one says *all* when one means *many*, this can be seen as a situation where the words say *more* than the person wants to say; if one says *none* when one means *few*, this, too, can be interpreted as a situation where the words say *more* than what the person wants to say. Given the Anglo practice of "understatement" (which I discuss in more detail shortly), the concern is that one should not exaggerate rather than that one should say strictly "no more and no less than what one wants to say." Rihbany is quite insightful in this regard (as he is in many others) when he says that "it is distressing to an Oriental to note how many things the Anglo-Saxon means but does not say" (Rihbany 1920, 77). This is largely what "understatement" as an Anglo speech practice is all about: expressing oneself in such a way that one's words say less than what one wants to say with these words. What is seen as important is that people should not *over*state—that is, should not exaggerate—rather than they should not *under*state what they really want to communicate.

Native speakers of English, including linguists, seldom seem to be aware of the extent to which English is perceived by cultural outsiders as the language of understatement. To quote one characteristic example—a comment on English Anglo culture by the German commentator H. Bütow:

> Everything is in the style of *understatements* [the English word is used here in the German original, A.W.], of downtoning, which the English conversation has over many generations brought to mastery. *Understatement* [again, in English, A.W.]— this is not only the opposite of what we call "Angabe" ["a full statement," A.W.], it is in England almost a worldview [*Weltanschauung*]. (Bütow 1961, 171)

In a similar vein, the Hungarian British writer, social commentator, and satirist George Mikes (1946) described "understatements" as a feature distinguishing native English speakers from foreigners (Huebler 1983, 2).

Comments of this kind could easily be dismissed as shallow stereotyping, were they not widely perceived as valid and useful by teachers of English as a nonnative language. For example, writing from a German perspective, Huebler comments:

Anyone progressing beyond the rudiments of learning English, certainly in Germany, soon finds that understatements are said to be typically English. Even someone who has not been exposed to English, if he has studied German literature at school, will come across the English word *understatement* as a literary term. The very fact that it is the English word *understatement* and not the German word *Untertreibung* that is used suggests a special affinity with the English way of life.

Attributing understatements to a predominantly English linguistic pattern of behaviour is documented in many works dealing with the English way of life. Amongst such books are those aimed specifically at teaching English as a foreign language. (Huebler 1983, 1)

Of course, it has often been pointed out that "understatement" is more characteristic of British English than it is of American English (and in Australia, it is often perceived as a feature of British English *distinguishing* it from Australian English). No doubt there is some truth in that, too. Nonetheless, downtoners, diminishers, minimizers, and deintensifiers of many kinds (to be discussed shortly) belong to the linguistic resources available to, and used by, speakers of American and Australian English, too.

Huebler (1983, 73) offers the following list of expressions commonly used in modern English as tools for understatement or downtoning (the labels are his; see also Quirk et al. 1972, 452):

compromisers:
> *comparatively, enough, kind of, more or less, quite, rather, relatively, sort of*

diminishers:
> *a little, in many/some respects, in part, mildly, moderately, partially, partly, pretty, slightly, somewhat*

minimizers:
> *a bit, barely, hardly, scarcely*

approximators:
> *almost, basically, nearly, practically, technically, virtually*

From a cross-linguistic perspective, it would be difficult not to admit that this list is very (or should I say, rather) extensive indeed. Furthermore, this wealth of downtoners is a relatively recent (roughly, post-seventeenth-century) development in English. For example, judging by Spevack's (1970) concordance to the works of Shakespeare, many elements included in the list are missing from Shakespeare's language. These missing elements include *comparatively, relatively, sort of* (as a hedge), *moderately, basically, practically, technically*, and *virtually*.

Where does the ideal of 'accuracy' or 'nonexaggeration' reflected in this wealth of 'downtoners' come from? To quote Rihbany again: "A Syrian's chief purpose in a conversation is to convey an impression by whatever suitable means, and not to deliver his message in scientifically accurate terms. He expects to be judged not by what he *says*, but by what he *means*" (1920, 81). The key word here is *scientifically*: given the central role of science in modern Anglo culture, it is understandable that scientific discourse has become in this culture, for many intents and purposes, the model of "good speech": rational, dispassionate, factually based, precise, and accurate.

One proviso, however, is needed: this is how one should speak about "things." When one speaks about people rather than things, other considerations come into play, and other scripts apply—scripts that may be alien to scientific discourse, which is about things, not people. When one speaks about people, 'tact' may be more important than strict accuracy. When one speaks about things, however, it is good to speak objectively, without undue emotion, without exaggeration, with care, with due caution, with precision, distinguishing facts from opinions, stating facts accurately, qualifying one's statements according to the strength of one's evidence, and so on. I discuss a number of these values in the subsequent sections of this chapter. Here, let me try to formulate, on the basis of the discussion so far, the cultural script for 'accuracy' and 'nonexaggeration'. I phrase these scripts in terms of certain prototypes:

> *the Anglo script for 'accuracy' and 'nonexaggeration'*
> [people think like this:]
> sometimes people say words like *all*
>   when they want to say something like *many*
> sometimes people say words like *many*
>   when they want to say something like *some*
> sometimes people say words like *none*
>   when they want to say something like *not many*
> it is not good to speak like this [i.e., to say things in this way]

The generalization suggested by these prototypes and alluded to in the phrase "speak like this" seems to be that in saying something about anything, it is not good to say "more" than what one really means—that is, than what one really wants to say about it. What is at issue here is the idea of the so-called "literal meaning" of one's words.

Although the matter requires further cross-linguistic investigation, arguably, this "literal meaning" can be interpreted as "what the words say" (see Goddard 2004a). If this line of interpretation proves tenable, we could suggest the following (generalized) Anglo cultural script:

> [people think like this:]
> when I want to say something about some things
> it will be good if I think about it like this:
>   "I will say some words now
>   I want to say something with these words
>   I don't want these words to say more"

Surely, it is this culturally inculcated disapproval of exaggeration that is responsible for the huge expansion of "hedges" of various kinds in modern English and, in particular, the great career of the word *rather*.

In older (pre-Shakespearean) English, *rather* meant "earlier" and was used in collocations like "rather or later" and "a little rather." Gradually, alongside this temporal sense of *rather* a nontemporal sense developed and spread, linked with the idea of choice (as in "this rather than something else" or "this rather than that"), including the choice of thoughts (as in "I rather think") and the choice of words (as in "or rather"). Apparently, it is only in eighteenth-century English (see Stoffel 1901, 134) that *rather* started to be used, and increasingly so, as an "anti-exaggeration device," as in the following examples from the *The Oxford English Dictionary* (the spelling of some older examples has been modernized):

> It would be rather inconvenient to you. . . . (1766)
> His appearance at the Baronet's must have been rather a silly one. (1778)

This new linguistic pattern—the use of *rather* with adjectives—suggests in itself a new cultural script: roughly speaking, an avoidance of an "unnecessary" use of the word *very* (and other words including *very* in their meaning, such as *extremely*, *highly*, etc.). This script can be formulated as follows:

> [people think like this:]
> sometimes when people want someone to know that something is big
>   they say words like "very big"
> sometimes when people want someone to know that something is bad
>   they say words like "very bad"
> it is not good if a person speaks [says things] in this way

I have chosen "very big" and "very bad" as the prototypes of exaggerated descriptions advisedly. First, "very small" can be regarded as a less clear example of exaggeration and indeed, in some contexts, as a possible tool for understatement. Second, "very good" can serve other Anglo scripts, especially those seen as conducive to harmonious social interactions, whereas in the case of "very bad," social pressures are likely to act in the opposite direction (e.g., "very good" can be useful for complimenting other people, whereas "very bad," which could be used for criticizing others or for complaining, might be seen as problematic).

Expressions like "rather big" or "rather nice" are clearly not a hallmark of scientific accuracy or precision. Nonetheless, the underlying cultural norm that "it is not good to exaggerate" is, I believe, related to the scientific revolution and to the intellectual climate that prevailed in its aftermath in the country of Bacon, Newton, Locke, and Hume. Interestingly, the words *accurate*, *accuracy*, and *precision* do not appear in Shakespeare's language at all; clearly, these words, and the meanings expressed by them, entered the English language only at the time of the scientific revolution. Since it is often assumed that the penetration of scientific ways of thinking and speaking into ordinary language is a "Western" rather than "Anglo" phenomenon, and that it affected English no more than other European languages, it is also worth noting that to this day there are no words corresponding to *accurate* and *accuracy* in German or French (although there are words corresponding to *exact* or *precise*).

The earliest example of *accurate* given by the OED is dated 1621. According to the OED, until the middle of the eighteenth century or so, *accurate* meant "careful, executed with care," as in the sentence: "An accurate diet is that when man taketh his meats in a certain measure, order, and number" (1650). Gradually, however, a new meaning developed and spread, described by the OED as "Of things . . . in exact conformity to a standard or to truth," "without special reference to the evidence of care." One example: "The term taste, like all other figurative terms, is not extremely accurate" (1756). The first OED example of *accuracy* is dated 1662, and out of context, its meaning is not quite clear. The second example, however, dated 1684, is both clear and highly instructive: "Experiments that require a greater accuracy" (1684). Here, *accuracy* does still imply care, but the link between a care for accuracy and interest in experimental science illuminates the historical process: in scientific discourse, the accuracy of results came to be seen as more relevant than the care of the scientist, and over time the meaning of the word shifted accordingly.

The history of the words *precise* and *precision* is also illuminating in this respect. The word *precise* is recorded in the OED as occurring in English from the early sixteenth century. The earliest example of the meaning defined by the OED as "neither more nor less than" comes from the end of the sixteenth century. The OED distinguishes this meaning, however, from a later one, defined as "stated with precision or exactness," and I think rightly so: *precise* in this more recent sense does not mean merely "neither more nor less" but rather "neither a little more nor a little less." The earliest example of this most recent meaning comes from the seventeenth century.

The noun *precision* (used by the OED in defining the adjective *precise*) made its appearance only in the eighteenth century, and its origin in the world of science is highlighted in the following (OED) quote from Thomas H. Huxley: "The precision of statement, which . . . distinguishes science from common information" (1877). The link between the notion of *precision* (in the modern sense) and the discourse of science—empirical and quantitative—is also well illustrated by the following OED example: "The comparison of observations is necessary in order to determine the relative degrees of precision of different sets of measurements made under different circumstances" (1885).

The current conversational routines including the words *precise* and *precisely* (as in *to be precise*, or "Precisely" used to express emphatic agreement) highlight the links between colloquial English and the values and standards of scientific discourse—links that are also reflected in the history of the English words *exact* and *exactly* and in contemporary conversational routines like *to be exact* and *Exactly!*

As documented by the OED, well into the eighteenth century *exact* meant something like "perfect" or "excellent," as in the following examples: "We all acknowledge both thy power and love to be exact, transcendent, and divine" (George Herbert, 1633) and "A very exact house and gardens" (1710).

In the eighteenth century, however, a new meaning of *exact* spread, closer to the modern meaning of *precise*, as in the following example: "The exact similarity of the two halves of the face" (1753). It is easy to see how this shift, too, could have taken place in the context of scientific discourse, as illustrated by the following example: "Having no instruments exact enough" (*Philosophical Transactions of the Royal Society of London*, 1665).

The rise of the collocations *exact science* and *exact sciences* is also illuminating in this regard, as is the subsequent reduction of *exact science* to simply *science*. In other European languages, science is divided into two kinds, "natural" (or "exact") and "human," but in English, the word *science* itself has incorporated into its meaning the notion of "exact," with the result that "the humanities" have been excluded from the realm of "science." In German, *Wissenschaft* ("science, knowledge") embraces *Geisteswissenschaften* on a par with *Naturwissenschaften*; in French, *la science* embraces *les sciences humaines* and *les sciences sociales,* as well as *les sciences naturelles* and *les sciences exactes;* but in English, *science* (without an adjective) refers normally to "exact sciences," and if other domains of human knowledge are to be regarded as science (e.g., political science, social science), they need to be seen as using the methods and standards of "exact sciences."

At this point, we may consider again the relationship between the cultural values of, on the one hand, scientific precision and accuracy and, on the other, "understatement," which might seem to be at odds. My argument that they are not can be supported with some quotes from the OED that illustrate the link between the ideal of 'precision' and the norm of "not saying too much." One characteristic example comes from Sir W. Hamilton's *Logic* (1837–1838): "A definition . . . should be precise, that is, contain nothing unessential, nothing superfluous." No mention is made here of the danger of saying "too little" — the whole emphasis is on the importance of not saying too much, and strikingly, it is the importance of not saying too much that is identified here with precision. Another example comes from L. Murray's *English Grammar* (also from OED): "Precision is the third requisite of perspicuity with respect to words and phrases. It signifies retrenching superfluities, and pruning the expression, so as to exhibit neither more nor less, than an exact copy of the person's idea who uses it" (1824). Thus, at the level of ideology, the goal is to say "neither more nor less" than what one means; in practice, however, what matters is to "retrench superfluities" and to "prune the expression," that is, to make sure that one says "no more" than what one needs to say. The implication is that saying less than what one means is not a problem and that, in fact, it may be an effective way of ensuring that one doesn't say more than what is actually meant.

The link between the ideal of precision and the practice of "understatement" is also highlighted by the nineteenth- and twentieth-century conversational strategy (noted by the OED) of saying "not exactly" to mean, ironically, "not at all" or "by no means." For example: "I wasn't exactly going to send in my checks this time" (1893), "the thought of prison doesn't exactly excite me" (1968). The OED includes also the following quote from Malcolm Muggeridge: "She was not exactly pretty even then. In fact, she was not pretty at all — which is what the use of the word 'exactly' usually signifies" (1949). This colloquial use of the expression *not exactly* illustrates both the Anglo practice of "understatement" and the saturation of colloquial English with words and notions deriving from scientific discourse. The person who says "not exactly" shows that he or she doesn't want to be "not exact," and thus is paying respect to the scientific ideals of precision and accuracy; at the same time, he or she is following the Anglo practice of "understatement."

Speaking of the rise of empiricism in seventeenth-century Britain, the Oxford philosopher and historian of ideas Felipe Fernández-Armesto remarked: "The ascendancy of senses over other means of truth-finding did not last long, even in the west, but while it endured, it made a vital difference: it gave science unique prestige — a place in the prevailing scale of values unmatched in other cultures" (1998, 155). Arguably, this unique prestige of science led to the unique prestige of scientific discourse and, consequently, of ways of speaking that imitate in some respects the norms of that type of discourse. To quote Bertrand Russell:

> Modern life is built on science in two respects. On the one hand, we all depend
> upon scientific inventions and discoveries for our daily bread and for our comforts
> and amusements. On the other hand, certain habits of mind, connected with a
> scientific outlook, have spread gradually during the past three centuries from a few
> men of genius to large sections of the population. (Russell 1948, 35)

If one thinks that it is essential to be careful not to say "all" when one means "much,"
it is easy to start saying "much" when one actually means "all," and this is what seems
to have happened in the English language. The development of new exponents of
negation such as *scarcely* and *hardly* is a good illustration of this process. If something
is "scarce," then there is very little of it, but there must be at least some. The adverb
scarcely, however, does not imply "not much"; rather, it implies "not at all." The adverb *hardly* reflects a similar process of negation arising through "understatement": if
something is "hardly possible," then it is likely to be (from the speaker's point of view)
not possible at all. Such uses of "understatement" are not regarded as inconsistent with
the value of accuracy, because the hearer is expected to be familiar with the conventions in question and to be able to interpret "not much" (in an appropriate context) as
"nothing," and "hardly" or "scarcely" as "not." The speech practice in question is not
universal, based on some putative universals of inference or politeness (along the lines
of Grice 1975; Leech 1983; Brown and Levinson 1987); rather, it is culture-specific and
rooted in culture-specific historically shaped assumptions and values.

   Thus, from a modern Anglo point of view, reflected in this history of English, it
is good to be accurate, but above all, it is good to be cautious in phrasing what one
wants to say: one needs to choose one's words carefully, one needs to "weigh" one's
words—and this means, in effect, that one must be careful not to allow one's words
to say more than what one is really prepared to say (and so to take responsibility for)
at any given moment.

   It is interesting to note in this context how guarded and cautious Anglo speech
appears from Rihbany's Middle Eastern point of view. This is not, Rihbany tells us,
how people speak in the Middle East. "Mere implications which are so common to
reserved and guarded speech leave a void in the Oriental heart" (1920, 126). Indeed,
sometimes Rihbany can't refrain from satirizing "the nice, cautious language of an
'up-to-date' [Anglo] thinker" (1920, 129), as when, for example, he tells the story of a
preacher "who was apparently [so] determined not to make 'rash statements' [that]
in speaking to his people about repentance he said this for his final word: 'If you do
not repent, as it were, and be converted, in a measure, you will be damned, to a certain extent.'" Words like *cautious*, *overcautiousness*, *guarded*, *removed*, and *qualified*
recur again and again in Rihbany's discussions of modern Anglo speech, as seen from
his native Syrian perspective. Again, comments of this kind could be seen as a case
of idle stereotyping, were they not so richly supported by linguistic evidence of the
kind cited, for example, by Huebler (1983).[4]

   The hedges chosen by Rihbany to illustrate the cautious and guarded ways of
speaking, which, from a Syrian perspective, strike him as exotic, point in particular
to an area of verbal caution that is especially characteristic of modern Anglo culture
and that highlights its close links with science, rationalism, and empiricism: the area
epitomized by modern English expressions like *to the best of my knowledge*, to which
I turn in the next section.

2.4. "To the Best of My Knowledge . . ."

In his preface to *The Syrian Christ*, Rihbany follows various cautious and modest authorial disclaimers with the following comment: "However, in Occidental, not in Oriental, fashion, I will say that to the *best of my knowledge* the statements contained in this book are correct" (1920, vii).

The cultural imperative of acknowledging the limitations of one's knowledge has a long history in Anglo culture—a history reflected in the English language and in Anglo discourse patterns. Again, Rihbany highlights the culture-specific character of this imperative by contrasting it with what he calls "Oriental speech":

> The fourth characteristic of Oriental speech is its unqualified positiveness. Outside the small circles of Europeanized Syrians, such qualifying phrases as "in my opinion," "so it seems o me," "as I see it," and the like, are almost entirely absent from Oriental speech. The Oriental is never so cautious in his speech as a certain Western editor of a religious paper who, in speaking of Cain, described him as "the *alleged* murderer of Abel"! (Rihbany 1920, 127–128)

This particular editor may indeed have taken certain Anglo cultural scripts a bit too far, but no one would deny that expressions like "the alleged murderer" are extremely important in modern Anglo discourse. It is interesting to note, therefore, that such expressions are virtually impossible to render (without long circumlocutions) not only in Arabic but also in most other European languages. For example, in Russian, the closest one could say would be, literally, "the person about whom some people say that this person killed [Abel]; I don't say that I know this" (but of course, no one would put it like this in ordinary language).

The need to distinguish, in rational discourse, between what one knows and what one thinks is one of the leitmotifs of John Locke 's *An Essay Concerning Human Understanding*. In fact, according to Locke, our knowledge ("true knowledge," 1959, 360; "clear" and "certain" knowledge, 1959, 188; "real" knowledge, 1959, 226) is extremely limited ("very short and scanty," 1959, 360). In most things that we say, therefore, we rely not on knowledge but on "judgment," and judgment involves, necessarily, many different degrees of assent.

> Our knowledge, as has been shown, being very narrow and we not happy enough to find certain truth in everything that we have an occasion to consider; most of the propositions we think, reason, discourse—nay, act upon, are such as we cannot have undoubted knowledge of their truth. . . . But there being degrees herein, from the very neighbourhood of certainty and demonstration, quite down to improbability and unlikeliness, even to the confines of impossibility, and also degrees of assent from full assurance and confidence, quite down to conjecture, doubt and distrust. (Locke 1959 [1690], 364)

Locke's ideas concerning degrees of probability and degrees of assent and the need to always distinguish between "knowledge" and "judgment"—that is, between knowing and thinking—have exercised, I believe, an enormous influence on modern English discourse and, indeed, on the English language.

Since throughout this chapter I will be quoting Locke, noting the resonance between his ideas and modern Anglo cultural scripts, I will adduce at the outset some critical assessments of the historical significance of Locke's *Essay* and its influence on modern Anglo culture.

To start with, the opening sentence of Kenneth Maclean's *John Locke and English Literature of the Eighteenth Century*: "The book that had most influence in the Eighteenth Century, the Bible excepted, was Locke's *Essay Concerning Human Understanding* (1690)." As Maclean notes, "so immediate was Locke's recognition that four editions of the *Essay* were required by 1700" (1962, 4–5). By 1710, the numbers rose to 11; by 1805, to 21; by 1860, to 32 (Aarsleff 1991). Sections of the *Essay* were frequently reproduced in the general journal of opinion *The Spectator*, and the popularity of Locke's book in society at large was quite unprecedented. According to Gabriele Jackson,"Locke's epistemology in the *Essay Concerning Human Understanding* influenced the language and the thinking of eighteenth century poets" (Ashcraft 1991, xv). Gabriele Jackson notes, "By the second quarter of the century he was generally considered . . . 'the light of the English race'" (Jackson 1991, 243), and she emphasizes that "the broad implications of Locke's epistemology fascinated not only discursive writers on specialised subjects but also authors of fiction, poetry and literary criticism, including commentators on literary style" (Jackson 1991, 246).

Locke's influence on language is emphasized by many other commentaries. To quote, for example, Yolton:

> One can find, in the tracts and pamphlets of the eighteenth century, frequent usage of Locke's terminology and concepts, . . . not only in the logic, but in works on science, in the sermons and books of theologians, in more general publications such as *The Annual Register, The Monthly Review, The Spectator*. The absorption of Lockean Language and Concepts occurred . . . almost as soon as the *Essay* appeared. (Yolton 1977, 8)

Locke's writings were also enormously influential in America, where he was widely referred to (inter alia, by leaders of the American revolution) as "the great Mr Locke." As Curti puts it, "the great Mr Locke," who "was America's philosopher during the Revolution period" (1991, 305), "in a real sense remained America's philosopher" (1991, 332).

Given the role that Locke's writings in general and his *Essay* in particular have played both in Britain and in America, it is hardly surprising that, as Ashcraft puts it, they "exercised a tremendous influence upon . . . the cultural consciousness of individuals several centuries after his death in 1704" (1991, xiii).

The parallels between the Anglo cultural scripts proposed here on the basis of linguistic evidence and the quotes from Locke's *Essay* with which this chapter is strewn provide, I suggest, striking new evidence of this influence.

To return to the topic of this section, I note that none of Locke's ideas was apparently more striking, and at the same time more persuasive, to his contemporaries than his view of human knowledge as inherently very limited. As Maclean puts it, "A principal object of the *Essay Concerning Human Understanding* is to make us realise 'what a darkness we are involved in, how little it is of Being and the things that are, that we are capable to know'" (1962, 160). According to Maclean, despite the controversy on many other points, on this main point—the limitations of human knowledge—"there was a universal assent" (1962, 160). Thus, the most immediate effect of Locke's *Essay* was "the smarting consciousness of the inferiority of man's mental endowments and the deficiencies of his knowledge" (Maclean 1962, 170). Arguably, the absence of "unqualified positiveness" in modern Anglo discourse, so striking from Rihbany's cross-cultural point of view, may well be a legacy of the "intellectual revolution" (Howell 1971, 7, quoted in Jackson 1991, 244), triggered by this main thesis of Locke's *Essay*.

Leaving aside the historical question of Locke's influence, from a cross-cultural perspective it is striking to what extent facts tend to be distinguished from opinions in modern English—striking not only from a Middle Eastern perspective, as discussed by Rihbany, but also from the perspective of other European languages—for example, Lithuanian (Drasdauskiene 1981, 57), Polish (Wierzbicka 1991, 41), and Swedish (Aijmer 1997). This emphasis on distinguishing what one knows from what one thinks is manifested, above all, in the spectacularly high frequency of the expression "I think" in spoken English. For example, according to the figures given in Aijmer (1997), in the London-Lund Corpus of English (of circa 500,000 words), there are an average 35 occurrences of *I think* per 10,000 words, and in conversational English, 51 occurrences per 10,000 words (according to the Cobuild data for "UK spoken," it would be 30 per 10,000 words), whereas in the comparable database of spoken Swedish (of circa 300,000 words) there are on average 2.6 occurrences of the closest Swedish counterpart *jag tror* (or *tror jag*), "I believe." In the Dutch databases, the highest figure for the closest Dutch expression *ik denk* is 9 per 10,000 words (Simon-Vandenbergen 1998, 311). Finally, in the Mannheim corpus of spoken German ("gesprochene Sprache"), the corresponding figures for the expressions *ich glaube* ("I believe"), *ich meine* ("I think/mean"), and *ich denke* ("I think") are, respectively, 5, 3, and 0.6 per 10,000 words. These differences—quite consistent with impressionistic observations expressed in the literature—are quite spectacular.[5]

Facts of this kind—remarkably consistent with the teachings of influential British thinkers like John Locke—suggest the presence of the following cultural script in modern Anglo culture:

> the Anglo "I think" versus "I know" script
> [people think like this:]
> if I think something about something, I can say "I think like this about it"
>   I can't say "I know it"
> it is not good if a person says about something "I know it" if they don't
>   know it

An unspoken assumption behind this script is that an unqualified statement such as "the Earth is flat" implies, indeed "says," that I know it (the meaning "I know it" being carried by the declarative mood unaccompanied by any "epistemic qualifier") (for discussion, see Wierzbicka 1998a).

This script is certainly consistent with the remarkably high frequencies of the expression *I think* in modern English Anglo discourse. Arguably, this "I know" versus "I think" script is closely linked with the accuracy and nonexaggeration scripts discussed in section 2.3—a link based on the belief that to know is "more" than to think. That belief itself is, of course, culture-specific, and it is no doubt related to the prestige of science and the cult of knowledge—especially empirical knowledge—fostered by the Enlightenment and the scientific revolution. Good (rational) thinking was also seen as valuable, but it was valuable mainly because it could lead to knowledge. By itself, thinking (no matter how good, i.e., how rational) was not enough: it needed to be combined with observation, with experience, with empirical evidence.

An opinion grounded in rational thinking is (in this cultural tradition) something valuable (most people's thoughts, Locke tells us, are not grounded in rational thinking and therefore are not really opinions, not even "wrong opinions"), and all people have the right to express their opinions. These opinions, however, should not be held out to be "more" than just that: opinions; they should not be presented as knowledge. Accordingly, when one wants to express an opinion, one should choose one's words carefully. The words should not be allowed to say more than what is really meant: they should say that this is what I *think*, not what I *know*.

The use of I *think* in modern Anglo discourse is also remarkable in another respect, in addition to its high frequency. As pointed out by a number of scholars, *I think* appears in spoken English in two variants, with and without *that* (I *think that* and I *think* Ø), and the "conversational force" of each variant (as well as its syntax and prosody) is different—so much so that Aijmer (1997) regards I *think* Ø, in contrast to I *think that*, as a discourse marker or a modal particle rather than a clause in its own right (see also Thompson and Mulac 1991).

Goddard (2003) has suggested that not only the grammatical status but also the meaning of I *think* Ø is different from that of I *think that*. I believe he is right on this point, and in proposing my explication of I *think* Ø (given later), I am following his insight that this expression does have a meaning of its own, distinct from that of I *think that*. This meaning of I *think*, which can be regarded as a downtoner, can be formulated as follows: I say: I think like this, I don't say more. This downtoner has two different interpretations and possibly even two distinct meanings, depending on the context: one in modally qualified or exclamatory (emotive) sentences, such as "I think we should go" or "I think this is awful," and another in unqualified declarative sentences, such as "I think he has left" or "I think Bill wrote it." In the modally qualified or exclamatory sentences, the component "I say I think like this, I don't say more" implies that what I say is my personal opinion, which doesn't have to be shared by others. In the unqualified ("plain") declarative sentences, however, I *think* Ø carries an additional implication: in saying I *think* Ø rather than I *think that*, the speaker disclaims knowledge—not by saying "I don't know" but by saying "I don't say: I know it."

As noted by Thompson and Mulac (1991) and others, in spoken English, I *think* Ø has an overwhelmingly higher frequency than I *think that*. For example, in Thompson and Mulac's data, I *think that* occurs 122 times (7% of the total I *think*), whereas I *think* Ø occurs 1,644 times (93%). If I am right in suggesting that in "plain" declarative sentences I *think* Ø carries the semantic component "I don't say: I know it," the high frequency of this expression is all the more telling.

It is interesting to note in this context the high frequency of the expression "I don't know" itself in English discourse and of its reduced variant "I dunno" (Scheibman 2000). For example, in Scheibman's database of American English conversation, *I don't know* (*I dunno*) is used in most cases as a "softener" indicating the speaker's uncertainty rather than lack of knowledge. Arguably, when used in such a softening way, *I don't know* (*I dunno*) qualifies the accompanying sentence with the component "I don't say: I know it."

The emergence of *I think* Ø and *I don't know* as discourse markers has been linked in the literature with universal linguistic processes of "grammaticization" and "subjectification" (see, e.g., Thompson and Mulac 1991; Scheibman 2000, 2001). Without disputing such views, I would propose that the emergence of new discourse markers in the function of epistemic qualifiers may also have culture-specific historical explanations and that this applies, in particular, to the history of epistemic qualification in the modern English language and Anglo discourse.

This brings us back to Locke's discussion of the limitations of human knowledge and the value of being cautious and tentative in one's statements. In most cases, Locke tells us, our judgments have more or less shaky grounds:

> It is unavoidable to the greatest part of men, if not all, to have several opinions, without certain and indubitable proof of their truth. (1959 [1690], 371)

> For where is the man that has incontestable evidence of the truth of all that he holds, or of the falsehood of all he condemns; or can say that he has examined to the bottom all his own, or other men's opinions? The necessity of believing without knowledge, nay often upon very slight grounds, in this fleeting state of action and blindness we are in, should make us more busy and careful to inform ourselves than constrain others. (1959 [1690], 373)

The idea of not imposing our own opinions on others, expressed in the last sentences of this quote, is another great theme in Locke's *Essay* and in modern Anglo culture as a whole. I will return to this theme later (in section 2.7). For the moment, however, I will focus on Locke's emphasis on the distinction between belief and knowledge and on the wisdom of acknowledging the limitations of one's knowledge and of refraining from saying "I know" when all one can say is "I think." What I am suggesting is that Locke's *Essay* may have contributed not only to the birth of the "I think versus I know" cultural script but also to a script suggesting that it might be good to accompany one's judgment with a disclaimer: "I don't say that I know it":

> [people think like this:]
> when I want to say to other people that I think something about something
> it can be good to say something like this at the same time:
>> "I say: I think like this
>> I don't say: I know it"

From Locke's point of view, it seems important not only to distinguish "thinking" from "knowing" but also to say openly, again and again, something like "I don't say: I know it." Furthermore, it is also important to view thinking as a matter of degree. It is knowledge that is our goal; thinking is our tool, but this tool itself has to be constantly scrutinized and evaluated in the light of our knowledge—and our ignorance. We want our opinions to be true; we know that they may not be true; accordingly, in forming and expressing opinions, we need to assess "probabilities."

> Probability is likeliness to be true, the very notation of the word signifying such a
> proposition, for which there be arguments or proofs to make it pass, or be received
> for true. (. . .) this sort of proposition is called belief, assent, or opinion, which is
> the admitting or receiving any proposition for true, upon arguments or proofs that
> are found to persuade us to receive it as true, without certain knowledge that it is
> so. (Locke 1959 [1690], 365)

According to Locke, then, to live rationally means to live largely in a world of probabilities—not in the essentially black-and-white world of "I know"–"I don't know,"
and not even in the potentially black-and-white world of "I think"–"I don't think,"
but in a gray world of probability.

> Probability wanting that intuitive evidence which infallibly determines the under-
> standing and produces certain knowledge, the mind, *if it will proceed rationally,*
> ought to examine all the grounds of probability, and see how they make more or
> less for or against any proposition, before it assent to or dissent from it; and upon a
> due balancing the whole reject or receive it, with a more or less firm assent, pro-
> portionally to the preponderancy of the greater grounds of probability on one hand
> or the other. (Locke 1959 [1690], 366)

As the grounds of probability, Locke tells us, "are the foundation on which our *assent* is built, so are they also the measure whereby its several degrees are, or ought to
be regulated" (Locke 1959 [1690], 369). Although Locke often speaks of "degrees of
assent," in fact he treats the word *degree,* I believe, as a metaphor. When it comes to
spelling out what he means by those "degrees of assent," he does not refer to different measures but to different qualitative "postures of the mind," such as belief, conjecture, guess, and so on. For example, he writes:

> As the arguments and proofs *pro* and *con*, upon due examination, nicely weighing
> every particular circumstance, shall to any one appear, upon the whole matter, in
> a greater or less degree to preponderance on either side; so they are fitted to pro-
> duce in the mind such different entertainment, as we call *belief, conjecture, guess,
> doubt, wavering, distrust, disbelief,* etc. (Locke 1959 [1690], 372).

Even in matters of religion and "divine revelation," Locke tells us, "our assent can
be rationally no higher than the evidence of its being a revelation, and that this is the
meaning of the expression it is delivered in" (1959, 383). Thus, our expressions—
our words—must not say more than what we ourselves can rationally say we think,
and what we can rationally say we think depends on the available evidence (see
Wierzbicka, Forthcoming). We can appreciate Locke's influence on Anglo ways of
thinking if we turn again, for example, to Bertrand Russell's *Sceptical Essays*, and
read Russell's definition of "rationality in opinion":

> I should define it merely as the habit of taking account of all relevant evidence in
> arriving at a belief. Where certainty is unattainable, a rational man will give most
> weight to the most probable opinion, while retaining others, which have an appre-
> ciable probability, in his mind as hypotheses which subsequent evidence may show
> to be preferable. (Russell 1948, 45–46)

This brings us to another feature of modern English discourse that from a cross-
cultural perspective is quite striking: the proliferation of various linguistic tools for

qualifying one's statements, for hedging one's assertions, and for differentiating the strength of one's assent to a proposition. This applies in particular to epistemic verbal phrases like *I suppose* and epistemic adverbs like *probably* (see chapters 7 and 8).

Thus, from the point of view of Rihbany's home culture, distinguishing between "I know" and "I think" and, in addition, qualifying one's statements in various ways appears to be a "highly differentiated and specialized" mode of thinking and speaking. From an Anglo cultural perspective, however, such distinctions are crucial.

2.5. Anglo Respect for "Facts"

English expressions like *to the best of my knowledge* or *as far as I can tell*, which are so striking from a Syrian and, more generally, cross-cultural point of view, point to the cultural emphasis on distinguishing not only what one thinks from what one knows but also what one knows oneself from what people in general can know. Roughly speaking, it is a distinction between 'personal knowledge' and 'public knowledge'. "Facts" do not always constitute widely shared knowledge, but they are always 'public' in the sense of being accessible *in principle* to public scrutiny and not subject to the vagaries of individual ways of thinking. Hence the perception is that they are "hard" ("hard facts"), "plain," and "stubborn" and that they "will not go away." They can be relied on and must be paid attention to. There are few features of modern Anglo culture as distinctive as its respect for "facts." (Cf. Shapiro 2000.)

How old is the notion of "facts" in Anglo culture? To many speakers of English, the question may seem strange. Haven't "facts" always been there? Aren't they simply a "fact of life," a notion as necessary and fundamental as time and place? To these people the news might come as a shock that there are no "facts" (in the plural) at all in Shakespeare. The word *fact* in the singular does occur in Shakespeare's works, but its meaning is different from that familiar from modern English discourse. The older meaning of *fact*, found inter alia in Shakespeare, is defined by the OED as "a thing done or performed" and is illustrated with the following example from an act issued by Henry VIII in 1539: "Every such . . . person shall be adjudged a traitor, and his fact high treason." The syntax itself ("his fact") shows clearly that the meaning of *fact* here must be different from the modern one. In modern discourse, facts do not belong to anyone; they are public. They must be anchored in people's experience and in observation, not just in someone's thinking (an inference is not a "fact"). They must be knowable, and they must be empirical. In essence, the definition of this modern sense of the word *fact* offered by the OED reflects all these aspects quite well:

> *fact*
>> 4. Something that has really occurred or is actually the case; something certainly known to be of this character; hence, a particular truth known by actual observation or authentic testimony, as opposed to what is merely inferred, or to a conjecture or fiction: a datum of experience, as distinguished from the conclusions that may be based upon it.

The OED says "the datum of experience," but presumably what is meant is not purely subjective experience (for example, a feeling or a sensation) but a "datum" that can be verified by other people, a "given"—presumably, "objectively given." It is interesting to note in this connection how factual the word *data* has come to sound in ordinary English. The philosopher's "sense data" can be subjective, but the ordinary English *data* sounds as objective and factual as *fact* itself.

The importance of facts in this new sense in modern Anglo culture can be gleaned from the following OED examples:

> These facts plainly show that. . . . (1745)
> Facts are stubborn things. (1749)
> The reader, instead of observations or facts, is presented with a long list of names. (1774)
> Facts are more powerful than arguments. (1782)
> It is an undoubted fact of human nature that the sense of impossibility quenches all will. (1809–10)
> One fact destroys this fiction. (1836)
> The very great advantage of being fact and not a fiction. (1875)

Thus, facts are stubborn, facts cannot be doubted, facts show things plainly, facts are more powerful than arguments, and so on. The birth and spread of new expressions based on *fact*, such as *in fact, a matter of fact, the fact of the matter, as a matter of fact, in actual fact*, and *in point of fact* (and also their extensions such as *a matter-of-fact tone, a matter-of-fact way*), provide striking linguistic evidence for the great cultural importance of this new concept. In particular, the expression *matter(s) of fact* started to be used in English in the seventeenth century to delimit "a sphere of knowledge that lay beyond dispute" (Bauman and Briggs 2003, 51). As Shapin and Schaffer (1985) have documented in detail, "matters of fact," which had a basis in experimental science, started to be sharply distinguished from "matters of opinion." They were "the foundations of proper natural philosophical knowledge" (p. 40), and they constituted "the property of the whole community that accepted them" (p. 321). The shift from the seventeenth-century "matter of fact" as a key philosophical notion to the present-day "semantically bleached" discourse marked *as a matter of fact* is a vivid illustration of the absorption of the Enlightenment thinking by everyday English. (Another interesting family of English expressions, semantically related to *fact*, has developed around the word *case*, as in *this is the case*, also without counterparts in other European languages.)

As a first approximation, I think we could explicate the concept of 'fact' as follows: to say that something is a fact is to say that it "really happened" and that "people can know it." This is not quite satisfactory, however, because, first, the word *really* requires an explanation no less than the word *fact* itself, and second, a fact doesn't have to be an event. For example, it is a fact that Paris is the capital of France (and it could be included as such in a brochure entitled, for instance, "Basic facts about France"), yet clearly, that Paris is the capital of France is not something that happened (an event). On the other hand, abstract truths that have nothing to do with times and places—for example, that 2 plus 2 equals 4—are less likely to be referred to as "facts." It would seem, therefore, that to be regarded as a "fact," a piece of knowledge cannot be based on thinking alone but must be somehow "empirical"—linked in some way with some people's physical experience—prototypically, with seeing (compare "evidence"). Furthermore, "facts" must be open to confirmation by other people; for example, a truth arrived at through an inner experience or regarded by the experiencer as revealed to them by God would not be referred to as a "fact." Thus, while a short definition of *facts* could be simply "things that people can know," a fuller definition would need to refer, in some way, to people's experience and also to some publicly available "verification procedure." This brings us to the following explication of the word *facts*, based on the prototype of such secure and verifiable knowledge:

> *facts*
> a. people can know that it is like this
> b. they can know it as they can know that something is in a place if they see that place
> c. if someone wants to know that it is like this they can do something
> d. other people can do the same

This definition shows that the word *facts* refers to human knowledge that is both shared (and therefore can be "objective") and regarded as rooted in experience. Arguably, the concept encapsulated in this word bears witness to the influence of empiricism and the scientific revolution on European and, in particular, Anglo thinking in modern times.

The eighteenth-century English writer Tobias George Smollett remarked: "Facts are facts, as the saying goes" (Stevenson 1958, 610), and it is interesting to see that at the time when he wrote, *facts are facts* was already regarded as a common saying. There is no such saying in Arabic, Chinese, Korean, Japanese, or Malay; for that matter, there is no similar saying in other European languages either. Similarly, the English collocation *hard facts* does not seem to have an equivalent in other languages—not even European languages.

For example, the *Langenscheidt Standard German Dictionary* (1983) glosses the expression *the hard facts* as "die nackten Tatsachen," literally, "the naked facts." The word *nackten* implies "nothing added" (no more, like English *bare facts*), but it loses the implication of the "power" of facts—a power that has to be acknowledged and cannot be resisted. Similarly, the *Collins Robert French Dictionary* (1990) glosses *the hard facts* as "la réalité brutale ou non-deguisée," literally, "the brutal, or undisguised, reality"—not a set and colloquial expression conveying respect and acceptance. The colloquial English expression *hard facts* is a telling example of British empiricism crystallized into a drop of everyday language and folk-philosophy.

The English expression *to know something for a fact* is also telling. *For a fact* is here an intensifier, vouchsafing the reliability of the knowledge: the implication is that if I "know something for a fact," I can be certain of it—more so than if I merely "know" it. Moreover, if I tell others about something that "I know it for a fact" then the information can count as more reliable than if I had merely said that "I know it." Again, there are no analogous expressions in other European languages.

Judging by the evidence from historical dictionaries, the concept of 'facts' spread in Europe in the eighteenth and nineteenth centuries, but nowhere did it seem to acquire the high status reflected, e.g., in the English saying *facts are facts*, in the collocation *hard facts,* or the expression *I know it for a fact,* not to mention more recent expressions like *fact-finding mission* or *misrepresent the facts* (cf. Shapiro 2000.)

Rihbany reminisces about his Syrian native village as follows:

> A neighbour of mine in a Mount Lebanon village makes a trip to Damascus and comes to my house of an evening to tell me all about it. He would not be a Syrian if he did not give wings to his fancy and present me with an idealistic painting of his adventure, instead of handing me a photograph. I listen and laugh and wonder: I know his statements are not wholly correct, and he knows exactly how I feel about it. We both are aware, however, that the proceedings of the evening are not those of a business transaction, but of an entertainment. My friend does not maliciously misrepresent the facts; he simply loves to speak in poetic terms and is somewhat inhospitable to cross-examination. (Rihbany 1920, 88)

Rihbany says that his friend "does not maliciously misrepresent the facts," and presumably the idea of a "fact" does not enter his friend's mind at all. What Rihbany is really trying to do in this passage is to explain that the Anglo ideal of faithfully and accurately "representing the facts" is culture-specific. As a first approximation, we can try to portray this ideal in the form of the following two cultural scripts:

> [people think like this:]
> if someone says to other people about something: "this happened"
>   it is good if these people can know because of this what happened
> [people think like this:]
> if someone says to other people about something: "it happened like this"
>   it is good if these people can know because of this how this thing
>   happened

These scripts may sound as if they were directed against lying, but in fact they are not based on the concepts 'true' and 'not true'. The primary concern reflected in them is not whether the speaker is telling the truth but rather whether he or she is a reliable source of knowledge about what happened and how it happened. What is at issue, then, is not truth but knowledge and, more precisely, the representation of "facts."

In the 1981 Paramount film *Indiana Jones and the Raiders of the Lost Ark,* the hero, a professor of archaeology, tells his students: "Archaeology is about facts. Not truth. If it's truth you're interested in, Dr. Tyree's philosophy class is down the hall." In the postmodernist atmosphere of many contemporary classrooms, the "hard facts" of yesteryear have also begun to melt, but in colloquial English and the mainstream culture reflected in it, the concept of 'facts' still appears to be going strong—and, judging by linguistic evidence, so are the cultural scripts based on it.

In Shakespeare's works, we find the tautology "truth is truth" (*Measure for Measure*) and also the rhetorical question "is not the truth truth?" (*I Henry IV*). It appears, however, that gradually the sense of certainty shifted from "truth is truth" to "facts are facts." For some time, the two—*truth* and *fact*—were used together as if they were complementary, as in the statement (cited by the OED) that "the said Commissioners are to report to this Board the Truth of the Fact." Later on, *truth* and *fact* could be used side by side as if they were virtually interchangeable, as in the words of the nineteenth-century English writer Thomas Carlyle: "Truth, fact, is the life of all things" (quoted in Stevenson 1958, 610). Gradually, however, the older respect for truth appears to have been replaced in Anglo culture with respect for facts (see Wierzbicka 2002d). In contemporary culture, "truth" is no longer seen as essential, at least not in interpersonal relations, as the expression *white lies* testifies. This is not to say that lying is no longer regarded in Anglo culture as something bad, but the meaning of *lying* appears to have changed—roughly, from saying, intentionally, something untrue to saying, intentionally, something untrue and presenting it as information about some facts. More precisely, the meaning of *lie* appears to have expanded to include the component indicated in bold in the formula below:

when X said it X was lying. =
a. X said something like this: "I want you to know that Z" to someone
b. X knew that Z was not true
c. **X wanted this someone to think that Z was true**

For example, if I say to the hostess "that was delicious," I may be saying, intentionally, something untrue without "lying," because my utterance is clearly offered as a compliment, not as a piece of information. (The conversational purpose of a compliment is to make the addressee "feel something good," not "know something.")

In her memoir *New York* (2001), the Australian writer Lily Brett (who was raised in Australia) writes: "Some untruths are essential. For example, compliments that are not entirely accurate, and other forms of kindness or flattery. Sometimes it doesn't make sense to tell the truth. Sometimes it would be just plain stupid" (p. 82). Brett contrasts these cultural assumptions, which she accepts, with those of her father—a Polish Jewish Holocaust survivor, of whom she says that "he is fond of the truth." Present at an interview given by his daughter, the father embarrasses her by interrupting and contradicting what she has said. Brett writes: "I couldn't believe it. 'It didn't happen the way you said it did,' my father said. I didn't want to start a family argument in front of the journalist. I glared at my father. He deflected my glare. 'The truth is the truth,' he declared" (p. 84). This saying corresponds to the Polish expression "co prawda to prawda" (lit. "what truth that truth"), which may have been at the back of her father's mind; from a contemporary Anglo perspective, however, it seems too inflexible and too absolute: "facts" are "facts" (because facts are "plain," "simple," and "hard"), but "truth" is no longer simply "truth."

It is interesting to note in this context that the expression *it's a fact that . . .* is used in contemporary English to insist that something is undeniable, whereas *it's true that . . .* is used as a partial concession and at the same time a likely prelude to disagreement: *it is a fact that . . .* precludes further discussion, but *it's true that . . .* is likely to be followed by *but* ("it's true that . . . but . . .")—another indication that facts are perceived as hard, but truth is not.

Jane Austen's novel *Pride and Prejudice* opens with the memorable sentence: "It is a truth universally acknowledged that a single man in possession of a good fortune must be in want of a wife." Today this sentence sounds dated because it is no longer widely assumed (in the world of Anglo discourse) that there are, or ever can be, any "truths universally acknowledged." On the other hand, linguistic evidence suggests that it is still widely assumed that if something is a "fact," then it does need and deserve to be "universally acknowledged," and also that "disregard for facts" is always reprehensible. Not so in many other cultures.

Rihbany contrasts the Anglo "respect for facts" with the Middle Eastern lack of such respect as follows:

> The Oriental's partial disregard for concrete facts has led his Anglo-Saxon cousin to consider him as essentially unveracious. . . . I have no doubt that the Oriental suffers more from the universal affliction of untruthfulness than does the Anglo-Saxon, and that he sorely needs to restrict his fancy, and to train his intellect to have more respect for facts. Nevertheless, I feel compelled to say that a clear understanding of some of the Oriental's modes of thoughts will quash many of the indictments against his veracity. (Rihbany 1920, 76)

The vignettes offered by Rihbany suggest that while in Syrian discourse truth is frequently appealed to, this is often done for emphasis, and that there is no expectation that what is being asserted, or even vouched for as "truth," would strictly correspond to "facts":

> I remember how those jovial men who came to our house to "sit"—that is, to make a call of indefinite duration—would make their wild assertions and back them up by vows which they never intended to keep. The one would say, "What I say to you is the truth, and if it is not, I will cut off my right arm"—grasping it—"at the shoulder." . . . To such speech we always listened admiringly and respectfully. But we never had the remotest idea that the speaker would carry out his resolution, or that his hearers had a right to demand it from him. He simply was in earnest. (Rihbany 1920, 83)

Such vignettes and such comments throw into relief the salience of "facts" in Anglo culture and the importance of a good understanding of cultural scripts concerning "facts" for successful cross-cultural communication.

2.6. "Cool Reason": To Think vs. to Feel

Commenting on his cross-cultural experience, Rihbany emphasizes again and again what he perceives as the relative absence of emotion in Anglo discourse. In particular, recalling Syrian ways of speaking, he marvels at what he sees as the ideal of "coolheadedness" in Anglo culture. I have already quoted his statement that—in contrast to an Anglo person—"a Syrian's chief purpose in a conversation is to convey an impression by whatever suitable means, and not to deliver his message in scientifically accurate terms" (Rihbany 1920, 81). In Rihbany's view, these different attitudes to the use of "scientifically accurate terms" are related to different attitudes to emotion. The Syrian

> does not expect his hearer to listen to him with the quizzical courtesy of a "coolheaded" Englishman, and to interrupt the flow of conversation by saying, with the least possible show of emotion, "Do I understand you to say," etc. No;

he piles up his metaphors and superlatives, reinforced by a theatrical display of gestures and facial expressions, in order to make the hearer *feel* his meaning. (Rihbany 1920, 83)

It would be easy to exaggerate the "antiemotionalism" of Anglo culture, and of course, here as elsewhere, one needs to recognize different strands in this culture, different registers, different genres, different subcultures, and so on. Nonetheless, linguistic evidence supports the impression of immigrants like Rihbany that there are in Anglo culture certain scripts cautioning speakers against showing—*in certain circumstances*—"unrestrained" emotion in their speech. The emergence in modern English of the word *dispassionate* is one such piece of evidence. The Concise OED defines this word, characteristically, as "free from emotion, calm, impartial," and the phrasing of this definition is revealing: not "*lacking* in emotion" but "*free* from emotion." The cultural message carried by the word *dispassionate* (and also by the OED definition of it) is that it is a good thing if one's speech is—at least under certain circumstances—free from emotion. Under what circumstances exactly? Rihbany's use of the word *coolheaded* gives us a clue as to his own interpretation of the main Anglo script directed against a show of emotion. Emotion can be seen as inimical to reason; "too much feeling" can be seen as an obstacle to "good thinking."[6] Speaking of cross-cultural misunderstandings arising in the interpretation of the Bible when it is read through the prism of modern Anglo culture, Rihbany comments: "Through our sacred Scriptures we hear the voices of those great Oriental prophets who spoke as they saw and felt; as seers, not as logicians" (p. 130), and he charges dominant modern approaches to the interpretation of the Bible with "an overstrained intellectualism" (p. 131).

As the English word *dispassionate* suggests, however, it is not thinking as such that should be (under certain circumstances) free from emotion but thinking expressed in speaking: one doesn't "think dispassionately" in English, one "speaks dispassionately." In particular, linguistic evidence suggests that it is seen as desirable that "heated arguments" should be avoided: when people express their opinions, they can disagree and they can argue, but it is good if they can "keep their cool" in the process. A "heated argument" suggests that the thinking expressed in that argument may not be good. A person described as "getting hot under the collar" is perceived as someone who is unlikely to be capable (at that moment) of rational thought.

Linguistic evidence suggests that there are probably several cultural scripts in Anglo culture that caution, in one way or another, about emotions. The topic is vast and cannot be discussed here in detail.[7] But I will suggest one particular cultural script, focused on the expression of opinions. Roughly speaking, this script says that if one wants to express an opinion about something, it is good to do it in a calm, cool fashion. More precisely:

[people think like this:]
when I say something because I want other people to know what I think
    about something
it will not be good if these people think that I say it because I feel
    something
it will be good if they think that I say it because I have thought about it
    for some time

This script suggests that when I want to let other people know what my opinion is, it is good to express this opinion calmly—without visible emotion (Rihbany says: "with the least possible show of emotion"). It also suggests that it is good to present one's opinion as a "considered opinion," that is, as something about which one has thought for some time.

There is a link between the "coolheadedness" of an utterance and prior thinking: if I don't speak "coolly," then what I say is likely to be rooted in my current feeling rather than in any prior thinking. If the opinion that I express is rooted in prolonged thinking, then I am likely to have considered it from different points of view and to have reached it on some rational grounds.

As we have seen, according to Locke (1959, 370–371), the majority of people "think they have formed right judgments of several matters . . . only because they never questioned, never examined their own opinions." Such lack of prior consideration leads people to be both dogmatic in their assertions and hotheaded: "And yet these, of all men, hold their opinions with the greatest stiffness; those being generally the most fierce and firm in their tenets, who have least examined them" (1959, 371). Thus, for Locke, fierceness in discourse tends to go hand in hand with stiffness in opinions, and both are combined with lack of critical thinking ("because they never thought otherwise"; that is, "because they never judged at all").

As we have seen earlier, Rihbany, in contrasting Anglo and Middle Eastern ways of speaking, describes the former as "cautious" (1920, 128, 129), "guarded" (p. 126), and "intellectual" and the latter as "impetuous" (p. 64) and "effusive" (p. 64), linking, in an insightful way, seemingly unrelated cultural scripts. For example, he writes: "The Oriental's impetuosity and effusiveness make his imprecatory prayers, especially to the 'unaccustomed ears' of Englishmen, bloodcurdling" (p. 4). More generally, "The language of the Oriental is that of sentiment and conviction, and not of highly differentiated and specialized thought" (p. 128). As discussed earlier, the "highly differentiated and specialized thought" is expressed in a kind of discourse that explicitly distinguishes "I think" from "I know" and links the "I think" with the grounds on which it is based and, consequently, with different degrees of probability. To examine the grounds and to assess the probabilities for one's "I think," one indeed needs to be "cautious," and if one takes a critical approach to one's opinions, one is unlikely to be "fierce" in their expression. One is also unlikely to be "impetuous," because one needs to control the degree of one's "conviction" (Locke says "assurance") in proportion to the estimated probabilities. According to Rihbany, this Anglo concern about control over one's words means also, in practice, control over one's feelings. By contrast, "the Oriental is never afraid to 'let himself go' and to give free course to his feelings" (p. 40).

Rihbany links the Anglo "coolheaded" ways of speaking with the traditions of scientific discourse, contrasting them in this respect with Middle Eastern ways: "the Oriental mind is that of the prophet and the seer, and not of the scientist and the philosopher" (p. 128). The Anglo emphasis on "intellectualism" leads to "caution" in speaking; the Middle Eastern emphasis on "sentiment and conviction" encourages "intimacy" and expression of "unrestrained affection":

> They ["Syrians"] talk to one another in terms of unbounded intimacy and unrestrained affection. The expressions, "My brother," "My eyes," "My soul," "My

heart," and the like, form the life-centres of the conversation. "My life, my blood are for you; take the very sight of my eyes, if you will." (Rihbany 1920, 45)

From an Anglo point of view, Rihbany observes, such effusiveness may seem excessive. "To the Oriental, on the other hand, the Anglo-Saxon seems in danger of becoming an unemotional intellectualist" (p. 40).

Peter Stearns opens his *American Cool: Constructing a Twentieth-Century Emotional Style* (1994) with the following sentence: "Cool. The concept is distinctly American, and it permeates almost every aspect of contemporary American culture" (p. 1). Stearns goes on to comment: "the positive connotation of 'cool,' along with its increasing usage, symbolizes our culture's increased striving for restraint." Stearns argues that this twentieth-century ideal of "emotional self-control" and "aversion to intensity" represents "a major break in what have been called 'feeling rules'—the recommended norms by which people are supposed to shape their emotional expressions and react to the expressions of others" (p. 2).

While accepting Stearns's observations concerning the growing emphasis on "cool is good" in twentieth-century American culture, we must also note the links between this ideal and the older Anglo notion that "coolheadedness" is good because "coolheadedness" is conducive to rational thought. A few examples from the OED:

> Upon cooler reflexion, I think I had done better to have left it alone. (1716–1718)
> The energy of the young prince had not then been found a match for the cool science of the veteran. (1848)
> The old, cool headed, general law is as good as any deviation dictated by present heat. (1777)

What applies to *cool* and *coolheaded* applies also to *dispassionate*: the lack of emotion is seen as conducive (if not downright necessary) to rational thinking.

> A critic on the sacred book should be candid and learned, dispassionate and free. (Cowper, 1780)
> They account it to be prime duty of a dispassionate inquirer. (1877)

The anthropologist Catherine Lutz writes this about American culture:

> One of the most pervasive cultural assumptions about the emotional is that it is antithetical to reason or rationality . . . To be emotional is to fail to rationally process information and hence to undermine the possibilities for sensible, or intelligent action. Mr. Spock of *Star Trek* fame, whose emotionlessness is part and parcel of his superior Vulcan intelligence, is one of many examples in contemporary popular culture which express the contradiction Americans see between rationality and emotion. (Lutz 1986, 291)

As the OED quotes adduced above illustrate, the "coolheaded Englishman" of whom Rihbany wrote in [1920] belongs to a tradition well entrenched in Anglo culture and going back at least to the eighteenth century.

It is interesting to note that, according to Thomas Kochman, the Anglo cultural assumption that reason and emotion "work against each other" also leads to misunderstandings and mutual distrust in communication between Anglo Americans and African Americans. For example, in his book *Black and White Styles in Conflict*, he writes:

The modes of behavior that blacks and whites consider appropriate for engaging in public debate on an issue differ in their stance and level of spiritual intensity. The black mode—that of black community people—is high-keyed: animated, interpersonal, and confrontational. The white mode—that of the middle class—is relatively low-keyed: dispassionate, impersonal, and non-challenging. The first is characteristic of involvement; it is heated, loud, and generates affect. The second is characteristic of detachment and is cool, quiet, and without affect. . . . Whites . . . regard the black argumentative mode as dysfunctional because of their view that reason and emotion work against each other; the presence of the latter militates against the operation of the former. This explains why discussion, the white mode for testing and validating ideas, is devoid of affect, and why its presence, to whites, automatically renders any presentation less persuasive to the extent that affect is also present. (Kochman 1981, 18–19)

No doubt the "black" cultural scripts described by Kochman (see also Wierzbicka 1994b) are different from the Middle Eastern ones discussed by Rihbany, but the perception of the mainstream Anglo scripts is similar. In both cases, this perception is based on lived cross-cultural experience; and it is consistent with the writings of Anglo thinkers and writers from John Locke to Bertrand Russell. It is also consistent with the existence of a tradition within Anglo academic psychology that tends to be hostile to emotions—a tradition psychologists Fehr and Russell have illustrated with the following characteristic sentences from an English-language introductory psychology textbook:

A state of emotion is recognized by its holder as a departure from his or her normal state of composure; at the same time there are physical changes that can be detected objectively.
　　When sufficiently intense, emotion can seriously impair the processes that control organized behavior. (Fehr and Russell 1984, 473)

Sentences of this kind, seemingly objective and scientific, reflect in fact an assumption that a person's "normal state" is a state of "composure" and that an emotion constitutes a departure from that "normal" (and presumably more desirable) state.

　　The script cautioning against "heat" in the expression of opinions is linked, logically, with a number of other scripts concerning opinions: that they should be rational, that they should have been arrived at by thinking and considering various possibilities, that one should be open-minded about them, and that one should not under any circumstances try to impose them on other people. This last point brings us to the last large theme to be considered in this chapter, the theme of "compelling," or "not compelling," other people to do something or think something.

2.7. To Compel or Not to Compel? The Value of Autonomy

One of the most central values of Anglo culture is, by all accounts, the value of personal autonomy. What exactly does this value mean, and how can it best be explained to speakers of languages with no words for either *personal* or *autonomy*? Trying to answer this question, let us start with Rihbany's reflections on Anglo and Syrian hospitality:

> To extend hospitality in genuine Syrian fashion is no small undertaking. Brevity on such occasions is the soul of stinginess. Oriental effusiveness and intensity of speech are never more strenuously exercised than at such times. The brief form of the English invitation, "I should be pleased if you would dine with us one night," however sincere, would seem to an Oriental like an excuse to escape the obligation of hospitality. Again, the ready acceptance of an invitation in the West would seem to the son of the East utterly undignified. Although the would-be guest could accept, he must be as insistent in saying, "No, I can't" as the would-be host in saying "Yes, you must." (Rihbany 1920, 146)

What is remarkable from a broad cross-cultural perspective is not the Syrian "you must," which has parallels in many other parts of the world (for parallels from Polish culture, see Wierzbicka 1985, 1991/2003; from Chinese, see Wierzbicka 1996a). Rather, what is remarkable is the Anglo avoidance of "you must," especially "you must" as a response to "I can't." As noted by Robin Lakoff (1973), it is not impossible for an Anglo American host to offer a guest some homemade delicacy with the words "you must try this," but should the guest clearly and firmly decline, a repeated "you must" would go against Anglo cultural scripts (and even the first time one could hardly say "you must eat this" using a verb of action like *eat* rather than a minimizer like *try*). Generally speaking, then, if a person says, "I don't want to do this," other people can't say to this person, "You have to do it because I want you to do it." A physical attempt to *force* another person to do something would normally be regarded as even more unacceptable than a verbal one, but both kinds would go against some very central Anglo cultural scripts. Not so in Syrian culture.

> Approaching his hoped-for guest, a Syrian engages him in something like the following dialogue, characterized by a glow of feeling which the translation can only faintly reveal:
> "Ennoble us [*sherrifna*] by your presence."
> "I would be ennobled [*nitsheeref*], but I cannot accept."
> "That cannot be."
> "Yea, yea, it must be."
> "No, I swear against you [*aksim 'aleik*] by our friendship and by the life of God. I love just to acquaint you with our bread and salt."
> "I swear also that I find it impossible [*gheir mimkin*] to accept. Your bread and salt are known to all."
> "Yea, do it just for our own good. By coming to us you come to your own home. Let us repay your bounty to us [*fadhlek*]."
> "*Astaghfero Allah* [by the mercy of God] I have not bestowed any bounty upon you worth mentioning."
> Here the host seizes his guest by the arm and with an emphatic "I will not let you go," pulls at him and would drag him bodily into his house. Then the guest, happy in being vanquished "with honour," consents to the invitation. (Rihbany 1920, 146–147)

As described by Rihbany, similar tactics apply in delaying the departing guest. What matters in the present context, however, is not Middle Eastern conventions of hospitality but the Anglo value of autonomy, overriding virtually everything else. The point is not that a person can do anything this person wants to do, or that no one has to do something he or she doesn't want to do, but rather that (roughly speaking) no one can impose her or his will on another person. More precisely, the scripts in question can be represented as follows:

> [people think like this:]
> no one can say to another person:
>> "I want you to do this
>> you have to do it because of this"
>
> [people think like this:]
> no one can say to another person:
>> "I don't want you to do this
>> you can't do it because of this"

These scripts don't say that people can do anything they want to do or that there can be no rules legitimately preventing people from doing what they want to do. Rather, they say that it cannot be another person's expression of will that prevents me from doing what I want to do or forces me to do what I don't want to do.

Linguistic evidence, however, suggests that modern Anglo scripts of personal autonomy go further than these two rudimentary formulae indicate. To say to another person "you have to do it because I want you to do it" is like giving orders. This is, generally speaking, unacceptable. But it is also unacceptable to put pressure on other people to do something that one wants them to do, and the modern English expressions *to put pressure on* and *to act under pressure* are highly revealing in this respect: these expressions did not occur in Shakespeare's language (in fact, the word *pressure* does not occur in the Shakespeare concordance at all), and there are no corresponding (colloquial) expressions in other European languages. (For discussion, see Wierzbicka, in press a). Thus, the unfavorable attention to "pressure from other people" is a distinctive feature of Anglo culture. ("Working under pressure" is not necessarily seen as bad, but "acting under pressure" *is*, because the latter implies pressure from other people.)

To *put pressure* on people does not mean to say to them that they "have to" do something but, rather, to say (or show) for some time that one wants them to do it and that one expects them to do it because of this. Clearly, this, too, is seen as inconsistent with the value of "personal autonomy": from the point of view of Anglo "autonomy scripts," it is good if, when I do something, I do it "freely," that is, because I want to do it, not because someone else wants me to do it.

> [people think like this:]
> when I do something it is good if I do it because I want to do it,
> not because someone else wants me to do it

This script would explain, among many other things, why not only "ordering people about" but also begging (imploring) is usually seen as culturally inappropriate in normal social interaction. Rihbany, trying to explain the norms of "Oriental speech" to speakers of English, gives a prominent place to the "habit of imploring 'in reason and out of reason' when asking a favour. To try to exert 'undue' influence, virtually to beg in most persuasive tones, is an Oriental habit which to an Englishman must seem unendurable" (Rihbany 1920, 124). Clearly, *imploring* or *begging* does not imply "you have to," yet it may well be seen as an "unendurable" assault on another person's autonomy: if I decide to do you a favor, I want to think that I'm doing it because I want to do it, not because you have tried to put "undue" pressure on me by begging. (The English word *undue* is well chosen by Rihbany in this context, as its most common use is precisely in combination with the words *pressure* and *influence*.)

This brings us back to the English whimperatives and the English speech act verbs that were mentioned in section 2.2. English verbs like *to offer, to invite,* and *to suggest,* used in frames like "she offered to do X," "she invited him to do X," and "she suggested that he could do X," all convey the message "if you want to" and in so doing show the speaker's special care not to "impose" on the addressee. It is interesting to note that the range of use of these verbs is wider than that of their counterparts in other European languages. In particular, the colloquial English use of the words *suggest* and *suggestion* (as in "I would suggest that you do X" or "it is only a suggestion") has no parallels in colloquial French, German, or Italian.

The whimperatives ("can you / could you / would you do X?" instead of "do X!" or "please do X") perform a similar function, insofar as they indicate (in contrast to the imperative) that the speaker doesn't know what the outcome of the request will be (see Wierzbicka 1991/2003a; Goddard and Karlsson 2004):

do X! =
I say: I want you to do X
I think that you will do it

can you / could you / would you do X? =
I say: I want you to do X
I think that maybe you will do it
I don't know

This conventionalized expression of our uncertainty in making requests serves to acknowledge, explicitly, the addressee's 'autonomy': whether or not the request will be complied with depends on the choice of the addressee.

There is, of course, a close link between the use of whimperatives in interpersonal interaction and the existence and use of speech acts verbs like *to suggest, to offer,* and *to invite.* Interrogative utterances such as "would you like to . . . ?" "how about . . . ?" and "why don't you . . . ?"—which can be interpreted as suggestions, offers, or invitations rather than requests—enable speakers to acknowledge the addressee's personal autonomy, while at the same time expressing their own desires and thoughts. (For discussion, see Wierzbicka 1991/2003a.) Among many other conversational routines that could be mentioned here in support of the proposed scripts, none is perhaps more telling than the common expression *it's up to you*—again, an expression with no exact equivalents in other European languages. In most languages, the closest counterpart that could be proposed would have to take the form of rather long-winded locutions like "if you want to do it, you can do it; if you don't want to do it, you don't have to do it." Not only are such locutions long and cumbersome but also they still lack a crucial semantic component of the English expression: roughly, that "it's your choice" and "no one can tell you otherwise." The emergence in English of such an expression (absent in Shakespeare's concordance and cited by the OED with the first date of 1908 and qualified as "American") witnesses to the growing salience of the "anti-compelling" scripts in modern Anglo culture.[8]

What is particularly striking from a cross-cultural point of view is that verbal routines of this kind that acknowledge everyone's personal autonomy are used even in the family circle. To quote Rihbany:

> From early childhood Westerners are as a rule taught to observe, even within the family circle, the niceties of "Please," "Thank you," "Pardon me," "I beg your pardon," "May I trouble you," and so forth. To a son of the East such a behaviour is altogether proper among strangers, but not among those who really *love one another*. Between husband and wife, parent and child, brothers and sisters, and true friends, such formalities appear to Easterners not only superficial, but utterly ridiculous. For such persons the most essential thing is that they should love one another. As lovers they have a right to *demand* favours from one another. (Rihbany 1920, 224)

From a cultural outsider's point of view, it may seem that what is involved here is a matter of superficial etiquette ("such formalities"), but attention paid in many Anglo families to such daily verbal routines suggests that it is, in fact, a question of deeply held cultural values. From a "Syrian" point of view (on Rihbany's account), it is important to show that one treats family members differently from strangers; from an Anglo point of view, on the other hand, it is important to habitually acknowledge that one sees them, too, as autonomous individuals. Rihbany's phrase *may I trouble you* sounds somewhat satirical in this context, but *please, thank you, sorry,* and *can you / could you / would you* are indeed important currency in the give-and-take of daily Anglo interaction between family members and friends—and they confirm the reality of the cultural scripts concerned with personal autonomy. A "thank you" exchanged between family members in the kitchen or at the table signals that even the smallest services are not taken for granted but are seen as given freely by one autonomous individual to another and therefore as something that the benefactee is grateful for (see Apte 1974).

Finally, it is important to recognize the links between the scripts of "autonomy" and "nonimposing" in the sphere of action and in the sphere of thought (see Wierzbicka 1994b; Goddard 2003). Just as it is unacceptable to try to force another person to do something we want them to do so too is it unacceptable to try to force another person to hold an opinion that we want them to hold. However attached we may be to our own opinions, and however convinced of their validity, we must not seek to "impose" those opinions on other people, and in speaking to others we must show that we respect their autonomy and their right to hold opinions different from our own.

We have already seen Rihbany's comments that English expressions like *in my opinion, so it seems to me,* or *as I see it* "are almost entirely absent from Oriental speech" (Rihbany, 1920, 128). The wealth and frequent use of such expressions in English discourse reflect the cultural emphasis on epistemological accuracy and precision. In the Anglo cultural tradition, this emphasis on epistemological accuracy and precision is linked with an emphasis on respecting other people's autonomy in thinking—on their right, that is, to think what they want to think and not what we might like them to think.

A key word in this tradition is *imposing*: we must not "impose" our will on other people, and we must not "impose" our opinions. Rihbany depicts these Anglo scripts in reverse, by presenting the contrasting way of speaking of "the Oriental": what strikes Rihbany about Anglo discourse is that in English (as he knows it), when one is expressing one's personal opinion, one is expected to make it perfectly clear that one is doing just that.

It is interesting to trace the origins of the autonomy cultural script in the writings of British philosophers and to see how Locke in particular linked rational thinking with tolerance for the diversity of opinions and the need to not "impose" our opinions on others:

> Since . . . it is unavoidable to the greatest part of men, if not all, to have several opinions, without certain and indubitable proof of their truth . . . , it would, methinks, become all men to maintain peace . . . in the diversity of opinions; since we cannot reasonably expect that any one should readily and obsequiously quit his own opinion, and embrace ours, with a blind resignation to an authority which the understanding of the man acknowledges not. (Locke 1959 [1690], 372)

Locke uses the word *impose* in this connection again and again. For example:

> Those who have not thoroughly examined to the bottom of their own tenets, must confess they are unfit to prescribe to others; and are unreasonable in *imposing* that as truth on other men's belief, which they themselves have not searched into, nor weighed the arguments of probability, on which they should receive or reject it. . . . and there is reason to think, that, if men were better instructed themselves, they would be less *imposing* on others. (Locke 1959 [1690], 374, emphasis added)

In addition to warning against "imposing" one's opinions on others, Locke speaks in a similar vein of "forcing" our opinions on others and of "constraining others" (p. 373). These warnings are consistent with the following cultural scripts:

[people think like this:]
no one can say to another person about anything:
"you have to think like this about it because I want you to think like this
    about it"
[people think like this:]
no one can say to another person about anything:
"you can't think like this about it because I don't want you to think like
    this about it"

Three hundred years after the first appearance of Locke's *Essay*, the norms articulated in these scripts are so well entrenched in Anglo culture as to seem self-evident— so much so that it may seem unnecessary to spell them out at all. Nonetheless, it is useful to formulate them as a possible starting point of a chain of scripts including also the following two (for discussion, see Wierzbicka 1991/2003a, 2002c; Goddard, in press):

[people think like this:]
no one can say to another person something like this about anything:
"I think like this about it, you have to think the same about it"
[people think like this:]
when I want other people to know what I think about something
it is good to say something like this:
"I think like this, I know that other people don't have to think like this"

Presumably, it is this last script (the script of "tolerance") that is reflected in expressions like *in my opinion, so it seems to me, as I see it,* and so on, cited by Rihbany as distinctly Anglo. In this connection, it is worth again quoting Bertrand Russell (1948, 165), who was clearly following in Locke's footsteps when he linked the weighing of evidence in expressing an opinion with tolerance (or "toleration"): "If there is to be toleration in the world, one of the things taught in schools must be the habit of weighing evidence, and the practice of not giving full assent to propositions which there is no reason to believe true."

The ideal of 'tolerance'—another key Anglo concept that can be traced in some measure to Locke 's writings (see in particular his A *Letter on Toleration* of 1689)— is related to the modern Anglo concept of "negative freedom" (Isaiah Berlin 1969), that is, "freedom from" as distinct from "freedom to" and of "individual rights." One expects to be "free from" other people telling one what one has to do or what one ought to think, and one assumes this freedom to be everyone's right. One expects this right for oneself, and one acknowledges that everyone else has this right, too. Everyday conversational routines such as the use of whimperatives and epistemological qualifiers allow and encourage the speakers of English to acknowledge this right on a daily basis.

It may even occur to some Anglo readers to ask: why don't other cultures have "anticompelling" scripts, too—or why are those scripts not equally salient in other cultures? Rihbany's "Syrian" vignettes are useful here in highlighting at least some of the costs involved (emotional costs). For example, a person who compels would-be guests to visit or departing guests to delay their departure can show in this way a great warmth toward these people and a great desire to do something good for them. Similarly, if one seeks to change the addressee's ways of thinking, one can show in this way that one cares what the addressee thinks—and that one cares for the addressee. Thus, "compelling" may be seen as a sign of love, and pointed "noncompelling" as a sign of indifference (see Kochman 1981).[9] From an Anglo point of view, the values of personal autonomy, freedom from pressure, and tolerance may be seen as worth paying almost any price for. It is good to recognize, however, that both compelling and noncompelling involve *some* costs, and it is good to see clearly what both the gains and the costs associated with each cultural choice are.

2.8. Conclusion

To deny the existence of Anglo cultural scripts means, in effect, to take these scripts as setting the standard of normal human thinking. But there are millions of people today who live through English and who nonetheless do not live and perhaps do not want to live by the cultural scripts described here. The testimony of bilingual writers who write predominantly in English but draw on the cultural traditions associated with their other language is particularly telling in this regard (see, e.g., Hoffman 1989; for discussion, see Besemeres 1998, 2002). As noted earlier, the German Arab writer Abdellatif Belfellah (1996) asks pointedly in the title of a recent article: "Wem gehört die deutsche Sprache?" ("To whom belongs the German language?"). A similar question is more and more often raised by immigrant writers writing in English. Monocultural people who live exclusively or mainly by Anglo cultural scripts do not "own the English language." But their expectations embedded in those scripts do much to determine the social context in which newcomers must live. It is important, therefore, to acknowledge that the scripts described here are real—that they do exist. It is particularly important that these scripts should be recognized and well understood in those parts of the world where English meets other languages—and where native speakers of languages other than English come into contact with the English language. Given the present spread and role of English in the world, this increasingly means everywhere.

Margaret Archer (2000, 92), in her otherwise impressively argued book *Being Human*, speaks dismissively of the "contentious proposition" that, as she puts it, partially quoting Harré (1998), "our tribal narrative conventions 'are like the "rules of grammar" of our native tongue.'" As grounds for this dismissal, she offers the observation that "globalization has weakened tribalism" and also that "'we' of the West are far too cosmopolitan to be bound to the conventions of our mother tongue, if such there be."

But if one doubts that English ("our mother tongue") may have any cultural conventions of its own and if one assumes that "we" of the English language are far too cosmopolitan for that, the result is that "being human" starts to look perilously close to "being Anglo."

For example, Spencer-Oatley writes with reference to Brown and Levinson's (1987) putative "universals of politeness":

> *Orders and Requests* can easily threaten rapport, because they can affect our autonomy, freedom of choice, and freedom from imposition, and this threatens our sense of equity rights (our entitlement to considerate treatment). They need to be worded, therefore, in such a way that we feel our rights to fair treatment have been adequately addressed, otherwise they may make us feel irritated or annoyed. (Spencer-Oatley 2000, 17)

Statements of this kind speak about "us," meaning, apparently, "us human beings." In fact, however, the whole thinking on which these statements are based is framed in terms, concepts, and assumptions that are language-specific. The key words and expressions used here—*autonomy, freedom of choice, freedom from imposition, equity rights, entitlement, fair treatment*—are quintessentially English, and they reflect Anglo cultural scripts of the kind investigated in this chapter. The idea that, for example, Middle Eastern speakers would also think about orders and requests in such terms is profoundly ethnocentric. (See Wierzbicka 1985, 1991/2003a.)

Consider also the following statement about "us" ("us, human beings"):

We have a fundamental belief that we are entitled to personal consideration from others, so that we are treated fairly; that we are not unduly imposed upon, that we are not unfairly ordered about, and that we are not taken advantage of or exploited. There seems to be two components to this equity entitlement: the notion of *cost-benefit* . . . and the related issue of *autonomy-imposition*. (Spencer-Oatley 2000, 14)

Again, the key words used in this passage—*entitled, consideration, fairly, equity, autonomy, imposition*—belong to the key words of the modern English language, words that epitomize, in various ways, Anglo cultural scripts. In the increasingly global world, these scripts need to be understood by all speakers of English—including monolingual Anglos who take them for granted and immigrants to English-speaking countries to whom they may be unfamiliar and alien. The use of simple and universal human concepts, shared by all speakers and learners of English, makes it possible to make these scripts understandable to anyone.

PART II

ENGLISH WORDS

From Philosophy to Everyday Discourse

Chapter 3

The Story of RIGHT and WRONG and Its Cultural Implications

3.1. Introduction

One of the most interesting phenomena in the history of the English language is the remarkable rise of the word *right*, in its many interrelated senses and uses. It is not the purpose of this chapter to document this rise in detail but rather to draw attention to it, to raise questions about its cultural underpinnings, and to formulate some hypotheses for future investigations.

I begin with two fragments from informal interviews tape-recorded by the sociologist Douglas Porpora, with the occurrences of *right* numbered:

> 1. I ask Peter why he feels he should treat people as he does. "You said you were raised to treat people like this?"
> "Right." (1)
> "Okay, that sort of explains why you have those values. . . ."
> "But why were they taught to me?"
> "No. Not why they were taught to you, but do you think those are values . . . I mean different people are taught different values, right?" (2)
> "Right." (3)
> "Somebody else might be taught a different set of values. . . ."
> "Mm-hm."
> "Than what you were taught. . . . So, do you think your values are right (4) rather than. . . . Do you think those are the right (5) values to have?"
> "I don't know if it's really a matter of right (6) or wrong." (Porpora 2001: 79)

> 2. "Go ahead," says Eli. "You tell me what you believe so maybe you'll give me a hint. I'll give you an answer from my . . ."
> . . . .
> "I believe in . . . Jesus. I believe that . . . uh . . . God is good, that there's a God who made the universe."
> "That's right (7)," replies Guzia. "One God is for everybody." (Porpora 2001, 111–112)

It would be very difficult to translate these fragments into other European languages because there would be no words in these languages to match *right*—in any of the senses illustrated here. All the bilingual native speakers of German, French, and Italian I've asked found themselves embarrassed and unexpectedly confounded by the task and proposed either renderings like *yes* and *true* (*ja, oui, sí; wahr, vrais, vero*) or various ad hoc solutions, for example, for German, *stimmt* (1), *oder?, ja* (3), *rechten* (4 and 5), *richtigen* (6), and *genau so* (7). Yet in English all these uses are very common, and all these senses function as basic tools for thinking, talking, and interacting with other people.

How many different senses of *right* are there? Leaving aside *right* as a countable noun (as in *human rights*), *right* as an adverb (e.g., *right then, right there*), and *right* as opposed to *left*, we can distinguish three major senses of *right*, all illustrated in the two previous fragments. For the sake of convenience, I will call these senses "moral," "intellectual," and "conversational."

The "moral" sense of *right* is linked, in particular, with the phrase "right or wrong" and related phrases like "a sense of right and wrong," "how to tell right from wrong," and so on. It is also manifested in sentences like the following one, which opens a book on ethics (based on a series of public lectures given at Columbia University in 1954): "In all the world and in all of life there is nothing more important to determine than what is right" (Lewis 1955, 3).

It has often been said, and justly so, that *right* in this sense refers to what a person does. To quote another philosopher, Ross (1955, 7), "'right' and 'wrong' refer entirely to the thing done." The "thing" in question can be mental rather than physical, as in the case of a *right choice* or *right decision*, but the mental acts involved can also be interpreted as a person *doing something*. To be called "right" or "wrong," however, the *doing* has to involve some thinking. To quote Lewis (1955) again, "No manner of behavior wholly untouched by thinking could be right or wrong" (p. 79), and "whatever is decidable or can be determined by deliberation is right or wrong" (p. 20).

The entry for *right* in *The Oxford Companion to Philosophy* (1995, 75) reads:

> *right, the.* What is right to do, as distinct from what is good to do. One of the traditional problems of moral philosophy is that of relating the right and the good.

What this entry doesn't say is that the problem of "relating the right and the good" is a problem restricted to *Anglo* moral philosophy: in other philosophical traditions, the problem does not present itself (at least not in this form) because there is no word corresponding to *right*. This is a good example of "philosophical problems" that originate in the philosopher's native language.

Similarly, the entry on *right action* in *The Oxford Companion to Philosophy* reads: "No subject is more central to moral philosophy or ethics than that of right and wrong action" (1995, 775). Expressing a certain impatience with the "linguistic philosophy" of the second half of the twentieth century, the author of the article goes on to comment:

> During the hey-day of Anglo-American meta-ethics, philosophers were often on principle more interested in defining ethical notions than in offering a substantive view of what actions are right and what actions are wrong. . . . But over the

longer history of philosophy and certainly nowadays as well, a greater interest has been taken in giving a substantive account of rightness.

The assumption behind these statements is that it is possible in principle to give a "substantive account of rightness" without paying any attention to the word *rightness* itself—as if "rightness" were a phenomenon "out there," independent of the English language, and one that could be discussed in any other language.

Philosopher Jonathan Harrison, in his book *Our Knowledge of Right and Wrong*, writes:

> The fact with which second-order moral philosophy starts is that we have in the English language, together with equivalents in other languages, words such as 'right' and 'wrong', 'good' and 'bad', 'duty', 'ought', and so on, which words have, roughly, the function of appraising people and things and the status of affairs and of directing behaviour. It is, of course, just a matter of fact that languages possess words which have this function. (Harrison 1971, 18)

Harrison is mistaken: it is actually a matter of fact that many languages *don't* have words like the English *right* and *wrong* (or, for that matter, *duty* and *ought*). They all have, however, equivalents of *good* and *bad*, and they also have equivalents of *true* (though not of *false*). I discuss these differences and similarities between different languages further in the next section.

The "intellectual" sense of *right* comes into play, above all, in the phrase *that's right*. Because this phrase is normally used in dialogue, as a response to somebody else's words, it may seem difficult to distinguish it from the use labeled here as "conversational." But "That's right" (unlike the purely conversational response "Right.") endorses a belief. For example, when Guzia says, "That's right. One God is for everybody," she is saying, in effect, that the *belief* expressed by her interlocutor is "right." By contrast, the conversational response "Right." may not indicate that the speaker regards the belief expressed by another person as "right" but only that he or she understands what the other person is saying. This potentially "noncommittal" character of "Right." is particularly clear in the following fragment:

> "Okay," Frederick continues. "The Old Testament. . . . but the book of Revelations only mentions twelve thousand from each tribe. Or a hundred and forty-four thousand."
> "Right." I am familiar with the belief among Seventh Day Adventists and some other fundamentalist groups that when Jesus comes again, there will be exactly one hundred and forty thousand Jews who will be saved by their conversion to Christ. (Porpora 2001, 143–144)

It is clear from the context that the interviewer does not share the interviewee's belief, and so cannot regard it as "right." What appears to be "right" in this third sense is neither an action nor a belief, but rather an understanding of what one's interlocutor is saying. As I discuss later, the conversational "Right." can also be seen as voicing the speaker's satisfaction with what has just been said, perhaps because it is clear.

In this chapter, I argue that the "moral," "intellectual," and "conversational" uses of *right* are related and that the emergence and expansion of the second ("intellectual") and the third ("conversational") are linked with the rise of the first ("moral"). More generally, I argue that salient conversational routines are related to deeply entrenched ways of thinking and that changes in conversational routines follow changes in attitudes, values, and worldview.

The rise of the conversational *right* in English is a language-specific and culture-specific phenomenon that could not possibly be explained in terms of supposedly universal rules of politeness, conversational logic, or maxims of interaction, in the spirit of Grice (1975), Brown and Levinson (1987), or Leech (1983). Of course, quasiparallels to the conversational *right* can be found in many languages, and without rigorous semantic analysis, such parallels may seem close enough for some pragmatic explanations to appear applicable to them all. But when one does engage in close semantic analysis, one discovers that the differences between the supposed parallels are as real as the similarities and that these differences can offer us valuable clues in our search for valid explanations.

When one looks from a broader European perspective at the rise of the distinction between *right* and *wrong* and the emergence of *right* as a discourse marker, both phenomena must be seen as innovations that set English apart from other European languages. Generally speaking, those other languages tend to rely, in moral discourse, on the universal concepts GOOD and BAD and, in conversational contexts, on the universal concept TRUE.

3.2. "Right" and "Wrong": A Basis for Ethics?

The distinction between right and wrong occupies a central place in the English moral lexicon and indeed in Anglo moral discourse generally—so much so that many Anglophone scholars, including even anthropologists, regard it as fundamental to human nature.

The very first example of the use of *right* offered by the *Shorter Oxford English Dictionary* (dated from 1737) reads: "You must acknowledge a Distinction betwixt Right and Wrong, founded in Nature." At the turn of the twenty-first century, the distinction between right and wrong continues to be invoked frequently in theoretical discussions and used as a frame of reference for talking about moral development and moral norms across cultures and societies—as if this distinction were indeed "founded in nature" itself. For example, philosopher Oliver Johnson, the author of a book entitled *Rightness and Goodness* (1959, 1), writes of "ethical intuitionism" as "the theory which holds that rightness—with its opposite, wrongness—is a fundamental, irreducible, and immediately apprehended ethical concept." Contrasting this theory with "axiological theories," which, he says, "make goodness—with its opposite, badness—the single fundamental ethical concept and rightness subordinate to, and derivative from it" (p. 1), Johnson affirms that "both concepts—rightness and goodness—are of fundamental importance to the moral life of man" (p. 2).

Psychologists, too, often take the notions of right and wrong for granted and regard them as human universals. For example, according to Kohlberg's (1981) "cognitive developmental theory":

The development of the idea of a moral obligation is related to the development of general skills of rational reasoning. . . . Movement through the stages is related to the cognitive ability to construct, and to transcend to, a detached, impartial vantage point from which one evaluates right and wrong objectively. (Shweder, Mahapatra, and Miller 1990, 131)

The point overlooked in such discussions is that "right" and "wrong" are not universal human concepts but English words without equivalents in other European languages, let alone in languages of more remote cultures and societies. To use these English words as one's basic tools for describing and comparing different cultures — or for talking about "children's moral development" (not English-speaking children but human children in general) — means to introduce into the discussion an unjustified Anglocentric bias.

I hasten to emphasize that in saying this I am not taking the position of a cultural, moral, or linguistic relativist. On the contrary: colleagues and I have tried to document in many publications the existence of linguistic universals, and we have argued, on the basis of empirical cross-linguistic research, that these universals include the concepts GOOD and BAD. We have also argued that while GOOD and BAD can be used across a wide range of domains and are by no means restricted to moral discourse, they can occur in all languages in combinations like "I (you, someone, this person) did something bad/good" or "it is good/bad if someone does something like this" (see Wierzbicka 2001, 161–169).

Moreover, we have argued that the concept TRUE is a linguistic universal and that in all languages people can say the exact semantic equivalent of "this is true" and "this is not true." Thus, the English words *good*, *bad*, and *true* can be seen as English exponents of the universal human concepts GOOD, BAD, and TRUE, with exact semantic equivalents in other languages. Table 3.1 shows some examples (see Goddard and Wierzbicka, eds., 1994, 2002).

But what applies to *good*, *bad*, and *true* does not apply to *right* and *wrong*,[1] and given the central role of *right* and *wrong* in Anglo moral discourse, the questions must be asked what precisely these two English words mean and how and why the language-specific concepts encoded in them have become so salient in modern Anglo culture.

Both 'right' and 'wrong' are modern Anglo concepts, conceptual constructs of Anglo culture and the English language. The words *right* and *wrong* are often used in English translations of classic Greek and Roman writers, but the words they are used to translate are usually the semantic equivalents of *good* and *bad* (or *better* and *worse*). One example (from Stevenson 1958, 1727):

I see the right, and I approve it too,
Condemn the wrong, and yet the wrong pursue.

TABLE 3.1 GOOD, BAD, and TRUE in Spanish, Malay, and Mandarin Chinese

	Good	Bad	True
Spanish	bueno	malo	verdad
Malay	baik	buruk	benar
Mandarin Chinese	hǎo	huài	zhēn

(*Video meliora probaque, deteriora sequor.*)
Ovid, *Metamorphoses*. Bk. vii, l.20. Translated by Samuel Garth)

The tendency to take the concepts 'right' and 'wrong' for granted, as if they were universal and not dependent on language and culture, can also be illustrated with standard definitions of concepts like "conscience." For example (*Oxford Companion to Philosophy* 1995, 152):

> *Conscience*. By "conscience" is meant the sense of right and wrong in an individual; described variously by philosophers as a reflection of the voice of God, as a human faculty, as the voice of reason, or as a special moral sense.

The author of this entry refers here to St. Thomas Aquinas's discussion of "conscience." But for Aquinas, conscience was *not* "the sense of right and wrong" but rather the sense of *bonum* and *malum*, that is, 'good' and 'bad' (*Summa Theologiae*, 1a, 2ae, Q, 19, arts. 5 and 6). For speakers of most modern European languages, too, 'conscience' is usually linked with the notions 'good' and 'bad', rather than 'right' and 'wrong'. Pope John Paul II's encyclical *Veritatis Splendor* (1993, 89) speaks about the "conscience" as follows (quoting the document of the Second Vatican Council entitled "Gaudium et Spes"):

> In the depths of his conscience man detects a law which he does not impose on himself, but which holds him to obedience. Always summoning him to love good and avoid evil, the voice of conscience can when necessary speak to his heart more specifically: "do this, shun that." For man has in his heart a law written by God. To obey it is the very dignity of man; according to it he will be judged (cf. Rom 2:14–6).

The English translation of the Latin original uses here the words *good* and *evil* (rather than *good* and *bad*), *evil* being a more specialized concept referring to "*wanting* to do bad things" rather than simply *doing* them. But again, in most other translations, the original simple equivalents of the Latin *bonum* and *malum* (i.e., *good* and *bad*) have been used (in German, *das Gute* and *das Böse*; in French, *le bien* and *le mal*; in Italian, *il bene* and *il male*; in Spanish, *el bien* and *el mal*, and so on) because, as noted earlier, GOOD and BAD—in contrast to 'right' and 'wrong'—are universal human concepts, with semantically equivalent exponents in all languages.

To speakers of English, however, 'right' and 'wrong' often appear to be fundamental, rooted in nature itself. According to some scholars, even animals have a sense of 'right' and 'wrong'. For example, Frans de Waal (1996, 2), the author of *Good Natured: The Origins of Right and Wrong in Humans and Other Animals*, states: "A society lacking notions of right and wrong is about the worst thing we can imagine—if we can imagine it at all." Well, sometimes our imagination needs to be stretched on the basis of cross-linguistic evidence; in this case, cross-linguistic evidence shows us that *most* societies don't have the notions of 'right' and 'wrong' and that in fact these notions are peculiar to, roughly speaking, Anglo culture. What may indeed be universal is the sense that "people can do bad things" and "people can do good things" (see Wierzbicka 2001, 165).

For example, from a "Russian" cultural point of view, the key choice is definitely that between *xorošo* ("good") and *ploxo* ("bad"), as set out in Mayakovsky's children's poem, "What Is Good and What Is Bad" (Marshall 1955, 80–83):

Tiny toddler told his Dad:
"I am puzzled so!
What is good and what is bad?
Answer if you know!"

The dad in the poem has some very definite answers to the question, with the desired result:

Tiny toddler understood.
Tiny told his Dad:
"I will always do what's *good*,
Never what is *bad*."

A Russian dad could not talk similarly to his child about *right* and *wrong*, because there are no such words in Russian.

Thus, I would not dispute de Waal's claim that "Morality is as firmly grounded in neurobiology as anything else we do or are" (1996, 217). But to make such claims plausible, one must be careful to find the right (!) way of expressing them. For example, when de Waal says, "Once thought of as purely spiritual matters, honesty, guilt, and the weighing of ethical dilemmas are traceable to specific areas of the brain" (1996, 217), he doesn't take into account the fact that 'honesty' and 'guilt', too, are culture-specific conceptual constructs, without exact equivalents in languages other than English. *Right* and *wrong* are, in this respect, like *honesty* and *guilt*. The question of whether they may be "traceable to specific areas of the brain" can be raised only by scholars whose native language includes the words *right* and *wrong*. A better (less language-dependent) question to ask would be whether the notion that "people can do bad [or good] things" can be traced to specific areas of the brain, or whether it has animal parallels.

Moral discourse based on the notions of 'good' and 'bad' is, of course, not absent from Anglo culture either. To take some examples from Stevenson (1958):

The Bad among the Good are here mixt ever:
The Good without the Bad are here plac'd never.
(Robert Herrick, "Good and Bad," seventeenth century)

There is no Good, there is no Bad; these be the whim of moral will.
(Sir Richard Burton, nineteenth century)

There are two kinds of people on earth to-day
Just two kinds of people, no more, I say.
Not the good and the bad, for 'tis well understood
That the good are half bad and the bad are half good. . . .
(Ella Wheeler Wilcox, nineteenth–twentieth centuries)

For good ye are and bad, and like to coins,
Some true, some light.
(Tennyson, nineteenth century)

The greater part of what my neighbours call good
I believe in my soul to be bad.
(H. D. Thoreau, *Walden*, nineteenth century)

It is interesting to note how often the contrasting use of the words *good* and *bad* in modern English (in a moral context) is linked with a desire to distance oneself from the use of these words as moral absolutes. By contrast, the words *right* and *wrong* are often contrasted in modern (at least pre-twentieth-century) Anglo discourse sharply and confidently, as the following quotes (also from Stevenson 1958) illustrate:

> My principle is to do whatever is right, and leave consequences to him who has the disposal of them. (Thomas Jefferson, eighteenth–nineteenth centuries)

> They say that if you do this you will be standing with the Abolitionists. I say stand with anybody that stands right. Stand with him while he is right and part with him when he goes wrong. (Abraham Lincoln, nineteenth century)

> The passionate love of Right, the burning hate of Wrong. (Lewis Morris, nineteenth century)

It is particularly interesting to recall here the following passage from the classic document of American culture, the *Autobiography of Benjamin Franklin* ("long regarded at home and abroad as the quintessential American," Bellah et al. 1985, 32), which was written in 1784:

> It was about this time I conceived the bold and arduous project of arriving at moral perfection. I wished to live without committing any fault at any time; I would conquer all that either natural inclination, custom, or company might lead me into. As I knew, or thought I knew, what was right and wrong, I did not see why I might not always do the one and avoid the other. (Franklin 1964, 148)

Admittedly, these quotes, which express their authors' confidence in their ability to distinguish the 'right' from the 'wrong', sound dated today: in the postmodern world, many people would hesitate to speak in similar tones. But if one looks at the use of *right* and *wrong* in English in the eighteenth, nineteenth, and early twentieth centuries, one is struck both by the ascendancy of *right* and *wrong* over *good* and *bad* and by the confident tone in which the former pair is often referred to, in contrast to the latter. Where did this confidence in the human ability to distinguish 'right' from 'wrong' come from in modern Anglo culture? And where did the interest come from for distinguishing right from wrong rather than simply good from bad?

We will consider these questions more closely in the next section. First, however, let us note that collocations linking *right* with *wrong* in English appear to have spread in English in the course of the seventeenth and eighteenth centuries. For Shakespeare, *wrong* was primarily a verb, or a noun derived from the verb, as in the following examples:

> He hath done me wrong.
> (Shakespeare, *I Henry VI*, Act IV, sc. i, l. 85)

> You wrong me, sir, thus still to haunt my house.
> (Shakespeare, *The Merry Wives of Windsor*, Act III, sc. iv, l. 67)

> Knowing my mind, you wrong me, Master Fenton.
> (Shakespeare, *The Merry Wives of Windsor*, Act III, sc. iv, l. 75)

At that stage, then, 'wrong' was not seen, primarily, as an opposite of 'right', and human conduct was not seen as, predominantly, a series of binary choices — choices between "wrong" and "right." Furthermore, the idea of "doing wrong (to someone)" was not linked, inherently, with the idea of "conscious choice"; it was only linked with the *ability to know* that one was doing something bad (to someone else). However, when the two words—*right* and *wrong*—were juxtaposed, an additional semantic element appears to have come into play: the element of *thinking*, of discernment. Presumably, the image behind the two words conceived of as a pair of opposites was that of a person's two hands and two sides, right and left, lending itself so readily to an interpretation in terms of a thoughtful binary choice: which of the two hands? which of two sides? which of the two ways ("good" or "bad")? To quote Bunyan's *The Pilgrim's Progress*:

> Better, though difficult, the right way to go,
> than wrong, tho' easy, when the end is woe. (Bunyan 1965, 74)

Here, it is not a question of wronging other people but of choosing, consciously, one of two (clearly distinguishable) ways to act.

A few early examples of the contrastive use of *right* and *wrong* (no longer linked with the idea of wronging someone) can already be found in Shakespeare, to wit:

> Force should be right, or rather, right and wrong,
> Between whose endless jar justice resides.
> (Shakespeare, *Troilus and Cressida*, Act I, sc. iii, ll. 116–117)

Later on in the seventeenth and eighteenth centuries, such a contrastive use of *right* and *wrong* appears to have increased.

Gradually, the image of two hands (or sides) and two ways (right and left, right and wrong) appears to have replaced in English an earlier image of a "right line" in the sense of a "straight line" and of possible deviations from that straight line. For example:

> Of lines there be two principal kinds, . . . a right or straight line, and . . . a crooked line. (1551, OED)

Thus, the right way was originally conceived of not as opposed to the symmetrical wrong way (one of the two possibilities) but as a kind of ideal that one should seek to approximate and that one may approximate to different degrees. Certainly, the use of the superlative (*rightest*) and comparative (*righter*) seems very common in English up to the seventeenth century.

> This is the rightest way and fittest order to serve God. (1561, OED)

> . . . then with a few to walk the rightest way. (1590, OED)

> That negative and contradictory humour, of thinking they are the rightest when they are unlikest the Papacy. (1599, OED)

> I would ask you whether in all these great points the Papists are righter than the Reformed Churches? (1665, OED)

> He observes that Hollenshede is righter than Parker. (1716, OED)

But as the pair of opposites "right" and "wrong" spread, the use of *righter* and *rightest* appears to have decreased, the idea of a binary choice gradually replacing that of trying to approximate an ideal. When the poet Cowper says at the end of the eighteenth century,

> Grace leads the right way: if you choose the wrong,
> Take it and perish. (1781)

he seems to be using *right* in the new sense, in which it is no longer gradable (as *right* and *left* are not gradable). How could life's choices appear to the seventeenth- and eighteenth-century speakers of English in the form of such clear-cut alternatives? The answer seems to be that life's problems came to be viewed increasingly as decidable by reason, like scientific problems, on the basis of clear, objective criteria.

3.3. The Link between "Right" and "Reason"

To pursue these questions further, we need to engage in a certain amount of careful semantic analysis. We can't ask what the words *good* and *bad* mean because these are (as colleagues and I have shown; see, e.g., Wierzbicka 1996c; Goddard 1998) unanalyzable conceptual primes. We can, however, ask about the meaning of the words *right* and *wrong* (as in the previous quotes), and here it can help to consider two expressions that do have equivalents in many other European languages: "you (we, they, etc.) are (were) right" and "you (we, they, etc.) are (were) wrong," that is, expressions that link the adjectives *right* and *wrong* used as predicates with human subjects. Interestingly, in several European languages, the literal equivalents of these expressions include a word that can also mean "reason." For example:

> *tu   as   raison* (French)
> you have reason
> "you're right"

> *[tu]   hai ragione* (Italian)
> [you] have reason
> "you're right"

What does it mean to say to someone "you're right" (*tu as raison, hai ragione*)? Roughly speaking, it means, I think, to express one's approval of this person's thinking, with reference to some potential interpersonal knowledge (or evidence). Thus:

> You're right. =
> a. you say: "I think (now) that it is like this"
> b. when you think like this you think well
> c. it is like this
> d. if someone thinks that it is not like this, this someone doesn't think well
> e. people can know that it is like this

Component (a) acknowledges the interlocutor's current opinion, component (b) approves of the interlocutor's thinking, component (c) confirms that this thinking corresponds to the way things are, component (d) contrasts this way of thinking with a different (wrong) one, and component (e) shows that this evaluation can be supported with reference to some interpersonally valid criteria (or reasons).

For a person to be "right" does not mean to think what most people think, because one can readily say in English: "I believe that she is right, although most people disagree with her." At the same time, the sentence "she is right" implies that what "she" thinks is objectively valid and that in principle other people *can* know this. If this is right, then what does it mean to say about something that "this is right" (an expression that, in contrast to "you/they/we etc. are right," does not have equivalents in other European languages)? Presumably, it means something analogous to "you (they, we, etc.) are right":

This is right. =
a. if someone thinks that it is like this, this person thinks well
b. if someone thinks that it is not like this, this person doesn't think well
c. it is like this
d. people can know that it is like this

I believe that this analysis can also be extended to English collocations like *the right decision* or *the right choice* or *the right solution*: the decision, the choice, or the solution is the outcome of someone's thinking, and in the speaker's view, this way of thinking about the matter at hand, in contrast to other ways of thinking about it, is good—an evaluation that, the speaker thinks, could be somehow objectively validated.

But if this is what *the right decision, the right choice*, or *the right solution* means, *the right thing to do* would seem to mean something very similar—or perhaps even the same. Jefferson's principle "to do whatever is right" seems to reflect a belief that in any given situation there is one good way of acting that can be reached by rational thought (i.e., by good thinking).

The importance of the idea of "good thinking" (i.e., of "thinking well") in Anglo folk philosophy is reflected in the colloquial conversational response "Good thinking!" that is without parallels in other European languages. For example (examples from a novel by Kathrine Kerr, taken from the Cobuild corpus of "UK Books"):

Enj considered for a moment. Since they hunt by sight, we should make a run for the base of the cliff now. "Good thinking," Rhodry said.

"We can send other men when I see the army approaching, for the final warning, like, but this way the banadar will know our situation." "Good thinking," Dar said.

"You know, I was thinking. We'd best tether the mule close, in here if that's possible. I don't want it being chased away in the night and having Otho insist on chasing after." "Good thinking. We'll do that."

It is particularly interesting to note cases where the phrase *good thinking* is combined overtly with the word *right* and used, as it were, as its partial folk explication, as in the following example:

"She know [*sic*] how you got the money?" "Oh, yeah. That was the whole idea. So the money couldn't be traced back to me." "Right," Kevin said approvingly. "Good thinking."

In this last example, *right* is used in a conversational sense, and the actions approved of by the speaker are not exactly "moral" in the usual sense of the word; yet the combination of approval for someone's actions and for the thinking behind the actions is very clear, and it illuminates other uses of the word *right* as well.

Another English conversational formula that expresses the speaker's approval for somebody else's thinking is "Good idea!", which also readily combines with "Right." as in the following examples from "UK Spoken":

> Right. . . . I think it's a very good idea.
> Right. And a year was also a good idea.
> Right. You use telekinesis to extend its range. Good idea.

One of the most intriguing aspects of the distinction between 'right' and 'wrong', so entrenched in the English language, is that these concepts appear to span moral and intellectual domains. Thus, one can "do the right thing," one can "do something wrong," but one can also "give the right (or wrong) answer" or "use the right (or wrong) method." The common denominator appears to be something like "problem solving": something to do with thinking, with procedures, with rules. It is interesting to recall in this context Benjamin Franklin's discussion of "the Science of Virtue," in which he likened "a Man of Sense," that is, "a virtuous man" (contrasted with "a vicious man"), to an arithmetician:

> There seems no necessity that to be a Man of Sense, he should never make a Slip in the Path of Virtue, or in Point of Morality; provided he is sensible of his Failing and diligently applys himself to rectify what is done amiss, and to prevent the like for the future. The best Arithmetician may err in casting up a long Account; but having found that Error, he *knows how* to mend it, and immediately does so; and is, notwithstanding that Error, an Arithmetician; But he who *always* blunders, and cannot correct his Faults in Accounting, is no Arithmetician; nor is the habitually-vicious Man a Man of Sense. (quoted in Levin 1963, 32)

Thus, the ascendancy of 'right' and 'wrong' over 'good' and 'bad' seems to reflect a more rational, more procedural, more reason-based approach to human life and a retreat from a pure distinction between GOOD and BAD unsupported by any appeal to reason, procedures, methods, or intersubjectively available evidence. An ethics of right and wrong is an ethics in which the choice between good and bad is seen as something that can be decided by reason, by good thinking, and something that can be interpersonally validated—like science. It is a rational ethics, an ethics that doesn't need to be grounded in metaphysics (in particular, in God) but can be grounded in reason.

Emphasizing the influence of the seventeenth and eighteenth centuries' British empiricism on the general intellectual climate of the time, Fernández-Armesto, the author of *Truth: A History and Guide for the Perplexed*, writes:

> Newton's work was both genuinely pioneering and embedded in a broader context of English and Scottish thought of the time: empiricism—the doctrine that reality is observable and verifiable by sense-perception. The success of science surely made possible this distrust of metaphysics. (Fernández-Armesto 1998, 153)

As I discussed elsewhere (Wierzbicka 2002d), this "distrust of metaphysics" may have contributed to the decline of British people's interest in "truth" and may have made them feel less comfortable with saying "that's true" than their contemporaries on the Continent did (and continue to do). Here, I would like to suggest that the same "distrust of metaphysics" may also have led to an avoidance of moral judgments unsupported by references to justification. The use of *right* may have been felt to be preferable to both the use of *true* and the use of *good*, for in contrast to both *true* and *good*, *right* appealed, implicitly, to some rational grounds for the expressed judgment. (I return to this convergence between *good* and *true* in *right* in section 3.6.)

Fernández-Armesto writes further: "The ascendancy of the senses over other means of truth-finding did not last long, even in the west, but while it endured it made a vital difference: it gave science unique prestige—a place in the prevailing scale of values unmatched in other cultures" (1998, 155). In my view, the "ascendancy of the senses" is better described in terms of knowledge finding than truth finding: in the climate of empiricism, people became increasingly inclined to replace the "search for truth" (the title of one of Descartes's works) with a "search for knowledge" (based on the evidence of the senses, as well as reason). The spread of "that's right" as a conversational response in modern English may be a reflection of this more general trend. (Another reflection of this trend is the rise of *really* and *evidence*; see Wierzbicka 2002d.) Note in this connection that in Britain, empiricism was not opposed to rationalism, as it often was elsewhere, but rather tended to be identified with it.

> Although the use of reason is as old as the history of mankind, its spells of preponderance succeed those of the truth you feel and the truth you are told. Reason provides a means of escaping from the constraints of belief-systems backed by authority and from the resentment which clever people feel at the power of their own passions. Because reason—in admittedly varying degrees—is available to everybody, it has a potential advantage over the truth you feel and the truth you are told. . . .
>
> Reason means different things to different people. To some people—a lot of them, a hundred years ago—it has meant thought purged of metaphysics and dogma. In the powerful tradition known as "pure rationalism" it means thought opposed to other kinds of experience. In that known as empiricism, it means the opposite: thought disciplined by the evidence of sense. (Fernández-Armesto 1998, 85–86)

The peculiar character of the British rationalism (rationalism cum empiricism), combining thinking with knowing, is reflected in the key English word *mind*. The meaning of this word is revealingly different from the French *esprit* or the German *Geist*, neither of which includes a similar combination. Only the English *mind* contrasts the "body" (matched by the French *corps* and the German *Körper*) with an organ of thinking and knowing. (For further discussion, see Wierzbicka 1992, chapter 1.)

The combination of empiricism with an emphasis on reason in British thought is stressed in Charles Taylor's classic *Sources of the Self*, with special reference to John Locke, of whom he wrote:

> What probably made Locke the great teacher of the Enlightenment was his combination of these two factors: that he offered a plausible account of the new science as valid knowledge, intertwined with a theory of rational control of the self; and that he brought the two together under the ideal of rational self-responsibility.

Many things have been declared authoritatively true, both in science and in practice, which have no real title to the name. The rational, self-responsible subject can break with them, suspend his adhesion to them, and by submitting them to the test of their validity, remake or replace them.

Holding the package together is an ideal of freedom or independence, backed by a conception of disengagement and procedural reason. This has given Locke's outlook its tremendous influence, not only in the eighteenth century, but right through to today. (Taylor 1989, 174)

Significantly, Locke's book on religion bears the title *The Reasonableness of Christianity* (1999 [1696]). For Locke, the empiricist, both ethics and religion had to be grounded in reason (as was science)—not speculative but procedural reason. They both had to be "reasonable."

The two key words of modern Anglo culture, *evidence* (in the modern sense) and *reasonable*, have spread in parallel in the intellectual climate created by the British philosophy of the seventeenth and eighteenth centuries. *Evidence* (in the modern sense of the word) has no semantic counterpart in other European languages at all (as discussed in Wierzbicka 2002d, forthcoming) and does not appear, for example, in Shakespeare's work. *Reasonable* and *reasonably* don't have exact counterparts in French, and in German, Italian, or other European languages, neither *reasonable* nor *reasonably* has any semantic equivalent at all (see chapter 4).

It is also interesting to note how "pragmatic" the words *reasonable* and *reasonably* sound in modern English. Fernández-Armesto (1998, 86) writes: "'Be reasonable,' we say when we want someone to sacrifice an opinion in the interests of consensus." This may not be a very accurate analysis of what *reasonable* means, but in essence, the observation is surely apt, pointing to a kind of convergence between folk rationalism and folk pragmatism in modern Anglo culture: to be "reasonable," one needs to know not only how to think well but also how to interact, pragmatically, with other people. As we will see when we look more closely at the conversational routines based on the word *right*, these routines point to a similar convergence.

3.4. "That's Right"

When a child does mathematical sums or answers questions about dates or capitals of far-away countries, the teacher can respond with the phrases *that's right* and *that's not right*. An Italian or French teacher could not make a similar response, because there are no similar phrases in these languages. What an Italian or a French teacher could say in such a situation would be *bene!* and *bien!* or "well" (and, if the response is 'wrong', *no* and *non* 'no'). Of course, an English-speaking teacher could also praise a student by saying "good!", but a "procedural," factual-sounding response "that's right" is also available. The availability, and wide use, of this response is a peculiarity of modern English, related, I would argue, to the intellectual climate influenced by empirical and "antimetaphysical" thinkers like John Locke and David Hume.

But before contemplating any further the cultural and philosophical underpinnings of the rise of the "that's right" routine, let us first examine the semantics of this expression. If one asks native speakers what *that's right* means, they are likely to reply either that it means "that's true" or that it means "I agree" (i.e., in universal concepts, "I think the same"). But while such ad hoc glosses may seem to fit some contexts, they would not fit others, and so they cannot represent the semantic invariant of this expression. For example, neither "that's true" nor "I think the same" could be substituted for "that's right" in the following exchange from the Australian writer Alex Buzo's play *The Front Room Boys*:

THOMO: Oh, you must be the new typist.

SUNDRA: That's right. [? I agree; ? that's true] (p. 28)

Neither would the glosses "I agree" or "that's true" fit the following exchange from the English playwright Simon Gray's play *Quartermaine's Terms*:

LOOMIS: Yes, yes, of course, you're right, my dear, thank you, thank you. And a little rest—and I'll try to make Thomas have one, too—

MELANIE: That's right [? that's true], Eddie, you both need it. (Gray 1986, 244)

Is "that's right" analogous to "you're right"? Yes and no. Of the two, "that's right" sounds more factual and also more conversational. Typically, the word *that* refers in this phrase to the interlocutor's *words* immediately preceding the response and only indirectly to the thinking behind it:

That's right. =
a. you say: "I think that it is like this"
b. when you think like this you think well
c. it is like this
d. people can know that it is like this

Component (a) shows that when used as a conversational response, *that's right* refers to the interlocutor's words. Component (b) refers to the thinking behind the words and expresses approval of this thinking, component (c) confirms that this way of thinking corresponds to the way things are, and component (d) shows that this approval is based on some generally valid standard. A symmetrical component "if someone thinks something else about this, this someone doesn't think well" has not been included in this explication, because the conversational response signal "that's right" does not have a negative counterpart ("that's wrong"). The absence of such a component contributes to the less "intellectual" and more "conversational" character of "that's right" as compared with either "you are right" or "this is right."

The spread of conversational routines based on *right* goes hand in hand in English with the ascendancy of *really* over *truly*. Arguably, both *really* and *right* have occupied in English some of the ground still covered in other European languages (and earlier, in English) by *truth*. In saying "that's right" rather than "that's true," the speaker implies that there is some evidence, some procedure, or some commonly recognized standard to appeal to. It is not a matter of some "metaphysical truth" but rather a matter of "facts" that the speaker has access to. It is not surprising, therefore, that "that's right" is often used in response to questions concerning the speaker himself or herself (as in Sundra's response to Thomo). In particular, this phrase is often used to confirm other people's suppositions concerning what we think or what we are trying to say. Some examples from Porpora's interviews:

> I try to bring the conversation back to God's collective purpose for us. "Why, do you think that God . . . You think that God created human beings?" "That's right," says Frederick. (Porpora 2001, 143)

> Like others, Martha has once again reduced the question of our collective human purpose to God's individual purpose for her. I try to make certain of her position. "Now, and when you say that we're all here for a purpose, you mean we each individually have a different purpose?" "That's right" says Martha. "I think . . ." "Yeah," Frederick echoes. "We each have a purpose to be here." (Porpora 2001, 143)

> "Do you remember when you first had that . . . belief?"

> "Yes, since I came here. I'm telling you." "What . . . Can you describe, though, the incident?" I'm pressing my luck. 'The incident? Yes, when my kid was born." 'That was the first time you started to believe in something?" "That's right. That's right. It was a miracle. I start building . . . what we lost in the old country. I start building a new generation." (Porpora 2001, 109)

As noted earlier, the conversational response "that's right," which, roughly speaking, endorses another person's belief, has no opposite; the expression "that's wrong" is not similarly used in English as a standard conversational routine. This asymmetry between "that's right" and "that's wrong" matches the increasingly asymmetrical use of *right* and *wrong* in a moral sense (a question to which I return later). With the growth of individualism and "decline of conviction" (see Bellah et al. 1985; Fernández-Armesto 1998), calling somebody else's thoughts "wrong" has increasingly come to be seen as inappropriate (even "totalitarian"; see Crossan 1980)—as inappropriate as calling somebody else's *actions* "wrong." To say to another person "that's wrong" could be offensive; saying "that's right" is not similarly offensive, because it supports the other person. Moreover, it does not sound patronizing because it implicitly appeals to some evidence.

3.5. An Illustration: English vs. Italian

Consider the use of the word *vero* ("true") in the following exchange from Giovanni Arpino's novel *La Suora Giovane*:

> "Non è peccato, vero?" "No," riuscii a spiccicare. (Arpino 1973, 45) "It is not a sin, true?" "No," I managed to utter.

Although literally *vero* would be translated as "true," normally "true" (or "is it true?") would not be used in English in such a context. Instead, a "reverse word order, opposite polarity" tag question would probably be used: "It is not a sin, is it?" A tag question of this kind would be checking the opinion of the interlocutor, not the truth of the sentence. Yet in Italian, the use of *vero?* in such nonfactual sentences is very common. A few more examples (from the same novel):

Sei mesi fa mia madre è venuta a trovarmi. . . . Pativo e mi vergagnavo con lei. È brutto questo, vero? (p. 54)
"Six months ago my mother came to visit me. . . . I suffered and was ashamed of her. This is pretty bad, isn't it?" (Lit. "true?")
Antonino, insegnami, ti prego. Vero che mi insegnerai? (p. 61)
"Antonio, teach me, I beg you. You *will* teach me, won't you?" (Lit. "True that you'll teach me?")
Per mesi ho sperato di vederti con loro. È stupido, vero? (p. 64)
"For months I hoped to see you with them. Stupid, isn't it?" (Lit. "It is stupid, true?")

As I have discussed in my *Cross-Cultural Pragmatics* (Wierzbicka 1991/2003a, 37), the extensive use of tag questions is a characteristic feature of modern English, with important cultural implications. But the semantic content of the typical (reverse word order, opposite polarity) English tag questions is as revealing as their frequency. In most other European languages (including Italian, Spanish, German, Polish, Russian, and Finnish), tag questions typically involve the word for *true*, as in Italian, and by using them, the speaker is asking the addressee to confirm that the sentence is true. In English, on the other hand, the speaker does not refer to the sentence's truth but rather asks the addressee to confirm (or disconfirm) the speaker's expectation that the addressee would say "it is like this" or "it is not like this." For example:

Stupid, isn't it? =
a. when I think about it I think that it is like this
b. I think that you will say: "it is like this"
c. I know that you can say: "it is not like this"

The tag question "right?" (which is less common in English and which is described by the OED as "originally US") sounds more forceful, sometimes even hectoring, because it refers, obliquely, to evidence: "right?" indicates that the addressee will have no choice but to confirm the speaker's expectation. I will propose two different (though symmetrical) explications for "right?" linked with different contexts.

A. with declaratives
Example
I mean different people are taught different values, right? (from Porpora 2001, 79)
Explication
(*I mean different people are taught different values, right?*) =

    a. when I think about it I think that it is like this [different people have different values]
    b. I think that you will say something like this now:
    c. "when you think like this you think well
    d. it is like this
    e. people can know that it is like this"
    f. I want you to say it

B. with instructions
Example

> ROBBO: Now, cross-check the registration column in that index and see if
> it matches up with the number of dates of reports received up until this date
> here, right? (from p. 26)

Explication
(Now, cross-check . . . and see . . . , right?)

> a. I think that you can know what I want to say
> b. I think that you can know what I want you to do
> c. I think that you will say something like this now:
> d. "when you think like this you think well
> e. it is like this
> f. I know what you want to say
> g. I know what you want me to do"

Because the word *right* implies the availability of rational justification when it is used
as a tag question, it does not combine with an expression of purely subjective opinion (see Wierzbicka 1991/2003a, 42), for example:

> She is nice, isn't she?
> She is nice, right?

As we have seen, the interrogative *right?* can be added to declarative sentences, too,
but only with reference to statements or instructions that imply a clear factual basis,
as in the following examples (from the OED):

> He was just doing his job, right? (1969)
> I was living alone on the West Side, in a one-room apartment . . . , right? (1977)
> You been here before, right? (1981)

"Right?" implies here that what the speaker says is verifiable, factual, precise — it can
be *known* rather than merely *thought*, as in the case of "she is nice." Thus, the use of
right as a tag presupposes a distinction between facts and opinions, a distinction that
is not similarly made in languages that use an equivalent of *true* for both opinions
and facts. I suggest that what applies to *right?* as a tag question applies also to *right* in
other contexts: it is a word that implies a possibility of interpersonal agreement based
on some objective basis, for example, on an explicit procedure for verification or
validation of what is being said.[2]

3.6. "Right" as a Neutral Ground between "Good" and "True"

In any language, assessments framed in terms of TRUE appear to be quite different
from those framed in terms of GOOD: there seems to be a clear-cut line between the
two. But phrases like *the right decision, the right answer,* or *the right solution* somehow cross that line: they seem to combine the element of approval (good) with an

element of intellectual judgment. At the same time, they seem to avoid both the "subjectivity" of (unsupported) moral evaluation and the "arrogance" of truth-judgments (as opposed to statements of opinion).

Consider, for example, the slogan *do the right thing, put it in the bin*. Clearly, the slogan does not present the action of putting some rubbish in the bin as a "good deed." Rather, the action of putting rubbish in the bin is presented here as something rational: it *is* a good thing to put rubbish in the bin but not because of any intangible moral imperative; rather, it is a good thing to do so—and a bad thing not to—because of certain rules that apply to everyone and that can be rationally explained and justified.

In this sense, it is comparable to arriving at the right answer to a problem in arithmetic: it is not a question of anybody's moral judgment but of certain objectively valid procedures, methods, and criteria. A person could reject metaphysics and religion and still say that putting rubbish in the bin is the right thing to do. From this perspective, reflected in modern English, human conduct can be seen and assessed "objectively," "rationally," and in accordance with "evidence." There are "rules," there are "procedures," and there are objective criteria that people can refer to. As the nineteenth-century English philosopher Herbert Spencer put it,

> *Rightness* expresses of actions, what *straightness* does of lines; and there can no more be two kinds of right action than there can be two kinds of straight line. (*Social Statics* 1892, chap. 32, sc. 4)

Many similar statements have come from the pens of English and American writers, with the word *right* both reflecting and presumably encouraging this culture-specific way of thinking: that deciding what to do—or what to say—can be a matter of following certain straightforward, public, rationally justifiable procedures; that ethics can be analogous to geometry (Emerson 1932, 52: "The axioms of geometry translate the laws of ethics"). Consider, for example, the following sentence (from spoken English): "I can't go [to tap dancing] because I don't have the right shoes." *Right* could be replaced here with *appropriate, suitable*, or *fitting*, but it is not a separate meaning of the word *right*. Rather, it is the same meaning as in the case of *a right decision, right answer*, or *right solution*: a meaning (unavailable in Italian, French, or German) that allows the speaker to stay on a "philosophically neutral" ground, without laying any claims to knowing what is true or what is (inherently, intrinsically, unaccountably) good. To identify a pair of shoes as "the right shoes," one needs to assess the fit between a kind of shoes and a kind of situation, between the features of the shoes and the requirements of the situation. Thus, the evaluation of the shoes has to involve some objective, interpersonally valid criteria.

> *These are the right shoes (for tap dancing).* =
> a. if someone says: "I think that these shoes are good (for tap dancing)"
> this someone thinks well
> b. it is like this
> c. people can know that it is like this
> d. people can say why it is like this

A particular kind of shoes is good for tap dancing because the properties of the shoes fit the purpose (tap dancing): these shoes are a good means from the point of view of the purpose, and people can say *why* they are a good means (because they can say how the properties of the shoes fit the purpose of tap dancing). The shoes are not intrinsically good, but they are instrumentally good; and the claim that they are good (for tap dancing) is not a matter of faith or taste but a matter that can be rationally justified. Evaluation and rational justification go hand in hand here. And so, it seems, is generally the case with *right*, as compared to *good*. The "right" answer and the "right" solution, too, are "good" because they can be rationally justified; and so is the "right" choice, the "right" decision, and also the "right" action. Truth doesn't come into it, not even in the case of the "right" answer: what matters is the justification. To do the "right thing" means to do something that is not simply "good" but something that can be rationally justified.

3.7. Procedural Morality

The ascendancy of *right* and *wrong* in the English language can be linked with the rise of "procedural morality" in Anglo culture. According to Porpora (2001, 72), "to say that modern morality is mainly procedural is to say that it focuses on the means we adopt to pursue our ends." For many of Porpora's respondents, ethics means not lying, cheating, or hurting other people, in accordance with the principle "Do your own thing as long as you don't hurt anyone." As long as they don't hurt other people, they think that everyone should be free to do their own thing. Porpora (2001, 72) comments:

> That is fine, but what should "our own thing" be? A morality reduced solely to procedural constraints totally removes "our own thing" from moral discourse. For such a morality, whatever "our own thing" is, it will by definition lack moral purpose. Instead, whatever ends we choose to pursue within the procedural constraints will have the appearance of morally neutral preferences.

In his discussion of this problem, Porpora (2001, 9) draws on the work of Charles Taylor, who argues that with regard to morality modern culture emphasizes "what is right or wrong to do" as opposed to "what it is good or bad for us to be." Taylor links "proceduralist ethics" with "a procedural conception of the right, whereby what we ought to do can be generated by some canonical procedure" (Taylor 1989, 503). Drawing on Taylor and speaking specifically about contemporary American culture, Porpora comments on the separation of morality from its religious roots—even among the religious (2001, 106). He links this separation with a pervasive loss of purpose and larger, moral vision and, among the Christians, who are some 85% of the population, "the routinization of Jesus' charismatic ethics" (p.166).

As I see it, the emergence of this "procedural ethics" is related to the linguistic phenomenon of the emergence and spread of the concepts of 'right' and 'wrong'. The rise of "procedural ethics" is linked with the rise of "rational ethics," and the separation of morality from its religious roots is linked with the idea that all beliefs require rational justification. A "right" decision is like a "right" solution to a problem (mathematical, logical, ethical, or practical): it can be justified with reference to a set of procedures, rules, or criteria. As Porpora argues, one's purpose in life can hardly be thought of in terms of "right" or "wrong"—or in terms of procedures, rules, and ethical "standards."

> To speak of the ultimate good is to speak of that good that concerns us ultimately, the good that constitutes the ultimate purpose of our lives. The problem in the modern or postmodern world is a pervasive loss of emotionally moving contact with a good that is ultimate, a contact that was once provided by the sacred. . . . As a consequence, the whole of our lives is without any overarching moral purpose. . . . This hardly means that we are all immoral. It does mean that our sense of morality has become largely procedural. (Porpora 2001, 71–72)

How exactly is the emergence and spread of procedural morality related to changes in the English language? Needless to say, I am not suggesting that the rise of 'right' and 'wrong' has somehow narrowed down English speakers' conceptual options or determined their ways of thinking. Rather, I am suggesting that the rise of new ways of thinking has led to the emergence of new linguistic and conceptual tools: *right* and *wrong* (not *instead of*, but *in addition to, good* and *bad*), *fair* and *unfair* (not *instead of*, but *in addition to, just* and *unjust*), and so on.

As discussed by Porpora, the Gospel ethics is not procedural ethics, and it is not an ethics of right and wrong. For example, the injunctions to turn the other cheek, to love one's enemies and to do good to those who hate us were not put forward as the right things to do. Rather, they meant, "it will be good if you turn the other cheek"; "it will be good if you love your enemies"; "it will be good if you do good to those who hate you" (Luke 6:27–29); not *right* but *good*, and the only reason offered for these injunctions is that this is what God wants and does ("be merciful, just as your Father also is merciful," Luke 6:36). There is no "rational" justification. (For discussion, see Wierzbicka 2004)

The idea of a "rational ethics," an ethics based on the notions of 'right' and 'wrong', was linked with the broader ideas of a "rational religion," favored by the Enlightenment and perhaps congenial to the "spirit of capitalism" (as suggested originally by Weber 1968 [1930] and discussed recently by Charles Taylor 1989). Locke argued in his Second Treatise (quoted by Taylor 1989, 238), that "God . . . hath . . . given them [mankind] reason to make use of it to the best advantage of Life, and convenience." According to Taylor (p. 239), Locke "is in fact a crucial hinge figure in the evolution of the ethic of ordinary life . . . , which has both facilitated and been entrenched by the rise of capitalism." Locke did not reject God but, as discussed by Taylor, he linked religion and ethics with "living rationally."

> Rising from passion, blind prejudice, and unthinking custom to reason confers the two related transformations: it gives our own productive life order and dignity, and it releases us from egoism and destructiveness to benefit others. Disengaged procedural reason raises us from destruction to beneficence because it breaks the shackles of illusion, blind custom, and superstition. . . . This high view of the morally transformatory power of reason . . . will be developed into one of the major organizing ideas of the Enlightenment. . . . Instrumental rationality, properly conducted, is of the essence of our service of God. . . . The rationality in question is now procedural: in practical affairs, instrumental, in theoretical, involving the careful, disengaged scrutiny of our ideas and their assembly according to the canons of mathematical deduction, and empirical probability. (Taylor 1989, 242–243).

Drawing on Weber, Taylor examines in considerable detail the links between the Protestant Reformation, the Enlightenment, the rise of capitalism, and changes in everyday ways of thinking. Weber saw in the Calvinist doctrine of predestination "the dogmatic background of the Puritan morality in the sense of methodically rationalized ethical conduct" (1989, 125), and he emphasized as "the most important result of ascetic Protestantism . . . a systematic, rational ordering of the moral life as a whole" (p. 126). Lutheranism, according to Weber, "lacked a psychological sanction of systematic conduct to compel the methodical rationalization of life" (p. 128). Invoking Weber's notion of a "disenchanted world," Taylor writes:

> The cosmos is no longer seen as the embodiment of meaningful order which can define the good for us . . . We demystify the cosmos as a setter of ends by grasping it mechanistically and functionally as a domain of possible means. Gaining insight into the world as mechanism is inseparable from seeing it as a domain of potential instrumental control. (Taylor 1989, 148)

Porpora (2001, 199, 200) summarizes Taylor's thesis as affirming that "ours is a disenchanted age that affirms ordinary life over transcendental meaning," "an age in which everyday life is valorized, not some higher plane of transcendent purpose." Taylor's thesis that modern (Anglo) culture emphasizes what is right or wrong to do as opposed to what it is good or bad to value or be closely accords with linguistic facts and, in particular, with the career of the words *right* and *wrong* in the English language. Especially, *right*.

3.8. "Right" and "Wrong": Increasingly Asymmetrical

As we have seen, for a long time the concepts 'right' and 'wrong' were perceived by speakers of English as symmetrical, and the two words were often juxtaposed, analogously to *right* and *left*. During the twentieth century, however (if not earlier), the use of *wrong* appears to have declined, in comparison with *right*, and many speakers of English appear to have become increasingly uncomfortable with the word *wrong*. One might venture to suggest that the decline of *wrong* (in relation to *right*) paralleled (and perhaps was related to) the spread of the pejorative word *judgmental*: it is bad to be judgmental, and to call anyone or anything wrong seems to have increasingly been felt to be smacking of judgmentalism. Consider, for example, the following fragment from one of Porpora's interviews:

> ". . . Let's say we were just talking about whether or not there is a supreme being."
> "Okay."
> "Do you think that there is . . . I have my opinion, you have your opinion. Do you think that one of us could be right and the other could be wrong?"
> "Sure."
> "Both of us could be wrong?"
> "We could both be right."
> "Oh," I agree, "and we could both be right."
> "Well, exactly. I mean, you know, but that . . . that's what this world is made up of: Different people with differences of opinions."

"And how do we arrive at the truth?"

"I have no idea. I think if we knew that, we'd be the supreme being." (Porpora 2001, 90)

Characteristically, the interviewee (not comfortable with the notion of "truth") does not feel any qualms about describing some opinions as possibly right; he does, however, seem reluctant to call somebody else's opinions "wrong": for him, two people who hold contrary opinions could both be "right," but they could not both be "wrong." The same reluctance to describe anything (and, in particular, any opinion) as "wrong" is reflected in the following interview:

> "I do," Peter says, "consider the two very similar: values and preferences. Just because some values aren't mine, that doesn't mean they're wrong or mine are more right than others."
>
> "So," I press him, "You wouldn't say that somebody who, who is a neo-Nazi . . . neo-Nazi values . . . You wouldn't say those values are wrong?"
>
> "Well . . ."
>
> "Any more than you wouldn't, you wouldn't say that I'm wrong if I didn't like vanilla ice cream, actually . . ."
>
> "Exactly . . . I'm going through the definition of how I see wrong in relation to my values. Believing in my values, neo-Nazis are wrong, but, I mean, who's to say? It's kind of difficult. I would say yes and no on that. neo-Nazis are not wrong, but in my value system they're wrong." (Porpora 2001, 80–81)

Fernández-Armesto notes the growing reluctance of many people in Western culture to call any opinion wrong and links it with what he calls "the retreat from truth":

> In a society of concessions to rival viewpoints, in which citizens hesitate to demand what is true and denounce what is false, it becomes impossible to defend the traditional moral distinction between right and wrong, which are relativized in turn. . . . Unless it is true, what status is left for a statement like "X is wrong" where X is, say, adultery, infanticide, euthanasia, drug-dealing, Nazism, paedophilia, sadism or any other wickedness due, in today's climate, for relativization into the ranks of the acceptable? It becomes, like everything else in western society today, a matter of opinion. (Fernández-Armesto 1998, 165–166)

The point is debatable: instead of saying, "The statement 'infanticide is wrong' is true," one might prefer to say, "It is bad to kill babies." But the observation that in Anglo societies many English-speaking people are increasingly reluctant to call any personal opinion wrong is indisputable (though politically correct injunctions and prohibitions may have come to form an exception to this). Above all, this applies, of course, to the opinions of one's interlocutors.

From a strictly logical point of view, it would seem that "right" and "wrong" should be—for anyone—equally acceptable or equally unacceptable. In fact, however, *wrong* appears to be, for many speakers, less acceptable than *right*—presumably, because *wrong* is more likely to give offense than *right*. What is involved, then, is not only the degree of confidence in one's ability to make moral judgments but also the cultural norms requiring the speakers to avoid unnecessary confrontation and offense and encouraging them to seek good relations with their interlocutors. From a modern Anglo point of view, there is a big difference between saying to one's interlocutor "you're right" and saying to them "you're wrong." Whatever one thinks of the merits of one's interlocutor's argument, "you're right" is culturally more appropriate than "you're wrong." The reason for this asymmetry lies not in any universal "logic of conversation" or "principles of politeness" but in culture-specific Anglo norms of social interaction. Again, Benjamin Franklin's *Autobiography* is highly illuminating on this point:

> I made it a rule to forbear all direct contradiction to the sentiments of others. . . .
> When another asserted something that I thought an error, I denied myself the plea-
> sure of contradicting him abruptly and of showing immediately some absurdity in
> his proposition; and in answering I began by observing that in certain cases or cir-
> cumstances his opinion would be right, but that in the present case there "appeared"
> or "seemed to me" some difference, etc. (quoted in Levin 1963, 20)

According to Franklin, this avoidance of a direct "you are wrong" approach proved, pragmatically, most effective in his interaction with other people:

> I soon found the advantage of this change in my manners: The conversations I
> engaged in went on more pleasantly; the modest way in which I proposed my opin-
> ions procured them a readier reception and less contradiction . . . And to this habit
> . . . I think it principally owing that I had early so much weight with my fellow
> citizens when I proposed new institutions or alterations in the old, and so much
> influence in public councils when I became a member. For I was but a bad speaker,
> never eloquent, subject to much hesitation in my choice of words, hardly ever cor-
> rect in language, and yet I generally carried my point. (quoted in Levin 1963, 20)

Presumably, large numbers of Franklin's compatriots must have shared his experience to some extent, for with time the avoidance of "you are wrong" and the like became a salient cultural script. To quote Eva Hoffman (1989), who as a teenager emigrated with her family from Poland to America and who had to learn the unspoken cultural scripts of her new country:

> I learn also that certain kinds of truth are impolite. One shouldn't criticize the
> person one is with, at least not directly. You shouldn't say, "You are wrong about
> that"—though you may say, "On the other hand, there is that to consider." You
> shouldn't say, "This doesn't look good on you," though you may say, "I like you
> better in that other outfit." I learn to tone down my sharpness, to do a more careful
> conversational minuet. (Hoffman 1989, 146)

It is interesting to compare Hoffman's perception of avoidance of "you are wrong" in Anglo-American culture with Blum-Kulka's (1982) comment on the use of *ata to'e* ("you're wrong") in Israeli culture:

> Generally speaking, Israeli society seems to allow for even more directness in so-
> cial interaction than the American one. . . . It is not uncommon to hear people
> around a conference table in Israel disagreeing with each other bluntly (saying
> things like *ata to'e* "You're wrong," or *lo naxon!* "Not true!"). Such directness in a
> similar setting in American society would probably be considered rude. (Blum-
> Kulka 1982, 30–31)

Both Hoffman and Blum-Kulka are talking here about saying "*you* are wrong," rather than "*he* or *she* is wrong," and in contemporary Anglo (American) culture the pressure to avoid "you are wrong" is no doubt stronger than that to avoid saying "he or she is wrong" or "it (e.g., infanticide) is wrong." It seems, however, that *wrong* in general tends to be increasingly avoided, as "presumptuous" and, as it were, "undemocratic." *Right* fares better: although there are some cultural scripts operating against both *right* and *wrong*, there are other scripts operating in favor of *right*—especially in conversational routines where *right* is addressed to the addressee, as in *that's right*, but also in conversational responses like *right, right you are, too right*, and so on. I discuss these conversational routines in more detail in section 10. First, however, I will present the reader with some statistics.

3.9. The Changing Frequencies of *True, Truth, Right*, and *Wrong*

Let us first compare in Table 3.2 the frequencies of the words *true, truth, right* (adjective), and *wrong* (adjective) in the concordances to the works of two English playwrights, separated by three centuries, Shakespeare (Spevack 1970) and Bernard Shaw (Bevan 1971) (figures per 1 million words).

What these figures suggest is that the use of both *true* and *truth* declined significantly, whereas the use of *right* and *wrong* (as adjectives) increased. They also suggest that *wrong*, which Shakespeare used primarily as a noun or a verb, over the centuries greatly expanded its use as an adjective—not on a scale comparable with the use of *right* as an adjective but nonetheless coming far closer to it than it was in Shakespeare's use. These figures are consistent with the hypothesis that the "discourse of truth" declined in English over the centuries, that the use of right and wrong as parallel concepts (and opposites) increased, and that the use of *right* as an adjective increased enormously in relation to the use of *true*.

If we now extend our comparison and include in Table 3.3 figures for spoken English ("UK Spoken") from the contemporary Cobuild Bank of English, we will see, first of all, that in comparison with Shaw (let alone Shakespeare) the figures for *true* and *truth* are extremely low. Furthermore, the figure for *right* is higher than in Shaw, and the figure for *wrong*, lower.

The very high frequency of *right* in contemporary spoken English differs markedly from its frequency in the contemporary corpus of written English (Cobuild's "UK Books"), as shown in Table 3.4.

Presumably, this explosion of *right* in spoken English is linked with the rise of conversational responses such as "that's right," "right you are," "too right," and simply "right." Of course, we do not have at our disposal a corpus of spoken English for

TABLE 3.2 Frequencies of *true, truth, right*, and *wrong* in Shakespeare and Shaw

	True	Truth	Adj. Right	(Total Right)	Adj. Wrong	(Total Wrong)
Shakespeare	959	391	180	(420)	17	(288)
Shaw	324	215	448	(890)	148	(206)

TABLE 3.3 Frequencies of *true, truth, right,* and *wrong*
in Shakespeare, Shaw, and Cobuild's corpus of
Spoken UK English

	True	Truth	Adj. Right	Adj. Wrong
Shakespeare	959	391	180	17
Shaw	324	215	448	148
Cobuild: UK Spoken	40	7	629	56

the times of Shakespeare, or even the times of Bernard Shaw, and dialogue in plays couldn't possibly be regarded as a functional equivalent of such a corpus. We cannot, therefore, prove an increase in the use of *right* in spoken English on a statistical basis. What we *can* show, however, is the emergence of new conversational routines in nineteenth- and twentieth-century spoken discourse.

These routines include, for one thing, the expression *all right* (used, according to the OED, "to express acquiescence or assent"), the first example of which cited by the OED comes from Dickens's *Pickwick Papers* (1837). Another important relatively recent conversational routine involves the expression *that's right* ("used to express affirmation or agreement," OED), the first example of which cited by the OED is dated as 1905:

> The President's address was frequently interrupted with applause and cries of "That's right."

Relatively recent conversational routines include also such expressions as "right you are!" (described by the OED as "recent slang use"), "too right" (labeled by the OED as "Australian and New Zealand colloquial"), "she'll be right" (also described as "Australian and New Zealand colloquial"), and the interrogative". . . . right?" ("inviting agreement or approval"), described by the OED as "originally U.S." and illustrated with only twentieth-century examples. In Australia, a particularly common conversational routine is the interactive-reassuring use of the phrase *you're right*, indicating that the speaker doesn't mind what the addressee is doing. I would argue that these recent conversational routines involving *right* include also several distinct uses of "Right" as a response in dialogue, to which I will now turn.

TABLE 3.4 Frequencies of *true, truth, right,* and
wrong in spoken and written UK English (from
Cobuild)

	True	Truth	Adj. Right	Adj. Wrong
UK Books	60	37	96	50
UK Spoken	40	7	629	56

3.10. "Right." as a Response in Dialogue

The use of "Right." as a "response signal" in dialogue goes back to sixteenth and seventeenth centuries, as the entry on *right* in the OED illustrates.

> Chiron: O 'tis a verse in Horace, I know it well . . .
> Aaron: Ay just, a verse in Horace; right, you have it.
> (Shakespeare, *Titus Andronicus*, Act IV, sc. ii, ll. 22, 24)

> Dalyell: She's . . . A princess of the blood, and I a subject
> Huntly: Right, but a noble subject. (Ford 1968 [1634], 22)

The OED defines this use of "Right!" as "You are right; you say well." I think this definition is, essentially, quite apt: the first speaker expresses an opinion, and the second approves of what the first speaker says and endorses it as true. Formulaically:

> A says to B: it is like this
> B says to A: you say something good (you speak well)
>   it is true

Seemingly, in contemporary English, the response "Right!" can still be used in a similar way (often with exclamatory intonation), as in the following example from the Donahue show (Carbaugh 1988, 28):

> AM: When we get to be senior citizens I think we should have the right to do what we want.
> DONAHUE: Yeah.
> A WOMAN SENIOR GUEST: Right!
> AM: And I'm for these people.
> AUDIENCE: (Applause).

Yet when we look at the whole spectrum of contemporary uses of *right*, it transpires that there are some important differences between the Shakespearean "Right!" of approval and the present-day one: whereas in Shakespeare's usage, "Right!" implies "you speak well, what you say is true," in present-day usage the approval refers to the previous speaker's thinking and to "the way things are": "you think well, it is like this."

What the OED doesn't make clear is that "Right." as a dialogical response has other uses and other meanings as well and that some of these uses are quite recent. The OED itself includes at least one (twentieth-century) example that appears to be different in meaning from the previous examples from Shakespeare and Ford. Roughly speaking, those earlier examples illustrate "agreement with a statement (regarded as true)," whereas the twentieth-century example illustrates "confirmation of a supposition":

> —"Have you ever thought of working for the Foreign Office?"
> —"The British one?"
> —"Right." (Gadney 1970)

Here, "Right." conveys something like "I confirm your guess." In the early examples, both speakers say what they think, not what they know; in the "confirmation" example, however, the person who says "Right." *knows* something that the other person doesn't know, and he or she confirms the other person's supposition or guess. Schematically:

A. I want to know what you wanted to say
   I think that you wanted to say this [the British one]
B. when you think like this you think well
   it is like this
   you know what I wanted to say

How far back does this use of "Right." as a confirmation go in the history of English? The matter requires investigation. It seems likely, however, that the earlier routine of "factual" confirmation of guesses or suppositions has led to routines of "conversational" ("metatextual") confirmation, as illustrated in the following exchange from Porpora's (2001, 79) interviews:

A. "You said you were raised to treat people like this?"
B. "Right."

Here, the interviewer (A) seems to be checking his understanding of what the interviewee (B) has said, in the spirit of conversational cooperation, and the interviewee confirms the supposition in the same spirit:

A. I want to know what you wanted to say
   I think that you wanted to say this [. . .]
B. you say "I want to know what you wanted to say
              I think that you wanted to say this [. . .]"
   when you think like this you think well
   it is like this
   you know what I wanted to say

This use of the response "Right." in the spirit of conversational cooperation brings us to a number of other apparently recent uses of this response, not documented in the OED at all, which can all be characterized, roughly, in terms of "cooperation." Consider, for example, the following four exchanges from a play by the contemporary English playwright Simon Gray (1986):

1. MELANIE (exiting): Off we go, St. John.

QUARTERMAINE: Right. (p. 274)

2. MELANIE (exiting): Jolly good—give her my love.

MEADLE: Right, Melanie, right. (p. 265)

3. WINDSCAPE (off): Actually, I've just finished [a game], I'm afraid—perhaps next week.

QUARTERMAINE (off): Right, I'll hold you to that. 'Night. (p. 239)

4. SACKLING: St. John, I'd be grateful if you'd stop referring to him as little Tom . . . —it makes him sound like something out of the workhouse.

QUARTERMAINE: O right—right. (p. 256)

What happens in such exchanges can be schematically summarized as follows:

A SAYS TO B: "I want something to happen
      I want you to do something because of this"

B SAYS TO A: you say: "I want something to happen
I want you to do something because of this
I think that you can know what I want you to do"
when you think like this you think well
I know what you want to say
I know what you want to happen
I know what you want me to do

It could be argued that here, too, the addressee approves of what the speaker has said, and of the thinking behind the words. But this characterization, lumping together the Shakespearean and the modern usage, would fail to show the specific features of this new usage. I would argue that it would also prevent us from gleaning the cultural underpinnings of the new conversational routine. The term *cooperation* is more useful here, because it points to new types of social relations in a democratic society: the use of "Right" in response to a request, suggestion, direction, or instruction signals a willingness to comply with another person's will while remaining on an equal footing. The assumption is that if I will do what you say you want me to do, I will do it because I know why you say it: I know that you are not trying to give me an order, to arbitrarily impose your will on me, but rather because you think it will be good if what you want to happen happens. I see your request is *rational*—not necessarily because I agree that it will be good if this thing happens but because I can know what you want me to do and why. I do not have to express any satisfaction at your request, but I do want to show that I know what you want to say and why. I accept your request as *reasonable*. (And so I will probably comply with it, though this is not as clear in the case of "Right." as it would be if I said "All right."

Here is a characteristic Australian example—an employee ("Robbo") speaking on the phone to his boss, Barry Anderson:

ROBBO: Hello? Oh, g'day. Yes. Can do. Will do. Right. Beauty. For sure. Right you are. See you. [Hangs up.] That was Barry Anderson. He wants report number 10777443101837392 taken to Alan White immediately. (Buzo 1973, 57)

Robbo is almost caricaturally eager to comply with his boss's wishes, and although he would never say to the boss anything like "Yes, sir," the expression "Right." serves him well. The use of "Right." indicates that both the boss and the subordinates link compliance with a spirit of equality and cooperation, rather than any submissiveness or subservience. The following exchange between another employee and their boss highlights the egalitarian character of the relationship:

GIBBO's phone rings.

GIBBO: Hello? Oh, g'day. Yes. Yes. Can do. Will do. Right. Beauty. For sure. Right you are. See you [Hangs up] That was Barry Anderson. Said he'd be down at the pub tonight for a few quiet beers. (Buzo 1973: 57)

Conversational routines expressing something like "cooperation" are useful in a society where people have to take directions and instructions from others without treating those others as their masters. By saying "Right." in response to somebody else's expression of will, the responder shows how he or she interprets that will: not as an order or a command but an understandable, rational thought that something is desirable. By saying "Right." in response, I acknowledge the first speaker's words as reasonable and as focused on a desirable state of affairs, rather than on any desire to impose their will on me.

There are several other conversational routines involving the response "Right." that can be seen as variations on the same theme. For example, the first speaker may want to do something himself or herself, and the second speaker may be simply expressing a willingness to help, as in the following exchange in the play *Who?* by the Australian playwright Jack Hibberd:

> PADDY: Think I'd better lie down for a while.
>
> ALEX: Right.
>
> [ALEX *helps* PADDY *to his bed*] (Hibberd 1973 [1970], 147)

Virtually the same formula applies here; the only difference lies in who is going to do what.

In addition to expressing a willingness to cooperate, "Right." can also be used to acknowledge cooperation that has already taken place and to express satisfaction at the completion of a task. For example, in Alex Buzo's play *The Front Room Boys*, Pammy is collecting money from her colleagues in the office for various "causes" (somebody's birthday, somebody else's new baby, and so on):

> PAMMY: Come on now . . . dig deep . . . pay up . . . Craig Hiscock's birthday. . . .
>
> PAMMY: That's all. . . .
>
> ALL: Thank you . . .
>
> PAMMY: Right, that's the lot. That's it for today. (Buzo 1973, 87)

Here, Pammy is acknowledging, with satisfaction, her colleagues' compliance with her expressed wish, and she interprets this compliance as based on the assumption that her wish was reasonable and made sense to them. At the same time, she is expressing satisfaction with her own thought processes: everything has gone according to plan.

> *Right, that's the lot.*
> a. I wanted something to happen
> b. I wanted you to do something because of this
> c. I thought that you could know what I wanted you to do
> d. when I thought like this I thought well
> e. it has happened now
> f. this is good

The last two components in this explication seem significant: the speaker's satisfaction ("this is good") is linked with the realization that what she wanted to happen has happened. And another analogous example from the same play:

THOMO: . . . Here, put those flowers round the wreath. . . . [they finish the wreath, GIBBO hands it to THOMO.]

GIBBO: Here you are, Thomo.

THOMO: Thanks, Gibbo. Right, now get your coats on and look smart. (Buzo 1973, 93)

This brings us back to the examples adduced at the outset of this chapter: "Right." as a conversational response expressing one's satisfaction with what one's interlocutor has just said in response to one's question. Here, too, cooperation is acknowledged, with a certain satisfaction, but this cooperation is purely verbal (at the level of saying rather than doing). As quoted earlier, in an interview with Porpora (2001, 143–144), one of the interviewees, Frederick, expresses his belief that 144,000 Jews will be saved, and the interviewer responds "Right." commenting for the reader's benefit that he is familiar with the belief in question. Here, Frederick has complied with the interviewer's wish to find out what he [the interviewee] thinks. If we replace "do" in the previous explication with "say," we can see that a similar explication applies there, too:

> *"Right." I am familiar with the belief . . .*
> a. I wanted you to say something
> b. because I wanted to know what you wanted to say
> c. I thought that you could know what I wanted you to do
> d. when I thought like this I thought well
> e. you said this now
> f. now I know what you wanted to say
> g. this is good

Thus, the interviewer acknowledges that the interviewee has done what the interviewer wanted him to do and that he has done it in the spirit of cooperation, on the assumption that the interviewer's wish made sense to him. In this case, the speaker's satisfaction ("this is good") is linked with the realization that his wish has been satisfied: he now knows that what he wanted to happen has happened; that is, he now knows what he wanted to know (i.e., what the interviewee wanted to say).

And two more examples (from a British novel)—seemingly dissimilar but in fact amenable to the same interpretation:

> "I'm not actually *from* India, you know," said Samad . . .
> Poppy Burt-Jones looked surprised and disappointed. "You're not?"
> "No. I'm from Bangladesh."
> "Bangladesh."
> "Previously Pakistan. Previous to that, Bengal."
> "Oh, right. . . ." (Zadie Smith 2000, 133)

Here, too, "Right." (often, *Oh, right*) implies "now I know [what you wanted to say], this is good." It also implies that Poppy's interlocutor (Samad) has interpreted her query as a reasonable and understandable quest for information and has responded to it in the spirit of cooperation. Essentially, the same applies to the following exchange from the same novel:

"... I was saying to my brother Abdul—"
"Which Abdul?" ...
"Abdul-Colin."
"Right." (Zadie Smith 2000, 186)

Here, "right" (which could be expanded to "Oh, right") conveys something like "now I know what you wanted to say." The utterance implies that there was something incomplete about the previous sentence (because there are several men named Abdul in the family) but that now the proper clarification has been supplied, and the interlocutor can be satisfied:

now I know what you wanted to say
this is good

Although the first part of the gloss offered for "Right" in the OED ("you are right") does not apply here at all, the second part ("you say well") does apply, to some extent at least, but it seems contrastive: "what you say *now* (in contrast to what you said before) is good (satisfactory)." For convenience, we could call this kind of use "the 'Right' of conversational satisfaction."

I wanted you to say something (more)
because I wanted to know what you wanted to say (what you meant)
you said this now
now I know what you wanted to say
this is good

3.11. "Right" and Cultural Scripts

As discussed in chapter 2, different cultures have different "cultural scripts"—different unwritten rules about how to behave, how to speak, and also how to think and how to feel. Often, these cultural scripts include guidelines concerning appropriate ways to respond to what other people say. In other cases, there are no specific scripts for how to respond to other people, but there are implicit norms that follow from certain more general scripts.

For example, the Russian language offers ample evidence for the existence, and salience, of the following cultural script:

[people think like this:]
people say two kinds of things to other people
things of one kind are true
it is good if a person wants to say things of this kind to other people
things of the other kind are not true
it is bad if a person wants to say things of this kind to other people

The existence and common colloquial use of the word *nepravda* ("untruth"), alongside *pravda* ("truth"), and the symmetrical use of phrases like *govorit' pravdu* ("to speak truth") and *govorit' nepravdu* ("to speak untruth"), is perhaps the clearest piece of evidence supporting this script; but there are others. (See V. Apresjan 2000; Wierzbicka 2002c.)

In Japanese culture, there is evidence for scripts that, roughly speaking, discourage expression of disagreement and encourage expression of agreement (see, e.g., Asano 2003):

> [people think like this:]
> when a person says to me about something: "I think about it like this"
> it is not good to say something like this to this person:
>> "I don't think the same"

> [people think like this:]
> when I say to another person about something: "I think about it like this"
> it is good to say something like this to this person at the same time:
>> "I think that you will say: 'I think the same'"

By contrast, Jewish culture (as described in Schiffrin 1984; see also Blum-Kulka 1982) places a special value on expressing disagreement—because it is good to say to another person what one really thinks, and also because it is interesting and enjoyable to talk with people who disagree with you.

> [people think like this:]
> when someone says something to me about something
> if I think that this something is not true
> it is good to say it to this person
> it is good if this person knows what I think

> [people think like this:]
> when someone says to me about something: "I think about it like this"
> if I think that this person doesn't think well
> it is good to say it to this person
> it is good if this person knows what I think

> [people think like this:]
> when someone says something to me about something
> it can be good if I say something like this to this person:
>> "I don't think the same"

In modern Anglo culture, the most salient cultural scripts are different again. One important script enshrines the belief in "freedom of expression":

> [people think like this:]
> if I think something about something I can say: "I think about it like this"
> everyone can do this

As noted by Carbaugh (1988), this script and its various offshoots are repeatedly rehearsed on popular American TV shows like Donahue. For example, "Donahue asked a woman audience member to react to a group of feminist guests: 'How do you feel about these women?' Her response was: 'Each woman has her own opinion, and if that's what they believe in, fine.' The tone of her utterance indicated an implicit

disagreement, but she stated explicitly the cultural premise: Everyone has the right
to say and do what they want" (Carbaugh 1988, 29).

> [people think like this:]
> when someone says to me about something: "I think about it like this"
> if I don't think the same
> I can say to this person: "I don't think the same"

But although disagreement can be voiced openly, there is also a script that says that
it is good to soften it with a partial agreement, along the following lines:

> [people think like this:]
> when I want to say to another person about something.
>   "I don't think the same [as you]"
> it is good to say something like this at the same time:
>   "I think the same [as you] about some of these things
>   I don't think the same [as you] about all these things"

But while one can voice disagreement (though preferably, only partial disagreement),
one cannot do it, to use Carbaugh's term, "impositionally":

> [people think like this:]
> when I say to another person about something: "I think about it like this"
> I can't say something like this at the same time:
>   "you have to think the same" / "I want you to think the same"

Furthermore, the marked asymmetry between the use of *right* and *wrong* in English
conversational routines suggests the following script:

> [people think like this:]
> when a person says to me about something: "I think about it like this"
> I can't say something like this to this person:
>   "it is bad if a person thinks like this"

What this means, in effect, is that although one can openly disagree with another
person's opinion, one can't criticize it or condemn it: to do so would mean to set oneself above the other person and to refuse them the right to have their own opinion.

As noted earlier, one might think that the same would apply to expressing *approval* of another person's opinion: whether I disapprove or approve of another
person's opinion, I can be seen as setting myself above this other person. In fact,
however, it doesn't work like that (in modern Anglo culture): there is no taboo on
expressing approval of another person's opinion—as long as this approval refers implicitly to some objective criteria. And this is what the expression *that's right* does: it
conveys approval of what the other person has just said and approval of the thinking
behind this person's words; at the same time, however, it appeals to some criteria,
some evidence, to which other people could have access.

The component "you think well" conveys, indirectly, a goodwill toward the
addressee and a friendly attitude, and the components "it is like this" and "people
can know that it is like this" suggest some objective factual basis for my endorsement
of your words and way of thinking, as well as the availability of a rational justifica-

tion. Thus, although my approval of your way of thinking suggests my personal good-will toward you, it doesn't really place me above you, because it appeals to some-thing rational and demonstrable. Implicitly, the speaker is appealing to a shared ground: a respect for rational thinking and for evidence. There is no pressure in modern Anglo culture to praise or endorse one's interlocutor's words regardless of what one thinks about them; presumably, a requirement of this kind would be felt as a restriction on one's freedom to say what one thinks. At the same time, however, it is seen as desirable that one should try to "validate" the interlocutor's words *if one can* — in the interest of conversational cooperation and good rapport. In expressing this validation, however, one must be careful not to appear to be patting the inter-locutor on the head, hence the need to appeal to some general criteria of good thinking and accountability.

3.12. Retrospect and conclusion: The Puritans, the Enlightenment, the Growth of Democracy

Let us try to sketch a short history of *right* (and to a lesser degree, *wrong*), in a very broad outline.

To begin with, *right* meant "straight," as in a *right line* ("straight line"). Figura-tively, perhaps, this *right* in the sense of "straight" was also used in an evaluative sense: "good," with an additional component building on the geometrical image: "clearly good," "demonstrably good," "one-could-say-why good." For example, spoken of somebody else's words, *right* was linked (implicitly or explicitly) with *true*, as in these three examples from Shakespeare:

> Thou'st spoken right. 'Tis true. (*King Lear*, Act V, sc. iii, l. 164)
> Most true, 'tis right, you were so, Alisander. (*Love's Labour Lost*, Act V, sc. ii, l. 566)
> Right, you say true. (*Richard the Second*, Act II, sc. i, l. 146)

Right appears to mean here, essentially, "good" or "well," "you speak well," "you say well" — an evaluation supported with a reference to truth: "because what you say is true."

But in the course of the seventeenth and eighteenth centuries, *right* appears to have begun to be used more and more with reference to thinking rather than speaking. The spread of the grammatical pattern linking *right* (and *wrong*) as a predicate with persons as subjects is a reflection of this new emphasis on "right thinking." A sentence like "you are right" (or "he is right," etc.) combines an approval of what someone says with an approval of their thinking ("you speak well, you think well") As noted earlier, the Shakespearean "'tis right" or "thou'st spoken right" was (implicitly or explicitly) truth-oriented and did not similarly refer to thinking. For a person, "being right" can be opposed to "being wrong." Although the earliest example of "you are right" included in the OED is dated 1597, the earliest examples that are cited in the OED of *wrong* referring to persons go back no further than the end of the seventeenth century.

Generally speaking, the association of *right* with thinking seems to have spread in parallel with a contrastive use of "right" and "wrong" — a trend apparently encouraged by the influence of the Reformation, especially within its Calvinist wing. The substitution of the Bible and the individual conscience for the church was a key feature of the Protestant Reformation, especially Calvinism. "In founding ethics on the Bible rather than on the leadership of the Catholic Church, Calvin opened the way to a decrease in the authority of human rulers and an increase in the authority of intellectual judgments" (Snell 1988, 24). This emphasis on individual conscience and judgment was very much part of the Puritans' stand in England and then America. "The Puritan could rely only on his own reading of Scripture and his own conscience for light" (Slotkin 1973, 52, quoted in Barnstone, Manson, and Singley 1997, xv). As vividly depicted in Bunyan's *The Pilgrim's Progress*, the key problem of every person's life is the great "either-or" of salvation versus damnation. This "either-or," which is a matter of supreme importance, depends on distinguishing "the right" and "the wrong": "Look before thee; dost thou see this narrow way? That is the way thou must go. . . . There are many ways but down upon this; and they are crooked and wide; but thus *thou may'st distinguish the right from the wrong* that only being straight and narrow" (Bunyan 1965, 59, emphasis added).

As Bunyan's key image of the two ways illustrates, the Puritans had a highly polarized view of human life, which they saw as a choice between, on the one hand, a progress toward the Celestial City, linked with "the right way to go," and on the other, the path toward damnation, that is, the "wrong [way], tho' easy, when the end is woe" (1965, 74). Not surprisingly, therefore, the Puritans—like the "just man" in Milton's vision in *Paradise Lost*—spoke much of right and wrong:

> Of middle age one rising, eminent
> In wise deport, spake much of right and wrong,
> Of justice, of religion, truth, and peace,
> And Judgment from above. (Milton 1989, Book XI)

And in the words of the eighteenth-century English poet, Cowper:

> Grace leads the right way: if you choose the wrong,
> Take it and perish. (1781, quoted in Stevenson 1958)

For Milton, as for other Puritans, religion was linked with the notions of 'right' and 'wrong'; reason, which was the basis for distinguishing between right and wrong, was sacred. (In *Paradise Lost*, Bk. VII, l.507, the first man, Adam, is described as "a creature . . . endowed with sanctity of reason.") As Edmund Morgan writes in his book *The Puritan Dilemma* (1958, 81), "the Puritans were extraordinarily reasonable men. The zeal with which they studied the Bible sprang from supreme confidence in the ability of reason to find the truth there. . . . Therefore they listened with respect to every man who could give reasons for his opinions, and if they thought his reason faulty, they used every possible argument to persuade him."

It is widely held that the impact of the Puritans on English culture went far beyond their purely religious influence. As Roger Sharrock (1965, 13) says in his introduction to *The Pilgrim's Progress*, "through their Calvinistic preaching and commenting on the English Bible they had effected a cultural revolution and created a new type of Englishman, endowed with an earnestness and a sense of mission not present in his medieval ancestors." The Puritans' polarized view of life, seen as

a choice between "the right way" and "the wrong way," may well have contributed
to the emergence of "right" and "wrong" as key opposites in the English language
and the world of thought associated with it. In this respect, as in others, their influence may have meshed well with the influence of the Enlightenment's emphasis on
'reason' (see Weber 1968, 198). In the age of Enlightenment, ethics came increasingly to be seen in terms of reason, and reason was linked with the notions of 'right'
and 'wrong'. In the words of the seventeenth–eighteenth century poet, Congreve:

> . . . Reason, the power to guess at right and wrong. (quoted in Stevenson 1958)

The close (perceived) link between the notions of 'right', 'wrong', and 'reason' is also
seen clearly in the following quote from the eighteenth–nineteenth century poet
Robert Southey:

> To prove by reason, in reason's despite,
> That right is wrong, and wrong is right,
> And white is black, and black is white. (Robert Southey, 1728, quoted in Stevenson
> 1958)

In eighteenth-century America, Benjamin Franklin, whose *Autobiography* has been
described as "the secular version of John Bunyan's *The Pilgrim's Progress*" (Bellah et
al. 1985, 32), preached "the reasonable Science of Virtue," likening "the Science of
Virtue" to other sciences (Levin 1963, 32–33); in nineteenth-century England, the
poet and essayist Matthew Arnold , in his work *St. Paul and Protestantism* (in which
he argues *against* the Puritans and *for* Anglicanism) ascribes "sweet reasonableness"
to Christ, using the phrase no fewer than eleven times in a short essay.[3]

Thus, for a long time *reason* became, for many speakers of English, a linchpin
holding together religion, morality, and a "modern" scientific outlook. The following late-nineteenth-century citation included in the OED is characteristic in this
respect:

> Clear and consecutive wrong-thinking is the next best thing to right-thinking.
> (Thomas Huxley 1877)

For Huxley, the quintessential agnostic scientist, 'right' and 'wrong' are primarily properties of thinking—and in a way, so they were for the Puritans and for Locke. The
Puritans wanted to think "rightly" (rationally) about God, Locke about both God
and nature, and Huxley wanted to think "rightly" (rationally) about nature, and nature alone.

It appears, however, that as democracy became more and more entrenched, first
in America and then in England, many speakers of English became less and less
interested in denouncing other people's opinions as "wrong," and freedom of thought
and expression began to be felt to be more important than the identification of any
"wrong" opinions. In the first half of the nineteenth century, the English historian
Thomas Macauley wrote in his *Essays: Southey's Colloquies*: "Men are never so likely
to settle a question rightly as when they discuss it freely" (quoted in Stevenson 1958).
Thus Macauley linked "right thinking" with freedom of discussion. In the early twentieth century, the American lawyer Harry Weinberger (1917; also quoted in Stevenson
1958) went further when he wrote: "The greatest right in the world is the right to be

wrong." This statement expresses the logical next step in the history of right and wrong: under the conditions of liberal democracy, it may be important to be right, but it is more important to be free to say what one thinks and to be able to hold on to one's opinions, whether others regard them as right or wrong.

There is an easy transition from thinking that everyone has the inalienable "right to be wrong" to thinking that no one can, or should, tell another person that he or she is wrong. As one of Porpora's interviewees puts it (2001, 90), "that's what this world is made up of: different people with differences of opinions."[4]

Thus, over the last two centuries or so, the discourse of "right" and "wrong" appears to have found a competitor in a discourse of cooperation and mutual concessions. Judging by both the frequency and range of its use, the word *right* flourished in this atmosphere, whereas *wrong* was increasingly left behind.

Speaking of the contemporary "death of conviction" and of the consequences of "classroom programmes, worthy in themselves, designed to equip students with . . . social virtues such as tolerance and mutual respect," Fernández-Armesto writes: "In a society of concessions to rival viewpoints, in which citizens hesitate to demand what is true and denounce what is false, it becomes impossible to defend the traditional moral distinctions between right and wrong, which are relativized in turn" (1998, 165). These remarks are consistent with the linguistic history of *right* and *wrong*. The great career that *right* has made in spoken English does not mean that people are necessarily more confident about what they regard, and want to defend, as "right." Rather, we are witnessing an explosion of a purely conversational "right" — a conversational routine serving a pragmatic goal of conversational harmony and cooperation unrelated to any deeper consensus or conviction.

Everybody can say what they think, and therefore, whatever they say can be responded to with the cooperative conversational "Right." It is not a question of truth and not even, primarily, a question of agreement. Rather, it is a question of getting along together. Two centuries ago, in his monumental study *Democracy in America*, de Tocqueville wrote:

> The political institutions of the United States put citizens of all classes in constant contact and compel them to carry out great undertakings together. People busy in this way have hardly time to think about the details of etiquette, and they also have too great an interest in living harmony to stop for that. (de Tocqueville 1966, 543)

The birth and triumphant spread (first in America and then elsewhere) of the various conversational routines based on the word *okay* (yet to be studied from a semantic point of view) clearly supports de Tocqueville's brilliant insight, but in a way, so does the expansion of the conversational *right* in the United States, Australia, and New Zealand (recorded by the OED). As we have seen, *right* can be used to acknowledge one's interlocutor's words as "good" and valid, not because they are true, and not even because one agrees with them, but because they express, quite legitimately, the other person's point of view. It can also be used to acknowledge and accept what another person wants us to do, on an "equal footing" and in the spirit of voluntary cooperation.

Donal Carbaugh rightly links the common Anglo American assumption that "individuals have rights" with common American conversational routines, when he says that "not only do individuals, or Americans, have rights, but also Americans, as individuals, preserve and protect their rights through their routine verbal performances" (1988, 25). The common conversational routine of responding to another person's expressed view with "Right." is, I suggest, one of those routine verbal performances. It is a response that reaffirms the value of the practice of expressing one's opinions and of listening, willingly, to other people's opinions. If I can't say that I think that "you think well," I can at least say that you have expressed yourself well because I now know what you think (or: want to say)—and "this is good, too."

The transition from (A) the Shakespearean response "Right." described by the OED as "you are right; you speak well," to (B) the present-day "Right." of noncommittal acknowledgment can be schematically represented as follows:

A. you say: "I think like this"
    you speak well
    [because what you say is true]
B. you say: "I think like this / want to say this"
    I now know what you think / want-to-say
    this is good

In Shakespeare's usage, the approval of someone else's words, expressed with "Right." refers, explicitly or implicitly, to truth; in present-day English, the approval of someone's else words expressed with "Right." refers to a successful act of communication. The implications are:

A. Right $\longrightarrow$ it is true (this is good)
B. Right $\longrightarrow$ I know what you think / want-to-say (this is good)

While noting these changes in the conversational routines involving the word *right*, we should at the same time note that the distinction between 'right' and 'wrong' as opposites continues to be taken for granted in the world of thought associated with the English language—both on the level of theory and scholarship (in philosophy, education, and so on) and in everyday life. To understand this peculiar feature of English and Anglo discourse, we need, inter alia, to take up some of Max Weber's searching questions and "attempt to penetrate into the peculiar characteristics of and the differences between those great worlds of religious thought which have existed historically in the various branches of Christianity" (Weber 1995, 45). To understand the continuing salience of the concepts 'right' and 'wrong' in English/Anglo discourse, we need to try to enter not only the world of John Locke, David Hume, and other British thinkers who influenced the intellectual climate in Britain in the seventeenth and eighteenth centuries (and, indirectly, in North America) but also the world of thought of the English and American Puritans (see Wierzbicka 2004).

In his well-known book *After Virtue*, Alasdair MacIntyre (1981) writes that "the Enlightenment project" of basing morality on reason has failed. Indeed, MacIntyre takes this failure for granted, as shown by chapter titles like "Why the Enlightenment Project of Justifying Morality Had to Fail" (chapter 5) and "Some Consequences of the Failure of the Enlightenment Project" (chapter 6). It should be recognized, however, that the continued use, in colloquial English, of the words *right* and *wrong* as a basic yardstick with which to evaluate human conduct continues, in a sense, "the Enlightenment project." For speakers of English, the opposites 'right' and 'wrong' are still important conceptual tools, available for use, and indeed widely used, in everyday life (not to mention Anglophone philosophy, education, developmental psychology, and so on). There is also the word *evil*, but this tends to be reserved for situations thought of as extreme. In daily life, human conduct still tends to be evaluated, by speakers of English, in terms of 'right' and 'wrong'. My point is that this way of speaking and thinking about human life is profoundly culture-specific. Three centuries after the Enlightenment, everyday moral discourse in French, German, and other European languages is still based on the notions GOOD and BAD, not on any putative equivalents of the English *right* and *wrong*. For this, there must be reasons; and these reasons appear to include the religious roots of modern Anglo culture and the influence of the Puritans. Both "the distrust of metaphysics" and the belief in reason as the basis for a "good life" continue to live on in everyday Anglo discourse in the form of the key cultural concepts 'right' and 'wrong'.[5]

The continued presence, and salience, of the words *right* and *wrong* in English/Anglo discourse suggests the continued presence of some cultural scripts linking evaluation of human action with critical thinking and the need for justification. The scripts appear to include these two:

> [people think like this:]
> when a person wants to do something
> it is good if this person thinks about it like this:
> > I want to know if it will be good if I do it
> > if I think about it I can know it

> [people think like this:]
> I can't say about someone: "I think that this someone did something bad"
> if I can't say why I think like this

The reliance on 'right' and 'wrong' and the apparent avoidance of absolute moral judgments unsupported by rational justifications highlight the absence from modern Anglo culture of the cultural script reflected in Mayakovsky's children's poem quoted earlier, and arguably very salient in Russian culture as a whole:[6]

> *The Russian "good versus bad" script*
> [people think like this:]
> people do things of two kinds
> things of one kind are good
> it is good if people want to do things of this kind
> things of the other kind are bad
> it is bad if people want to do things of this other kind

In its polarized dichotomy, this script parallels the Russian script opposing truth to untruth. (For discussion of polarized dichotomic models of thought in Russian culture, see Uspenskij 1996; for discussion of the penchant for absolute moral judgments reflected in the Russian language, see Wierzbicka 1992, 435–440, and 2002c.)

The English language—in contrast to Russian—does not encourage this type of extreme and absolute moral evaluation, and it does not provide its speakers with convenient colloquial tools for evaluating human conduct in this way. To illustrate, let me quote the following sentence from a Russian novel (Solzhenitsyn's *Cancer Ward*) and its English translation:

> *I udivilsja by on [Efrem] esli b drugoj mužik stal emu ser'ezno dokazyvat', čto on ploxo postupaet s babami.* (Solzhenitsyn n.d., 116)
> And he'd been amazed if some other fellow had seriously tried to tell him he treated women badly. (Solzhenitsyn 1969, 104)

The Russian sentence refers, in simple colloquial words, to a man's (Efrem's) moral conduct and condemns it, unequivocally, as "bad." The judgment is as clear and as simple as the judgment that "he did something bad," but it is extended to the man's conduct as a whole (in relation to women). There is no way to convey the same absolute judgment in colloquial English. Perhaps the following would be the closest: "his moral conduct in relation to women was bad." But this is, of course, not colloquial, and a simple uneducated man like Solzhenitsyn's Efrem could neither speak nor think in such terms. The word for women used in the Russian sentence is crude and slangy. The focus of the Russian sentence is not on how Efrem treats women (as in the English translation "he treated women badly") but on the fact that what he is doing is "wrong"—except that in Russian, it is not "wrong" but "bad." The Russian verb *postupat'* is not transitive, like the English *treat*, but intransitive, like *behave*. One could therefore try to convey the sense of the Russian sentence by saying of Efrem that "he behaved badly (in relation to women)" or that "his behavior in relation to women was bad." This, however, would not convey the moral force of the Russian sentence. *Behavior*, unlike *conduct*, is a word that can be used about animals ("animal behavior" vs. "*animal conduct*"). One could also say of a little boy that he "behaved badly" but not that "his conduct was bad." *Postupat'* is, in this respect, like *conduct*, not like *behavior*. Thus, *postupat' ploxo* conveys a negative moral evaluation that simply cannot be conveyed in colloquial English. It would not help to say "he treats women like dirt" because this, too, would refer to how he treats others, not to his own moral conduct as such.

A folk ethics based on the notions of 'right' and 'wrong' does not encourage categorizing people, as well as actions, into two diametrically opposed categories: one cannot speak in English of "right people" and "wrong people," one can speak only of "good people" and "bad people"—a categorization lying outside an "ethics of right and wrong." By contrast, Russian cultural scripts are fully compatible with such a categorization. To illustrate again from the *Cancer Ward*:

> *èto byl daleko ne samyj ploxoj čelovek, iz vstrečavšixsja Olegu v žizni.* (Solzhenitsyn n.d., 31)
> he was far from the worst man he'd met in his life. (Solzhenitsyn 1969, 209)

Significantly, modern English—unlike Russian—doesn't have words evaluating people as "very bad people" (or, indeed, "very good people"), that is, semantic equivalents of descriptive Russian words like *podlec, negodjaj, merzavec*, although it does, of course, have, as does Russian, swearwords like *bastard*, animal metaphors like *swine*, and the like. (Note also the archaic status of words like *rascal, scoundrel*, or *villain*; cf. Wierzbicka 1992: 436.)

Nor does English have a verb like the Russian *osuždat'*, which combines in its meaning semantic components of several English verbs (*to judge, to try, to condemn,* and *to convict*), and which can refer to both everyday talk (as in "she judges / condemns / convicts him") and to court activities (as in "Joe Bloggs was tried, convicted, and sentenced").

I have mentioned earlier, with reference to Porpora, that an ethics based on the concepts 'right' and 'wrong' is different from the ethics presented in the Gospels. It hardly needs to be added that an ethics of "judging and condemning" (*osuždat'*) other people is also different from the ethics of the Gospels and that dividing people into two categories, "good people" and "bad people," is in fact incompatible with it. (For detailed discussion, see Wierzbicka 2001.) From a semantic point of view, however, we need to note that the expressions *good people* and *bad people* seem possible in all natural languages and, from a cultural point of view, that the English words *right* and *wrong* and the Russian word *osuždat'*, *podlec, merzavec,* and *negodjaj* point to different cultural traditions.

The extreme moral absolutes of Russian folk ethics go no doubt beyond the cultural scripts found in many other European languages, but English differs from those other languages, too, in basing its folk ethics on 'right' and 'wrong' rather than 'good' and 'bad'. The result is that to speak, for example, of Hitler, Stalin, and Pol Pot, English speakers have to go beyond their basic concepts of 'right' and 'wrong' and reach for the more extreme word *evil*. The implication seems to be that (for English speakers) truly terrible actions and regimes are beyond the ordinary human world, where 'right' and 'wrong' can be used as basic guideposts.

In her essay "Losing Your Concepts," philosopher Cora Diamond explores the idea of "living with concepts" and speaks of "a human good of our having a range of concepts through which the characterizing facets of human life enter our sense of who we are and what we experience" (1998, 269, quoted in Besemeres 2002, 25). For speakers of English, living means, inter alia, living with the concepts 'right' and 'wrong'.[7] It also means living with cultural scripts related to these key concepts. Culture-specific key concepts and cultural scripts are usually interrelated, and often the links between the two are most clearly visible in everyday conversational routines: in greetings, in swearing, in forms of address, in the give-and-take of everyday verbal exchanges. The use of *right* in English conversational routines is related to the use of *right* and *wrong* in English folk philosophy. Conversational routines—like key cultural concepts—reflect historically shaped values, attitudes, and ways of thinking.

Chapter 4

Being REASONABLE

A *Key Anglo Value*
and Its Cultural Roots

"The definition of *reasonable* is almost impossible to define." (*sic*; Cobuild corpus)

"Reasonableness, as a concept employed in modern legal systems, is both elusive and multifaceted." (Saltman 1991, 107)

4.1. Introduction

Every society has certain evaluative words that provide a frame of orientation in daily life and guide people's judgment and behavior. Sometimes speakers are very conscious of some of these guiding words and regard them as a badge of belonging. Some members of other societies, too, may become aware of that society's guiding words and borrow them as tools for describing modes of behavior or thought.

Sometimes, however, a guiding word is so ingrained in the thinking of a speech community that it is not perceived as distinctive but, rather, taken for granted like the air that people breathe. Presumably, words of this kind, which the speakers themselves are not conscious of as distinctive, are also less likely to be perceived as such by outsiders.

One striking example of a ubiquitous yet oddly invisible guiding word is the English *reasonable*. The fact that this word has seldom been the focus of special attention and reflection may have contributed to its enduring power. Well-known badges of cultural distinctiveness—for example, the English concept of "gentleman"—can be more or less consciously rejected, even scorned, together with the ideals and values they represent. But values and attitudes associated with words that are constantly used but never noticed or recognized as culturally distinctive are less likely to be consciously rejected. The words themselves—unsuspected, ordinary, everyday words—pass these ideals on and ensure their continued influence on people's lives.

At the turn of the twenty-first century, many English speakers would dissociate themselves from the ethos of the *gentleman*. But how many would doubt the value of "being reasonable" and the undesirability of having one's conduct judged as "un-reasonable"? How many would wince at phrases like *a reasonable person, within reasonable limits, a reasonable price, a reasonable time, a reasonable assumption,* or *a reasonable offer*?

The words *reasonable* and *unreasonable* carry with them a framework of evaluation that plays an important part in Anglo/English discourse—and therefore, presumably, in the lives of its practitioners. This framework of evaluation is language- and culture-specific and historically shaped. Broadly, it is a post-Enlightenment framework. But because we do not find the same framework operating in other European languages (with the apparent, but only apparent, exception of French, to which I return later), its roots must be sought in the *British* Enlightenment rather than in the Enlightenment as a whole.

Before turning to the historical roots of this framework, however, we need to try to understand the framework itself. The key to such an understanding lies in the meaning or meanings of the key word *reasonable* and its relatives *reasonably* and *unreasonable*.

4.2. The Pre-Enlightenment Uses of "Reasonable"

The distinct post-Enlightenment character of the word *reasonable* as it is now used emerges clearly from a comparison with its earlier use. Shakespeare's usage gives us a good sense of how it has changed.

First of all, in Shakespeare's corpus, *reasonable* was still very closely associated with *reason*. For example:

My reasonable part produces reason
How I may be deliver'd of these woes
And teaches me to kill or hang myself (*King John* act III, scene iv)

The "reasonable part" seems to stand for the power or ability to think. There is no whiff here of the modern Anglo connotation of "moderation," which would prevent extreme actions like killing or hanging oneself from being associated with the word *reasonable*. Another example:

It is a quarrel fair and reasonable,
To be revenged on him who slew my husband. (*King Richard III*, act I, scene ii)

In this scene, Lady Anne expresses her thirst for revenge, and she spits at Gloucester, wishing that her spit "were mortal poison" and that her eyes "were basilisks" ("to strike thee dead"), and in doing this she describes her attitude as "reasonable"—not the word that would come to mind in such a context now.

Again, in *The Merry Wives of Windsor* (act IV, scene ii) one of the characters, Ford, describes his jealousy as "reasonable" ("my jealousy is reasonable"), clearly not implying that it is not excessive but rather that, great as it is, it is fully justified.

In another play, the words *great* and *reasonable* are in fact linked in one phrase:

The perdition of th' adversary hath been very great, very reasonable great. (*King Henry V*, act III, scene vi)

Some Shakespearean uses of *reasonable* seem consistent with modern usage but in fact do not mean what the modern reader might think they do. For example:

> Ay, sir, you shall find me reasonable; if it be so,
> I shall do that that is reason. (*The Merry Wives of Windsor*, act I, scene i)

As we have seen, doing "that that is reason" (that is, what is "reasonable" in Shakespeare's sense) could include suicide or murder. If this is to any extent a change in social norm, it is also a change in language—in this case, in the usage of the word *reasonable*.

Similarly, when (in the same play, act IV, scene iv) a reference is made to a clown "who wants but something to be a reasonable man," the phrase *a reasonable man* may seem to be consistent with the present-day usage; in fact, however, it occurs in Shakespeare's language side by side with *a reasonable creature* (*Much Ado About Nothing*, act I, scene i), in other words, a creature endowed with reason (with a capacity to think). In contemporary English, the collocation *a reasonable creature* is no longer possible, because, as I discuss later, to be seen as "reasonable" in contemporary usage requires more than being simply "endowed with reason" (as any member of the species *Homo sapiens* would be). This shows that *a reasonable man* did not mean for Shakespeare what it does today.

Clearly, between Shakespeare's time and our own, a change has occurred in Anglo ways of thinking, and this change has found its reflection in the semantics of the English language. And it is not just a change in the prevailing conception of what is and what is not "reasonable." Rather, it is a change in the basic kit of conceptual tools used for making judgments and evaluating actions and events. The word *reasonable* with its modern family of interrelated senses is a new tool in the kit.

4.3. The Main Themes in the Modern Meanings of the Word *Reasonable*

As it is used in contemporary English, the word *reasonable* appears to have several different meanings. Used in at least one of these meanings, *reasonable* has an opposite, *unreasonable*, whereas in some others, it has no such opposite. For example, a request can be described as either reasonable or unreasonable; similarly, one can speak of reasonable and unreasonable prices or charges, reasonable and unreasonable expectations, and so on. On the other hand, there is a *reasonable guess* but not an **unreasonable guess*. Similarly, the phrase *beyond reasonable doubt* has no negative counterpart (**beyond unreasonable doubt*), and observations, explanations, or hypotheses can be readily described as reasonable but not unreasonable. How can we generalize from these examples to a limited number of identifiable distinct meanings?

Reflecting on the use of the word *unreasonable* may provide us with a useful starting point: if someone is said to be unreasonable, this seems to imply, first, that this person is not thinking well and, second, that he or she "wants too much." If we now look, in the light of this observation, at phrases like *reasonable expectations*, *reasonable prices*, and *reasonable requests*, we note that they all appear to imply (in addition to something like an absence of good thinking) the opposite of "wanting too much": to be reasonable (as opposed to being unreasonable) appears to imply "not wanting too much." Furthermore, we can note that "being reasonable" is not a solitary virtue but one that has something to do with other people. The following examples from Cobuild are quite characteristic in this regard:

> Let's make a deal. Let's be reasonable. You wanted Eva. Well, you got her. Okay. Take off and let's call it quits. Be reasonable, George, and settle for half a loaf now.

> Look at Hitler or Stalin. . . . Boy, if they could have been reasonable, they would have divided this whole earth up between them.

One can be "rational" or "irrational" on one's own, but one is usually being "reasonable" or "unreasonable" when one is interacting with other people.

Before we try to identify the different meanings of *reasonable* more precisely, let us consider some further examples, putting some of them in groups in a preliminary way. One distinct group or type can be illustrated with the following phrases (from Cobuild):

reasonable results

a reasonable service

reasonable conditions

reasonable prospects of success

a reasonable location

to keep a person in reasonable health

a reasonable command of language

a reasonable support

a reasonable standard of living

meetings with reasonable attendance

Roughly speaking, *reasonable* could be replaced in all these phrases with *reasonably good*, and it certainly could not be replaced with *reasonably bad*: consider *reasonably good location* versus **reasonably bad location* and *reasonably good results* versus **reasonably bad results*. (It is interesting to note that in some collocations where *reasonable* cannot be replaced with the phrase *reasonably good* it still means, roughly, something like that. For example, the phrase *reasonable comfort* cannot be replaced with *reasonably good comfort*, but this is because the semantic component "good" is included in the meaning of the word *comfort* itself [compare *?reasonable discomfort*].)

Used in this way, then, *reasonable* suggests limited praise: in the speaker's view, the results and so on can perhaps be described as "good," but not as "very good," and the living conditions can perhaps be described as "comfortable" but not "very comfortable"; furthermore, they can be described as "good" only if one does not want too much—if one limits one's expectations "in a reasonable way." It would seem, then, that it is "reasonable" not to expect too much—if one can think well, one can perhaps accept some things as good even if they are not very good. It is good to be pragmatic, to accept that one cannot have everything that one might want to have, that things can be seen as good even if they are not "very good," and, especially, that such moderation may be needed in our relations with other people.

Consider, for example, the following two sentences (from Cobuild):

I'm paid a reasonable (if not extravagant) salary.

So I'll be reasonable, we'll compromise.

On the one hand, the meaning of *reasonable* in the two sentences is clearly different, as can be seen from the fact that in the second sentence, *reasonable* is opposed to *unreasonable* (*I won't be unreasonable*), whereas in the first one it is not (?*I'm paid an unreasonable salary*). On the other hand, however, some themes are clearly shared: the references to something good, to one's ability to think well, to moderation (in the sense of not wanting too much), and to an interest in what other people would say, think, want. At least some of these themes—an ability to think well, moderate praise, and other people's opinions—appear to be also involved in phrases like *a reasonable guess* or *a reasonable comment*. It is particularly noticeable how often the use of the word *reasonable* is linked with a normative spatial metaphor of "how far one can go," as in the phrases *within (the) reasonable limits, within reasonable bounds, beyond reasonable doubt, (gone) beyond what is reasonable, (you can certainly go) so far as is reasonable* (examples from Cobuild), and so on.

Can these various themes be clearly and precisely articulated in the form of semantic components—or do they have to be seen, rather, as some vague, impossible-to-pinpoint family resemblances?

To answer this question, we need to construct some explications and validate them through testing. But to develop plausible explications, it will be helpful first to take a brief look at the broader history of ideas and try to get some insight into the cultural background of the contemporary usage of the word *reasonable* and its derivatives. A reasonable place to start may be the culturally laden phrase *a reasonable man*.

4.4. "A Reasonable Man"

The concept of a 'reasonable man' is one of the most important concepts in British and British-derived common law. Roughly speaking, 'a reasonable' man is, as a British judge famously put it, "the man on the Clapham omnibus"—that is, an ordinary man, a humble commuter, who epitomizes an ordinary person's putatively sound judgment. 'A reasonable man' is not an intellectual, not a theoretician, and yet he is seen as someone whose judgment can be trusted—perhaps more so than that of a theoretician, a philosopher, a professional thinker or scholar.

There is of course a link—not only etymological but also semantic—between *reasonable* and *reason*. But the 'reason' attributed to 'a reasonable man' is not an abstract reason, linked with systematic thought, with sustained logical reasoning, with an ivory-tower search for knowledge or with hair-splitting speculations. The 'reason' of 'a reasonable man' is akin to common sense; and the 'reasonable man' himself is a 'common man', not a member of any elite.

The concept of 'a reasonable man' is democratic, as well as pragmatic: it is linked with the belief that most ordinary people are 'reasonable people' and that their thinking is essentially good and trustworthy—not because these ordinary people will always know the truth in some absolute sense, but because in most situations they will be able to think well enough for practical purposes.

Although the concept of 'a reasonable man' is a vital legal concept, it is not a purely technical one. If ordinary people like jurors could not understand this concept (via ordinary language), it could not play the role in law that it does. It is a concept that is expected, inter alia, to guide communication between the legal profession and ordinary people. To make sense to 'ordinary people', the phrase *a reasonable man* (as it is used in law) must be intelligible to 'an ordinary man'.

With these points in mind, let us consider some definitions and explanations from a standard law textbook, from a section entitled "The Reasonable Person":

> The standard of care to be expected of a person subject to a duty of care depends on what *a reasonable person* would have done about a foreseeable risk of injury. . . .
> We need to consider more closely the nature of the "prudent and reasonable man" to whom Alderson B referred . . . In English jurisprudence this person has traditionally been described as "the man on the Clapham omnibus" (the origin of the phrase attributed to Lord Bowen, 1903). (Luntz, Hambly, and Hayes eds. 1985, 154–155, emphasis added)

Thus, 'a reasonable man' (or person) sets the standard of behavior by which anyone's behavior can—and should—be judged: this standard is not based on any empirical studies of most people's actual behavior, and neither is it based on any opinion polls. It is a hypothetical standard: "the standard of the 'reasonable' person tends to be an idealized, ethical standard, rather than the behavior of the actual 'man in the street'" (Luntz, Hambly, and Hayes, 1985). The judgment of 'a reasonable man' is fallible, and reasonable men may disagree with one another. For example:

> The law reports in recent times have been filled with accounts of road accident cases. These illustrate that often the same facts are viewed differently by different judges concerned to determine culpability. It may seem remarkable that *reasonable men* should differ so often, and so markedly, as to what would in given circumstances be expected of *a reasonable man*. But this merely demonstrates that reasonable prudence is an indefinite criterion of conduct. From this appeals multiply: lawyers flourish. . . . (J. Windeyer in *Edwards v. Noble* 1971, 125 CLR, in Luntz, Hambly, and Hayes 1985, 156, emphasis added)

Thus, any knowledge based on the hypothetical judgment of 'a reasonable man' can only be seen as probabilistic, limited, fallible. It is always open to debate and open to question. It is never definitive or absolute, and it depends on the circumstances. For example:

> Take a case like *Richards v State of Victoria* [1969] VR 136 (FC). A schoolboy was very severely injured when struck a blow in the classroom by a classmate, who was 18 years old, six foot (180 cm) in height and weighed 12 stone (76 kg). One major issue was whether the teacher should have prevented it. What would *the reasonable person* have done in the circumstances? It is accepted that in this context the man on the Clapham omnibus is irrelevant and the question becomes what *the*

reasonable schoolteacher would have done. In this case the teacher was male; would it have made a difference if the teacher had been a woman? The teacher was 25 and "no match physically for either" of the boys; can the court take into account the physique of the particular teacher or is *the reasonable teacher* assumed to be at least as big as the pupils? (Luntz, Hambly, and Hayes eds. 1985, 156–157, emphasis added)

To say that the concept of 'a reasonable man' (as illustrated in these quotes) plays a key role in British and British-derived law does not mean that it belongs only to the language of law and is not used or relied on in ordinary language. On the contrary, as the corpora such as Cobuild demonstrate, it is also used widely in ordinary English—and, it appears, essentially in the same sense. For example (from Cobuild):

To have been anything but satisfied would have been highly unreasonable, and Alistair, for a professor, was a rather reasonable man.

Have no more fear of sleeping with your mother: How many men, in dreams, have lain with their mothers! No reasonable man is troubled by such things.

. . . the stepfather seemed to take over the role of being the good and reasonable person in the house.

The history of the collocation *reasonable man* in English highlights the distance that separates the modern Anglo concept of 'reasonable man' as a pragmatic standard for human life and judgment (a paradigmatic modern juror) from the older concept of 'reasonable man' as a species endowed with reason (an equivalent of the Latin *animal rationale*). To quote some earlier examples (from OED):

Man is a reasonable two footed beast. (Chaucer, 1374)

Man, a reasonable creature, whose dignity doth come so near the Angels. (1588)

Let your employment be such as may become a reasonable person. (1650)

For man is by nature reasonable. (1791)

The emergence of the modern concept of 'a reasonable man' is causally linked with the British Enlightenment. The Age of Enlightenment was seen, and saw itself, as the Age of Reason; *reason* was clearly a key word and a key ideal of the period. Isaac Watts proclaimed in the early eighteenth century, "Reason is the glory of human nature" (quoted in Porter 2000, 48), and this statement was typical of his times. But the reason cherished by the most influential figures of the British Enlightenment was not "pure reason," the reason of syllogisms, the reason of metaphysics and aprioristic logic, the reason of Descartes's "homo rationalis." It was a reason focused on empirical reality, on "facts," on "common sense," and on probabilistic thinking, not expecting absolute certainty in anything.

As in many other areas of modern Anglo culture, a key role must be attributed here to John Locke. As the British historian Roy Porter put it in his magisterial *Enlightenment: Britain and the Creation of the Modern World*, "Locke was far and away the key philosopher in this modern mould" (2000, 60); "his philosophy proved a great watershed, and he became the presiding spirit of the English Enlightenment" (p. 66). The fact that the word *reasonableness* appeared in the title of one of Locke's major works (*The Reasonableness of Christianity*) is symptomatic in this respect. In

Locke's book, the word *reasonable* was not yet used in any of the senses it has now in either legal or ordinary language; and yet his view of "reasonableness"—which linked it with "mutual toleration" (1999, 120) and with "diversity" ("since we cannot reasonably expect that anyone should readily and obsequiously quit his own understanding and embrace ours," *Essay*, 1959, 372)—has left a noticeable imprint on the subsequent history of the word *reasonable*. To quote Porter:

> In stark contrast to Descartes, Hobbes and the other rationalists, Locke's truth claims were models of modesty. To the Galileo-idolising Hobbes, reason could range omnipotent; for Locke, any straying from the empirical straight and narrow led into mental minefields. While Hobbes proposed proofs modo geometrico, Locke saw no scope for Euclidian certainty. Man was a limited being, and reason just sufficient for human purposes. (Porter 2000, 60)

Many passages in Locke's writings show the new, post-Enlightenment meanings of the word *reasonable* in *statu nascendi*:

> Locke shared Bacon's impatience with scholastic syllogisms which chopped logic "without making any addition to it." Empirical knowledge, by contrast, traded in honest matters of fact and though limited, could be cumulative and progressive. (Porter 2000, 63)

Empirical, "demonstrable" knowledge was only probable knowledge, but it was nonetheless practically useful:

> While inevitably lacking the certitude of revelation or intuition, this formed the main stock of truth available to mortals. Locke agreed with Sydenhaus, Boyle, Newton, and their peers in stressing the limits of man's powers, but that was no insuperable problem: "our business here is not to know all things, but those which concern our conduct." (Porter 2000, 63)

> Though "demonstrable" knowledge, the harvest of experience, could never be more than probable, it was nevertheless useful and progressive. (p. 65)

Given that the quotes from Locke adduced by Porter read like sketches for a semantic history of the word *reasonable*, it is not surprising that Porter's conclusion about Locke's impact is framed in precisely such terms:

> Alongside his defences of toleration and political liberty Locke thus set the enlightened agenda with his endorsement of the mind's progressive capacities. In dismissing Platonic and Cartesian apriorism, in asserting that knowledge was the art of the probable and in holding that the way forward lay in empirical inquiry, *he replaced rationalism with reasonableness* in a manner which became programmatic for the Enlightenment in Britain. (Porter 2000, 66, emphasis added)

The British philosophical tradition that lies behind the folk value of 'reasonableness' reflected in modern English is, of course, not restricted to Locke alone. It embraces several different (and often mutually critical) strands, including the seventeenth-century "constructive skepticism" of John Wilkins (the founder of the Royal Society), Hume's "naturalism" (which made room for beliefs that are not rationally justifiable but that nevertheless leave no room for doubt), and the Scottish "common sense philosophy" of Thomas Reid. (See, e.g., Ferreira 1986; Shapiro 1983, 1991;

van Leeuwen 1963; Livingston and King, eds., 1976.) But Locke's impact on the general intellectual climate in both Britain and America was by far the greatest.

A key role in the evolution of the word *reasonable* was undoubtedly played by the emergence in the eighteenth century of the legal doctrine of "beyond reasonable doubt," which I discuss more fully in section 4.6. In that same section, I comment on the link between the phrases *reasonable doubt* and *reasonable man* as they were used in Britain and America in the eighteenth century, discuss the meaning of *a reasonable man* in eighteenth-century English, and attempt to show that it represented an intermediate stage between Shakespeare's use and twentieth-century use. For the moment, however, let me try to explicate its contemporary meaning.

a reasonable man (X)
  a. sometimes when things happen to a person this person has to think like this:
  b. "I want to know what is a good thing to do now"
  c. when something like this happens to X, X thinks about it like this:
  d. "I know some things about things like this
  e. when I think about these things well I can think like this about something:
  f. it will be good if I do this
  g. I can say why I think like this"
  h. if someone else knows the same things about it when they think about these things well they can think the same about it
  i. it is good if someone is like this
  j. I don't want to say more
  k. I don't want to say: not many people are like this

Components (d) and (e), focused on good thinking grounded in knowledge, relate the concept 'reasonable' (as used in the collocation *a reasonable man*) to 'reason', in the procedural sense: a 'reasonable man' can think well. But the first two components (a) and (b) suggest, contrary to appearances, certain limitations on this ability: X's ability to think well is not absolute but relative to the subject matter, contingent. Although he is not a narrow specialist and can think well about many (different) things, X cannot necessarily think well about everything. He is not a "thinker" tout court or a person of outstanding general intelligence; he is simply someone who can think well in a concrete situation, when he needs to know what to do. Hypothetical collocations like *a reasonable teacher*, quoted earlier, are *not* used in modern English in the same sense as *a reasonable man*. A *reasonable teacher* would have to mean *a reasonably good teacher*. A phrase like *a reasonable boss* (or *employer*) can have also another sense: roughly, a boss (or employer) who doesn't require too much from his or her subordinates (employees). But the phrase *a reasonable man* (or *person*) is different—because it links X's ability to think well with his experience: his is not necessarily an ability to think well about abstract problems, or about logic, but an ability to think well in concrete situations, when something happens to him (component c).

Components (b) to (g) link X's ability to think well with an ability to know what to do in a given situation ("now"). The standard set by the 'reasonable man' has to do with human conduct, not with thinking about the universe or about formal logic. It also has to do with an ability to think about a particular set of circumstances: X can know what to do in a particular situation because X is good at thinking about particular situations.

Component (j) ("I don't want to say more") introduces an element of limitation: the speaker does not want to present X as an intellectual giant, standing head and shoulders above other people. On the contrary, the speaker is keen to portray X as an ordinary person or, rather, to avoid creating an impression that X is necessarily someone outstanding. Hence component (k): "I don't want to say: not many people are like this."

In fact, it is important for the speaker to validate X's judgment with reference to other people. Because the speaker does not say that X *always* thinks well (about *all* matters) and because he or she explicitly denies that X is someone outstanding, where else could the speaker's trust in X's judgment come from? Component (h) suggests that it comes precisely from the speaker's trust in ordinary people's capacity to arrive at a sound judgment. But of course there is no guarantee that, having considered the matter, other people will think the same as X does (about what is a good thing to do in that particular situation), though they certainly *can* come to the same conclusion: (h) "if someone else knows the same things, when they think about these things well, they can think the same."

The overall evaluation (component i) is optimistic: "it is good if someone is like this." The grounds for optimism are limited, for the speaker does not say that X actually "*knows* what is a good thing to do" or that other people will *necessarily* agree. Yet limited as human knowledge is—empirical, probabilistic, prone to error—in most situations, for most practical purposes, "a reasonable man" can make "a reasonable judgment," and, from the cultural point of view reflected in the phrase *a reasonable man*, "this is good."

As a whole, this explication reflects the British empirical tradition with its emphasis on the link between good thinking and experience and on practice rather than theory; and it also reflects faith in democracy and in the trustworthy (if not infallible) judgment of "ordinary people."[1]

Let me close this section with a characteristic and telling quote from a pamphlet entitled "The Law and the Reasonable Man" published by the British judge Lord Reid (and originally delivered as a lecture at the British Academy):

> We are a democracy and I would say that a large majority of the voters are, as individuals, reasonable men and women. . . . The law departs at its peril from the views of the reasonable man. He could not give a definition of what he means by justice and neither can I. But that does not prevent him from saying that particular things are clearly unjust. We as lawyers and legislators can go far but we cannot afford to go so far that we offend his sense of justice. We may try to educate our masters, but we shall do incalculable harm if we try to override the views of the average reasonable man. (Reid 1968, 204–205)

4.5. "It is Reasonable to" Think (Say, Do) . . .

Let us now explore, from a semantic point of view, the common syntactic frame "it is reasonable to," with its modally (and epistemically) qualified variants (examples from Cobuild):

it would be reasonable to suppose

it seemed reasonable to assume

it is reasonable to suppose

it was quite reasonable to be worried

it seems reasonable to say

it is reasonable to speculate

it seems reasonable to think

it is reasonable to consider

it is reasonable to ask

it is reasonable to wonder

In legal literature, it appears to be assumed that this sense of *reasonable* corresponds closely to that in the phrase *a reasonable man (person)*. Phrases like *reasonable doubt*, *reasonable fears*, and *reasonable expectations* (as well as *reasonable care*) are used in that literature alongside the phrase *a reasonable man* as if exactly the same concept were involved in all these cases. In fact, though, this is not so. To clarify the relations between the different senses, however, we need to consider each type separately.

Thus, the type linked with the frame "it is reasonable to" takes verbs that are predominantly verbs of thinking. Furthermore, it is, characteristically, *tentative* thinking—thinking associated with the limitations of a person's knowledge ("it is reasonable to suppose / assume / speculate"). The prevalence of the copula *seem* is consistent with this uncertainty: it *seems* good to think like this, but since one doesn't really know, one prefers to be cautious and tentative. For the same reason, no doubt, the copula tends to be hedged: not just "it is reasonable" or even "it seems reasonable" but often "it would be reasonable" or "it would seem reasonable." The tentativeness characteristic of the prevalent use of the frame "it is reasonable to . . ." is also characteristic of the use of *reasonable* with the corresponding abstract nouns: "a reasonable hypothesis," "a reasonable guess," "a reasonable judgment."

In addition to verbs of thinking (especially tentative ones), some verbs of speaking or feeling can also occur as complements of the clause "it is reasonable to . . ." but only if they can be understood as implying thinking—either inherently (as in *to worry*) or in the given context. For example, one can readily say "it is reasonable to ask why . . ."—implying that the speaker has thought about the possible reasons or causes. But a purely factual question does not easily lend itself to such use (e.g., ?it is reasonable to ask what time it is). Similarly, speech act verbs referring to social routines such as *apologize*, *greet*, or *thank* are normally not used in the frame in question (there are no examples like "it is reasonable to apologize" in the Cobuild corpus). On the other hand, it would be okay to say "it is reasonable to expect an apology in the circumstances," because *expect* implies a thinking process.

Sometimes, the frame "it is reasonable to . . ." can even be combined with a verb of doing—but again, only on the condition that this "doing" can be understood as implying thinking. For example (from Cobuild):

Such arguments, convincing as they may be, may dictate that it's reasonable to remove life-support systems—in spite of the fact that to do so would be active Euthanasia.

Whilst it is reasonable to take an occasional tablet to relieve them, there is increasing evidence that "popping" too many aspirin or paracetamol can actually increase the frequency of headaches to the extent that they occur every day.

What is being described here as *reasonable* is a physical action but an action that implies thinking ("should we continue with this life-support system, or should we remove it?" and "should I take a tablet or is it better not to?"). Hence, in these sentences, too, the judgment "it is reasonable" can be taken to apply to someone's thinking.

What does it mean, then, to say that "it is reasonable to think like this"? Clearly, it is, first of all, a judgment concerning the compatibility of a given thought with someone's ability to think well: in the speaker's opinion, a person who can think well can think like this. Does this mean that the speaker agrees with the view assessed as "reasonable"? Not necessarily. The speaker acknowledges that the view in question is consistent with an ability to think well—and stops there, denying any desire to go further in supporting that view: "I don't want to say more"; that is, "I don't want to say: it's good to think like this."

And yet the epistemic reserve of the frame "it is reasonable to . . . " does not commit the speaker to a position of complete uncertainty and profound lack of confidence. On the contrary, the phrase "it is reasonable to think . . . " (even when modally qualified) implies a degree of confidence.

This sense of confidence comes from two sources. First, the speaker ("I") has grounds for the expressed judgment—grounds that could be made explicit ("I can say why I think like this"). Second, my judgment, fallible as it is, but also justifiable as it is, can, I think, be shared by other people—if these people consider the matter carefully (as it is implied I have done).

In Gilbert and Sullivan's operetta *Trial by Jury*, the judge says to the lawyer for the plaintiff that what the defendant proposes ("I'll marry this lady today, and I'll marry the other tomorrow") "seems to be a reasonable proposition with which I think your client may agree." While the humor turns on the fact that the suggestion is wholly unreasonable, the reference to expected agreement is as characteristic here as the verbal caution ("seems to be").

These considerations bring us to the following explication:

a reasonable hypothesis (it is reasonable to think that)=
a. I know some things about it
b. when I think about these things well I think that it can be like this
c. I can say why I think like this
d. if someone else knows the same things about it when they think about these things well they can think the same about it
e. I don't want to say more
f. I don't want to say: it is like this

If we now compare the explications of the two senses of *reasonable*—that in *a reasonable man (person)* and that in *it is reasonable to . . .*—we will see a number of differences, as well as a number of links. As for links, they both share references to an ability to think well and to a possible consensus, and they both express a certain reserve on the part of the speaker (the speaker does not want to go overboard in making a positive assessment). But there are also clear differences.

First of all, the phrase *it is reasonable to think* does not refer in any way to an "ordinary person": the image of the man on the Clapham omnibus is not there. Although a consensus is still expected, there is no longer an implication that the person who thinks what is being described as "reasonable" is someone like many other people.

Second, the phrase *it is reasonable to . . .* does not seem to be limited to the world of common human experience: it is not linked necessarily with specific situations where something happens to someone and could also apply to abstract, theoretical thinking, as in the following examples from the OED:

> It is reasonable to attribute these changes to the high dose of radiation delivered to the host-animal . . . (1956)

> It is reasonable to expect the biochemical variability of the parasite to be statistically correlated with other features. (1988)

> It is reasonable to fix the real change from pre-human to human social life by reference to the beginning of language. (1958)

Third—and this is obviously a related point—the phrase *it is reasonable to . . .* does not imply, specifically, an ability to know what to do. Examples like "it is reasonable to remove the life-support system" are, of course, consistent with such an implication, but a sentence like "it is reasonable to assume/think" can also be used in theoretical discussions; it does not seem related, specifically, to the practical world and to a specific set of circumstances in the way *a reasonable man* (or *person*) is.

Fourth (and this is also a related point), the phrase *it is reasonable to . . .* appears to be linked semantically with *reasons*: if I say that "it is reasonable to think like this," I seem to be implying that I could state the reasons for thinking like this ("I can say why"). On the other hand, the "reasonable man" on the Clapham omnibus is not necessarily expected to be able to state the reasons for his judgment. Thus, the component "I can say why," assigned to *it is reasonable to . . .* , has not been assigned to *a reasonable man (person)*.

It is particularly interesting to note that this use of *reasonable* as an epistemic hedge (diminisher, downtoner) appears to be a relatively recent development in English and that 100 or 150 years ago a phrase like *reasonable assumption* did not imply the reserved noncommitment that it does now. Examples like the following one (from the OED) can be misleading in this regard:

> . . . the reasonable assumption would be that this bullet would range a greater distance if projected at the same velocity. (1877)

If *reasonable* as used here included the component "I don't want to say more" then it could hardly be used in the following sentence (also from the OED):

> The conviction would be reasonable, for it would be based upon universal experience. (1877)

In contemporary English, "convictions" can hardly be described as "reasonable"—
presumably because they are not compatible with the component "I don't want to
say more," which in the course of the last century and a half became incorporated in
the word's very meaning. (I return to this point in section 4.6.)

All in all, the phrase *it is reasonable to . . .* appears to belong to the world of
epistemic modifiers characteristic of modern Anglo discourse. As I have argued, this
world, too, has its roots in the intellectual climate that can be traced, inter alia, to
John Locke's *Essay on Human Understanding*.

Both *rational* and *reasonable* have their starting point in the concept of "reason," but two centuries ago (if not earlier), their paths parted, and *reasonable* went
its own way. One of the sentences cited in the Cobuild corpus reads: "Are these assumptions reasonable, rational?" In this context, the two adjectives are brought together (without *and*) as if they were near-synonyms. In fact, however, their meanings
are substantially different, as highlighted by another example from Cobuild:

> The retreat from reality, like neurosis, met a real psychic need, Dwight wrote. . . .
> Irrational modes of thought were increasing. . . .

"Modes of thinking" can be described as rational or irrational but not as reasonable
or unreasonable, because, first, the assessment "reasonable" applies always to a particular thought, not to some mode of thinking in general, and, second, because *reasonable* refers inherently to a potential discussion or debate with other people and
implies an expectation that if they considered the matter, they could think the same.

By contrast, *rational* has nothing to do with other people and refers precisely to
a way of thinking rather than to a particular (and not recurring) thought. Thus, we
can have *irrational fears* (implying an irrational way of thinking) but not *?an irrational assumption* or *?an irrational guess*; we can also say *it is reasonable to suppose* but
not *?it is rational to suppose*: a single act of thinking (supposing, guessing) is not a
sufficient basis for identifying and judging a way of thinking.

Without attempting full explications, I would propose the following as a starting point (the arrow indicates a partial explication):

> *irrational fears* =>
> when someone thinks like this, this someone is not thinking well
> when someone is thinking well, this someone cannot think like this

As we have seen, the explication of *reasonable* (in the meaning under discussion)
includes quite different additional components suggestive of intellectual restraint ("I
don't want to say more"), a perceived need for evidence ("I can say why I think like
this"), and an interest in other people's judgment ("I think that other people can think
the same").

The distinction between the concepts "rational" and "reasonable" has often been
discussed in philosophical literature. A good example is of such discussion is Sibley's
(1953) article "The Rational versus the Reasonable," which, as Rawls (2001, 7) puts
it, "connects the distinction closely with the idea of cooperation among equals" and
"is of central importance in understanding the structure of justice as fairness." I believe that such philosophical discussions would benefit from careful semantic analy-

sis of the word *reasonable* in all its different though interrelated meanings. We will come back to this point in section 4.10.

4.6. "Reasonable Doubt"

The momentous phrase *beyond reasonable doubt* entered the English language some time in the seventeenth century (see van Leeuwen 1963, Shapiro 1983)[2] and became well established in the eighteenth century. As noted by Morano in his important paper "A Reexamination of the Reasonable Doubt Rule" (1975), it was used in the Boston Massacre trials of 1770, where the prosecution appealed to the jury's "Cool and Candid Reason," telling them that if the "Evidence is not sufficient to Convince beyond reasonable Doubt," the accused must be acquitted. At the same trials, a judge instructed the jury in the following words: "If upon the whole ye are in any reasonable doubt of their guilt, ye must then, agreeable to the rule of the law, declare them innocent" (Shapiro 1991, 22).

The phrase *any rational doubt* was also used in other late-eighteenth-century trials, for example, in the so-called Irish trials of 1795, as was also the phrase *rational men*. But eventually, the language of *reasonable doubt* replaced that of *rational doubt*, and it was often linked with the phrase *reasonable men*.

Thus, in the Trial of Weldon (1795), the judge indicated that if the jury had "any rational doubt" in their minds, they must acquit. Another judge said that if the jury felt "such a doubt as reasonable men entertain," they had to acquit. In another trial of the same year (Trial of Leary), the judge told the jury that they must acquit . . . if you should have any doubt, such as reasonable men may entertain"; and in the Trial of Glenman (1796), the judge used jointly the following formulations: "if you have a reasonable doubt" and "you are rational men" (Shapiro 1991, 23).

Thus, both *rational* and *reasonable* were used at the time, in similar contexts, and two centuries later, the two words are still used interchangeably in some scholarly commentaries on the history of the notion of "reasonable doubt" in Britain and America. In fact, however, the two words did not mean the same, and, as Porter (2000) notes in his book on the British Enlightenment, the victory of *reasonable* over *rational* was highly significant. I would add that no less significant were the changes in the meaning of the word *reasonable* itself, and I will argue that the phrase *beyond reasonable doubt* has also changed in meaning, and that due to its continuous use over more than two centuries, this fact has largely gone unnoticed.

What was the difference in meaning between the two phrases *rational men* and *reasonable men*, as used, for example, in late-eighteenth-century instructions to jurors? Roughly speaking, it appears that the phrase *reasonable men* limited the expected "good thinking" to the domain of a person's experience and at the same time implied confidence in that experience as a possible source of practical wisdom (or "prudence"). To quote Morano, "the concept of the 'reasonable man'— whose conduct was the standard against which allegedly negligent actions would be judged—developed during the eighteenth century . . . the concept of the 'reasonable man of ordinary prudence' was first mentioned in a 1738 English case" (1975, 514).

Thus, when the model of *a reasonable man* was set before the eighteenth-century jurors, I would hypothesize that it was understood along the lines of the following formula:

a reasonable man (eighteenth century) =
a. when this person wants to know what is good to think about something this person thinks about it like this:
b. "I know some things about it
c. I want to think about these things well
d. I want to know what I can think because of these things"
e. because this person thinks like this this person can know many things
f. it is good if someone is like this
g. not everyone can be like this

As this explication shows, the eighteenth-century model of *a reasonable man* was closely related to "reason," and it was not restricted to concrete situations, personal experience, and the need to "know what to do." Rather, it was concerned with "knowing what to think" and how to arrive at new knowledge on the basis of thinking well about what one already knows. Furthermore, that model of *a reasonable man* did not yet necessarily include the assumption that *a reasonable man* was an ordinary person (the average commuter on the Clapham omnibus). Accordingly, instead of the last two components of the explication given in section 4.4 ("I don't want to say more," "I don't want to say: 'not many people are like this'") this explication includes an "elitist" component, "not everyone can be like this."

In the new jury system that developed during the eighteenth century, "jurors sit as fact evaluators who assess both the direct testimony of eyewitnesses and indirect circumstantial evidence. The beyond reasonable doubt doctrine evolved as judges came to inform jurors that they must evaluate the testimony of witnesses" (Shapiro 1991, 244). To evaluate the testimony of witnesses and the circumstantial evidence means to think well about what one hears and what one sees, and to draw from this appropriate conclusions.

From their evaluations, jurors were expected to draw inferences. Because they were no longer (as in earlier centuries) "important local men who presumably would possess the requisite local knowledge" (p. 244) but rather evaluators of evidence, "jurors by that time could make little claim to independent knowledge, that is, to knowledge brought to, rather than gained in, the courtroom" (p. 244). The knowledge gained by the jurors in the courtroom was limited; and it had to rely, to a large extent on their judgment.

In the older jury system, jurors had to rely, above all, on their conscience and personal beliefs. For example, Shapiro (1991, 260) notes: "in the Trial of Sir Thomas More (1535) jurors were told that the decision about witness credibility rested on the 'conscience and discretion' of the jury. . . . More was informed by the judge that the jury had found him 'Guilty in their Conscience.'"[3] In the new system, which developed in the eighteenth century, jurors were no longer seen as "good men and true" (as Shakespeare puts it in *Much Ado about Nothing*), that is, as people who could rely on their own knowledge and conscience. Instead, they were people who had to rely on the careful, critical, and conscientious consideration of evidence. To quote Shapiro again:

> The language of satisfied conscience conceivably might have been useful even when jurors thought of themselves as self-informing, but the beyond reasonable doubt language suggests a standard to be attained after a rational consideration of evidence. . . . Armed with the formula "beyond a reasonable doubt and to a moral certainty" and a circumstantial evidence doctrine to replace the self-knowledge that had itself replaced God's knowledge, the criminal trial jury thus could maintain its role as the central actor and legitimator of the Anglo-American justice system. (Shapiro 1991, 245)

It is widely accepted that the legal principle of "beyond reasonable doubt" is closely linked with the philosophical ideas that developed in England at the end of the seventeenth century (in particular, but of course not only, Locke's ideas). Morano puts it as follows:

> The philosophical origins of the reasonable doubt rule can be traced to late seventeenth century England. During that period, a group of English philosophers—including John Wilkins, Robert Boyle, Joseph Glanville and John Locke—rejected the prevailing doctrine that equated moral certainty with absolute certainty. This group argued that one could not be absolutely certain of anything and that the concept of moral certainty could not demand such a high degree of proof. Instead, moral certainty required only that one have no reasonable doubts about one's beliefs. (Morano 1975, 513)

As Shapiro (1991) documents, from Sir Geoffrey Gilbert's authoritative *Law of Evidence* (1770) onward, the development of the beyond reasonable doubt principle was linked in particular with Lockean empirical philosophy and with Locke's conception of degrees of probability. Justified in these terms, this principle provided a secular moral standard on which, it was felt, law could be based in the Age of Reason. It was also a concept that by the late eighteenth century had reached the educated public, first in Britain and later in America, and become part and parcel of public discourse—and of the modern English language.

Given how entrenched the concept has become in English—not only in the legal system and in philosophical discussions but also in popular thinking—it is important to recognize that the meaning of the phrase *beyond reasonable doubt* has changed by imperceptible stages in the course of the last two centuries.

At the time when the phrase *beyond reasonable doubt* entered the English language, the word *reasonable* did not mean exactly the same as it does today. As noted earlier, today *reasonable* readily combines with verbs and nouns implying an absence of conviction (e.g., *it is reasonable to suppose / assume / wonder / fear / speculate / hypothesize*, etc.), and older collocations like *reasonable conviction* sound odd today—precisely because they are not compatible with an absence of conviction, a noncommittal implied today by the word *reasonable*. But when at the end of the seventeenth century John Tillotson, Archbishop of Canterbury, argued: "The laws of God are reasonable, that is, suitable to our nature and advantageous to our interest" (quoted in

Porter 2000, 3), he was clearly indicating conviction, not a lack of conviction — and the sentence sounds odd today.

At the end of the eighteenth century, when the phrase *reasonable doubt* took root in the English language, and the doctrine of beyond reasonable doubt, in Anglo/ American law, phrases like *reasonable conviction* or *reasonable belief* were still common, as was indeed the phrase *reasonable certainty* — not in the modern sense of "I'm reasonably certain," that is, "not quite certain," but on the contrary, in the sense of "quite certain." To quote a legal document from as late as the mid-nineteenth century (quoted in Shapiro 1991, 24): "the evidence must establish to a reasonable and moral certainty; a certainty that convinces and directs the understanding and satisfies the reason and judgment. . . . This we take to be proof beyond a reasonable doubt."

As pointed out by Morano (1975), the beyond reasonable doubt test was originally introduced by the prosecution, and it was actually designed to provide less protection to the accused than the earlier "any doubt" test, which did not require that doubts be reasonable.

> The reasonable doubt rule had the effect of reducing the prosecutor's burden of proof in criminal trials. . . . It informed the jurors that they needed to be persuaded only beyond reasonable doubt — not beyond any doubt. . . . the rule helped reduce the potential for irrational acquittals and to that extent operated to the prosecution's advantage. (Morano 1975, 515)

In the first half of the eighteenth century, that is, before the reasonable doubt rule was adopted, the jurors' personal "belief" and "satisfaction" (as well as "conscience") were seen as the decisive factors. "A guilty verdict was appropriate if the jurors 'believed,' an acquittal if they were not satisfied" (Shapiro 1991, 20). In the second half of the century, judges still made appeals to the jurors' "belief" ("most cases . . . still exhibited the familiar formulas emphasizing belief" p. 20). Although the words *mind*, *understanding*, and *judgment* started to be used more frequently than *belief* and *conscience*, the new language of "understanding" and "judgment" did not imply that rational arguments were to *replace* personal belief. As one judge put it, "the understandings of the jury must be 'absolutely coerced to believe'"(Shapiro 1991, 20).

Thus, the shift from "any doubt" to "any reasonable doubt" did not mean that the requirement of subjective personal conviction was to be *replaced* with objective rational arguments ("reasons") but rather that it was to be supplemented in this way. *Reasonable doubt* implied "reasonable belief" and not merely "a tenable line of argument," as it might today.

Morano's reexamination of the reasonable doubt rule is consistent with the semantic observations made here. In present-day English, the phrase *beyond reasonable doubt* suggests a doubt that can be weak and hypothetical, and it implies that even a weak and hypothetical doubt should be able to be rejected (before the verdict guilty can be reached); it provides more protection for the accused, not less. By contrast, at a time when *a reasonable doubt* could be taken to refer to strong personally held doubt, the proviso could have indeed worked against the interests of the accused: it implied that even a strong personally held doubt (with respect to the prosecution's case) was not sufficient, that reasons were needed as well.

Reasonable doubt was initially expected to be "serious" and "substantial," as well as real (that is, actually held). As a judge put it to the jurors in the 1798 American trial of Matthew Lyon, "you must be satisfied beyond all reasonable substantial doubt that the hypothesis of innocence is unsustainable" (Shapiro 1991, 24). Half a century later, in the *Commonwealth v. Harman* trial in Pennsylvania, the court defined *reasonable doubt* as "serious and substantial — not the mere possibility of a doubt" (Morano 1975, 522). But in twentieth-century usage, *reasonable doubt* is no longer understood as necessarily "serious and substantial."

For example, in the legal thriller entitled *Beyond Reasonable Doubt*, the author, a practicing attorney, has his lawyer for the defense address the jurors as follows:

> When it's over, you take the prosecution's claim, and you take the evidence, and you ask yourself, "Do I have any doubt that this happened exactly the way the prosecutor said it did?" And if you have any doubt, then you have to acquit Jennifer Ryan. Not a big doubt. Just a *reasonable* doubt.
>
> The judge is going to tell you about that, too. He'll tell you a reasonable doubt is any doubt you can assign a reason to. That doesn't mean a detailed reason like a specific theory of how the crime happened or who did it. It means any reason you might have, to doubt any part of what the prosecution is telling you. To doubt the elements that make up his case, or to doubt the conclusion he wants you to reach. Any reasonable doubt at all. (Friedman 1990, 481)

It is striking how close Friedman's "reasonable doubt" comes to "any doubt" — at least any doubt for which some logically defensible reason can be offered:

> Proof beyond a reasonable doubt is not proof beyond any doubt or proof beyond the shadow of a doubt. A doubt is reasonable if it is a doubt for which a reason can be given, a doubt which a reasonable person would have, acting in a matter of this importance. (Friedman 1990, 506)

The claim that *a reasonable doubt* is "a doubt which *a reasonable person* would have" comes, I believe, from the earlier legal tradition, but the assertion that "a doubt is reasonable if it is a doubt for which a reason can be given" does capture a real component in the present-day meaning of the phrase *a reasonable doubt*. In fact, it is one of the components that would distinguish the meaning of this phrase from that of the phrase *a reasonable man*: as mentioned earlier, "a reasonable man" does not need to be able to say why he thinks what he does; an intuitive sound judgment (as to what ought to be done in a given situation) may be sufficient for "a reasonable man."[4] But an intuitive doubt would not be sufficient to qualify as *reasonable doubt*: it must indeed be "a doubt for which a reason can be given."

In eighteenth-century usage, the principle of beyond reasonable doubt was also linked with statable reasons but was not limited to them; rather, it was still linked with the notions of conscience and moral certainty. For example, in the 1796 (Irish) Trial of Glennan, the judge told the jury that they should acquit "if you have a reasonable doubt, not such as the idle or fanciful may take upon remote probabilities, but such as cannot satisfy your judgment upon your oath. . . . You are rational men and will determine according to your consciences, whether you believe these men guilty or not." As Shapiro, who quotes this passage, comments, "here the languages

of belief, the satisfied conscience, and beyond reasonable doubt are all linked together" (1991, 23).

It is worth pointing out in this context that in eighteenth-century trials the phrase
reasonable doubt was often linked syntactically with someone's (a juror's) personal
belief: the question was not whether "*there is* a reasonable doubt" but whether "*you
have* a reasonable doubt" (or "if *you are in* any reasonable doubt"). Today, the phrase
if you have a reasonable doubt sounds a little odd.

As noted by Shapiro, "by the late eighteenth century the concepts of moral certainty and reasonable doubt were tightly linked in philosophical literature, in legal
treatises, and in legal discussions designed to reach the educated public" (1991, 29).
Indeed, Shapiro suggests that "moral certainty and beyond reasonable doubt were
originally viewed as synonymous" (p. 274). In twentieth-century usage, however, *reasonable doubt* is not intimately linked to the jurors' personal convictions, the question is whether a "reasonable case" can be made, not whether the jurors have any
subjective "moral certainty" as to the truth of the matter. The change in the grammatical frame, from a personal to an impersonal one, reflects this change in the
understanding of *reasonable doubt*. Roughly, this change can be portrayed as follows:

> (*I have*) *a reasonable doubt* (*eighteenth century*)
> a. I know some things about it
> b. when I think about these things well I think that maybe it is not like this
> c. I think that it is good to think like this
> d. I can say why I think like this
> e. if someone else knows the same things about it when they think about
>   these things well they can think the same about it
>
> (*there is*) *a reasonable doubt* . . . (*twentieth–twenty-first centuries*)
> a. I know some things about it
> b. when I think about these things well I think that maybe it is not like this
> c. _____
> d. I can say why I think like this
> e. if someone else knows the same things about it when they think about
>   these things well they can think the same about it
> f. I don't want to say more
> g. I don't want to say: I know that it is not like this

Thus, I am suggesting that in present-day usage *reasonable doubt* is understood along
the same lines as *a reasonable assumption* or *a reasonable hypothesis*—that is, as
something for which tenable reasons can be offered, not something that one feels
necessarily committed to.

Fernández-Armesto's (1998, 165) phrase "the death of conviction," used as a
characterization of our times, may be somewhat hyperbolic, but the fact that the words
conviction and *reasonable* have ceased to be combinable is noteworthy. They were
certainly combinable when John Locke was writing his *Reasonableness of Christianity*
and when the phrase *reasonable doubt* became established in the English language.
For Locke, "reasonableness" was consistent with both tolerance ("toleration") and
conviction: tolerance for other people's opinions, belief in one's own.

To recapitulate, the meaning of the word *reasonable* has changed. As a result, the meaning of the phrase *beyond reasonable doubt* has also changed, roughly speaking, from a "belief consistent with reason and sincerely held," to a "supposition consistent with reason and put forward as a logical possibility," but because this phrase was continually used for over two centuries and became entrenched in Anglo/American law as well as in ordinary language, and because the older meaning of *reasonable* is no longer known to most speakers, the change has, generally speaking, gone unnoticed.

4.7. "Reasonable Force" and "Reasonable Care"

Reasonable force seems to be related to the notions of *a reasonable assessment* or *a reasonable estimate*. If a person is said to have used *reasonable force*, this appears to mean that it is reasonable to think that under the circumstances that person had to use that much force. Some examples from Cobuild:

> By my understanding, it is okay to use reasonable force to protect life and property though no one is exactly sure what is meant by reasonable force.

> When I asked a police officer to define reasonable force he said it depended on circumstance.

> The main thing to remember is to use only reasonable force.

> At present, the law allows for a person to use "reasonable force" in defence of himself or his property.

> The Law Society said: "People are entitled to use reasonable force. But their actions must be proportionate to the threat against them.

> Mr Grant was detained while officers considered if he had used reasonable force for a valid citizen's arrest.

> The law also recognizes that people cannot make decisions about what is reasonable force when they are being attacked.

> British parents can use "reasonable" force to discipline their children.

Who decides whether the force applied in a given situation was reasonable? If we accept that the verdict should take into account the defendant's perspective as well as that of other people, we can propose an explication along the following lines:

> *(when X did it) X used reasonable force.* =
> a. when X did it, X knew some things about it
> b. when X thought about these things well, X could have thought like this:
> c. "this person is doing something now
> d. something very bad can happen because of this
> e. it will not happen if I do something to this person's body
> f. I know that if I do it something bad can happen to this person
> g. because of this I can't not do it
> h. I have to do it

    i. I don't want to do more"
    j. I can say why X could have thought like this
    k. if someone else knew the same things about it
       when they thought about these things well
       they could have thought the same about it
       [because of this they could have done the same]

For example, if some parents are using "reasonable force" in disciplining their child, their actions must be consistent with the following mental scenarios: (c.) "This child is doing something now," (d.) "this can be dangerous" ("something very bad can happen because of this"), (e.) "this very bad thing will not happen if I restrain the child," (f.) "if I restrain the child something bad can happen to the child's body," (g.) I can't not do it because of this," (h.) "I have to do it," (i.) "I don't want to do more." Thus, these parents' actions are seen as consistent with careful consideration of the matter and a desire to be moderate and to avoid excessive force.

    The prominence of the "body" in this explication is of course due, partly, to the word *force*. The phrase *reasonable force*, which plays an important role in Anglo/American law, has a meaning of its own that cannot be fully derived from the meanings of its parts, but is clearly related to them and built on them.

    The same applies to another important legal concept, that of "reasonable care," which is also focused prominently on the human body.

    First some examples from Cobuild:

> today's juries are broadening in a dramatic way the legal notion of "reasonable care" as it relates to health and safety precautionary practices.

> these training steps must be in place to legally demonstrate [that] "reasonable care" has been taken in providing for patrons' health and safety.

> judged by proper professional standards in the light of the objective facts about the individual patients the dental treatments criticised as unnecessary [were] treatments that no dentist of reasonable skill exercising reasonable care would carry out

Again, if we assume that the judgment as to whether the person involved did or did not take reasonable care should take two perspectives into account (a "subjective" as well as an "objective" one), we can propose the following explication:

X *took reasonable care (in doing it)* =
    a. X knew some things about it
    b. when X thought about these things well X could have thought like this:
    c. "I have to so some good things for this person for some time
    d. during this time I don't want something bad to happen to this person's body
    e. something is happening to this person now
    f. I know that if I don't do something now
       something very bad can happen to this person's body
    g. because of this I have to do it

h. I don't have to do more"
i. I can say why X could have thought like this
j. if someone else knew the same things about it
   when they thought about these things well
   they could have thought the same about it
   [because of this they could have done the same]

The phrase *reasonable care* is also sometimes used in relation to physical objects (other than people's bodies), as in the following example from Cobuild:

Under the Supply of Goods and Services Act, the dry cleaners had a duty to take reasonable care of your trousers while they were in their possession.

With minimal changes, the explication previously proposed would apply to such uses of *reasonable care*, too (except, of course, for the references to a person's body).

4.8. "A Reasonable Time," "A Reasonable Amount"

In the Cobuild corpus, by far the most common collocation linking the word *reasonable* with a noun (apart from *reasonable prices*, which I discuss in section 4.10) is *a reasonable time*, and the next one, *a reasonable amount*. To understand the meaning of these collocations, we need to consider them in context. Here are some characteristic examples (also with *period*):

And we expected we'd all be home within a reasonable time.

In addition the Act stated that all contracts for the supply of a service should be carried out in a reasonable time to a reasonable standard and at a reasonable price if one had not been previously agreed.

Any skin problem that does not go away within a reasonable period of time or recurs requires an expert's evaluation and diagnosis.

Testosterone is a naturally occurring hormone in men and women and an explanation is required for why this ratio was high and Diane Modahl must be given reasonable time to do this.

Such a dismissal must be for some specific reason, e.g. theft, damage to machinery or persistent absenteeism, and the employee must receive a reasonable period of notice before the dismissal occurs.

Since Autumn was supposed to be a stranger in town, she had to avoid Ella and her family until she had lived there a reasonable length of time.

Clearly, in all these examples the expression *a reasonable time* refers to duration (rather than to a particular point in time). Is this duration relatively long or relatively short? Paradoxically, in some cases, it seems to mean "reasonably short" and in others, "reasonably long." Thus, if something is to be done *in* or *within a reasonable time*, this means "reasonably short," whereas if it is to be done *for a reasonable time*, this is more likely to be understood as *reasonably long* (with verbs like *to give* and *to receive* being usually also interpreted as implying *fairly long*). But whether *a reasonable time* is interpreted as a reasonably long time or a reasonably short time, the duration in question is evaluated as satisfactory: if possible, the speaker is willing to be satisfied ("I want to say: this is good"). This brings us to the following explication:

(for, in, within) a reasonable time =
a. I know some things about it
b. when I think about these things well I think about it like this:
   "it was a good time"
c. I can say why I think like this
d. if someone else knows the same things about it when they think about these things well they can think the same about it
e. I don't want to say more
f. I don't want to say: "very good"

The cultural concerns reflected in this explication are very striking. First, the speaker is weighing his or her words very carefully: this is a guarded, reflective, cautious way of speaking ("I think I can say this," "I don't want to say that"). Second, the speaker wants to avoid exaggeration: special store is set by not saying more than what is justified ("I don't want to say more") and, consequently, by avoiding the word *very*, or not using it lightly ("I don't want to say: 'very'"). Third, there is an aspiration to "good thinking" ("if someone can think well . . ."). Fourth, there is a willingness to say that one is satisfied, even if to do so one has to compromise ("it was a good [amount of] time").

We will see the same cultural concerns in another (clearly related) use of *reasonable*, in which it means, essentially, "reasonably good." Before turning to that use, however, we need to consider briefly the implications of another related usage, as in the phrase *a reasonable amount*. Comparing this phrase with *a reasonable time*, we note that while the latter is open to two interpretations ("reasonably long" or "reasonably short"), *a reasonable amount* seems to have only one interpretation:

a reasonable amount =
a. I know some things about it
b. when I think about these things well I think about it like this:
   "it is a good amount"
c. I can say why I think like this
d. if someone else knows the same things about it
   when they think about these things well they can think the same about it
e. I don't want to say more
f. I don't want to say: "very good"

The collocation *a reasonable amount* would tend to be interpreted not only as a desirable amount but also as a rather large amount. Given an appropriate context, *reasonable* can also refer to desirably small amounts, but without context, the normal interpretation would be "a reasonably large amount." Presumably, this effect is due to the component "I don't want to say more," which can be interpreted as restricting the amount as such, rather than indicating that it is less than ideal.

4.9. "Reasonable" as "Reasonably Good"

Let's consider the following sentences from Cobuild:

> I am a reasonable left-handed player, with a good short game.

> The pacey wing, who also enjoyed a reasonable afternoon as goalkicker, rattled up 19 points with flanker Markus Van Greunen the other tryscorer.

> 1986 was a reasonable year and the picturesque Erden village had produced a stylish wine from late harvested grapes.

Clearly, a "reasonable left-handed player" does not mean a reasonable person: *reasonable* means here, roughly, "reasonably good." A judgment is involved in all these examples, but it is the speaker's judgment, and it is a judgment concerning positive evaluation.

If we compare the meaning of *a reasonable year* with collocations like *reasonable force, reasonable amount, reasonable doubt*, or *a reasonable goal* (diverse as the latter are), it will be clear that it differs from them all. The word *reasonable* always seems to carry with it some reference to a positive evaluation, but this evaluation does not always fit in the same way in the semantic structure of different phrases. For example, *reasonable force* is not exactly "a good force" or *a reasonable doubt*, "a good doubt." A *reasonable year*, on the other hand, is (all things considered) "a good year." I would propose the following explication for *reasonable* in this sense:

> *reasonable year / location / attendance / health etc =*
> a. I know some things about it
> b. when I think about these things well I think about it like this: "it is good"
> c. I can say why I think like this
> d. if someone else can knows the same things about it
>   when they think about these things well they can think the same about it
> e. I don't want to say more
> f. I don't want to say: "very good"

In most respects, this explication is parallel to those of *a reasonable time* and *a reasonable amount*. Here, too, the speaker's attitude is guarded, cautious, deliberately restrained. Here, too, the speaker is weighing the words carefully and avoiding what could be seen as exaggeration ("very"). Here, too, the speaker uses the model of a hypothetical person who can think well, and here, too, the tone is somewhat worldly wise: not only the words but also the expectations and requirements are consciously limited.

And yet there does seem to be one respect in which the semantic structure of *reasonably good* diverges from that of *a reasonable time* or *a reasonable amount*. In the latter two, the speaker is willing to see the situation in a positive light ("I want to say: this is good"). In the case of phrases that amount to *reasonably good*, this is also the case. At the same time, however, there seems to be an implication that the speaker is consciously choosing to be satisfied with something that is less than very good and, moreover, that the attitude displayed in this way is part of the meaning of the expression *reasonably good* itself, as well as of all the other collocations with *reasonable* where *reasonable* can be understood as standing for *reasonably good*.

Arguably, the idea that it is good, and wise, not to want or expect too much was linked with the philosophy of "reasonableness" from its inception. When Locke asserted that the limited certainty that can be derived from empirical knowledge is sufficient for ordinary purposes, he was effectively advocating this very attitude.

I have already quoted Porter's (2000, 60) observation that "Locke's truth claims were models of modesty. . . . Man was a limited being, and reason just sufficient for human purposes." But although it was only *just* sufficient, it was nonetheless *sufficient*. In fact, for Locke the awareness that human knowledge was only "probable knowledge" and that human access to truth was limited was not necessarily a bad thing, for it provided a protection against dogmatic thinking and intolerance. Thus, his ideal of "reasonableness" went hand in hand with his ideal of "toleration" ("those who have not thoroughly examined to the bottom of their own tenets . . . are unreasonable in imposing that as truth on other men's belief which they themselves had not searched into"; Locke 1959, 374). It was "reasonable" not to want and expect too much in one's quest for truth and knowledge, and it was reasonable to be satisfied with that which *can* be reached. The aura of wise and contented self-limitation became associated, in one way or another, with most, perhaps all, the uses of the word *reasonable*. To recall a characteristic example from the Cobuild corpus, quoted earlier:

> To have been anything but satisfied would have been highly unreasonable, and Alistair, for a professor, was a rather reasonable man.

In the collocations *reasonably good* and *reasonably well* and also in *reasonable* used as a substitute for *reasonably good*, this philosophy of a wise and contented limitation of expectations and desires appears to have become explicitly encoded in the semantic structure, hence the last component (e) of the explication: "I don't want to think that if I don't want to say 'very good' I can't say 'good'."

Finally, it should be pointed out that *reasonable* in the sense of "reasonably good" can be used when the speaker thinks that something *is* very good—as a tool of culturally valued understatement. (The sentence "I am a reasonable left-handed player" may be a case in point.) The lists of English diminishers and downtoners given in Quirk et al.'s (1972, 452) *A Grammar of Contemporary English* or in Huebler's (1983, 73) *Understatements and Hedges in English* do not include *reasonable* and *reasonably*, but these two words are both widely used in that function alongside *rather, fairly, enough, pretty, quite, basically*, and so on. In fact, given their etymological and semantic links with "reason" and their connotations of careful, sustained, dispassionate thinking, they can be seen as particularly effective as devices used for the purposes of understatement. At the same time, their use for understatement is related to their use for other ends—including those to be discussed in the next section.

4.10. "Reasonable" and "Unreasonable"

Some of the most common collocations with the word *reasonable* include words like *fees, charges, rates, interest, rent*, and, above all, *price(s)*, that is, collocations pointing to moderation in demands for payment. For example, a "reasonable price" suggests that, roughly speaking, the sellers do not want too much money for their merchandise.

The idea of "not wanting too much (from another person)" applies also to many other collocations, including, for example, *reasonable request*. (To quote Phyllis from Gilbert and Sullivan's *Iolanthe*, "No. You're quite right—it's asking too much. One must be reasonable.") More generally, it also applies to *reasonable* used by itself when it is used as a predicate and when it refers to people. In particular, "being reasonable"—with the implication of not wanting too much—tends to occur in the imperative and in exhortations:

Be reasonable!

Let's be reasonable!

Characteristically, this sense of *reasonable* is linked with the presence of an opposite, *unreasonable*. There are "reasonable prices (fees)" and there are also "unreasonable prices (fees)," and a person can be described as either reasonable or unreasonable:

You are being unreasonable.

Don't be unreasonable.

Sentences appealing to the addressee to be "reasonable" (of which there are very many examples in the Cobuild corpus) point to a particularly interesting feature of this sense of the word: its inherent reference to wanting someone else to do something.

The relation between a seller and a buyer, or between a provider of a service and a client, gives us a good clue to the meaning of *reasonable* that we are now discussing. If one's price is not "reasonable," one is not simply being greedy but may also be acting against "reason"—and thus against one's own interest. This element of enlightened self-interest, often linked with the use of *reasonable*, is clearly visible in the following dialogue between Sherlock Holmes and a criminal count:

> "That's the hand I play from," said Holmes. "I put it all upon the table. But one card is missing. It's the king of diamonds. I don't know where the stone is."
> "You never shall."
> "No? Now, be reasonable, Count. Consider the situation. You are going to be locked up for twenty years. So is Sam Merton. What good are you going to get out of your diamond? None in the world. But if you hand it over—well, I'll compound a felony. We don't want you or Sam. We want the stone. Give that up, and so far as I am concerned you can go free so long as you behave yourself in the future." (www.online-literature.com)

Collocations like *reasonable price* have been around for a long time, but their meaning has, I would suggest, subtly changed. To take an example from Benjamin Franklin's *Autobiography* (OED):

> All forage is to be taken for the use of the army and a reasonable price to be paid for the same. (1755)

Reasonable does not have here the implications that it would in a similar context today: it does not include the point of view of the other party. The same applies to the following example (also from OED) from a later period:

> They were determined to prosecute . . . unless a reasonable sum were forthcom-
> ing, and . . . by a reasonable sum was meant seven thousand pounds. (1849)

From today's perspective, the rigidity of the requirement ("seven thousand pounds")
sounds somewhat incongruous in combination with the word *reasonable*, which has
come to imply something like a willingness to take some account of the other party's
wants and interests.

The difference between *a reasonable request* (or *reasonable price*) and, say, *a
reasonable location* (or *reasonable results*) may seem to be contextual rather than
semantic, as they both appear to be consistent with the idea of "not wanting too much."
For example, *a reasonable location* may not be "a very good location," but it could
be "unreasonable" to want more (i.e., an even better one).

Yet although the two meanings are closely related, they cannot be reduced to
one semantic formula without a loss: *a reasonable location* (or *attendance*) is a reasonably *good* location (or attendance), whereas *a reasonable fee*, *a reasonable charge*,
or *a reasonable rent* could not be described as "reasonably good." Nor could a *reasonable request* be regarded as in any sense "a good request." Furthermore, as pointed
out earlier, one can hardly speak of an *unreasonable location* or *unreasonable attendance*, whereas one can certainly speak of *an unreasonable request*.

I conclude, then, that *reasonable* as in *a reasonable request/ price/ fee*, and so on
is a distinct meaning of the word, linked in a special way with human interaction
and also that it is the same meaning we find in the predicative use of the word in
sentences about people (as in "be reasonable!").

an unreasonable request =
[X wants Y to do Z]
  a. I know some things about it
  b. when I think about these things well I think about it like this:
  c. "it is not bad if X wants Y to do some things
  d. it is bad if X wants Y to do more
  e. X wants Y to do more
  f. this is bad"
  g. I can say why I think like this
  h. if someone else knows the same things about it
    when they think about these things well
    they can think the same about it

Reasonable can be explicated in exactly the same way, except that (e) will be negated
and in (f) "bad" will be replaced with"good."

"A reasonable request" has to be persuasive to the addressee: the addressee has
to come to think that it would be good to follow it and to be willing to do so. From
the point of view of the ethos reflected in this meaning of *reasonable*, if one stays
within these limits, it is not bad to want other people to do some things; it is bad,
however, to go beyond these limits — to want other people to do more than what they
can be persuaded to do. What these limits are, in a given situation, is something that
all people who can think well can be expected to agree on.

The ethos that opposes "reasonable" interpersonal behavior to what is "unreasonable" can be stated in terms of an Anglo "cultural script"—a script that stigmatizes "unreasonable" demands on, and expectations of, other people:

> A *cultural script associated with 'unreasonable' demands and expectations*
> [people think like this:]
> it is not bad if a person wants another person to do something
>   if this other person can think about it like this:
>   "I know why this person wants me to do it
>   it will be good if I do it
>   I want to do it because of this"
> it is bad if a person wants another person to do more

If the explications proposed here (together with the associated cultural script) are right, they would explain why *reasonable* tends to co-occur with *fair*, as in the following examples (from Cobuild):

> The second requirement is that the judge should be seen to be even-handed, fair and reasonable.

> There are others with fair and reasonable claims to the job.

> Yesterday UCL said the decision to increase rent was "fair and reasonable."

> We believe we are being fair and reasonable to all parties.

They would also explain why *reasonable* in the relevant sense tends to co-occur with words like *deal, settlement, compromise, negotiate, agreement, cooperation*, and *terms*. For example:

> When the delegates had met at Philadelphia, instead of settling a reasonable plan of accomodation with the parent country, they employed themselves in censuring acts of the British parliament.

> Rather than coming on tough and aggressive, you appear reasonable, willing to compromise. . . .

> Be reasonable, George, and settle for half a loaf now.

> So I'll be reasonable, we'll compromise.

> I think we made a reasonable compromise.

> I found a certain amount of resistance to what I would have thought . . . was reasonable cooperation.

> We tried to negotiate a more reasonable fee, but they weren't prepared to budge.

The idea that "a lean compromise is better than a fat lawsuit" (George Herbert, *Jacula Prudentum*, quoted in Stevenson 1958) had been for centuries an important theme in Anglo culture. During the Enlightenment, it became closely associated with reason, increasingly the subject of aphorism, and a well-established cultural script, as the following two eighteenth-century quotes (also from Stevenson 1958) illustrate:

Life cannot subsist in society but by reciprocal concessions. (Samuel Johnson, Letter to Boswell, 1766)

All government—indeed every human benefit and enjoyment, every virtue and every prudent act—is founded on compromise and barter. (Edmund Burke, Speech on Conciliation with America, 1775)

By the twentieth century, the ideology linking a willingness to compromise with reason and an enlightened self-interest had become so entrenched in Anglo culture as to be encoded in a distinct sense of the word *reasonable*, a sense manifested (inter alia) in its collocations with words like *deal, settle, negotiate*, and, of course, *compromise* itself.

Thus, the sense of *reasonable* illustrated by the quotes adduced in this section implies a whole ideology of social interaction. First of all, it implies that in telling other people what we want them to do we should appeal to their thinking and not only to their will: we should allow them to do what we want them to do voluntarily because they have themselves come to think that it is a good thing to do, and not only because *we* want them to do it. Second, it implies that it is good to limit our claims on other people's goodwill and not to request too much, and third, it implies that in expressing our wishes it is good to take into account the other person's point of view (and consequently, to cooperate, to compromise, to reach a deal or an agreement, to "settle"). It is good to act in this way not only on moral grounds but also because this is what reason dictates. Or rather, reason and morality are seen as converging in the ideal of cooperation with other people: after all, this is what is good for everyone, as anyone can see if they can think well. To be "unreasonable," like being "unfair," is a transgression against good relations with other people and also against reason (including enlightened self-interest)—a transgression against rational ethics and against rational rules of conduct in a democratic society.

I quoted earlier Rawls's (2001) comments on the importance of the distinction between "the rational" and "the reasonable" to philosophy in general and the philosophy of justice in particular. We can now see that the sense of the word *reasonable* that Rawls primarily has in mind is that which has its opposite in *unreasonable*. It is precisely this sense that is linked with the idea of "cooperation between equals" and with the notion of "fairness." We will return to these links in chapter 5, in the context of a discussion of "fairness."

Finally, it is worth noting that some words that by themselves do not imply human interaction—for example *goal, target*, or *risk*—can also be used in combination with *reasonable* in the sense under discussion, if in a given context they can have such an implication. For example, in the Cobuild corpus we find the following sentences:

. . . dozens of these artificial languages were created for good reasons seeking a very reasonable goal.

. . . if we were to go down the route of trying to increase retail sales what would be a reasonable target percentage-wise?

What may seem to be too risky to the managerial mind may appear to be a reasonable risk to the specialist mind.

Words like *goal, target,* or *risk* can refer to solitary activities, but then they would be unlikely to be combined with *reasonable* (or *unreasonable*). A goal or target that someone proposes to others can be described as *unreasonable*, but a goal or target that one sets for oneself would be more likely to be described as *unrealistic*, and if someone is said to be taking an *unreasonable risk*, this tends to suggest that somebody else's life may be affected (for example, a doctor may take *unreasonable risks* in regard to a patient's life).

It also seems that while the phrases *a reasonable request* and *an unreasonable request* are equally acceptable in English, the phrase *unreasonable demands* is more felicitous than ?*reasonable demands*: as an opposite to *unreasonable demands*, many speakers would prefer *justifiable demands* (as if *demands* were too categorical to qualify as "reasonable"). For similar reasons, *a reasonable request* sounds better than *a *reasonable order.* On the other hand, although *a reasonable compromise* sounds perfect, ?*an unreasonable compromise* sounds rather odd. Through asymmetries of this kind, phraseology reflects the ethos of the speech community, shaped by its history and culture.[5]

In sixteenth-century English, a "creature" or a "beast" could be "reasonable"; today, a dog can be "clever" but not "reasonable." To call it reasonable would be like calling it a gentleman: *reasonable* has become saturated with Anglo culture.

4.11. An Internal Reconstruction of the Semantic History of "Reasonable"

Leaving aside the collocation *reasonable man*, which has already been discussed in some detail, let us try to identify the main turns in the history of the word *reasonable* and suggest how changing ways of thinking and speaking could have crystallized into new meanings. I will represent this hypothetical history in stages, while noting that in actual usage the meanings assigned to different stages can co-occur and also that the meanings assigned to stages I and II are no longer in use but those assigned to stages III, IV, V, and VI are all richly represented in present-day English. Thus, the hypothetical sequence outlined here is meant to be, above all, logical rather than demonstrably chronological; certain meanings are hypothesized to have developed out of certain other meanings.

Stage I

The word *reasonable* is used in the sense of, roughly, "endowed with reason," as in the phrase *a reasonable creature.*

Stage II

The word *reasonable* starts to be linked not only with the ability to think but also more specifically with the ability to think well. For example, the sentence cited by the OED (and dated 1636), "Reasonable and judicious readers will not dislike the same digression," appears to refer to readers who "can think well." Locutions like *it is reasonable to conclude* (as used by Locke 1690) also link the word *reasonable* with the ability to think well and, in particular, to think well about what happens to one and to draw inferences from this. At that time (seventeenth–eighteenth century), *reasonable* can be linked not only with thoughts that are hypothetical (assumptions, suppositions, and the like) but also with belief, conviction, certainty, and substantial doubt. Christianity is defended as "reasonable" by those who wholeheartedly embrace it. At the same time, *reasonable* is seen as "compatible with reason" rather than "required by reason." The claim is that someone who thinks well *can* think like this, not that they *have to* think like this. Thus, the ideal of "reason" is felt to be consistent with both conviction and "toleration" (tolerance for other people's convictions) and inconsistent with dogmatism, absolutism, and intolerance (this is the era of the British Enlightenment).

Stage III

The word *reasonable* continues to imply the ability to think well, but it becomes increasingly associated with an emphasis on the limitations of one's knowledge and on the lack of certainty. Conviction is no longer described as *reasonable*, and *a reasonable doubt* (with the emphasis on *reasonable*) becomes reinterpreted as *any reasonable doubt* (with the emphasis on *any*). The semantic component "I don't want to say more" becomes part of the semantic invariant: the ability to think well becomes associated with the concern about not saying more than one has evidence or justification for.

Stage IV

The self-limitation inherent in collocations like *it is reasonable to suppose* (where *reasonable* is no longer compatible with *conviction*) leads to the rise of *reasonable* as a more general tool of "moderation," as a device for avoiding an "excessive" (unjustified) use of words like *much* (a lot) and *very*. As a result, we witness the spread of collocations like *a reasonable time* and *a reasonable amount*—clearly distinct in meaning from *a reasonable assumption* or a *reasonable hypothesis*.

Stage V

Reasonable as an "anti-*much*," and "anti-*very*," device becomes linked, in a particular way, with avoiding "excessive praise": it becomes increasingly used as a device for not saying "very good." At the same time, however, it becomes associated with a willingness to say a qualified "good" even when one cannot say "very good," that is, to be satisfied with less, to be "realistic" and "pragmatic."

Stage VI

The willingness to accept things as "reasonably good" even if they are not "very good" becomes linked in a special way with interpersonal relations and, more specifically, with what one wants from other people. Collocations like *a reasonable request* and *a reasonable deal* spread, collocations like *reasonable demands* decline, and sentences like "Be reasonable!" start to be interpreted as a call for a "reasonable compromise."

Looking back at the semantic history of the word *reasonable* in the English language and at the ascent of the value of "reasonableness" in Anglo culture, it is important to bear in mind that as Porter (2000, 99) emphasizes, in Britain "Enlightenment . . . took place within, rather than against, Protestantism" and that "as the seventeenth century drew to its close, one call was heard ever louder: religion and reason were one and must pull together." "Reason" did not mean at that time skepticism or rejection of religion but rather antidogmatism and "toleration."

> Enlightenment minds ceased to equate religion with a body of commandments, graven in stone, dispensed through Scripture, accepted on faith and policed by the Church. Belief was a matter of private judgment, for individual reason to adjudicate within the multi-religionism sanctioned by statutory toleration. (Porter 2000, 99)

It is in this atmosphere that the Anglo value of "reasonableness" developed and took root: the value of "reasonable beliefs," "reasonable doubts," "reasonable expectations," "reasonable attitudes," and finally "reasonable compromises."

4.12. "Reasonable" and Anglo Cultural Scripts

The word *reasonable* (as it is used in modern English) is crucially involved in a number of cultural scripts. To begin with, it is linked with the central strategies for interpersonal interaction in modern Anglo society. In any society, one of the key problems is getting other people to do what one wants them to. In many societies, this problem tends to be solved on the basis of power differentiation. Hierarchical structures and accepted patterns of inequality often make it clear who can give orders to whom. From the point of view of the powerless, the answer may often lie in begging, imploring, and the like, that is, in putting pressure on the powerful by appealing to their feelings. It may also lie in a system of asymmetrical relationships of "patronage"—a pattern of care and responsibility for others (one's "dependents") that is associated with a higher status.

In democratic societies like Britain or America, other patterns have come to the fore, patterns based on assumptions and values of equality, individual autonomy, voluntary cooperation, mutual concessions, and so on. In this cultural climate, the scope for orders and commands is limited, and at the same time there is less room for patronage, begging, imploring, pleading, and appealing to mercy. The idea of "sweet dependency" (comparable to Japanese *amae*; see, e.g., Doi 1981; Wierzbicka 1997) is also culturally alien; on the contrary, value is placed on independence and self-reliance. But if one can neither give orders and commands nor beg, implore, plead, or appeal for mercy, help, or patronage, how does one get others to do what one wants them to do?

The modern use of the word *reasonable* and of the phrases based on it suggests that Anglo strategies in this regard include limiting one's claims on others and at the same time appealing to reason. These two strategies can be implemented jointly by means of the word *reasonable*. A sentence like "Be reasonable" appeals both to the ideal of limiting one's claims on other people and to the ideal of acting according to reason. To reject such an appeal is to reject some of Anglo culture's central cultural scripts.

In Anglo culture, the word *reasonable* is also a powerful ethical tool—a lever, a principle, and a court of appeal. To take a literary example, in Galsworthy's *The Forsyte Saga*, Soames Forsyte asks his daughter Fleur to "be reasonable" and to accede to his request to give up her first love:

> "Listen!" he said. "You're putting the feelings of two months—two months—against the feelings of thirty-five years! What chance do you think you have? Two months—your very first love affair, a matter of half a dozen meetings, a few walks and talks, a few kisses—against, against what you can't imagine, what no one could who hasn't been through it. Come, be reasonable, Fleur! It's midsummer madness!"
> Fleur tore the honeysuckle into little, slow bits. (www.online-literature.com)

The many such examples in modern English literature suggest that people may take, or expect others to take, crucial decisions in their lives on the basis of the standard of "reasonableness." The importance attached to this notion is also very clear in the following passage from Virginia Woolf's novel *Voyage Out*:

> She became absorbed in the book. Helen meanwhile stitched at her embroidery and thought over the things they had said. Her conclusion was that she would very much like to show her niece, if it were possible, how to live, or as she put it, how to be a reasonable person. (www.online-literature.com)

Here the heroine, Helen, explicitly equates ethics (knowing how to live) with "knowing how to be a reasonable person."

The examples from Galsworthy and Virginia Woolf are of course quite old and reflect ways of thinking that in many respects would now be seen as obsolete. "Being reasonable," however, seems to be as important at the turn of the twenty-first century as it was a century before. Judging by the material in the Cobuild corpus, the use of *reasonable* in contemporary English not only is very extensive but also often relates to questions of crucial importance, including, quite literally, matters of life and death (as when someone says, for example, that "it's reasonable to remove life-support systems").

One could even venture the suggestion that in interpersonal relations, the ethics of "reasonable" and "unreasonable" may have replaced, to some extent, the earlier form of "rational ethics," that is, the ethics of "right and wrong." Although the ethics of "right and wrong" based on reason could be seen for a long time as a "rational" alternative to the "absolutist" ethics of "good and bad" based on religion, with time, an ethics of "right and wrong" appears to have come increasingly to be itself perceived as "absolutist." An ethics based on the more limited, more pragmatic, more negotiable notions of "reasonable" and "unreasonable" appears to have an increasingly growing appeal in modern Anglo society. In a secular society, where many traditional virtues (for example, *goodness, fidelity, mercy, valor, selflessness, self-denial, innocence, humility*, and *modesty*) and sins (for example, *infidelity, pride, vanity, shamelessness, lust, self-indulgence, gluttony*, and *intemperance*) have increasingly come to be seen as obsolete, sometimes even ridiculous, what is there to appeal to as a basis for ethics? One of the most important notions to appeal to appears to be that of 'reasonableness'.

For example, in a recent best-selling novel by the British writer Nick Hornby, the hero is trying to save his marriage by offering to meet his estranged wife's wishes — if they are reasonable:

—What am I allowed to ask for?
—Anything you want. And if I don't think it's reasonable, we'll talk about it. (Hornby 2001, 208)

In the same novel, in the conflict between the parents, a child, Molly, takes her father's side because, the mother complains:

Molly has never been able to see her father as anything less than a perfect and perfectly reasonable man. . . . (p. 74)

The combination of two attributes, "perfect" and "perfectly reasonable," is very telling, and it is reminiscent of the example from Cobuild quoted earlier: "the stepfather seemed to take over the role of being the good and reasonable person in the house." "Good and reasonable," even "perfect and perfectly reasonable" — apart from a vague reference to an unspecified "goodness" or "perfection," the one and only essential value that readily comes to mind appears to be "reasonableness."

Another aspect of English discourse where the use of the word *reasonable* reflects some important cultural scripts is that of the tone of voice. The collocation *a reasonable tone of voice* is well established in modern English, as are its variants like *a reasonable-sounding voice, a reasonable voice,* or *a reasonable intonation.* Clearly, speakers of English recognize — and value — a certain tone of voice as "reasonable." They often appear to use it deliberately, to project a desirable image at important times and for important conversational purposes. For example (from Cobuild):

Chuck, you are not ready to give up on this marriage[?], asked the counsellor. Petra looked away. We see things differently, said Chuck in a reasonable voice. I always put you and the children first. I always did what I promised, I was there for the children's birthdays and your book launch parties, for God's sake.

"If they arose to restore balance," Olly said in her most reasonable voice, "then they must have made some changes."

"I'd like you to think about it. To think hard about it. That choice." There was a long pause. Somehow, . . . His father stopped. Then started again. He had made his voice gentle and reasonable. "You're the oldest one home now, Mack. The way you handle things sets an example for the rest. I'd like you to be asking a bit more of yourself."

And yes, maybe she had gone out with Leo once or twice in college. "But don't you think that was something you should have told me?" Gretchen had demanded, though in what she hoped was a reasonable tone of voice.

Often, "a reasonable voice" is linked explicitly with emotional self-control, as in the following example:

He said: "The sun's all right for you, isn't it?" She raised her head, set her chin on two small fists. "Go away," she said. He did not move. "Listen," she said, in a slow reasonable voice, where anger was kept in check, though with difficulty. . . .

Clearly, both the perception that there is a special, "reasonable" tone of voice and the value attached to this kind of voice are related to the "antiemotional" cultural scripts discussed in chapter 2. We may note in this connection that although the word *reasonable* appears sometimes in English translations of Russian novels (as a translation of the word *razumnyj*) there is no collocation in Russian corresponding to the English *reasonable voice*. The reason for this is not only that *razumnyj* does not mean the same as *reasonable* but also that there is no corresponding cultural script linking good thinking with emotional self-control (or indeed, a script encouraging emotional self-control in the first place). Although as I mentioned at the outset French may seem closer to English than Russian as far as the appeal of reasonableness is concerned, in fact, the collocation *une voix raisonnable* ("a reasonable voice") is not used in French either.

In her book *Let's Be Reasonable: A Guide to Resolving Disputes*, the Australian lawyer and community legal educator Margaret White recommends "being reasonable" as the most effective answer to the problems of "living and working together"(1997, vii). "Being reasonable" includes, according to this guide, "stating your case moderately," "trying to see the problems from their [the other side's] point of view," and using a "lubricant demeanor" in "the manner of your approach, the tone of your voice" (p. 5). The back cover describes *Let's Be Reasonable* as "an invaluable guide and reference for every household and business . . . a layperson's guide to resolving disputes of all sorts as quickly, efficiently and effectively as possible." Without disputing the publisher's description of the book, one might add that it is also an invaluable (if inadvertent) guide to some key Anglo cultural scripts.

4.13. Is the Anglo Value of "Reasonable" Unique? English vs. French

I have said that other European languages do not have words corresponding in meaning to the English word *reasonable*. I have also noted one seeming exception to this generalization: French. If we consult bilingual dictionaries, we will find that they match the English *reasonable* with the French word *raisonnable*. But do the two words really mean the same thing?

A closer inspection of the two words' use shows that they do not: first, because the range of use of the French word is much narrower and, second, because even in those combinations in which both words are possible, the range of contexts available to them is different.

For example, *raisonnable* cannot possibly be used in the French counterparts of English phrases like *a reasonable time, reasonable limits, a reasonable chance*, or *reasonable results*, not to mention *reasonable doubt, reasonable force*, or *reasonable care*.

As for English phrases that do appear to have exact French counterparts, the impression of equivalence is generally misleading. For example, while the *Collins Robert French Dictionary* (1990) glosses *a reasonable person* as *une personne raisonnable* and vice versa, in fact some of the examples cited offer evidence to the contrary. For example:

Elle devrait être plus raisonnable à son age.
"She should know better (or "she should have more sense") at her age."

One cannot say in English "she should be more reasonable at her age," because "reasonableness" has nothing to do with age. Clearly, both the French and the English words refer to an ability to think well, but the pragmatic components of the phrase *reasonable person*, discussed in this chapter, are missing from the French word.

Similarly, the fact that *Collins Robert* glosses *reasonable* used in combination with *price* and *offer* as *raisonnable* does not prove that *a reasonable price* means the same as *un prix raisonnable*. According to the French-English part of the dictionary, French does have collocations linking the words *prix* ("price"), *demande* ("request"), *salaire* ("salary"), and *quantité* ("quantity, amount") with the word *raisonnable*, which is glossed in these contexts as "reasonable, fair." I would argue, however, that despite appearances, *un prix raisonnable* does not mean the same as *a reasonable price*. A closer English gloss would be here *justifiable*: *un prix raisonnable* can be justified. The phrase is linked with an ability to think well ("if someone can think well . . . ") and with an ability to state one's reasons ("I can say why I think like this"), but there is no reference here to moderation, to the value of a willingness to say: "I don't want more" or "I don't want to say more." As evidence for this claim, I would point out that although a request (*une demande*) can indeed be described in French as *raisonnable*, a compromise, an agreement, or a deal cannot:

?un compromis raisonnable

?un accord raisonnable

?un marché raisonnable

It is also significant that unlike *reasonable*, *raisonnable* has no opposite in French. An *unreasonable price* would be translated into French as *excessif, démesuré, exorbitant*, or *exagéré*. As these glosses indicate, the "excessiveness" implied by the English word *unreasonable* has to be stated in French by a separate word. The reason, I suggest, is that *raisonnable* itself does not imply any absence of excessiveness. Should the phrase *an unreasonable price* be translated into French as *un prix qui n'est pas raisonnable* ("a price that is not *raisonnable*"), this could, of course, be interpreted as implying that the price was excessive, but this implication would be due to inference, not the meaning of the word *raisonnable* as such.[6]

Furthermore, the French sentence "*Soyez raisonnable*" ("Be *raisonnable*") could no doubt be translated in some contexts as "be reasonable," but in fact the two sentences do not mean the same, and the Collins Robert dictionary is quite helpful to the English user in suggesting here the gloss *sensible, sane* rather than *reasonable*. The English sentence "Be reasonable" refers, indirectly, to other people (and appeals to the ideals of moderation, cooperation, willingness to reach compromises or make concessions, and so on). The English sentence "Be sensible" does not, and neither does the French sentence "*Soyez raisonnable*."[7] When one pleads with a person, "*Soyez raisonnable*," one is appealing to a different ideal than when one pleads with another person, "Be reasonable." Differences of this kind are not only differences in the meaning of words ("mere semantics"). They are also differences in cultural ideals, traditions, and attitudes.[8]

The Anglo value, or complex of values, reflected in the word *reasonable*, with its large family of interrelated meanings, is indeed unique, and it tells us a great deal about Anglo culture.

Let me close with an extended quote from a book entitled *Basic Concepts of Legal Thought* by the legal scholar George Fletcher:

> One of the striking features of legal argument in English is our pervasive reliance on the term "reasonable." We routinely refer to reasonable time, reasonable delay, reasonable reliance, and reasonable care. In criminal law, we talk ubiquitously of reasonable provocation, reasonable mistake, reasonable force, and reasonable risk. Within these idioms pulse the sensibilities of the reasonable person. Without this hypothetical figure at the center of legal debate, we would be hard pressed to mount an argument about responsibility or liability.
>
> As Anglophone lawyers negotiate in the language of reasonableness, French, German, and Russian lawyers argue in a different idiom. Their languages do deploy a concept of reason, and their terms for "reason"—*raison*, *Vernunft*, and *razumnost'*—readily yield corresponding adjectives. Yet these parallels to our term "reasonable" do not figure prominently in legal speech on the Continent. The French civil code uses the term *raisonnable* precisely once; the German and Soviet codes do not use the term at all. The criminal codes—the natural habitat of the reasonable person—are barren of these derivatives of reason. . . . The adjectives describing a faultless mistake in Continental languages do not translate as "reasonable" but as "invincible," "unavoidable," and "non-negligent." All these emanations of the reasonable person find diverse translations in Continental legal discourse, a distinct word for every context. (Fletcher 1996, 64)

What Fletcher says about Anglo/American law applies also to virtually every other aspect of Anglo life. But it is not only the pervasive use of the word *reasonable* that is a unique and salient aspect of Anglo discourse: it is also its very meaning or, more precisely, its family of meanings. For example, *raisonnable* is not only far less common that *reasonable* but also a word with a different meaning and different cultural implications.

Chapter 5

Being FAIR

*Another Key Anglo Value and
Its Cultural Underpinnings*

5.1. The Importance of "Fairness" in Modern Anglo Culture

Fairness is one of the most important values in modern Anglo culture. The exclamations "That's not fair!" and "It's not fair!" are often heard in daily life, not only from adults but also from young children, and they can appear in children's books. Here are two characteristic examples from a recent children's book, *Snot fair!* (Montano 2003):

> It's just snot fair when I have to go stay at my Nonno and Nonna's place, 'cause my mum and dad think I'm too young to stay home alone and babysit me and Bianca.

> I think that it's snot fair when your birthday is at the end of the year and everyone gives you a Christmas and birthday present combined. I want two presents, not one, right? Hey, I *deserve* two presents. Everyone else gets two presents. Bianca my sister gets a present for her birthday, and then another present for Christmas, so why 'cause my birthday's the day before Christmas do I get tricked?

Remarkably, the phrase *that's not fair!* can often be heard on television programs for preschool children, such as the British program *Angelina Ballerina* or the Canadian program *Babar*.

The ubiquity of the words *fair* and *unfair* in modern English discourse, across a wide range of registers, is all the more remarkable given that these words have no equivalents in other European languages (let alone non-European ones) and are thoroughly untranslatable. To quote the legal scholar George Fletcher:

> Remarkably, our concept of fairness does not readily translate into other languages. While the concept of justice appears, it seems, in all cultures, it is virtually impossible to find a suitable translation for fairness in European or Semitic languages. As a result, the term is transplanted directly in some languages such as German and Hebrew, and absent in others, such as French that are resistant to adopting loan words that carry unique meanings. Why has Anglo-American culture cultivated this distinct concept of fairness? (Fletcher 1996, 81)

In fact, the concept of 'justice' does not appear in all cultures—a point to which I return later. He is right, however, about 'fairness': it is indeed a uniquely Anglo concept, without an equivalent in any other language, and the question of why Anglo culture has created this concept is an important one.

The frequency of the word *fair* in modern English is extremely high. For example, in the Cobuild "UK Spoken" corpus (excerpted on November 1, 2004), there were 101 occurrences of *fair* per million words, whereas the corresponding figures for *just, reliable, truthful, thoughtful,* and *considerate* were, respectively, 33, 9, 3, 1, and 1.

The high frequency and colloquial character of the expressions "that's not fair!" and "it's not fair" are reflected in the existence of the reduced version "s'not fair!" used by children, as in the book title previously quoted. At the same time, *fair* and its derivatives are used widely in other registers of English, including the language of scholarly works, government publications, public administration, business, trade, and law. For example, in the bookstore on my university campus, the following titles are listed as currently available:

Fair

Australia's Choices: Options for a Fair and Prosperous Society

It's Not Fair

Not Fair Won't Share

Constitutional Right to a Speedy and Fair Criminal Trial

Fair Division & Collective Welfare

Fair Cop: Learning the Art of Policing

Snot Fair

Fair Game

Where's the Fair Go: The Decline of Equity in Australia

What's Fair

Lies and The Lying Liars Who Tell Them: A Fair and Balanced Look at the Right

You Know the Fair Rule

Fair Enough: Egalitarianism in Australia

Playing Fair Game Theory and the Social Contract, Vol. 1

Good Sports: The Myth of the Fair Go in Australian Sport

It's Just Not Fair

Fair Trade: No Nonsense Guide

Elections: Full Free & Fair

Fair Trial Rights

Unfair

Moneyball: The Art of Winning an Unfair Game

Unfair Dismissal in New South Wales

Law of Unfair Dismissal

Trademark and Unfair Competition Law

Law of Unfair Contracts in NSW

Fairness

Justice as Fairness: A Restatement

Justice & Fairness in International Negotiation

Capitalism & Justice: Envisioning Social & Economic Fairness

Managing Fairness in Organisations

The various pages in the *Australian Law Online* Web site yield a similarly rich harvest. To give some examples: "NSW Department of Fair Trading," "Fair Go documents," "Fair Dismissal Laws for Small Business," "Fair and Open Elections and Referendums," "Unfair Dismissal Legislation," "Complaints of Unfair Government Competition with the Private Sector," and "Unfair Market Practices."

The centrality of the pair *fair* and *not fair* (or *unfair*) in modern Anglo discourse can be compared with that of *right* and *wrong* (or *not right*) and *reasonable* and *unreasonable* (or *not reasonable*). In fact, *fair* often co-occurs with *right* and with *reasonable* and is seen by the speakers as closely related to those two other English key words.

Both the centrality of *fair* to the modern Anglo system of values and its status as a close relative of *right* are reflected in the following passage from Paul John Eakin's (1999, 160) book *How Our Lives Become Stories*, in which the author reflects on the ethics of life writing: "What is right and fair for me to write about someone else? What is right and fair for someone else to write about me?"

The close link between the value of "fairness" and that of "reasonableness" can be illustrated with numerous examples from John Rawls's book *Justice as Fairness*, to which I return later. Here, let me just give one example of the close company that the words *fair* and *reasonable* (and their derivatives) keep in Rawls's discussion. According to Rawls, "the fundamental idea of a society as a fair system of social cooperation" means that:

> reasonable persons are ready to propose, or to acknowledge when proposed by others, the principles needed to specify what can be seen by all as fair terms of cooperation. . . . It is unreasonable not to be ready to propose such principles, or not to honor fair terms of cooperation that others may reasonably be expected to accept. (2001, 7)

Given the frequent co-occurrence of *reasonable* and *fair* in Rawls's book, it is not surprising to see the two words repeatedly used together in the editor's "Foreword," which summarizes the book's ideas. For example: "According to justice as fairness, the most reasonable principles of justice are those that would be the object of mutual agreement by persons under fair conditions" (Kelly 2001, xi). "Rawls presents justice as fairness as the most reasonable form of political liberalism" (p. xii).

The collocation *fair and reasonable* is also well attested in the Cobuild corpus. For example:

> People should have rights to directly negotiate (individual contract) terms subject to fair and reasonable minimum standards.

> His view of the Chamberlain case was not only accurate but also fair and reasonable.

> . . . legislation enabling leaseholders who are owner-occupiers to purchase the freehold of their homes at a fair and reasonable cost.

> Industrial democracy—one of Lewis's favorite phrases—was the CIO's chief goal, posed as a fair and reasonable solution to the economic crisis.

> The words in our brochures speak for our attitude: our aims include a fair and reasonable policy on fees.

> The second requirement is that the judge should be seen to be even handed, fair and reasonable.

> There are others with fair and reasonable claims to the job.

> We stand by our decisions and we believe we are being fair and reasonable to all parties.

Thus, along with *right* and *reasonable, fair* is one of the most important "guiding words" in modern English, and in speakers' minds, it is closely related to the other two. The fact that the abstract noun *fairness* (in contrast to *rightness* and *reasonableness*) is also widely used in modern English suggests that the value of 'fairness' is particularly salient in modern Anglo consciousness. Perhaps more than any other value, fairness is taken for granted—a fact reflected, for example, in the English tautological expression "fair's fair," referring to a supposedly indisputable truism (compare "what's done is done"; "business is business"; "war is war"; for discussion, see Wierzbicka 1991/2003a; Davis 1998). If we want to understand Anglo culture, we have to try to understand the concept of 'fairness'. The best starting point is provided, I think, by the phrase *that's (it's) not fair,* which appears to be more common in everyday language than its counterpart without negation (*that's fair*). The word *fair* has or has had at least three clearly distinct meanings in English, as in *fair maiden* (archaic), *fair hair* (restricted), and *fair trial* (very common). Here, I focus on the last of these three, that is, on that meaning of *fair* that has its opposite in *unfair* and that underlies the abstract noun *fairness* (as it is currently used).

5.2. The Meaning of *Fair* and *Not Fair*

A sentence like "That's not fair" implies that someone was "not fair" *to someone else. Fair* differs in this respect from both *good* and *right*: one can be "good" or do something "good" or "right" on one's own (so to speak), whereas *fair*, like *kind*, is inherently relational: one can be 'fair' only in relation to someone else. It is, of course, possible to say simply that someone (e.g., a head of department) is "very fair" (in general), but this usually means that in making decisions he or she is always careful not to be unfair to anyone.

The relational character of 'fairness' does not mean that one is, necessarily, doing something *to* another person; it can also mean that what one is doing *affects* another person in British and Australian English (though not in U.S. English): one can do something that is *unfair on* another person, as well as *unfair to* another person. Generally speaking, to do something that is 'not fair' implies (although, of course, cannot be reduced to) doing something that is bad for another person.

Admittedly, the words *fair* and *unfair* are also used with respect to things that simply happen to us, without anybody "doing" anything, as in the common complaint that "life is unfair." This, however, is an extension of the primary meaning of *fair*, based on a personification of life: the speaker thinks of life as being like a person who treats some people unfairly.

This, then, is one semantic component of *fair* and *not fair*: doing (or not doing) something that is bad for another person. Another component that we can isolate at the outset involves doing something *with* another person or other people. The importance of this component becomes clearer when we try to compare *fair* with *just*. For example, a king or a ruler (in a traditional society) could be described as 'just' but not as 'fair'. On the other hand, a teacher (in modern society) can be described as 'fair' but not 'just'. The reason—or at least one reason—is, I suggest, that a king is not thought of as "doing things *with* his subjects," whereas a teacher can be thought of as doing things (together) *with* his or her students (roughly, cooperating with them).

"Doing things with" has to be understood in a very broad sense, which includes any kind of interaction or dealings with another person, not necessarily on an equal basis. For example, a "fair teacher" interacts with his or her students without having the same role, or position, in the interaction as the students have.

This is not to say that the idea of 'equality' or 'sameness' is not relevant to "fairness" at all, but it is not necessarily an equality of role or position. Rather, what is "the same" about all the interactants who can be described as "fair" or "not fair" is that they are all bound by certain generally recognized rules—*regardless* of their role or position. For example, students can be "unfair" to the teachers by criticizing them "unfairly," and vice versa.

It is also interesting to note that rules can be described as either *fair* or *not fair* but cannot be described as *just* or *not just*, whereas with laws, it is the other way around. Roughly speaking, rules are for people who want to do things together. For example, the rules of the game are for people who want to play a game together. In a sense, people who want to play (or do other things) together accept a set of rules as binding for them all. This is not the case, however, with laws: whether the laws are just or unjust, they bind people subject to them as if they were imposed on them from above. The rule of law (which has no plural: *the rules of law) is comparable to a ruler (just or unjust) rather than to a set of rules (fair or unfair).

The concept of 'rule' is relevant to that of 'fairness' in more than one way. In a sense, *fairness* implies that there are certain rules known to and recognized as good by all those who are willing to do things with one another. The link between *fairness* and *rules* highlights the fact that *fairness* implies a certain consensus. I suggest that this can be captured in the following pair of semantic components:

> when people want to do some things with some other people
> they know that they can do some kinds of things
> at the same time they know that they can't do some other kinds of things
>   because if they do things like this it will be bad for these other people

The interaction—doing things together—is voluntary ("when people want to . . ."), but within the framework of voluntarily undertaken interaction certain rules are obligatory, "binding" ("they have to" or "they can't"). A game is a good model of such a collective undertaking: people enter the game voluntarily, but within a given game, the rules are binding—otherwise, there would be no game. This is an essential aspect of 'fair play': acting according to the rules, 'above board'—without seeking for oneself an advantage that would be against the rules.

The positive component "when people want to do some things with some other people, they know that they can do things of some kinds" is important, because it accounts for the conceptual links between *fair* and notions like *fair play* and (Australian) *fair go*. From the point of view of the person who uses such expressions, the emphasis is not only on what one *cannot* do but also on what one *can* do (within the limits of the rules): "fair" is not inimical to enterprise, initiative, games, sports, business, and so on.

At the same time, however, it is crucial (from the speaker's point of view) that all such activities should be conducted within the "rules of the game," that is, that the "players" should think about some other things like this: "people can't do things like this." The rationale for such restrictions is clear: those "other things" are bad for some of the players, and those players could legitimately protest against them (they could say: "you can't do things like this").

What a person in a given community can and can't do is, so to speak, the content of the rule. But the "rules of the game" linked with the idea of "fairness" are not arbitrary; rather, they wear on their sleeve their own justification: a person can't do some things because if they did it would be bad for someone else (within the circle of interactants).

These are, then, the background assumptions of the judgment "that's not fair." What the speaker who makes such a judgment is asserting can be spelled out as follows (where "like this" refers to the kinds of things that interactants "can't do"):

> people can know that when this person (X) did it (W),
> X did something bad
> because when X did it, X did something like this

It is often assumed that "fairness" needs to be understood in terms of equality, equity, or nondiscrimination, but that is not so. It is true that common collocations like *unfair competition, unfair comparison, unfair advantage,* or *your fair share* imply that everyone (in a given group) should be treated in the same way, but this is not always the case. Consider, for example, the collocation *fair prices.* Here, the focus is not on prices being the same for everyone but rather on prices being such that they could be judged, by the general consensus, as justifiable (in terms of what is reasonable for both sellers and buyers). It is unlikely that the collocations *fair prices* or *unfair prices* would be used with respect to a vendor in a Moroccan or Indonesian market, who can quote different prices to different buyers and who can always arbitrarily change his or her prices. Vendors who are acting in this way are not being "unfair" to their customers because the background assumptions of "fairness" do not apply in this case, and it would be ridiculous to complain that their prices were not fair.

The phrase *fair prices* implies that (as the speaker sees it) both the seller and the buyer belong to a community of people who want to cooperate and who accept that they have to cooperate according to statable, constant, and recognizable rules—rules that are assumed by all concerned to be good and that are voluntarily accepted.

Statements like "that's not fair" are commonly followed by an explanation or by a "why?" from the interlocutor, to which the first speaker is expected to have a ready answer. The explanation will have to refer to a clear rule that, in the speaker's view, has been violated. If one child is given more sweets than the others, the protest "that's not fair" probably refers to the rule that if a parent or teacher does something good for one child, they should do the same for the other children. But the notion of an 'unfair price' does not refer to an equal distribution of goods to all people. Rather, it expresses the speaker's judgment that the sellers are doing things that would be bad for the buyers and that could not be justified in terms of some generally accepted standards. Similarly, expressions like *a fair comment* or *a fair criticism* do not refer to an equal distribution of goods but rather to the possibility of saying things that are harmful to some people in the speaker's community and that are not justifiable with reference to some generally accepted standard.

Trying to generalize from the examples so far, we could say that the concept of 'fairness' refers to a potential tension between what one person wants to do and what can be bad for another. One assumption is that it is good if a person can do what they want to do—but a second, concomitant assumption is that attention must be paid to whether the intended action is not bad for someone else (in the group of people with whom one interacts).

This does not mean that it is necessarily deemed "unfair" for people to pursue their own interests if it can be disadvantageous for someone else. Rather, it means that when I want to do something that may be bad for someone else, there are limits to what I can legitimately do. Certain rules apply that limit my freedom of action when it may come into conflict with other people's interests.

Consider, for example, a father described by his only child as "strict but fair." If there were other children in the family, it could be expected that they would all be treated by the father in the same way, but this cannot be the intended interpretation of "fair" as applied to the father of an only child. Can "fair" imply, in this case, that the same rules apply to the father and to the child? Yes and no. If one of the rules is "no television before homework," then clearly this rule applies to the child, not to the father. At the same time, if the father is "fair," this rule binds the father, too: the child who has done the homework then has "the right" to watch the television, and the father can't (justifiably) say no.

Consider next the case of someone saying that Joe Bloggs is rather lazy (or "doesn't pull his weight") and someone else describing it as a "fair comment." What does it take for a comment to be "fair"? Presumably, the comment needs to be true, but this cannot be the only condition. I say that Joe Bloggs is lazy ("doesn't pull his weight") because I want to do so, and it is bad for Joe Bloggs that I say so, even if it is true. Under what conditions would it be a "fair" comment to make? Presumably, there must be some reason for my saying so, a reason that can be stated in general terms and that would be recognizable by other people as valid, over and above the statement being true. For example, if I am acting as a referee in relation to Joe Bloggs's application for a promotion, it is my obligation to give a "fair assessment." In this context, saying that Joe Bloggs "doesn't pull his weight" could be regarded as a "fair comment." Presumably, in this case, the rule—recognizable as general and valid— would be that when one undertakes to write a reference for an applicant for a promotion, it is good to say (in some form) all that is relevant, even if it is bad for the applicant. (It is "fair" to the employer and "not unfair" to the applicant.)

Consider, further, the following passage from a story by David Malouf (about an Australian "comfort girl" for American troops):

> They were just boys, she knew that, but they made her mad. She often quarrelled with them and said things that were mocking and cruel, but only in her head. Laying the responsibility for their feelings on her, making her responsible for their weakness, was unfair. They did not play fair. (Malouf 2000, 78)

It is clear that the girl who is thinking these thoughts is not thinking about equity or equal distribution of goods. Rather, she is thinking about the way these men are dealing with her, and she thinks that in their relation to her they are breaking certain general rules for dealing with other people: one should not lay the responsibility for one's failings and weakness on other people.

And another passage from the same book: "They struggled, the man cursing, and at last he wrenched it [a magazine] away. The boy yowled, saying over and over with a deep sense of grievance: 'It's not fair, it's not fair, Kenny, I'm the one that found it. It's mine.'" (Malouf 2000, 110).

Again, this boy's grievance has nothing to do with equal distribution of goods. Rather, he is appealing to a rule of human interaction that he regards as generally accepted: "if I have found something, it's mine; nobody else can take it away from me." The word *grievance* used in this passage is particularly illuminating, as it implies all at once several components postulated here: "you did something bad," "this is bad for me," and "you can't do things like this."

To say that someone or something is "not fair" is not to make an absolute moral judgment but rather to express a protest, an objection, a grievance. What is at issue is not simply that "someone did something bad" but rather that "they did something bad because what they did is bad for me" and that I have the right to say to this person: "you can't do things like this." If the "unfair action" is not directed at me personally, by saying "that's not fair" I protest, as it were, on behalf of the person at whom it is directed: in my judgment, the "unfair" doer is doing something that is bad for that other person, and this other person can legitimately say "you can't do things like this"—such is my (the speaker's) judgment, which I can justify with reference to some generally accepted rule, and I am confident that other people would agree with me.

The content of a given rule seen by the speaker as generally accepted is not specified by the word *fair*. It would be a mistake to try to reduce the meaning of *fair* to a simple rule that "it is bad if someone wants to do something that is bad for someone else." For example, in a lawsuit a lawyer who represents the interests of one party against those of another can want to do something that is bad for that other party. This is not necessarily "unfair"; it would be "unfair" only if in pursuing the interests of one party, the lawyer were to break some generally recognized rules. What these rules are is not specified by the meaning of the word *fair* as such.

Let us consider a few more examples from the Cobuild corpus.

> It is deemed fair to suspend the person on full pay while the investigation goes on.

Presumably, according to the speaker, it would not be "fair" to suspend a person on less than full pay while the investigation goes on. Here, the assumption is that in a democratic society based on cooperation, people have to (can't not) treat the person under investigation as innocent (until proven guilty); to do otherwise would be generally regarded as doing something that is bad for that person and against which this person could rightfully protest. Again, it is not a question of equal distribution of goods but rather of human rights: everyone has the right to be regarded as innocent unless and until proven guilty. The same applies to the following example:

> I think it's fair on the day he's about to leave the company that we recognize him and give praise where praise is due.

The first assumption that is clear in this example is that the departing member of the company is "one of us": we have been doing things together, and we have to act toward this person accordingly. Second, in this circle of interactants (the company), we have to give praise "where praise is due": we can't do some things (e.g., fail to give due praise) to one of us. If we failed to give due praise to this person, we would be doing something that is bad for this person. Third, the rule is general, constant, and recognizable: if someone deserves praise, this praise should be given. Fourth, if we didn't, this person could rightfully protest. Another example:

> . . . my nan's constantly undermining my authority. And it's not fair on [X] as well as not being fair on me.

Here the assumption is that in the family, a parent has the right to have a position of authority. If someone undermines a parent's authority, it is not simply "bad" but "not fair." Thus, when the (male) speaker implies that his nan is doing something bad, he is referring, implicitly, to a norm that he assumes to be generally held. The person "unfairly treated" is not simply *complaining* but *protesting*, or at least implying that he has the right to protest.

A reference to "human rights" is also clear in the following sentence:

> What I'm asking really I think is for parent governors who are out there listening or any governors at all is to keep a good track on what's happening in your school. Be informed about it and make sure that any extra money that's spent on setting up the tests extra help in supply teachers is logged and that we send off to the Department of Education and Science after this sort of farce has been gone through this time and we really make them see that it is impossible—it's an unfair strain on teachers. It's unfair on the children and it's an absolute waste of time all round. I'd really ask school governors not to sort of put it under the carpet.

In this case, someone (the Department of Education and Science) is doing some-thing bad to the teachers and is not taking them into account in its decisions. There is a general rule involved here: an employer shouldn't make decisions without tak-ing into account the fact that these decisions may be bad for some of the employees; if an employer does make decisions in this way, one can say: "I think it is bad and I expect that other people will think the same." Above all, the employees themselves can say to the employer: "you are doing something bad, you can't do it," because their rights are being violated. And one last example:

> I really would love to give a home to some of these children because I feel myself
> I could you know give them an awful lot but it would be unfair to my husband
> because he needs the quiet, he needs the peace of mind and [laughter] no way
> could he tolerate young children.

Here, the speaker feels that she can't do what she would like to do because this would be bad for her husband and because her husband would have every right to say: "you can't do it." The assumption is that if the speaker and her husband want to do things together (live in a partnership, as it were), they have to agree on some things. One of these things is that one spouse cannot unilaterally make decisions that would be bad for the other spouse. In the speaker's judgment, if she were to do what she wants to do—give a foster home to some young children—it would be bad; she can say why she thinks like this, and she expects that other people would think the same.

All these considerations allow us to attempt a definition of the word *fair* (to begin with, in the negative frame "that's not fair"). This definition will have three parts. The first part, in the frame "I say," expresses the speaker's judgment. The second, indented part displays the background assumptions behind the concept 'fair'. The third part justifies the speaker's judgment with reference to those background assumptions.

> *That's not fair.*
> a. I say: people can know that when this person (X) did it (W),
>   X did something bad
> b. if other people know about it they will say the same
>   because they all think about some things in the same way
> c. they think like this:
> d. "when people want to do some things with some other people
>   they know that they can do some kinds of things
> e. at the same time they know
>   that they can't do some other kinds of things
> f. because if they do things like this,
>   it will be bad for these other people
> g. they know that people can think that no one will do things like this"
> h. people can know that when this person (X) did it (W),
>   X did something like this
> i. because of this, other people can say to X:
>   "you can't do things like this"

The positive phrase *that's fair* can be explicated as, essentially, *not not fair*. Accord-ingly, the background assumptions (components c.–g.) are the same, and the only difference is the presence of negation in the components at the beginning and the end (the first, fifth, and sixth components).

That's fair.
a. I say: people can know that when this person (X) did it (W),
  X did NOT do anything bad
b. if other people know about it they will say the same
  because they all think about some things in the same way
c. they think like this:
d. when people want to do some things with some other people
  they know that they can do some kinds of things
e. at the same time they know
  that they can't do some other kinds of things
f. because if they do things like this,
  it will be bad for these other people
g. they know that people can think that no one will do things like this
h. people can know that when this person (X) did it (W),
  X did NOT do anything like this
i. because of this, other people can NOT say to X:
  "you can't do things like this"

These explications do not seek to specify what kinds of things would be regarded as "not fair," which would be an impossible task. As we have seen, the range of situations about which such judgments can be made is very broad and cannot be reduced to some simple formula like "the same for all" (for *fair*) and "not the same for all" (for *not fair*). Instead, the proposed explication articulates the assumptions on the basis of which such judgments are made, and the judgment itself is explicated in only very general terms.

In contemporary Anglo societies, values like "equity" and "equal distribution of goods" have become so important for many people that they have come to see them as the essence of "fairness," and when they try to define *fairness*, many people do so along the lines of "equity." As we have seen, however, the words *fair* and *unfair* continue to be used in ways that do not fit the model of equity at all. To define *fairness* as, essentially, "equity" is like defining *good* in terms of love, happiness, sex, food, or whatever else may be seen as the main "good" in human life. In fact, as argued by, for example, Prichard (1935), the question of the meaning of *good* must, of course, be distinguished from people's ideas of what the "supreme good" in life is.

Mutatis mutandis, the same applies to "fairness." The two cases are not parallel in all respects, because *good* is an unanalyzable conceptual prime, occurring as a word in all languages, whereas *fair* is a complex concept, which has emerged in Anglo culture and found its expression in an English word with no equivalents in other languages. Nonetheless, the two cases are parallel in one important respect: the meaning of *good* does not tell us which things are good and which are not, and neither does the meaning of *fair* tell us which things are fair and which are not. If something like "equity" is the most salient example of what most speakers of English regard as "fair," this does not mean that the word *fairness* means the same, or very nearly the same, as *equity*. On a conscious level, many speakers of English may indeed believe that "fairness" boils down to "equity"; on an unconscious level, however, they continue to interpret *fairness* far more broadly and to use the words *fair* and *unfair* in ways which have little or nothing to do with "equity." This shows us once more that (as Franz Boas [1911] argued a century ago) language as it is actually used is often a better guide to people's ways of thinking than their consciously held views and opinions.

The unconscious cultural assumptions underlying the concept of "fairness" could be informally stated as follows: human interaction, which is based largely on what people as individuals want to do, needs to be regulated, in everyone's interest, by certain rules. These rules cannot be all stated in advance – presumably, because life is too complex and varied for that. In most situations, however, it is possible to appeal to a general rule that would be seen by most people as generally applicable and also as "reasonable."

The regulation of life effected by stated and unstated rules of interaction is not seen as imposed on the society from outside but rather as something that all its members would bind themselves by voluntarily. The rules are seen as general, the same for everyone ("democratic"), and voluntary. The approach is pragmatic and flexible (the rules are not necessarily all stated in advance). It allows for free pursuit of one's wants (it is "liberal"), but within limits. It also allows for a conflict of interest: an individual is not necessarily precluded from doing things that are bad for other people, but again, within limits. These limits cannot always be set in advance, but they can be expected to be agreed on in concrete situations by an appeal to what is "reasonable" — justifiable on grounds that can be recognized by "everyone" (that is, by "the-person-in-the-street") as valid.

5.3. "Fairness" and Anglo Political Philosophy

Where does the concept of "fairness," which occupies such an important place in the everyday philosophy of the speakers of English, come from? When we compare the folk philosophy embedded in the word *fair* with the political philosophy of "fairness" developed in works such as Rawls's classic, which was mentioned earlier, the consonance between the two is very striking. One way of looking at this consonance is to say that the everyday word *fair* has crystallized in its meaning political and philosophical ideas that were developed in the seventeenth and eighteenth century by the thinkers of the British Enlightenment and that have become entrenched in modern Anglo consciousness. Another way of looking at it is to say that theoretical reflection on "fairness" such as Rawls's (which is building on those earlier political and philosophical ideas) is in fact guided by the meaning of the word *fair*.

Rawls's formula "justice as fairness" is not entirely felicitous because, strictly speaking, "fairness" is not "justice" but rather a new concept that has developed in the last three centuries or so and that has come to play a central role in modern Anglo consciousness — to some extent, alongside "justice" and to some extent, in place of "justice." I take a quick look at the concept of "justice" in the next section. Here, I briefly present Rawls's ideas about "fairness" and show how these ideas correspond to the everyday concept as discussed in the preceding section.

The key ideas in Rawls's discussion are that "fairness" is linked with a democratic conception of society, that it has its origins in the idea of social contract, that it is linked with the idea of cooperation and mutual agreement, and that it presupposes publicly recognized and generally accepted rules. Rawls himself summarizes his conception of "justice as fairness" as follows:

> (a) Social cooperation is distinct from merely socially coordinate activity—for example, activity coordinated by orders issued by an absolute central authority. Rather, social cooperation is guided by publicly recognized rules and procedures which those cooperating accept as appropriate to regulate their conduct.
> (b) The idea of cooperation includes the idea of fair terms of cooperation: these are terms each participant may reasonably accept, and sometimes should accept, provided that everyone else likewise accepts them. Fair terms of cooperation specify an idea of reciprocity, or mutuality: all who do their part as the recognized rules require are to benefit as specified by a public and agreed upon standard.
> (c) The idea of cooperation also includes the idea of each participant's rational advantage, or good. The idea of rational advantage specifies what it is that those engaged in cooperation are seeking to advance from the standpoint of their own good. (Rawls 2001, 6)

Rawls's idea of "social cooperation" corresponds to the component "when people want to do some things with other people." His "publicly recognized rules and procedures" correspond to "when people want to do some things with some other people, they know that they can do things of some kinds" and "at the same time they know that they can't do things of some other kinds." The idea of "the public and agreed upon standard" finds also its echo in the component "if other people know about it they will say the same": the speaker's confidence that other people will share his or her evaluation of an act described as "fair" or "not fair" is based on the existence of such a public and agreed upon standard ("people can know that").

The component "when people want to do some things with other people, they know that they can think that no one will do things like this" (i.e., things of these other kinds) corresponds to Rawls's reference to "trust and confidence" (not mentioned in the preceding summary but stipulated elsewhere [p. 196]).

I have not included in the explication a reference to the idea of "each participant's advantage, or good," because I think that this idea may belong to the philosophy of social contract rather that to the concept of 'fairness' as such. I have, however, included a reference to the *disadvantage* of some of the participants as a rationale for the constraints on the actions of others ("because if they do it it will be bad for these other people"). This is consistent with Rawls's observation that in a society conceived of as "a fair system of cooperation," the "fair terms of cooperation" are not specified by reference to "a moral order of values" or "to God's law" but rather to the participants' agreement based on their perceived "reciprocal advantage, or good" (pp. 14–15).

> . . . The fair terms of social cooperation are to be given by an agreement entered into by those engaged in it. One reason it does this is that, given the assumption of reasonable pluralism, citizens cannot agree on any moral authority, say a sacred text or a religious institution or tradition. Nor can they agree about a moral order of values or the dictates of what some view as natural law. So what better alterna-

tive is there than an agreement between citizens themselves reached under conditions that are fair for all? (Rawls 2001, 15)

As this passage makes clear, the emergence of "fairness" as a modern Anglo ideal
can be seen as related to the post-Enlightenment move away from metaphysics and
to the shift from an ethics based on religion to a "procedural morality" and to an
ethics based on "reason," "social cooperation," and "each participant's rational advantage" (see chapters 3 and 4).

I have not tried to formulate the explication of *fair* in such a way as to make it
maximally close to Rawls's discussion of a "fair system of cooperation," because the
purpose of Rawls's discussion is different from mine. Nonetheless, there is a striking
correspondence between the explication of *fair* proposed here, which was arrived at
by analysis of linguistic usage, and Rawls's analysis rooted in political philosophy and
history of ideas. The historical phenomenon of the emergence of what Rawls calls
"justice as fairness" has found its expression in an unprecedented semantic phenomenon: the emergence of the concept of 'fair' in everyday English.

In developing his theory of "justice as fairness" Rawls (1999, xviii) sought, as he
put it, "to generalize and carry to a higher order of abstraction the traditional theory
of the social contract as represented by Locke, Rousseau and Kant." But judging by
linguistic evidence, this concept of "justice as fairness," based on the theory of social
contract, is akin to the conception embedded in ordinary language in the English
word *fair* and its derivatives. Since *fairness* has no colloquial equivalents in either
French or German, once again we can surmise that Locke's ideas to which Rawls
refers (in particular those developed in his *Second Treatise of Government* [1960])
have had a greater impact on the English language than Rousseau's or Kant's ideas
of social contract have had on either French or German.

In any case, there is, according to Rawls (2001, 2) "a divide between the tradition
derived from Locke, which stresses . . . freedom of thought and liberty of conscience,
certain basic rights of the person and of property, and the rule of law and the tradition derived from Rousseau, which stresses . . . the equal political liberties and the
values of public life."

Speaking of a "well-ordered," "civil" society, Locke (1960 [1690]) tends to use
the word *just* rather than the word *fair*. Yet it is easy to discern behind his statements
the key elements of the modern Anglo concept of 'fairness': "common consent"
(p. 396), "standard of right and wrong" (p. 396), "standing rules" (p. 404), "agreeing
with other men to join and unite into a community" (p. 379), "equal and free," and
"trust" (p. 476). Two quotes:

On freedom, equality, and social contract

Men being, as has been said, by Nature, all free, equal and independent, no one
can be . . . subjected to the Political Power of another, without his own *Consent*.
The only way whereby any one divests himself of his Natural Liberty, and puts on
the bonds of Civil Society is by agreeing with other Men to joyn and unite into a
Community, for their comfortable, safe, and peaceable living one amongst another.
(Locke 1960 [1690], 374–375)

On a "common standard of right and wrong"

The great and chief end therefore, of Men's uniting onto Commonwealths, and putting themselves under Government, is the Preservation of their Property. To which in the state of Nature there are many things wanting. *First*, There wants an establish'd, settled, known Law, received and allowed by common consent to be the Standard of Right and Wrong, and the common measure to decide all Controversies between them. (Locke 1960 [1690], 395–396)

As Bauman and Briggs (2003, 5–6) note in their *Voices of Modernity*, "The second of his [Locke's] *Two Treatises of Government* (1960 [1690]) is credited with constructing the notions of civil society, individual rights, and government that have shaped modern societies up to the present." Although the matter requires further investigation, I would conjecture that Locke contributed to not only the shift from "rationalism" to "reasonableness" in Anglo consciousness and culture (as suggested by Porter 2000, 66) but also a shift from "justice" to "fairness."

Locke himself appears to have often used the word *fair* in a sense closer to general commendation (roughly, "good") than to the full-fledged modern meaning as explicated here. For example, *men of fair minds* (read in context) appears to mean for him, roughly, "men of good minds," and *to live upon fair terms with someone* (read in context) appears to mean, roughly, "to live on good terms." In his *Two Treatises of Government*, however, the word starts to be used in collocations like *a fair and equal representative* (of a community) and *fair and impartial execution of the laws*, where a semantic shift seems to start taking place—from, roughly, "good" in general to "fair" in the modern sense.

No doubt the salient modern Anglo concept of 'fairness' has other sources, in addition to seventeenth-century political philosophy (including, most probably, "Protestant ethics and the spirit of capitalism," in the sense of Max Weber 1968 [1930]). But when political philosophy reaches a wide audience of educated readers (as Locke's writings did), it may help, as Rawls puts it, to "orient" the public "in the (conceptual) space, say, of all possible ends, individual and associational, political and social" (Rawls 2001, 3). "Political philosophy, as work of reason, does this by specifying principles to identify reasonable and rational ends of those various kinds, and by showing how those ends can cohere within a well-articulated conception of a just and reasonable society" (p. 3). Arguably, 'fairness' is one of the aspects of the conception to which Rawls is here referring.

5.4. "Fairness" vs. "Justice"

A comparative and historical study of the concept of 'justice' is a topic for future research. There is, of course, already an extensive literature on the subject of "justice," but, generally speaking, this literature is based on the assumption that the concept of 'justice' is either entirely language-independent or at least is shared with all European languages and that it can be discussed from a philosophical point of view without any special attention to the semantics of individual languages in which this and related concepts are encoded. For example, when Mautner's *Dictionary of Philosophy* (1996, 218) discusses different "conceptions of justice" from Plato to the modern era, this is done as if there were a concept of 'justice' independent of the Greek word *dikaiosyne*, the English word *justice*, the German word *Gerechtigkeit*, and so on.

Similarly, when *The Cambridge Dictionary of Philosophy* (Audi 1999, 456) defines *justice* as "each getting what he or she is due," it does not specify whether this is intended as a definition of the English word *justice*, of some language-independent Platonic idea, or both. In fact, since the discussion in the entry opened with this definition embraces Plato and Marx, it can hardly be expected to reflect, specifically, the concept of 'justice' encoded in ordinary English and operative in the culture reflected in that language, so presumably it is meant to refer to some language-independent, universal human idea.

It is an illusion, however, to think that the concept of 'justice' is universal and can be discussed, fruitfully, in a linguistic vacuum. It is also an illusion to think that it is a concept shared by all the European languages. It is true that unlike 'fairness', which is distinctively Anglo, 'justice' belongs to a common European heritage with its source in Greek philosophy and in the Bible, and that for centuries there was a common European discourse about a complex of ideas that in English was linked with the word *justice*. It is also true that the English word *justice* has relatively close parallels in many other European languages. Nonetheless, these parallels do not amount to full semantic identity. For example, while (as noted earlier), in contemporary English a teacher or parent cannot be described as *just* (or *unjust*), in contemporary Polish they could well be described as *sprawiedliwy* (or *niesprawiedliwy*). In the brief remarks on justice that can be made within the confines of this chapter, I will start with the word *justice* as it was used in English in the past—a usage that is still familiar to contemporary speakers of English, and especially to readers of English literature, whether or not they have it in their active repertoire themselves. Here are three examples from Shakespeare.

> I beg for justice, which thou, prince, must give: Romeo slew Tybalt, Romeo must not live. (*Romeo and Juliet*)

> F. Peter [to Isabella]: Now is your time: speak loud and kneel before him.

> Isabella: Justice, O royal duke! Vail your regard upon a wrong'd I'd fain have said, a maid! O worthy prince, dishonour not your eye By throwing it on any other object, Till you have heard me in my true complaint, And given me justice, justice, justice! (*Measure for Measure*)

> Antipholous of Ephesus: Justice, most gracious duke, oh, grant me justice! . . . Justice, sweet prince, against that woman there she whom thou gave'st to me to be my wife That hath abused and dishonour'd me Even in the strength and height of injury! Beyond imagination is the wrong that she this day hath shameless thrown on me.

> Duke: Discover how, and thou shalt find me just. (*Comedy of Errors*)

As these examples suggest, *justice* refers to a society where some people have power over other people and can make decisions that influence other people's lives for the good or for the bad. In the following explication, this is represented in terms of a "place" where "many people live" and where "some people are above other people." (The vertical metaphor expressing a vertical view of a society can be rendered in explications in this way because it appears to be available in all languages; see Lynch 2000). Thus, we could start our explication of the English word *justice* with the following components:

> [people think like this:]
> when many people live in a place it can be like this:
> some of these people are not like other people,
>> they are above other people
> if these people say some things,
> good things can happen to other people in this place
> if these people say some other things,
>> bad things can happen to other people in this place

The concept of 'justice' implies that the people whose decisions can influence other people's lives (judges, rulers, etc.) should be motivated in their pronouncements by a desire to do what is good for all people, not by anything else (e.g., not by a desire for personal gain, fame, or popularity; not by partiality to some and indifference to others; not by arbitrary whims). Thus:

> it is good if these people say things like this because they want to do good
>> things for all people,
> not because they want something else

More specifically, the desire of the "just" rulers and other privileged decision makers to do what is good should be associated with a desire to ensure that, as *The Cambridge Dictionary of Philosophy* (Audi 1999) puts it, "each gets what he or she is due"—above all, in the sense of consequences of bad deeds: if someone did something very bad to other people, something very bad should happen to them because of that (for example, if Romeo slew Tybalt, Romeo should be killed himself). Thus:

> it is good if these people think like this:
> "I want people to know that if someone in this place does something very
>> bad to some other people
> something very bad will happen to this person because I say something"

The *Cambridge Dictionary of Philosophy*'s (Audi 1999) definition, "each gets what he or she is due," implies also a symmetrical notion of reward:

> "I want people to know that if someone in this place does very good
>> things
> something good will happen to them because I say something"

In fact, however, *justice* does not imply such a notion. Rather, as the example from the *Measure for Measure* illustrates, *justice* implies that wrongs will be redressed, that is, that if someone has been wronged, the "just" ruler or judge will ensure that something good will happen to the wronged person because of that:

it is good if these people think like this:
"I want people to know that if something very bad happens to someone in
      the place because someone else did something very bad
something good will happen to this person because I say something"

In practice, the punishment of the guilty and the compensation for the wronged can
often go hand in hand, as in the example from the *Comedy of Errors*.

Furthermore, *justice* implies that if the privileged and powerful decision makers do not think in those terms, this can have very negative consequences for the people
dependent on their pronouncements:

if these people don't think like this it is very bad
many very bad things can happen to many people in this place because
      of this
This brings us to the following overall explication:[4]

justice (as in *a just king*)
 a. [people think like this:]
 b. when many people live in a place, it can be like this:
 c.   some people in this place are above other people in this place
 d.   if these people say some things,
       good things can happen to people in this place because of this
 e.   if these people say some other things,
       bad things can happen to people in this place because of this
 f. if it is like this in a place, it is good if these people say such things
       because they want to do good things for all people,
       not because of something else
 g. it is good if these people think like this:
 h. "it is not good if in this place some people do very bad things
       to some other people
 i. because of this, I want people to know
       that if someone in this place does something very bad
         to some other people
       something very bad will happen to this person
         because I say something
 j. at the same time, I want people to know
       that if something very bad happens to some people in this place
         because someone did something very bad
       something good will happen to these people
         because I say something"
 k. if these people don't think like this, it is very bad
 l. people can't live well in this place if these people don't think like this
 m. many very bad things can happen to many people in this place
       because of this

If we compare this explication of *justice* with that of *fairness* proposed earlier, several differences stand out. One is the nonegalitarian character of *justice*: the notion
implies that there are some people in the society who are in a position of power and

privilege ("above other people") and whose judgments and pronouncements can have an impact on many other people's lives. When the words *justice, just,* and *unjust* are used with reference to the past, they are often applied to individuals, especially rulers. When they are used with reference to modern democratic societies, they are used most often with reference to abstractions such as "the system" or "the society." Two examples from Cobuild:

> I just went on doing it because it was something to do, a way of kicking back at the injustice of the system.

> . . . how Americans perceived the sources of justice and injustice in their society and acted upon those views.

In the Cobuild corpus, the vast majority of all the sentences with *justice* refer to the law. For example:

> I think that the best way of handling this would be to have an independent unit an independent body that examines allegations of miscarriage of justice.

> He says the pilots must face justice.

> But of course, with capital punishment, justice delayed is always justice denied.

Although the explication of *justice* proposed here in relation to "just" rulers or judges may require certain adjustments to fit the use of this word in relation to law ("the system of justice"), in principle it is applicable here, too: the representatives of the law such as judges and magistrates can still fit the description of people whose decisions can cause good or bad things for many other people in the place that is under the law (although in a modern democratic society, it is not judges and magistrates as individuals who are seen as being "above" other people but the law they represent).

Apart from "the law," "the society," and "the system," various other extensions of the old concept of 'justice' can be encountered in modern usage, but they are often accompanied by a reference to *fairness*, as if a conceptual shift was in progress. For example:

> They make conditions unfair and unjust.

> . . . the Hayden-Cartwright Act agreed that using motor vehicle taxes for something other than building or maintaining highways was "unfair and unjust."

> . . . if right now there were within you inner feelings of unfairness, injustice, imbalance . . . then not all at once but over perhaps some eight- nine- at the outside ten-month period many if not all of those inner feelings are going to be blown away.

The shift from 'justice' to 'justice' and 'fairness' (and to 'fairness' tout court) is no doubt related to the fact that 'justice' as applied to individuals has a ring of an absolute moral judgment: the idea that a "just person" (e.g., a "just king") makes some decisions because he (or, more rarely, she) "wants to do good things" sounds uncongenial to many present-day Anglo speakers, who (as noted by Charles Taylor 1989 and others) tend to value "procedural" rather than "absolute" morality and who are more concerned about mutually advantageous cooperation between individuals than about absolute ideas like 'goodness' and 'truth' (a point to which I return in section 5.7). It is significant that the notion of 'fairness', in contrast to that of 'justice', is related to the notion of 'rights'. 'Justice' can be contrasted not only with 'injustice' but also with 'mercy'. For example:

> And earthly power doth then show likest God
> When mercy seasons justice (Shakespeare, *The Merchant of Venice*)

Justice could be "seasoned" with *mercy*, but it would be impossible to say the same about *fairness*. *Mercy* implies inequality: the giver of mercy is in some sense above the recipient, who depends on the giver's benevolence. The phrase *earthly power* rightly links both *justice* and *mercy* with power. *Fairness*, on the other hand, implies equal standing of all the parties—at least in the sense that they are all bound by the same rules.

Given the relatively small overlap between 'justice' and 'fairness' as explicated in this chapter, it is all the more striking that in the literature fairness is often presented as a *variety* of 'justice' or a specific conception of 'justice'. In fact, the perceived closeness of the two concepts should be explained in structural rather than substantive terms: in modern Anglo society, the ideal of 'fairness' has supplanted, to some extent, the ideal of 'justice', largely restricting the domain of 'justice' to a public sphere and linking it with personified abstractions—especially the law—rather than with individual human beings.

5.5. The Illusion of Universality

As mentioned earlier, 'fairness' is a uniquely Anglo concept, without equivalents in other languages, except, as for example in German, as a loan from English (*das is nicht fair*, "that's not fair"). At the same time, in Anglo culture this concept is so central that many speakers of English imagine that it must be universal, perhaps even innate. For example, in a recent article in the British newspaper *The Guardian*, Polly Toynbee (2002) argues for the innateness of some basic moral code by using as her prime example the supposedly innate principle of fairness ("morality is plainly inborn in every child as soon as it cries 'unfair'").

Similarly, Steven Pinker, in his 2002 book *The Blank Slate*, includes 'fairness' on his list of putative human universals. Pinker's list is derived mostly from Donald Brown's 1991 book *Human Universals* and from Brown's entry in *The MIT Encyclopedia of the Cognitive Sciences* (1999). "Donald Brown's List of Human Universals" includes many items that, as the empirical investigations carried out within the NSM framework have established, are indeed universally attested (see Table 1.1). Among them are, for example, "one" and "two," "same" (i.e., "the same"), "good," and "bad." The list includes also some spurious universals, such as "white" and "black," which were posited as such in Berlin and Kay's 1969 classic, and which are now known not to be universal (for discussion e.g., Wierzbicka 1996, in press b,c) but which are nonetheless not uncommon in the languages of the world. But the presence of *fairness* on the list is remarkable, given that *fairness* is a unique conceptual invention of modern English. Remarkable, that is, from the point of view of native speakers of languages other than English. For native speakers of English, however (including many scholars), it is simply unimaginable that 'fairness' should not be a universal human concern. This is a good example of how people's native language can shape their ways of thinking and their assumptions about what is natural and universal. It is also a good illustration of the dangers of a monolingual perspective in discussions of "human nature" and "the human mind."

Many scholars working in English simply refuse to believe that "fairness" is not a universal human concern. Some appeal in this context to Aristotle and to Piaget. For example, James Wilson, the author of *The Moral Sense* (1994, 10) (apparently, the source of *fairness* on "Donald Brown's List of Human Universals") writes: "Perhaps the first moral judgment uttered by the child is, 'That's not fair!'" (Note: not "an English-speaking child" but simply, "the child.") Wilson elaborates: "By the time that they are in elementary school, the idea of fairness has acquired a fairly definite meaning: people should have equal shares" (p. 11). According to Wilson, this corresponds to Aristotle's concept of "distributive justice":

> A vast body of research on adult behaviour provides compelling evidence for the importance of fairness as a guide to how we behave. In these studies (and here as well), fairness is defined much as Aristotle defined distributive justice: "What is just . . . is what is proportionate" (*Nichomachean Ethics* 1131b17)—that is, things should be divided among people in proportion to their worth or merit. (Wilson 1994, 12)

The "vast body of research on adult behaviour [which] provides compelling evidence for the importance of fairness as a guide to how we behave" is no doubt right—if by "we" one means "we Anglos," rather than "we human beings." But "fairness" can hardly guide the behavior of people who have no such concept, that is, speakers of most, if not all, languages other than English, for example, Polish, German, or French, not to mention Australian Aboriginal languages, to which I will return shortly.

What applies to Aristotle (as a thinker who was supposedly keenly interested in "fairness") applies also to Piaget. When Piaget's classic work, *The Moral Judgment of the Child*, was translated into English (by Marjorie Gabain; Piaget 1950), Piaget's French word *juste* was in most contexts rendered in English as *fair*. It is an illusion, however, to think that when Piaget was studying the emergence of the concepts of *juste* and *justice* (French words) in French, he was studying the emergence of the concept of 'fairness', as the reader of the English translation, unaware of the semantic differences between the French word *juste* and the English *fair*, may unsuspectingly assume. For example, when Piaget asked (French-speaking) children to give examples of what is not *juste* (*pas juste*) (1969, 250), they cited lying, stealing, breaking things, and so forth, as well as cheating in games or giving a big piece of cake to one person and a small piece to another (p. 250). Clearly, this is a concept different from that encoded in the English word *fair* (although Piaget's English translator did render *pas juste* in this context as "not fair").

In fact, the French word *juste* could be compared not only with the English *fair* but also with the English word *right*, for example, "it's not right (or it is wrong) to lie or steal." It is an altogether different concept, which doesn't necessarily imply "reciprocity" or "cooperation" any more than the English words *just* and *right* do. For example, while in English one can describe office bearers in democratic institutions as "fair" (e.g., "she is very fair," "she was a very fair chairperson/head of department"), one could not use the French word *juste* in such a context: "*elle *est très juste," "*Madame la Présidente est très juste."* The English *fair* and the French *juste* overlap in meaning, but they do not match.

The projection of the modern Anglo value of "fairness" onto other epochs and other cultures is well illustrated by a passage from the Bible story of the Prodigal Son, as retold in English for young children in the series *Usborne Bible Tales: The Prodigal Son*. (As the cover puts it, "Usborne Bible Tales have been specially written, staying close to the original stories, for young children who are just beginning to read.") In the New King James version of the story, the words of the contrite prodigal son are "Father, I have sinned against heaven and before you, and I am no longer worthy to be called your son. Make me like one of your hired servants." In the Usborne version, on the other hand, we read: "Forgive me, father. It isn't fair for me to be your son anymore. Please let me be one of your servants." Although the value of forgiveness is indeed central to the story and to New Testament ethics in general, the value of fairness is, of course, totally alien to that ethics.

A particularly spectacular example of mistaking the historically shaped Anglo concept of 'fairness' for a human universal is provided by a recent book entitled *Natural Justice* (Binmore 2005). The author of this book acknowledges that "fairness norms can differ in different times and places" (p.17), but insists that the concept of 'fairness' as such is "biologically determined" (p.18), and "is one of those few characteristics of our species that separates us from other animals" (p.18). Indeed, "fairness is evolution's solution to the equilibrium selection problem for our ancestral game of life" (p. 14). The book completely misses the point that the very phrase "fairness norms" imposes an Anglocentric perspective on what he calls "our [human] ancestral game of life."

Both the nonuniversality of the Anglo concept of 'fairness' and its links with, as Rawls (2001, p. 6) put it, "social cooperation guided by publicly recognized rules" are clearly visible in the following vignette from Australia (where Ann is an Australian Aboriginal woman and Janet, an Anglo Australian):

> It was Saturday afternoon and the shop was closed. Jimmy's mother Ann needed some food. She went to see her friend Janet who was the storekeeper's wife.
>
> Ann went to Janet's house. After sitting for a while she asked her, "Janet, can you open up the shop for me? My little girl's been sick and I need to buy some food now."
>
> Janet answered, "I'm sorry, Ann, but I can't do that. You know we tell everybody they can't buy food on Saturday afternoon. They have to buy their food on Saturday morning. If I open up the store for you, lots of other people will want to buy things too."
>
> Janet gave Ann some of her own bread, but Ann was not happy. Janet was a "sister" to Ann, and they visited each other a lot. Ann thought Janet was not being a good sister to her. (Hargrave 1991, 19)

As this vignette illustrates, "fairness" (invoked here implicitly) is essentially about rules ("social contract") that are the same for everyone, publicly recognized, and generally accepted. Clearly, there is no such concept in Ann's culture, just as there is no concept of kinship-based obligations in Janet's culture. As I have argued elsewhere (Wierzbicka 2001), there are indeed some universal moral norms and values, but to think that "fairness" is among them is an Anglocentric illusion.

The culture-specific character of the Anglo concept of 'fairness' and of the values attached to it is highlighted by the experience of many immigrants to Anglophone countries. Drawing on my own experience as a Polish immigrant in Australia, I can testify that this concept was often a source of tension in our cross-cultural and bilingual family. Thus, in the past, my daughters, growing up in Australia, used to say to me (in Polish), *to nie fair* ("that's not fair!"), and I used to reply, in exasperation, that I didn't think in such terms. These bilingual children, who were speaking both English and Polish every day and who were thinking in terms of the English word *fair* (a key concept of their dominant Anglo Australian culture), *knew* that there was no Polish word for *fair*, so they used the English word *fair* in their Polish sentence. And I, as a bilingual but culturally predominantly Polish person, *knew* that I found the concept of 'fair' both alien and (in a family situation) offensive and hurtful. One of my daughters used to say, with some resentment, "You hate the word *fair*." (This is a good example of how cultures clash in cross-cultural and bilingual families.)

It should be pointed out here that judging by linguistic and other evidence, in Australia 'fairness' is even more important than in other traditionally English-speaking countries (see for example the *Australian National Dictionary* for the evidence of its linguistic elaboration). The Australian writer David Malouf has recently commented on this as follows:

> The one word that sums up what Australians demand of society, and of one another, is fairness, a good plain word that grounds its meaning in the contingencies of daily living. It is our version of liberty, equality, fraternity and includes everything that is intended by those grand abstractions and something more: the idea of natural justice, for instance. It's about as far as most Australians would want to go in the enunciation of a principle. (Malouf 2004)

5.6. "Fairness" and "Fair Play": A Historical Perspective

When exactly did the concept of 'fairness' enter the English language (and collective Anglo thinking)? The question is not easy to answer, because the words *fair* and *unfair* (in other meanings) are attested in English from the nineth century and because their earlier meanings and the changes in their meanings have not yet been investigated.

According to OED, the word *unfair* in the relevant sense entered the English language in the eighteenth century. The OED defines this sense as follows: "not fair or equitable; unjust; of actions, conduct etc, specifically of (business competition)," and the earliest examples cited to illustrate this sense are the following four:

> This shifting, unfair method of yours (Berkeley, 1713)

> If indeed it were so abridged as to alter the sense, that would be unfair. (Wesley, 1746)

> This conclusion appeared so unfair . . . that she burst into tears. (S & Ht. Lee, 1798)

> There was a very unfair review in the Athenaeum. (E. Fitzgerald 1859)

It is very likely, however, that the word *unfair* was not used in these sentences exactly in the same sense in which it was used in late nineteenth- and twentieth- century examples with the phrase *unfair competition*, cited by the OED under the same definition, because its range of use was in the eighteenth century much wider. One example (from a judge's speech to the jury):

> I find it difficult to suppress my feelings. As, however, to say anything of the distinguished talents and virtues of that excellent man, might tend to excite improper emotions in the minds of the jury, [I] would withhold these feelings which pressed for utterance from my heart, and leave you, gentlemen, to form your judgement upon the evidence which has been adduced in support of the case, undressed by any unfair indignation which you might feel against his murderer.

"Unfair indignation" is seen here as an improper emotion in the minds of the jury—an understandable but not longer possible use of the word *unfair*. Thus, it would appear that the familiar twentieth-century sense of *unfair* (as, for example, in *unfair competition*) emerged and spread widely only in the nineteenth century.

As for *fair* in the relevant modern sense, the OED goes even further back and, indeed, opens its entry devoted to this sense with an example dated 1340! In fact, however, the examples predating the eighteenth century are open to many different interpretations. It is clear that before the eighteenth century, *fair* was used widely as a fairly general word of commendation and that the interpretation imposed on some earlier examples by the OED projects on them the modern meaning rather than identifying what they meant at the time. In fact, even eighteenth-century examples such as "words which have the fairest Right to each Class" indicate that *fair* in the relevant sense—which was then gradable—was different from the modern sense.

The range of collocations of *fair* was also different from what it is now. Modern-sounding collocations like *a fair question* are deceptive in this regard, because in the eighteenth century (in contrast to the present usage), not only a question but also an answer could have been described as 'fair'. Other collocations common then but impossible now include *a fair proof, a fair disclosure,* and *a fair confession*. To illustrate from *The Proceedings of the Old Bailey*:

> That is a very fair answer, and just such an one as I expected you to give; you have told us very fairly that you are uncertain. (1785)
> There was a fair proof against the prisoner, who but denied the fact, and the jury found him guilty to the value of 10 d. (1716)
> I ask you, whether the confession she made was a free and fair confession; or whether it was extorted from her by any hope or promise, or any thing of that sort? (1782)
> He has given a fair evidence. (1784)

The earliest examples that sound "modern" in their use of *fair* are those with the phrase *fair play*, attested from the end of the sixteenth century onward. In fact, however, even the phrase *fair play* is misleading as putative evidence for a pre-eighteenth-century emergence of the modern concept of 'fairness': *fair play* had its opposite in *foul play*, not in *unfair play*, whereas *fair competition* has its opposite in *unfair competition*. There is undoubtedly a historical link between *fair play* and *fair competition*, but as the different opposites of *fair* in these two collocations indicate, the two senses of *fair* (as in *fair play* and *fair competition*) are by no means identical.

In fact, one can speculate that the notion of 'fair play' as a whole played a significant role in the emergence of the new concept of 'fair': in *fair play*, the notion of, roughly speaking, rules was part of the meaning of the word *play*, whereas in *fair competition* (and other comparable modern collocations), it became part of the meaning of *fair* itself. To put it differently, the notion of 'fair play' appears to have become absorbed, as it were, in the meaning of *fair* itself: the meaning of *fair*, as applied to all types of human interaction, appears to have been built on the model of 'fair play'. Indeed, the OED cites several sentences—from the seventeenth, eighteenth, and nineteenth centuries—in which the phrase *fair play* is used in what the OED calls a "transferred meaning," for example:

> Fear of the future shut his eyes to all sense of justice and fair play. (1882)

(Recall, for comparison, the example from Malouf cited earlier: "Laying the responsibility for their feelings on her . . . was unfair. They did not play fair.")

5.7. "Fairness" and "Procedural Morality"

"Fair play" as a model of human interaction highlights the "procedural" character of the ethics of fairness. Arguably, the emergence of the concept of "fairness" reflects a shift away from absolute morality to "procedural (and contractual) morality," and the gradual shift from *just* to *fair* can be seen as parallel to the shifts from *good* to *right* and also from *wise* (and also *true)* to *reasonable*: in all cases, there is a shift from an absolute, substantive approach to a procedural one.

Speaking of the conceptions of justice central to Western law, the legal scholar George Fletcher quoted earlier contrasts the categories of "distributive" and "corrective" justice, bequeathed to us (as he puts it) by Aristotle, and the closely related categories of "retributive" and "commutative" justice, which were (as he puts it) added later, with the modern Anglo 'procedural' conception reflected in the word *fairness*.

> All four of these [classical] forms of justice—distributive, corrective, retributive, and commutative—are substantive as opposed to procedural. They all speak to the result rather than the process by which the result is achieved. A distinct form of justice addresses itself to the question of how this result is realized. The central term in the discussion of procedural justice is "fairness." (Fletcher 1996, 81)

Fletcher's definitions of *fairness* and *fair procedures* are circular, but they are nonetheless instructive:

> Our notions of fairness and fair play draw heavily on the analogies from competitive sports and gaming that pervade idiomatic English. Fair procedures are those in which both sides had an equal opportunity of winning. Fairness consists in playing by the rules that are fair to both sides. Neither side hits below the belt. No one hides the ball. Idioms like these inform the way Americans think about procedural justice. (Fletcher 1996, 81)

The phrasing "the way Americans think about procedural justice" is, in my view, somewhat unfortunate, because neither Americans nor other ordinary Anglos think in terms like "procedural justice." But they undoubtedly think about "fairness" and often do so in terms of sporting metaphors.

Jeremy Paxman, the author of *The English: A Portrait of a People* (1999), states that "while the French Revolution invented the Citizen, the English creation is the Game" (p. 194) and "certainly, sport came to occupy a central role in English culture" (p. 196). He also quotes a characteristic comment by the writer Vita Sackville-West (1947)[2] that links the English preoccupation with games and sport with the concept of 'fairness':

> The English man is seen at his best the moment that another man starts throwing a ball at him. He is then seen to be neither spiteful, nor vindictive, nor mean, nor querulous, nor desirous of taking unfair advantage; he is seen to be law-abiding, and to respect the regulations which he himself generally has made; he takes it for granted that his adversary will respect them likewise; he would be profoundly shocked by any attempt to cheat; his scorn would be as much aroused by any exultation displayed by the victor as by any ill-temper displayed by the loser . . . It is all quite simple. One catches, kicks, or hits the ball, or else one misses it; and the same holds for the other chap. It is all taken in good part. (Paxman 1999, 196)

Paxman comments: "What she is talking about is something whose importance cannot be exaggerated. It is the significance to the English of the idea of the *Game*. The thing is loved for its own sake" (1999, 196).

In a way, sport—especially team sport—provides a perfect model for "fair" interaction because the emphasis is on rules and procedures, which are blind to the individual players' interests and which everyone voluntarily accepts. To quote Fletcher again:

> In its pure form, a fair procedure is all that is needed to generate a just result. Systems of perfect procedural justice are illustrated by flipping a coin to resolve a dispute or the venerable method for fairly dividing a piece of cake, namely, letting one person cut and the other choose his preferred slice. These are procedures that do not admit of mistakes; no one can complain about the outcome as unjust. (Fletcher 1996, 81)

Here, the "fairness" of the procedure is that all the participants who want to do something together (share a cake) know in advance what they can do (either cut the cake or choose a slice) and what they can't do (both cut the cake and choose a slice), and they know that if someone both cut the cake and chose a slice, this could be bad for the other participant(s), and the other participant(s) could protest.

The cultural assumptions of "fairness" as outlined here reflect a specific, historically shaped, political and social philosophy. Once this is recognized, it should no longer be surprising that most languages of the world do not have words corresponding to the English words *fair, fairness,* and *unfair* (in the relevant, modern sense). The concept of 'fairness' is an artifact of modern Anglo culture and one of the key concepts that speakers of Anglo English live with and see as the best basis for social life and interpersonal interaction.

In his much-discussed book *Trust*, Francis Fukuyama (1995, 34) defines *culture* as "inherited ethical habit." Distinguishing "ideologies," which are conscious, from "cultural habit" and "unwritten moral rules," Fukuyama writes:

> The most important habits that make up cultures have little to do with how one eats one's food or combs one's hair but with the ethical codes by which societies regulate behaviour—what the philosopher Nietzsche called a people's "language of good and evil." Ethical systems create moral communities because their shared languages of good and evil give their members a common moral life. (pp. 35–36)

Ethical codes binding large groups of people into "moral communities" are conveyed across generations through particular words—of course, not exclusively through words, but largely through words. The shared use of words like *fair* and *unfair* both reflects and transmits the "habit" of thinking in such terms.

Fukuyama links aspects of Anglo-American culture such as practices and principles of voluntary association, cooperativeness, combining for business purposes (p. 273), generalized social trust (p. 281), the primacy of rights, and adherence to democratic political institutions with the development of certain "ethical habits" entrenched in a shared ethical language. I would add that the English words that best epitomize the ethical code in question are the distinctively English and untranslatable words *fair* and *unfair*.[2]

PART III

ANGLO CULTURE REFLECTED IN ENGLISH GRAMMAR

Chapter 6

The English Causatives
Causation and Interpersonal Relations

6.1. The Cultural Elaboration of Causation

6.1.1. Ethnosyntax: Links between culture and grammar

While obviously words are carriers of meaning, it is less obvious that grammatical categories of a language also encode meaning. But in fact this is what grammar is all about: certain meanings are so important to communities of speakers that they become not just lexicalized (linked with individual words) but grammaticalized, that is, embodied in the language's structural patterns.

Languages differ widely not only, as Sapir (1949 [1924], 27) put it, in the nature of their vocabularies but also in the nature of their grammar. Sapir's dictum "Distinctions which seem inevitable to us may be utterly ignored in languages which reflect an entirely different type of culture, while these in turn insist on distinctions which are all but unintelligible to us" (p. 27) applies equally to vocabulary and to grammar.

Clearly, the reason why a notion like "an alternating generation" is encoded in the grammar of some Australian languages—but not, for example, in the grammar of English or Russian—is that this notion plays a role in the Australian Aboriginal societies in question (where, for example, the generations of one's grandparents or grandchildren are expected to be treated differently from those of one's parents, great-grandparents, or great-grandchildren). Similarly, it is clearly not an accident that, for example, the Hanunóo language of the Philippines has dozens of words for different kinds of rice (see Conklin 1957), and to anyone who knows anything about Russian culture, it is clearly not an accident that Russian has an extremely rich and elaborate system of expressive derivation applicable to proper names (names of persons), whereas in languages like English the corresponding system of expressive derivation is extremely limited (compare, e.g., *John* and *Johnny* in English, vs. *Ivan* and *Vanja, Vanečka, Vanjuša, Vanjuška, Vanjušečka*, and so on in Russian; for discussion, see Wierzbicka 1992, chapter 7; also Friedrich 1966). In this chapter, I focus on one area of "cultural elaboration" in grammar, namely, on the elaboration of causal relations in modern English.

If one looks at English in a comparative perspective, one is struck by its extremely rich repertoire of causative constructions. This wealth is concealed, to some extent, by the use of the same key words, such as *make, have,* or *let,* in many different constructions, all of which may appear to be examples of a single *"make-*construction," *"have-*construction," or *"let-*construction." In fact, there are reasons to distinguish, on both semantic and structural grounds, more than a dozen different *make-*constructions in English (for evidence and argumentation, see Wierzbicka 1998c) and probably more than a dozen different *have-*constructions (see Wierzbicka 1988). As this chapter seeks to demonstrate, English has also a wide range of different *let-*constructions. To give just a few preliminary examples of the wealth of causative constructions found in English, let me mention the following eleven (for further discussion, see Chappell 1978; Wierzbicka 1988):

X made Y do something *intentionally* (e.g., X made Y wash the dishes)

X made Y do something *unintentionally* (e.g., X made Y cry)

X made Y *adjective* (e.g., X made Y furious)

X had Y do something (e.g., X had Y wash the dishes)

X had something done to X's Z (e.g., X had her boots mended)

X had Y doing something (e.g., X had Y staying with her)

X got Y to do something (e.g., X got Y to wash the dishes)

X got Y *adjective* (e.g., X got Y furious)

X got herself *participle* (e.g., X got herself kicked out)

X *verb*ed Y into doing Z (e.g., X talked/tricked Y into resigning)

X *verb*ed Y doing something (e.g., X kept Y waiting)

As mentioned earlier, grammatical elaboration of conceptual domains often goes hand in hand with lexical elaboration. Kinship in Australian languages is one case in point (see, e.g., Hale 1966; Dench 1982, 1987; Heath, Merlan, and Rumsey 1982). Causal interaction in English is, I think, another. For example, if one compares English and Russian speech acts, one will discover that the English lexicon pays more attention to different strategies of human causation—just as English grammar pays more attention to this area than Russian grammar. Other semantic areas are more elaborated in Russian than in English (see, e.g., Wierzbicka 1992, chapter 12; 1997, chapter 2).

In trying to understand the extraordinary wealth of causative constructions found in modern English (not only in comparison with other European languages but also in a universal perspective), we should ask, I think, for its cultural roots. Why is it that so much attention is focused in English on the precise nature of causal relations between various actions and various events? I would like to put forward two interpretive hypotheses in this regard.

First, as democracy developed in modern society—initially, in America (see de Tocqueville 1966 [1848])—a new style of human relations evolved, which had to accommodate an increased scale of interpersonal interactions and put those interactions on a new footing (see Stearns and Stearns 1986). The new managerial type of society, too, needed an increased scale of interpersonal causations: for the new society to function smoothly and efficiently, lots of people had to be told what to do. This had to happen, however, in the context of a democracy, where people might be willing to take "directions" or to follow "instructions" but not to obey "orders" or "commands."

But to talk of a shift from "orders" to "directions" and "instructions" is an over-simplification. In fact, a whole range of new concepts has developed and become socially salient, concepts to do with different kinds of interpersonal causation. For example, there are significant differences between "telling" someone to type up some letters, "ordering" someone to do so, "directing" them to do so, and "having some letters typed up." In modern Anglo society, the idea of "having things done" has become increasingly important; it suggests a setup that doesn't involve one person bending to the will of another and where many people are willing—in various spheres of life, such as office work or interaction at a service station—to do things that someone else wants them to do, while at the same time preserving their personal autonomy and full control over other areas of their personal lives.

The cultural emphasis on personal autonomy, characteristic of modern Anglo society and reflected in many ways in modern English (see, e.g., Wierzbicka 1991/2003a, 1996a), is no doubt closely related to the expansion of causative constructions in modern English, as is also the marked emphasis on the need for voluntary cooperation among equals (see Fukuyama 1995). In a large-scale society, where service encounters have come to occupy a vital role in everyday life and where people are acutely aware of their right to, and need for, personal autonomy, the nuances of causation assume an extraordinary importance.

For example, if I am working in a service profession (say, waiting tables or driving a taxi), my livelihood depends on my willingness to do what other people want me to do (and to do it because they say they want me to do it), but the relationship with my customers has to be negotiated in such a way that I don't abrogate my personal autonomy in the process. I am willing to "serve" my customers, but I am not willing to treat them as my superiors. If I am working in an institution such as a university or in public administration, I may well have "bosses," "superiors," or "heads of department," whose will I may have to bow to on an everyday basis. But if I am a modern Anglo person, I will not want to abrogate my personal autonomy because of this, and I will follow my bosses' will only in a context that ensures the recognition of both my autonomy and my essential "equality" with them. Even in the realm of family interaction, it has become crucial in the modern Anglo world that parental authority has to be exercised, and indeed conceived of, in ways that are consistent with the children's right to, and need for, personal autonomy.

All these modern ideas and expectations needed new ways of speaking and, I suggest, found their expression in the plethora of causative constructions so characteristic of nineteenth- and twentieth-century English. It is, of course, true that democracy reaches wide outside the Anglo world, and that so does the ethos of equality, of the rights of the individual, and of personal autonomy. It is not true, however, that the cultural emphasis on personal autonomy in the "Anglosphere" (cf. Bennett 2004) is equally characteristic of the German-speaking, Spanish-speaking, or Russian-speaking world (see, e.g., Wierzbicka 1998b).

There are considerable and partly grammaticalized differences in ways of speaking separating English from most other European languages, above all, differences in the use of the imperative. The extraordinary growth of various "whimperatives" in modern English (see chapter 2), linked with the growing avoidance of the straight imperative, is an unparalleled phenomenon, with obvious cultural significance. In fact, the growth of conventional expressions such as "would you do X," "will you do X," "could you do X," and "would you mind doing X"—all aimed at avoiding the impression that one is trying to impose one's will on somebody else—seems to have proceeded in parallel with the growth of causative constructions and the emergence of new varieties of *make*-constructions, *have*-constructions, *get*-constructions, and especially *let*-constructions in modern English. (For further discussion, see Wierzbicka 1998c.) Before discussing these constructions in detail, we need to consider some methodological issues.

6.1.2. The meaning of causatives in a cross-linguistic perspective

The literature on the syntax of causative constructions in different languages is huge; the literature on their semantics is relatively modest. But the use of such constructions is largely determined by their meaning. Since little is known about their meaning, a language learner looking for some guidelines to the actual use of such constructions can seldom find any statements anywhere that are clear, precise, and reliable. But it is not just the language learner who would be disappointed by the literature on causatives. The area of causation is of enormous inherent interest for the "philosophy of grammar" and social psychology; after all, a language's causative constructions show how its speakers draw distinctions between different kinds of causal relations and how they perceive and interpret causal links between events and human actions. And yet our understanding of "ethnocausology" is far behind that of, for example, ethnozoology or ethnogeology.

Folk interpretations of causal links are less accessible to direct observation than those of more concrete phenomena, but they can be empirically investigated. The syntax of a language provides a wealth of evidence in this regard—if we can find ways of analyzing it in an illuminating and systematic way.

I believe that here as elsewhere the key to such analysis lies in the choice of a suitable semantic metalanguage. In the existing literature on causatives, the semantics of different constructions is usually discussed in terms of ready-made labels such as "direct versus indirect causation," "contactive versus distant causation," "strong coercion versus weak coercion," "authority versus absence of authority," "factitive versus permissive causation," or "manipulative versus directive causation." But labels of this kind can often be misleading and don't have much explanatory or predictive power, because the meaning of the constructions to which they are applied differs from language to language.

The use of ready-made labels such as "direct versus indirect causation" or "contactive versus distant causation" is based on the mistaken (in my view) assumption that there are certain types of causation that can first be described a priori and then identified in individual languages. But detailed semantic analysis shows that the actual causative constructions are often unique in the meaning they encapsulate. What is called "direct causation" or "strongly coercive causation" in one language usually differs from what bears the same label in another. This is not to say that there are no recurring motifs, no cross-linguistic similarities in the area of causation. Rather, the point is that causative constructions usually encapsulate a unique combination of components. Individual components—such as, for example, "Y wanted it" or "Y didn't want it"—frequently recur in the world's languages. But the configurations of such components tend to be unique and cannot be adequately captured in global labels such as "indirect," "manipulative," and "distant."

As I see it, establishing the configuration of universal concepts encoded in a given causative construction is not a final touch that can be added to the results once the main analysis has already been completed. Rather, it is the essence of the analysis. Assigning to a construction a label such as "coercion," "authority," or "contact" does not really bring us any closer to understanding its meaning.

What applies to the cross-linguistic comparison of causative constructions applies also to the comparison of different causative constructions within one language. For example, in English, "interpersonal causation" can be described by means of several different causative constructions:

a. Mary had John return the money.
b. Mary made John return the money.
c. Mary got John to return the money.
d. Mary forced John to return the money.
e. Mary talked John into returning the money.

Each of these sentences means something different, and no labels such as "direct," "indirect," "strong," "weak," "coercive," "manipulative," or "contactive" can clarify the nature of these differences (any more than they could clarify the differences between these constructions and the German *lassen*-construction or the Japanese *o-* and *ni*-constructions).

In what follows, I first briefly discuss constructions (a), (c), and (e), and then more extensively construction (b). Finally, I compare the meaning of the *make*-causative illustrated in (b) with that of the *force*-causative illustrated in (d).

6.1.3. *Three English causatives:* Have, get, *and* into

6.1.3.1. HAVING SOMEONE DO SOMETHING

The following sentence from a novel nicely illustrates the contrast between *make* and *have* causatives:

> "She had the girls clean his bicycle and made Anand pump the tyres every morning." (Naipaul 1969, 481)

In the novel, the wife, Shama, is trying to please and appease her husband in various ways and, in particular, by getting the children to do things for him. The girls are expected to be compliant and willing to do what their mother wants them to do, whereas the boy, Anand, has to be "made" to pump the tires every morning. The meaning of the *have*-construction can be portrayed as follows:

> *Person X had person Y do Z.* =
> a. X wanted something to happen (to W)
> b. because of this X wanted Y to do Z (to W)
> c. because of this, X said something to someone
> d. because of this Y did Z
> e. X could think about it like this:
>   when I say something like this (about something like this)
>   Y can't say: "I don't want to do this"

The *have*-construction does not imply that the causee didn't want to perform the action. Nor does it imply that the causee *had to* do it. It does imply, however, something like a hierarchical relationship, within which the causer can say that he or she wants the causee to do something, and the causee can't say in response, "I don't want to do it."

This doesn't mean that the causer has complete power over the causee and that the causee has to do whatever the causer wants. The compliance may well be limited to some particular sphere (such as the professional duties of a secretary to whom her boss can give directions). Within this sphere, however, the causer doesn't have to exert any special pressure to achieve the desired effect: simply saying what he or she wants is enough. In fact, the causer's will does not even have to be expressed directly to the causee; it can be conveyed via another person. Because the causee doesn't really have to do what the causer wants, it might seem that it would be better to phrase component (e) as "Y wouldn't say: 'I don't want to do it.'" This alternative formulation, however, could apply also to situations when the causer is counting on the causee's good heart ("when I ask her to do something she will not say no"), and it is therefore inappropriate in the case of the *have*-construction. In a hierarchical relationship, a person *can* think that someone in a subordinate position "can't" refuse to take directions.

Thus, in the *have*-causative, the causer assumes the causee's "readiness to take directions"; the causee is treated here as a cooperative performer of the causer's will, as someone to whom the causer's will can be communicated (either directly or by an intermediary) and who will be both able to understand it and willing to perform it. This explains why, as pointed out by Talmy (1976, 107), the causee of the *have*-causative normally has to be human:

> *I had the squirrel leave its tree.

> The trainer made/?had the lion dance.

One could say, vaguely, that both the *make*-causative and the *have*-causative imply some sort of "power" relation between the causer and the causee. But clearly, the nature of this relation is in each case perceived differently. The *make*-causative implies that the causee is acting under pressure (what exactly this means is discussed later). The *have*-causative doesn't imply that; here, the causee is expected to comply with the causer's will, and there is no assumption, or expectation, of unwillingness on his or her part. Nonetheless, the expected compliance of the causee is not seen as due entirely to good will: there is also an assumption of dependence reflected in the component "Y can't say: I don't want to do this."

Finally, the *have*-construction does not imply that the causer is seeking to control the causee's actions, and it is not compatible with a situation where someone is seeking to impose her or his will on another person just to enjoy arbitrary power. Rather, the *have*-construction implies a goal that transcends the causee's actions; from the causer's point of view, the causee is like an instrument in achieving some objective (as signaled in the component "X wanted something to happen") rather than as the target of the causee's will. Presumably, this is the reason why the *have* causatives normally occur with transitive rather than intransitive verbs:

X made Y wait (sit still).

?X had Y wait (sit still).

Furthermore, the transitive verbs in the *have*-construction usually take definite rather than indefinite objects:

a. X made Y eat fish.
b. ?X had Y eat fish.
c. X had Y return the fish to the shop.

The *have*-construction implies that the causer wants something to happen to some object (in this case, the fish) rather than to the causee as such. The *make*-construction, however, is quite compatible with exercises in arbitrary power, deliberate cruelty, malice, punishment, and so on:

[She] used to make us kneel on graters for a thing like that. (Naipaul 1969, 236)

?She used to have us kneel on graters for a thing like that.

It is also interesting to note that in (partial)[1] contrast to the *make*-construction, the *have*-construction does not allow the passive (with the causee being put in the subject position):

a. He was made to pump the tyres every morning.
b. *He was had to pump the tyres every morning.

The causee of a *make*-construction can be "topicalized" in this way because the causee *is* the target of the causer's action and so is potentially worthy of interest, but the causee of the *have*-construction is not the target of the causer's action but a mere "instrument."

6.1.3.2. GETTING SOMEONE TO DO SOMETHING

The interpersonal causative construction based on the auxiliary verb *get* can be illustrated with the following sentence:

. . . Anand got Shama [his mother] to bring a coloured print of the goddess Lakshmi from Hanuman House. (Naipaul 1969, 383)

The boy Anand has no authority over his mother, and he can't "have" or "make" her do anything. Nevertheless, he can "get" her to do something for him.

The *get*-construction illustrated in this sentence is not the only *get*-causative available in English. Causative *get*-sentences with an inanimate causee are also possible (for example, "she got the sauce to thicken"), but the semantic conditions on such sentences are different from those on the interpersonal sentences with a human causee and a verb of action, that is, of the type "someone (X) got someone else (Y) to so something," with which we are concerned here.

The *get*-causative of the type discussed here implies that the causees do something not because they want to do it but because somebody else wants them to do it. At the same time, the action is not imposed on the causee by virtue of the causer's power or authority. The causer realizes that the causee may not want to comply, and, unlike the case of the *have*-causative, the causer has no power or authority over the addressee to overcome his or her possible reluctance or unwillingness to do what the causer wants. Because of this, the causer does (typically, says) something to the causee in the expectation that this might influence the causee's will and that as a result the causee will do the desired action willingly. And indeed, this happens: the causee does what is wanted by the causer and does it willingly. The causer "gets" something out of it: often because what the causee does can be seen as good for the causer, and always because the causer can think that what he or she wanted to happen has happened (see component g in the explication below).

How does one "get" another person to do something that one wants them to do? Usually, by saying something, as in the case of the *have*-construction, but not necessarily so. For example, one can "get" a dog to swallow a pill by putting it in a piece of meat or by smearing it with jam. The *get*-construction can also be used with reference to machines that appear to have "a will of their own," for example:

How did you get the washing machine to go? I couldn't.

The *have*-construction, which relies on a speech act, and on conscious acceptance of somebody else's authority, cannot be used like that.

?She had the dog swallow the pill.

?She had the washing machine go.

Thus, the overall semantic conditions on the *get*-constructions (with a human or humanlike causee) can be summarized as follows:

Person X got person Y to do Z. =
a. X wanted Y to do Z
b. X knew that if Y didn't want to do it Y would not do it
c. X thought about it like this: "if Y wants to do it Y will do it"
d. because of this X did (said) something to Y
e. because of this after this Y wanted to do Z
f. because of this Y did Z
g. because of this X could think like this:
   "I wanted something to happen
   it happened"

Although the action is done willingly (component e), the strategy used by the causer smacks a little of manipulation, for the causee's action is brought about by the causer's, rather than the causee's, will. Nonetheless, "getting" someone to do something cannot be seen as real manipulation, for the causer does not conceal his or her goal, and the causee is not acting *against* his or her will (there is no assumption that the causee doesn't want to do what the causer wants, and it is assumed that a causee who didn't want to do it would not do it). In both these respects, "getting" people to do something differs from the truly "manipulative" scenario discussed in the next section and linked with yet another—semantically more complex—causative construction.

6.1.3.3. MANIPULATING SOMEONE "INTO DOING SOMETHING"

The construction discussed in this section is identified not in terms of a causative verb (such as *make*, *have*, or *get*) but rather in terms of a preposition: *into*. But the set of main verbs that can be used in this construction is quite limited and gives a clear clue to this construction's meaning. Thus, one can not only "talk" someone "into" doing something but also "trick" them, "maneuver" them, or "push" them. On the other hand, one cannot "encourage" or "induce" someone "into" doing anything. Roughly speaking, the generalization seems to be as follows: the *into*-construction takes verbs that either imply or at least are compatible with the idea of manipulation (tricking, maneuvering, and the like). More precisely, the meaning of the *into*-construction can be portrayed as follows:

Person X VERB-*ed person Y into doing Z.* =
a. X wanted Y to do Z
b. Y didn't want to do Z
c. X didn't say to Y: "I want you to do Z"
d. X thought about it like this: "if I say this, Y will not do Z"
e. because of this X did something else
f. because of this after this Y did Z
g. Y didn't do it because Y wanted to do it
h. Y did it because X wanted Y to do it

There are some clear similarities, as well as some clear differences, between the *into*-construction and the *get*-construction. The main differences are: first, in the case of the *into*-construction, the causee *originally* didn't want to do what he or she did, whereas in the case of the *get*-construction there is no such assumption; second, in the *into*-construction the causee's action is "triggered" by the causer's will, not by the causee's own will, whereas in the *get*-construction the causee is acting in accordance with his or her own will, as well as the causer's will; and third, in the *into*-construction, the causee is unaware of what is happening (namely, that his or her action is "triggered" by the causer's will), whereas in the *get*-construction, there is no such assumption.

Given these differences, it is not surprising that one can use the *get* causative, but not the *into* causative, as a request, for example:

I'll get you to sign this.

*I'll talk you into signing this.

The speaker of a *get*-sentence does not seek to conceal his or her wish for the causee to do something, although he or she does not regard the mere expression of the wish as a sufficient "trigger" for the causee's action. For this reason, an "I'll get you" re-quest may even be used in the service of politeness, for it sounds less presumptuous than a bare expression of the causer's will: "I want you to sign this." By using a sen-tence like "I'll get you to sign this" rather than simply "I want you to sign this," speakers signal that they don't regard their want as a sufficient reason for the causee to act, and also that they expect the causee to act willingly (in accordance with the speaker's wishes, but "freely").

6.1.4. Making something happen or someone do something

English has many different *make*-constructions. The meaning of each of these con-structions constitutes a unique configuration of components; it appears, however, that some components may be shared. Roughly, the overall semantic "theme" of *make*-constructions can be represented as follows:

A happened
because of this B happened
B wouldn't have happened if A had not happened

The precise meaning of a *make*-construction depends on the following factors: Is the causer different from the causee? Is the causer a person? a thing? an event? Is the causee a person? a thing? an event? Does the causer *do* something? Does the causee *do* something? If the causee does something, is this something that can be done only intentionally (e.g., *write, read*) or is it something that doesn't have to be done inten-tionally (e.g., *cry, laugh*)? Does something *happen* to the causee? Does the causee *think* something?

Leaving aside sentences in which either the causer or the causee is not human, we can say that there are six subtypes of the *make*-construction of the "interpersonal" kind, that is, of the kind where both the causer and the causee are human and where they are different persons. These six subtypes can be illustrated with the following sentences:

a. Person X made person Y fall.
b. Person X made person Y feel guilty.
c. Person X made person Y think about Z.
d. Person X made person Y want something.
e. Person X made person Y cry (laugh).
f. Person X made person Y apologize.

In type (a), something *happens* to the causee, and the causee doesn't have to feel anything or do anything. In type (b), nothing happens to the causee (apart from what the causer does or says), and the causee doesn't do anything, but he or she *feels* something. In type (c), nothing happens to the causee, and the causee neither does nor feels anything, but he or she has to *think* something. In type (d), nothing happens to the causee, and the causee doesn't have to do, feel, or think anything, but he or she has to *want* something. In type (e), the causee *feels* something and because of this *does* something, but something that he or she *does not want* to do, that is to say, something that can be done involuntarily (and that, presumably, is triggered by something happening in the person's body). Finally, in type (f), the causee *does* something that can be done only *intentionally* (even if it is done unwillingly—a distinction that will be discussed in some detail later). Here, I examine only type (f). Let us start by considering a few examples (again from Naipaul):

1. When we were small Mai used to make us kneel on graters for a thing like that. (Naipaul 1969, 236).
2. He . . . made her learn the quotations hanging on the walls, and made her sit still while he unsuccessfully tried to sketch her. She was dispirited and submissive. (Naipaul 1969, 222)
3. Granny is making me eat fish. I hate it. (Naipaul 1969, 186)

As these examples suggest, being "made" to do something implies doing something unwillingly under pressure from somebody else. Formulaically, this can be spelled out as follows:

Person X made person Y do Z. =
a. X wanted Y to do Z
b. because of this X did (said) something to Y
c. because of this, Y thought like this: I have to do it
d. because of this Y did Z
e. Y didn't do it because of anything else

The action that the causee is "made" to perform does not have to be inherently unpleasant (as in the case of kneeling on graters), and the causer can in fact be solicitous and concerned about the causee's welfare, as in the case of the grandmother making a child eat fish, but even then, the construction itself implies that the action was not performed willingly. Consider, for example, the following passage (from the same novel):

He was tired; she made him rest. He was hungry; she gave him food. He had nowhere to go: she welcomed him. (Naipaul 1969, 484)

In this case, rather atypically, the causee appreciates the causer's pressure. Yet here, too, given the situation described in the book, it is quite plausible that he wouldn't have rested, had his mother not urged him do so, and that he gave in to his mother's solicitous pressure in recognition that, given her attitude, he had to let her take care of him. Thus, he did it because he thought: "I have to," not because of anything else.

How does one "make" another person do something that this person is apparently unwilling to do? Presumably, by "doing something to this person" (usually, verbally): by threatening them, pressuring them, nagging them, or perhaps cajoling them. Typically, the causer's words are directed at the causee, and typically they refer to some possible consequences of the causee's action (or inaction). What does it mean, however, that the action is not performed willingly? Does it mean that the causee doesn't want to do what he or she is doing?

At first sight, a component along these lines ("Y didn't want to do it") seems apt, but when one examines a wide range of *make* sentences (with an intentional-verb complement), it emerges that not all of them are entirely consistent with such a component. Sometimes the implication seems to be that the causee was passive and submissive, rather than (outright) unwilling, as in the following sentence:

> My wife made me go to the doctor. I was planning to go anyway, but I
> kept putting it off, so she rang and made an appointment for me.

The component "Y didn't want to do Z" would be "too strong" to account for such sentences.

The solution I would propose is this: We cannot say that the causee "didn't want to do what he (she) did," but we can say that the causee thought, at some point: "I have to do it," and did it because of this—and *only* because of this. If we put it in that way, we will be showing that the action was not due to the causee's own volition, without going so far as to say that he or she "didn't want to do it."

It is interesting at this point to compare the "*make* of coercion" with the lexical verb *force*. What is the difference, for example, between "making someone eat fish" and "forcing" them to do it? I believe that comparing *make* and *force* is particularly useful in that it throws light on the nature of the "unwillingness" implied by *make*. For clearly, *forcing* does imply that the causee didn't want to do whatever he or she ultimately did, and because *force* is, intuitively, "more coercive" than *make*, comparing the two helps us see that it would not be wise to attribute the same component ("Y didn't want to do it") to the "*make* of coercion" construction as well. Both the differences and the similarities between *force* and "*make* of coercion" can be accounted for if we propose the following explication for *force*:

> *Person X forced person Y to do Z (e.g., they forced me to eat fish)* =
> a. X wanted Y to do Z
> b. X knew that Y didn't want to do this
> c. because of this X did something to Y
> d. because of this Y had to do Z
> e. because of this Y did Z
> f. when Y was doing Z Y thought like this: "I don't want to do this"

If we compare this explication with that of the *make*-construction (as in the sentence *Granny made me eat fish*), we will see two main differences. First, *make* implies, as it were, "subjective necessity": the causee thinks "I have to do it," whereas *force* implies "objective necessity": the causee had to do it. Second, *force* implies that the causee thinks "I don't want to do it," whereas in the case of *make*, there is no such implication; rather, the causee thinks "I have to do it."

6.1.5. *Interim conclusion*

As we have seen, English has a broad spectrum of causative constructions available for talking about one person wanting another person to do something. These constructions distinguish between various conceptual scenarios that have not been similarly differentiated in other languages. The cultural elaboration of the area of interpersonal causation manifests itself both in the English lexicon and in English grammar. I examined the lexical elaboration of interpersonal causation in detail in my 1987 *English Speech Act Verbs: A Semantic Dictionary*. In this chapter, I have looked at only the lexical verb *to force*, which does have semantic equivalents in many other languages. In contrast to *force*, the verbs *get*, *have*, and *make* act as auxiliary verbs in English grammar. For example, although they appear to take a direct object (the causee), they do not passivize, at least not straightforwardly, as the following contrasts show:

    a. John forced Mary to do it.
    b. Mary was forced by John to do it.
    a. John got Mary to do it.
    b. *Mary was got by John to do it.
    a. John had Mary do it.
    b. *Mary was had by John to do it.
    a. John made Mary do it.
    b. *Mary was made by John do it.
    (Compare: Mary was made by John to do it.)[2]

All these auxiliaries focus on the precise relationship between the person who wants someone else to do something and the person who is doing it, and on the pressure applied by one person on the other. The cultural elaboration of this theme in the area of causative constructions parallels its elaboration in the area of "directives," that is, various conventional substitutes for the straight imperative (see chapter 2). The great cultural importance of this theme also finds its expression in the area of causative constructions and expressions based on another auxiliary verb, *let*—the most important one of all, to which we now turn.

6.2. The English "Let"-Constructions and the Cultural Ideal of "Noninterference"

6.2.1. *Introduction*

The verb *let* plays an extremely important role in the field of English causatives. A whole family of different constructions (or, if one prefers, subconstructions) are based on it. All these subconstructions appear to share a common theme that could be articulated as follows:

X let Y do Z. =
a. X knew that if X didn't do (say) something to Y
   Y would do Z
b. at the same time X knew that if X did (said) something to Y
   Y would not do Z
c. X didn't do (say) anything to Y
d. Y did Z

Given the existence of this common theme, it may seem unnecessary to list any subconstructions or subtypes of the *let*-construction at all, beyond noting that there are two variants of this construction, one with *do* and one with *happen* ("X let Y do Z" or "X let Z happen to Y"), and also that the causee Y can be either a person (or an animal) or a thing. But a description of this kind would not have full predictive power and thus would be inferior to one that recognizes the whole family of *let*-subconstructions, which have a common semantic theme but many differences, too—differences that are not fully predictable from the context or from the lexical meaning of the verb.

For mnemonic purposes, we can distinguish the different types of the *let*-construction by means of labels such as "permission," "noninterruption," "indifference," "nonprevention," "nonintervention," "negligence," and "tolerance," but these are not expected to have much predictive power or explanatory value by themselves. To see what the differences really are, we need not labels but explications.

In this part of chapter 6, I examine in some detail a range of English causative constructions and expressions based on the verb *let*. (For a more comprehensive discussion, see Wierzbicka 2002b.) To get a better perspective on *let*, however, I will first examine a parallel from German, based on the causative auxiliary *lassen*.

6.2.2. *The German* lassen-*constructions*

German has a number of causative constructions based on the auxiliary verb *lassen*. In this section, I consider only the use of *lassen* in combination with a human causee and a verb of intentional action, according to the schematic formula:

Someone (X) *ließ* someone else (Y) do something.

In different contexts, the *lassen*-construction is best translated into English with different constructions, based on the verbs *make*, *have*, *get*, *cause*, or *let*, but as this very fact shows, it cannot be semantically equated with any one of these constructions. For example:

Ich	habe	mir	Bleistift	und	neues	Papier	geben	lassen.
I	have	to-me	pencil	and	new	paper	to give	let/have

(Speer 1975, 19)
"I have asked for a pencil and new paper."

The verb *lassen* does not mean "ask for," but how else can one render in English the meaning of the phrase *geben lassen* when it refers (as in this case) to a request from a prisoner to the prison authorities? Clearly, the prisoner can neither "make" the guards give him new writing paper nor "have" them give it to him. He could perhaps "get" them to do it, but by translating *lassen* as *get* we would significantly distort the meaning of the original sentence, for "getting someone to do something" implies something like overcoming some actual or potential unwillingness on the part of the causee, and there is no trace of this in the German sentence.

In this example, then, and also in the following one, the best translation might be one relying on speech act verbs such as *ask for* or *request* rather than on any general causatives:

> Vom Doktor eine Schlaftablette geben lassen. (Speer 1975, 44)
> from doctor one sleeping.tablet to give let/have/make/get
> "[to ask] the doctor for a sleeping tablet (and get one)." [A note in a diary]

But a translation based on the verb *ask for* or *request* is not accurate either, for it doesn't convey the idea that the request was effective.

Consider also the following sentence:

> Im Anschluß an seinen Monolog drückte Hitler auf den Klingelknopf und
> ließ Bormann kommen. (Speer 1975, 101)
> "Having completed his monologue Hitler pressed the bell and [thus]
> summoned Bormann."

In this case, the speech act verbs *ask for* and *request* are inappropriate, and *summon* is much more suitable; but clearly, *summon* brings with it presuppositions that are absent from the earlier two examples.

In the following example, in which the causee is the causer's personal assistant, the English *have*-construction seems to fit the context best:

> Im Jahre 1938 hatte er [Streicher] ihm durch seinen persönlichen
> Adjutanten zum Geburtstag demonstrativ einen großen Distelstrauß
> überreichen lassen. (Speer 1975, 173)
> "In 1938, Streicher [Gauleiter of Nuremberg] had his personal assistant
> deliver to him [Leibel, mayor of Nuremberg] on his birthday, demonstra-
> tively, a large bunch of thistles."

As we have seen then, the range of the *lassen*-causative is so broad that it can accommodate requests from a prisoner to the prison authorities, instructions from a district chief to his assistant, and orders from a dictator to his underlings. There is no causative verb or construction in English that would fit a range of relations as broad as that.

> Ich ließ die Studenten eher nach Hause gehen, weil ich krank war.
> a. I let the students go home earlier because I was sick.
> b. I "had" the students go home earlier because I was sick
>   (i.e., I sent the students home earlier because I was sick).

As these glosses indicate, from an English speaker's point of view, the German sentence has two distinct interpretations, which can be roughly identified by means of the causatives *let* and *have*. On the (a) interpretation (*let*), it is assumed that the students wanted to go home earlier and that the teacher yielded to the students' wishes.

On the (b) interpretation, however, it is assumed that the teacher wanted the students to go home earlier and that she simply acted on her own "want" (without considering the students' wishes at all).

If we interpreted the German sentence through the prism of the English language, we would say that it is ambiguous, and we would have to assign to it two alternative interpretations. From a German point of view, however, the sentence is not ambiguous, and the question whether the students wanted to go home or not simply doesn't arise. What matters is that the students' earlier departure would have happened because of something that the teacher did and also that the teacher was aware of this causal link between her own action and the students' action. More precisely, this can be represented as follows:

    a. X (the teacher) did (said) something (W)
    b. because X did (said) this, Y (the students) did Z (went home early)
    c. X knew that if X did (said) this, Y would do Z

We must conclude, then, that the semantic invariant of the *lassen*-construction (with a human causee and a verb of action) includes only the three components postulated here—(a) X did (said) something (W), (b) because of this Y did something (Z), (c) X knew that if X did W, Y would do Z—and does not include any references to either the causee's or the causer's wanting.

6.2.3. *The English* let-*constructions*

6.2.3.1. INTRODUCTION

The common theme of English *let*-constructions articulated in section 6.2.1 is different from the common theme behind the German *lassen*-constructions. As we have seen in the preceding section, the German *lassen*-construction implies that the causer *did* something, whereas *let*-constructions imply, generally speaking, that the causer did *not* do anything. In some situations, a person's behavior can be interpreted as either a case of "doing something" or as a case of "not doing something," and in such situations both *let* and *lassen* can be used, for example:

    a. Mary let the children watch television.
    b. Mary ließ die Kinder fernsehen.

Sentence (a) implies that Mary didn't stop the children from watching the television, whereas (b) implies that she allowed, or even instructed, them to do so. When the difference between "letting" (not stopping) and "allowing" (giving a nod) is only a matter of interpretation, both *let* and *allow* can be used in English, and *lassen* can be used in German. When, however, the situation can be construed only in terms of "doing something" rather than "not doing something," *let* cannot be used at all, whereas *lassen* can. For example, in the sentence in which Hitler "summoned" Bormann by pressing a bell, *lassen* can be used but *let* could not.

Generally speaking, then, the common theme of English *let*-constructions involves the idea of "refraining from doing something" and, in the case of human causees on which this chapter focuses, the notion of "refraining from doing something to other people"—a notion that I suggest has a great deal of cultural significance. By grammaticalizing this notion in a variety of *let*-constructions. English grammar suggests, so to speak, that it may be important at times to refrain from doing anything to other people—a suggestion highly consonant with the modern Anglo ethos of "noninterference," "nonimposition," and "negative freedom" (see I. Berlin 1969; Wierzbicka 1997, chapter 3). Often, "letting someone do what they want to do" involves saying something that amounts to giving them permission to do so, but although I have called the construction in question "the *let* of permission," the *let*-construction differs in this respect from speech act verbs like *permit*: to *permit* someone to do something, one has to say something, whereas to *let* them do what they want to do, one doesn't have to do anything.

In some situations, "letting someone do something" may seem to imply doing something physically rather than "not doing anything," but if so, then the implication is deduced from the context rather than from the meaning of *let*. For example, if person X is holding person Y tightly by the wrists and thus preventing Y from going somewhere, Y may beg X: "Let me go!" and expect that X will do something (take her hands off Y's wrists). The sentence doesn't *mean*, however, that X should take her hands off Y's wrists but rather that she shouldn't prevent Y from going: taking her hands off Y's wrists is a *situational* requirement, independent of the meaning of the sentence as such. The sentence *Let me go!* is different in this respect from the expression *Let go!*, which does encode in its meaning the idea of doing something (physically, not by speech): taking one's hands (or some other body parts) off someone or something.

I will not discuss here *let*-constructions with an inanimate causee, such as, for example, "He let the vegetables rot"; note, however, that although these don't share the full theme of "refraining from doing something to other people," they, too, reflect an interest in the significance of "people *not doing* something (rather than *doing* something)." I return to this point in the last section of the chapter.

Anticipating the discussion in the final sections of this chapter (6.2.3.4–6.2.3.8), I will also mention another important theme emerging from the examination of different *let*-constructions: the theme of "cooperation," visible in constructions such as "let's do Z," "let me know/see/have a look," or "let me propose/suggest/conclude." The two themes (roughly, "noninterference" and "cooperation") are related because, as we will see later, the main concern of the "cooperative" *let*-constructions is how to "cooperate" while acknowledging the rights of the addressee as an autonomous and free individual, on an equal footing with the speaker.

6.2.3.2. LET OF "PERMISSION"

Example:

> She let him go to the party (once). (Compare "She allowed him to go to the party").

In this subconstruction, one person (X) "lets" another person (Y) do something of the kind that can be done only intentionally. Verbs of "happening" (such as *fall* or *trip*) are not included, and neither are verbs of "involuntary action" (such as *moan* or *giggle*).

The semantic conditions on the "*let* of permission" are as follows: (a) the causer knows that the causee wants to do something and will do it if he or she only can; (b) the causer knows that he or she can prevent the causee from doing it (e.g., by saying "I don't want you to do this" or something to that effect) and that the causee knows it; (c) the causer refrains from doing so; (d) the causer's nonaction is intentional; (e) because of the causer's intentional nonaction, the causee can do what he or she wants to do; (f) and after this the causee does it. Unlike the case of the verb *permit* (X permitted Y to do Z), the causer doesn't have to *say* anything; what matters is that the causer intentionally refrains from saying "No" and that because of this the causee can (and does) proceed.

Person X let person Y do Z (once). =
a. X knew that Y wanted to do Z
b. X knew that if X didn't say anything about this to Y, Y would do it
c. at the same time X knew that if X said to Y: "I don't want you to do this"
   Y could not do it
d. X didn't say anything like this to Y
e. because X didn't say anything like this to Y, Y could do Z
f. Y did Z

What this explication shows is that, from the speaker's point of view, person X enabled person Y to do what Y wanted to do by refraining from interfering with Y's actions.

Let us now compare, in the light of this discussion, two superficially similar sentences, one English and one German:

(a) Mary let John come (go).
(b) *Mary ließ John kommen (gehen).*

On the face of it, we have here two analogous constructions, and given that dictionaries treat *let* and *lassen* as translation equivalents, the meaning of A and B could be expected to be the same. But the use of NSM explications allows us to show precisely in what way the meaning is not the same: in A, we know that it was John who wanted to come (or go), and Mary didn't do anything to prevent him, whereas in B we don't know what John wanted, but we do know that Mary did (said) something, knowing that if she did, John would come (or go), and that John came (or went) because Mary had done it.

Thus, the English construction (in contrast to the German one) encodes the idea of refraining from doing something to another person—and thus enabling this person to do what she or he wants to do, highlighting in this a major Anglo cultural theme.

To see that the general theme of "refraining from doing something to other people" is a modern development in English, consider the following examples of *let*-sentences from earlier epochs (from the OED):

(a) He let make a proclamation throughout all his Empire. (c. 1440)
(b) On my arrival at her house I was not let to wait long. (1781)

In (a), the king clearly does something, rather than refraining from doing anything, so that the proclamation is made through all his empire. In contemporary English, *let* could not be used in this way. In some (but by no means all) comparable contexts, a *have* causative could be used instead.

In sentence (b), *let* is also used to imply action rather than inaction, and so the sentence could not be used in present-day English. The closest present-day counterpart would be "I was not made to wait long," but this would introduce the idea that "I had to wait," absent from the older use of *let*.

The OED lists these examples under the heading "To cause," which it treats as a separate meaning, alongside a supposed meaning described as "Not to prevent; to suffer, permit, allow." This latter (supposed) meaning is illustrated with examples such as the following ones:

    c. Ye Kyng gave him fair words, and let him depart home. (1548)
    d. Your son Thomas will not let us work at all. (1602)

However, there are no compelling reasons to posit polysemy here: all the examples given, including (a), (b), (c), and (d) cited here, lend themselves to a unitary interpretation in terms of the causer "doing something," which in fact is rather similar to the use of the causative *lassen* in German discussed earlier. (On the use of *let* in Middle English and in earlier Modern English, see, e.g., Fischer 1992; Visser 1973).

6.2.3.3. *LET* OF "TOLERANCE"

Examples:

    Let her be!

    Live and let live!

    Let me finish!

    Let her do as she pleases.

The "*let* of tolerance" is normally (or at least typically) used in the imperative: it would be unusual to say, for example,

    ?He let her be.

    ??She let him live.

Let be and *let live* could be regarded as frozen expressions, and verbs other than *be* and *live* can be used in a wider range of forms (not necessarily in the imperative) to produce the "*let* of tolerance" effect, but normally they, too, require some modals or at least some speech act verbs implying "want" or "can (cannot)," for example:

    You've got to let her make her own mistakes.

    He vowed to let her make her own mistakes.

    ?He let her make her own mistakes.

    ?Yesterday he let her make her own mistakes.

What the "*let* of tolerance" pattern does is acknowledge a certain ideology, roughly speaking, the ideology of tolerance, and so it is normally not used for purely factual statements. For example, the sentence "Let me finish!" implies not only a desire not to be interrupted but also a hint of disagreement: "you may not like or agree with what I am saying, but nonetheless you've got to let me finish."

Similarly, the sentence *Let her be!* hints at a possible disapproval of whatever the person referred to is or is not doing. Nonetheless, disapproval or not, this person, too, deserves some tolerance. The phrase *Let her (him, etc.) be!* is different in this respect from the apparently similar-in-meaning phrase *Leave her (him, etc.) alone!* Both convey, roughly speaking, the message "Don't do this to her any more; she doesn't want this," but in addition, the first, in contrast to the second, implies that the addressee should desist even if there *are* some possible grounds for disapproval. For example, if X is tormenting Y out of sheer cruelty and malice, one would say to X *Leave her alone!* rather than *Let her be!* On the other hand, if Y is doing something that the speaker slightly disapproves of but doesn't want to oppose (acknowledging Y's right to decide for herself whether she wants to do it), then *Let her be!* can be seen as more appropriate. (In the following formula and in the subsequent ones, I have used prime marks to draw attention to the added semantic components, and lines, to the subtracted ones.)

> *Let her be! (Let her make her own mistakes!)* =
> a. you know that Y wants to do Z
> a'. maybe you think that if Y does Z it will be bad
> b. you think that if you don't do anything to Y, Y will do Z
> c. at the same time you think that if you do (say) something to Y, Y will not do Z
> d. I say: it will not be good if you do (say) something to Y
> d'. it will be good if you don't do (say) anything to Y
> d". you know that when a person wants to do something
>   it is not good if other people say to this person "you can't do it"
> e. _____
> f. _____

One thing that clearly distinguishes this formula from the others is the component labeled here a' ("maybe you think that if this person (Y) does this (Z) it will be bad"), which can be regarded as a hallmark of tolerance: the ideal embedded in the word *tolerance* requires that we will not try to stop other people from doing what they want to do, even if we think that is not good (as long as it is not bad for other people).

Another distinguishing feature of the present type, also related to the ideal of tolerance, is a hint of disapproval from the speaker for the addressee, reflected in the component "it will not be good if you do something to Y (because you think these things)," and also the admonition related to it: "you know that when a person wants to do something it is not good if other people say to this person 'you can't do it.'"

All in all, it can be said that the "*let* of tolerance" incorporates in its very meaning an important Anglo cultural script and thus provides further evidence for the validity of this script in contemporary Anglo culture. In a sense, the whole family of modern *let*-constructions discussed here provides evidence for Anglo cultural scripts (of "autonomy," "noninterference," and so on), but the "*let* of tolerance" construction does so in an especially striking way, because it not only *serves* a particular cultural norm but also in fact *articulates* its very meaning.

6.2.3.4. *LET* OF "SHARED INFORMATION"

In some cases, a *let*-construction can also refer to an intended result of the causer's action. One case in point is the expression *let (someone) know*, similar in meaning to *inform* but sharing some components with the other *let* types discussed here. Typically, *let know* is used in the imperative, interrogative, or hypothetical, rather than the indicative mood:

> Let me know (what happened).
>
> Did you let her know?
>
> It would be good to let them know.

The *let know* expression, although superficially similar in meaning to *inform*, can perhaps be seen as reflecting the cultural assumption enshrined in modern Anglo culture that it is natural for people to want to know all sorts of things and that in principle people have the right to have their questions answered (except for so-called personal questions, which shouldn't be asked in the first place; see Eades 1982). By the same token, telling people something that they want to know can be seen as simply not preventing them from knowing it (i.e., not withholding information).

Looked at from this perspective, the *let know* expression, although implying action, can be seen as a natural extension of the *let*-construction of "inaction." According to the *The Oxford English Dictionary* (1989), *let* in the sense of "cause" is archaic in English and has survived only in the expression "let someone know." It is certainly true that in Middle English *let* could be used in the sense of "positive causation," as *lassen* can be used in contemporary German (see section 2). But this doesn't prove that the expression *let me know*, as used in contemporary English, is an archaism rather than an innovation.

In Shakespeare's English, *let* could indeed be combined with *know*, but not in the sense in which these words are combined in the modern expression *let me know*, as the following example (from OED) illustrates:

> If your name is Horatio, as I am let to know it is. (1602)

Here, "to let to know" means something close to "to tell" or, as the OED puts it, "to inform." In some nineteenth-century examples quoted by the OED as examples of the same sense of *let*, *let know* means in fact something closer to "to give to understand," for example:

> There was always some body of Churchmen which disliked them, and took every opportunity of letting them know it. (1883)

But the present-day expression *let me know* (and its variants, such as "could you let me know") has a distinct meaning implying cooperation among autonomous individuals, a meaning incompatible with contexts like that in the 1883 example. In fact, even sentences with the imperative *let me know* such as the following one from Shakespeare:

> What is the end of study, let me know.

sound odd to present-day speakers of English, because they do not conform to the present-day meaning of the "let me know" construction. In this sentence, *let me know* implies something like "tell me," but in contemporary English *let me know* doesn't mean "tell me," and in particular, it cannot apply to something that the addressee knows now (as in "let me know what your name is"). *Let me know* implies that when you know something in the future, I want you to share this knowledge with me (and not withhold it from me) and that I assume you will do it, not because you will have to do it but because you will be willing to do it, in the spirit of cooperation between autonomous persons.

> *let me know* (compare "tell me") =
> a. I want to know something (Z)
> a'. I think that you will know it some time after this time (i.e., later)
> b. I think that you know that if you don't say it to me I will not know it
> c. at the same time you know that if you say it to me I will know it
> d. I think that you will not say "I don't want to do it"
> d'. I know that you don't have to do it
> d". I think that you will do it because you will want to do it
> e. after this I will know it

In further support of this analysis, I would note that it is not true that *let know* is the only "causative *let*-expression" in contemporary English, as the OED implies. There are other expressions, especially "imperative" ones, that can be seen as expressing "causation by action," and these may throw some light on the meaning and cultural role of the expression *let know*, as it is used in modern English. Consider, for example, the following sentences:

> Let me have a look.
>
> Let me see it.
>
> Let me have a copy.

What sentences of this kind do is convey a directive without apparently "imposing." They sound as if the speaker were only asking the addressee for permission to do something, whereas in fact the addressee is also required to do something. A straight imperative or an overt *I want*-sentence could seem, in a similar situation, an act of forceful self-assertion and imposition:

> I want to have a look.
>
> I want to see it.
>
> Show it to me.
>
> Give me a copy.

The *let*-construction—rather like a whimperative (see Wierzbicka 1991/2003)— allows the speaker to avoid giving such an impression.

It could be said that the *let*-construction under consideration is the only one in which the causer is actually required to *do* something. In fact, however, the emphasis is not on "doing" but on "knowing": the way the speaker presents the request suggests that its goal is the sharing of information. This is why it would be unusual to use the *let*-construction when asking for food or other material things unrelated to knowledge:

?Let me have a pencil/an apple/ten dollars.

In the Cobuild corpus there are (at the time of writing) 38 imperative sentences of the form "let me have [a Noun]," and of these not a single one requests a physical object other than a written document (a catalogue, a leaflet, or some other potential source of information). Although there are a few apparent exceptions, they are more apparent than real. In particular, sentences with the word *my* in the object phrase suggest that the speaker is demanding access to an object (often, his or her own property) rather than asking for it. One example:

She sobbed, a cry of more than physical pain. 'Please, let me have my needle.'
'Not until you tell me what you did with my baby.'

The expression *let me have a copy* (of your article) is sayable (as a request) because it can be construed as a request for information (I want to read the article). The assumption is that the addressee can be expected to be willing to give the speaker access to some information.

Let me have a copy =
    a. I want to have something (Z) because I want to know some things (W)
    a'. I know that you can know these things
    b. I know that if you don't do something I will not have Z
    c. at the same time I know that if you do something I can have it
    d. I think that you will not say: "I don't want to do it"
    d'. I know that you don't have to do it
    d". I think that you will do it because you will want to do it
    e. after this I will have Z
    f. because of this I will know W

As this explication suggests, the speaker is not saying (even implicitly), "I want you to do it—I think that you will do it because of this," which could sound hectoring and "imposing." Rather, he or she is saying (implicitly), "I want to have something because I want to know something," "I know that if you do something I will have it," plus "I think that you will not say: I don't want to do it," thus indicating that he or she is counting on the addressee's cooperation, while politely acknowledging the addressee's right to prevent the speaker from getting access to the desired information.

6.2.3.5. LET ME DO Z FOR YOU (OFFERING TO
PERFORM A SERVICE)

Example:

Here—let me open the door for you." (Malouf 1985, 19)

English has a common conversational routine in which the speaker proposes to perform some small service for the addressee and in doing so verbally goes through the motions of asking for the addressee's permission. The speaker is not really asking for permission and is not anticipating any opposition, yet symbolically at least he or she is giving the addressee a chance to decline the offer and in this way is acknowledging the addressee's autonomy and right to do things for herself or himself.

A sentence like *let me open the door for you* sounds more "polite" in English than its counterpart that simply declares the speaker's intention ("I will open the door for you" or "I want to open the door for you"). The "let me do X for you" routine does not apply to future situations and future actions but only to present ones, and it is normally restricted to doing something that otherwise the addressee would need to do and would "have trouble" doing. For example, sentences such as:

> Let me carry it for you.
>
> Let me write it down for you.

can refer only to the immediate situation, as the infelicity of the following sentences shows:

> ?Let me carry it for you tomorrow.
>
> ?Let me write it down for you when I find it.

But just sparing the addressee the trouble of doing something by doing it oneself is not enough for the *let*-routine under discussion to be felicitous. For example, it is appropriate for the host to say (a) but not (b) to a guest who is about to leave:

> (a) Let me open the door for you.
> (b) ?Let me close the door for you.

If the host doesn't do anything, the guest will have to first open the door and then close it (from the other side), so it would seem that the host has two ways of sparing the guest a bit of trouble: either by opening the door before the guest leaves or by closing it afterward. But the "let me do X for you" routine is appropriate only in the former case.

One reason seems to be that the speaker wants to do something that will be "good for the addressee," and it is good for the addressee to have the door opened, so that he or she can leave. On the other hand, having the door closed is something that is good for the host, not for the guest—and so the "let me do X for you" routine is not appropriate.

This is still not the whole story, however, and the missing aspect is highlighted by the common phrase *Let me help you*. As this phrase suggests, what the speaker is trying to be seen as doing is cooperating with the addressee rather than doing the addressee a favor: the assumption is that the addressee has a goal and that the speaker wants to be given the green light to assist the addressee in achieving that goal. For example, if the addressee is leaving, I can assist him or her by opening the door, but not by closing the door, for having the door closed is not instrumental in the addressee's overall goal of leaving, whereas having the door open is instrumental. This leads us to the following explication:

Let me do Z for you. =
  a. I say: I want to do something good (Z) for you now
  a'. I know that you want to do something now
  a". because I know this I think that it will be good for you if I do Z now
  b. I want you to know that if you don't say "I don't want you to do it" I will do it
  c. at the same time I know that if you say it I can't do it
  d. I think that you will not say it
  e. because you will not say it I will know that I can do it
  f. I will do it now

6.2.3.6. *LET'S* DO Z!

Examples:

Let's go. Let's do it. Yes, let's.

The expression *let's* (contracted from *let us*) differs in meaning, as well as in register, from the somewhat archaic or elevated *let us* (e.g., *Let us remember! Let us pray*). Roughly speaking, *let us* assumes authority and expects compliance; by contrast, *let's* envisages a joint action that is based on consensus and cannot proceed if any of the prospective participants voices any objections to it, and so it implies an egalitarian rather than authoritarian attitude.

The archaic *Let us do Z!* construction implies that the speaker, who is a member of a group, wants the group to do something and assumes that if he or she voices this, the group as a whole will comply. More precisely:

Let us pray! (*Let us remember!*) [*archaic:* "guidance"] =
  a' I think that it will be good if we do Z
  a I say: I want us to do it
  f' I think that because I say this it will happen

Presumably, the construction seems dated partly because its meaning is inconsistent with the modern Anglo democratic ethos: normally, it is no longer expected that groups will "follow the leader" and do some things simply because of what the leader thinks and wants.

On the other hand, the common modern *Let's do Z!* construction reflects a different ethos: an ethos valuing voluntary cooperation of free and equal individuals. The construction *Let's do Z!* shares with the *Let us do Z!*-construction two components: "I want us to do Z" and "I think it will be good if we do Z." It adds to it, however, two further "addressee-oriented" components: "I think that you will say 'I want the same'" and "I know that if you say: 'I don't want the same' we can't do it." It also expresses the speaker's confidence in the addressee's cooperation: "I think that you will not say this." Thus:[3]

Let's do Z! ["suggestion"] =
  a'. I think that it will be good if we do Z now
  a. I say: I want us to do it

    a". I think that you will say "I want the same"
    b. I know that if you say it it will happen
    c. at the same time I know that if you say "I don't want it to happen" it
       can't happen
    d. I think that you will not say it
    e. _____
    f. _____

6.2.3.7. *LET* OF COOPERATIVE DIALOGUE

Examples:

> Let me conclude by saying. . . .
>
> Let me explain/suggest/assure you. . . .
>
> Let me start by saying this. . . .
>
> Let me propose a toast for. . . .
>
> Let me ask you. . . .
>
> *Let me order you. . . . (Compare I order you. . . .)
>
> ?Let me beg you. . . . (Compare I beg you. . . .)

The formula "Let me Verb" normally includes a verb of speech (Vsay) or a verb that can at least be interpreted as such, as a verb of sequence (e.g., Let me start with . . ; let me now turn to . . .).

Clearly, the most obvious semantic component of the "let me Vsay" construction is "I want to say something." At the same time, however, the speaker signals his or her wish to involve the addressee in the speech act and to acknowledge the addressee's (real or imaginary) presence and rights as a participant in the communication process. More precisely, the semantic structure linked with this formula can be spelled out as follows:

Let me conclude. =
    a. I say: I want to say something (Z) now
    b. I want you to know that if you don't say: "I don't want it to happen"
       I will say this thing
    c. I know that if you say it I can't do it
    d. I think that you will not say it
    e. because I think that you will not say it I think that I can do it
    f. I will do it now

Again, Shakespearean sentences like

> Let me ask my sister pardon.
>
> Let me entreat you.

sound odd to a modern ear, because they do not conform to the cultural logic underlying the present-day array of *let*-constructions: *let me ask you* would be acceptable because it would comply with the principles of nonimposition and cooperation between the speaker and the addressee, but *let me ask my sister pardon* does not have the same justification and sounds odd.

The sentence "let me entreat you" does involve interaction between the speaker and the addressee, but it also sounds odd, and not only because *entreat* is now an archaic word. *Let me beg you* would also sound odd, although *I beg you* is still quite acceptable, as is also *let me suggest* or *let me explain*. Here, the reason for the incongruity lies in the inequality between the speaker and the addressee, implied by the verb *beg*, and the implication of "equal rights" of the interlocutors, implied by the "let me Vsay" construction. (Compare also *let me ask you* vs. **let me order you*).

Both from a formal and a semantic point of view, there is a similarity between sentences like *Let me explain* and those like *Let me finish* discussed earlier. But in the case of *Let me finish*, there is a real danger that the addressee may try to prevent the speaker from having his or her say. In the case of *Let me explain*, however, there is no such danger, and there is no implicit appeal to people's right to do what they want to do and say what they want to say.

Of course the expression "let me Verb" is only a formula, one might even say an "empty formula"—a conventional speech routine. But formulae of this kind are seldom really "empty." Even if the speaker doesn't "mean" what the formula conveys, this fact cannot detract from the significance of the ritual reenacted each time a formula of this kind is used (see Ameka 1987, 1994, 1999).

The fact that one doesn't say in English *let me go now* or *let me have a cup of tea* to announce one's intention of doing something, whereas one does say *let me explain* or *let me propose* requires an explanation. My explanation is that in the case of speech acts the speaker's action affects the addressee, and so the formula "let me Vsay" implicitly acknowledges the addressee's rights in the speech situation. This explanation is consistent with the explanation I have proposed for a wide range of other phenomena, such as, above all, the wealth of whimperatives in contemporary English (see chapter 2). It is also consistent with the fact that one can say *let me suggest* or *let me ask* but not **let me order you* or **let me beg you*: the addressee's rights are acknowledged if the addressee is seen as an equal, not as someone below or above the speaker.

6.2.3.8. LET OF COOPERATIVE INTERACTION

Consider the following three sentences:

Let me talk to him.

Let me get back to you on this.

*Let me apologize to her.

Why is it that the first two sentences are fully acceptable, whereas the third one sounds odd? The reason seems clear: the first two can be construed as referring to "cooperative interaction" between the speaker and the addressee, whereas the third one cannot be so construed because it concerns the relationship between the speaker and a third party and has nothing to do with the addressee. In the first sentence, the addressee is not mentioned either, but it is easy to construe the talking to a third party as involving some matter of joint concern to the speaker and the addressee. Thus, what is relevant in the present construction is, first, that the speaker and the addressee have a shared goal (they both want the same thing to happen); second, that the speaker offers to do something to bring this goal about; third, that the speaker is going to proceed only if the addressee does not object; and, fourth, that the speaker assumes that the addressee will not object.

> *Let me get back to you on this* =
> a'. I know that you want something to happen
> a". I know that I want the same thing to happen
> a. because I know this I think that it will be good if I do something
> a'''. I say: I want to do something (Z)
> b. I want you to know that if you don't say: "I don't want you to do it" I will do it
> c. at the same time I know that if you say it I can't do it
> d. I think that you will not say it
> e. _____
> f. _____

6.2.3.9. *LET* OF COOPERATIVE THINKING

The *let* of cooperative thinking, which could also be called "*let* of deliberation," can be illustrated with the following examples:

> Let me see . . . (*Let you see . . .)
>
> Let me think . . .

Since thinking is, above all, an individual rather than social activity, it may seem odd that verbs of thinking occur in the frame "let me V" at all: if I want to think, nobody could stop me, and my thinking doesn't require other people's cooperation. When, however, sentences like "Let me see . . ." or "Let me think . . ." are seen against the background of the "*let* of cooperative interaction" and, especially, the "*let* of cooperative dialogue," their function becomes clear: they imply, so to speak, a request for an interruption in our ongoing interaction (so that the speaker can think for a while), and because such an interruption would affect not only the speaker but also the addressee, it does make sense for the speaker to ask for the addressee's "cooperation." As in the case of the "*let* of cooperative dialogue," such a request can be regarded as a pseudorequest, simply enacting a certain conventional conversational routine. But, as noted earlier, conventional conversational routines reflect culturally important attitudes and assumptions about social interaction.

> *Let me see . . .* =
> a. I say: I want to think about it for some time now
> b. I want you to know that if you don't say: "I don't want you to do it" I will do it
> c. I know that if you say it I can't do it
> d. I think that you will not say it

e. because I think that you will not say it I can do it

f. I'm doing it now

6.2.4. A comparative glance at Russian

The extraordinary wealth of sentence types based on *let* in modern English points to one of the cultural preoccupations of modern Anglo culture. As Matsumoto (1988, 404) observed, Anglo culture assigns a key role to "the want of every 'competent adult member' that his actions be unimpeded by others" (Matsumoto is quoting here Brown and Levinson 1987, 67) and "his freedom of action unhindered and his attention unimpeded" (Brown and Levinson 1987, 134). Matsumoto argues, convincingly, that Anglo theorists in general, and Brown and Levinson in particular, have mistakenly attributed to these concerns a universal significance. The story of *let* is linked, I believe, with the story of such cultural preoccupations, reflected in Anglo conversational norms (see Wierzbicka 1985, 1991/2003a) and with the role of concepts like 'freedom', 'tolerance', and 'noninterference' in English discourse (see Wierzbicka 1997, chapter 3).

For example, it is surely not an accident that most of the *let*-constructions identified here for English have no counterparts in either German or Russian and that in fact many of the *let*-sentences adduced in this chapter cannot be translated idiomatically into either German (see section 6.2.2) or Russian.

Thus, the closest Russian counterpart of the English *let*-family is the family of causatives based on the verb *dat'*, literally, "to give" (for a detailed study of *dat'*-constructions in modern Russian, see Podleskaya 2004). But the range of the *dat'*-family in Russian is much more restricted than that of the *let*-family in English. Only a few of the types identified here for English could be translated into Russian by means of a *dat'* causative, and those that could—like for example the "*let* of noninterruption"—would by and large be limited (except for contrastive uses) to modally qualified predicates, and especially to negative or imperative uses. For example:

Ona   ne dala emu   spat'.
she.*nom neg* gave him.*dat* sleep.*inf*
"*She didn't let him sleep.*"

Daj   emu spat'.
give.*imp* him sleep.*inf*
"Let him sleep."

?Ona   dala   emu   spat'.
she.*nom* give.3sg.*past* him.*dat* sleep.*inf*
"She let him sleep."

Furthermore, one could hardly use a *dat'*-construction to translate a sentence of the "*let* of nonprevention" type:

She let him fall.

?Ona dala emu upast'.

although, again, a negative sentence would sound better:

Ona ne dala emu upast'.

She didn't let him fall.

By and large, the same applies to the "*let* of tolerance" type. The exact meaning of a sentence like *Let her be!* cannot be expressed in Russian at all, the closest approximation being *Ostav' ee* "leave her (alone)." As mentioned earlier, however, *Leave her alone!* doesn't mean the same as *Let her be!* and doesn't appeal to a general ideology of tolerance.

Similarly untranslatable is the general slogan *Live and let live!* although a negative declarative sentence meant as a complaint or criticism is possible:

Ona mne   žit'   ne daet.
she me.*dat* live.*inf* neg gives.*3sg.pres*
"She doesn't let me live."

The "*let* of intentional interpersonal causation" does have a counterpart in Russian but one restricted to agentive verbs like *posmotret'* ("to look") or *poslušat'* ("to listen") and excluding nonagentive verbs like *znat'* ("to know") or *videt'* ("to see"):

Daj   mne   posmotret'/poslušat'.
give.*imp* me.*dat* look.inf/listen.*inf*
"Let me have a look/listen."

On the other hand, sentences like *Let me know, Let me see,* or *Let me have a copy* cannot be exactly translated into Russian at all (although the sentence *daj mne znat'* does have a restricted use as an idiomatic expression, not equivalent to *let me know*). The closest one could do is to use an imperative: *skaži,* "tell (me)" or *pokaži,* "show (me)," or *daj,* "give (me)." Of course, a straight imperative doesn't have the same "tactful" and "nonimposing" connotations as expressions like *let me know* or *let me see* do:

*Daj   mne   videt'.
give.*imp.pl* me.*dat.pl* see.*inf*

Nor could one use a *dat'*-construction to offer to perform a service, as in the English sentence *let me open the door for you.*

?Daj   mne   otkryt'   tebe   dver'.
give.*imp* me.*dat* open.*inf* you.*dat* door.*acc*

The closest one could do would be to use the verb *razrešit'* (or *pozvolit'*), "to allow" (with a "polite" plural form), thus substituting lexical for grammatical means:

Razrešite   mne   otkryt'   vam   dver'.
allow.*imp.pl* me.*dat* open.*inf* you.*dat.pl* door.*acc*
"Allow me to open the door for you."

Nor could one render in Russian the exact sense and tone of English sentences like "let me explain . . . ," "let me assure you . . . ," or "let me propose a toast to . . ." In Russian, in corresponding situations one would simply say *ja xoču . . .* ("I want . . .").

One generalization that suggests itself very strongly on the basis of a comparison of the English *let*-constructions and the Russian *dat'*-constructions is that the English constructions reflect the general theme of "negative freedom" (that is, roughly, noninterference), so characteristic of modern Anglo culture (see I. Berlin 1969; Wierzbicka 1997, chapter 3), whereas the Russian *dat'*-constructions do not reflect any such theme. The *let* family implies, roughly speaking, "not doing something," whereas the *dat'* family (in accordance with the basic lexical meaning of *dat'*) implies "doing something." Consider, for example, the following sentences:

Maša   dala Petru   počitat' svoj   dnevnik.
Mary.*nom* gave Peter.*dat* read.*inf* own-*acc* diary.*acc*

This sentence could be translated, roughly, into English as "Mary let Peter read her diary," but it could also be translated as "Mary gave Peter her diary to read." The English sentence "Mary let Peter read her diary" suggests that Mary didn't stop Peter from reading her diary rather than that she actively encouraged him to do so. But the Russian sentence suggests that Mary *did* something, and in this it is similar to the English sentence "Mary gave Peter her diary to read" rather than to "Mary let Peter read her diary."

Similarly, the Russian sentence:

Maša   dala Petru   est'.
Mary.*nom* gave Peter.*dat* eat.*inf*

is virtually impossible to translate into English, because it implies not only that Mary set some food in front of Peter but also that as a result of her action Peter ate it. Mary didn't simply "let" Peter eat; rather, she "caused" him to eat, she ensured that he ate, she almost "made" him eat (although in Russian the implication is that Peter was willing rather than unwilling to do so).

To undertake a survey of the different causative uses of the Russian verb *dat'* (in an NSM framework) would require a separate study, but the preliminary discussion given here should be sufficient to throw into relief—by way of contrast—the focus on "negative freedom," on "noninterference," so characteristic of the English *let*-causatives.

Of course, the preoccupation of modern Anglo culture with "noninterference" and "personal autonomy" can only explain the wealth of *let*-constructions involving both a human causer and a human causee. One can speculate, however, that once the idea of the consequences of inaction becomes salient in a language's semantic system, it can easily spread from the interpersonal realm to the realm of inanimate causees. If the speakers' attention is focused on the question of "letting" (or "not letting") other people do things, it may also come to be focused on the question of "letting" (or "not letting") things happen (to things). There may be other explanations as well, including some addressing, more generally, the extraordinary elaboration of the theme of "cause and effect" in modern Anglo culture (see Wierzbicka 1992, chapter 2). I cannot, however, pursue this theme any further in the confines of this chapter.

Nor can I undertake here a truly comprehensive discussion of the German *lassen*-causatives, which also deserve a full-scale study based on the same common measure (the empirically established set of lexicogrammatical universals). All I can do here is remind the reader of the wide range of the German *lassen*-causatives, glossing over any distinctions based on the wants of the addressee (see section 6.2.2), and also mention that German has no equivalents of English *let* causatives and quasicausatives such as "let me know," "let me have a look," "let me open the door for you," or "let me explain (suggest, assure you, etc.)." Instead, one would say, idiomatically, *Sag mir bescheid* (lit., "tell me with certainty"), *Kann ich mal sehen?* (lit., "could I have a look?"), *Warten Sie—ich öffne Ihnen die Tür* (lit., "wait [polite form]— I open the door for you"), *Ich möchte erklären, daß* . . . (lit., "I would like to explain that . . ."), or *Ich würde vorschlagen* . . . (lit., "I would propose . . ."). The general point I want to make here is that to undertake such comparisons between English and other languages, we must first disentangle the complex network of various English constructions and expressions in which *let* is involved and elucidate their meaning. For this, a rigorous and universally applicable semantic framework is indispensable.

The semantic history of *let*-constructions in English is a vast and fascinating topic that requires a separate study. But the general trend is fairly clear: it is, on the whole, a shift from positive causation, in a very broad sense (often spanning, effectively, "action" and "inaction") toward "negative causation," that is, to "enabling by not preventing."

As Fischer (1992, 29) puts it, *let* was "the central causative verb" in Middle English, and it had a distinct sense of "cause, allow," that is, a sense apparently spanning (like the German *lassen* still does) "positive" and "negative" causation, but in fact interpretable in *all* cases in terms of "doing something." This is clearly not the case in contemporary English, in which *let* refers, by and large, to abstention from action rather than to action. Apparent exceptions such as "let me know" or "let me have a look" confirm, in their own way, the cultural logic behind this general trend, because they imply something like cooperation among autonomous individuals and focus on shared knowledge rather than on the action required from the addressee.

6.2.5. Summing up

English causative constructions, whose cultural elaboration is a distinctive typological feature of the English language, focus, as we have seen, on the freedom and autonomy of the person who is performing the action. It might be suggested that, leaving aside the lexical verb *to force*, the causative auxiliaries could be arranged on a scale from *let* to *make*, with *get* and *have* closer to *make*. As I have shown, however, the differences are qualitative rather than quantitative, and to portray them adequately, we need to present each construction as a unique bundle of semantic components.

Arguably, the central question behind all these constructions is whether the person who is doing something is doing it out of his or her own volition. Thus, in the case of the main *let*-construction (as in "X let Y do Z"), person Y is doing something because he or she wants to do it, while another person, X, doesn't prevent Y from doing it. In the case of *get*-constructions, person Y is doing, voluntarily, something that another person, X, wants her or him to do. In the case of *have*-constructions, person Y is also doing something that another person, X, wants her or him to do, and in this case the relations between X and Y are such that Y cannot say (about something of this kind) "I don't want to do it"; here, too, Y is doing it "voluntarily" in the sense that Y doesn't think "I have to do it." In the case of *make*-constructions, Y is doing something that someone else, X, wants Y to do, and in this case Y does think: "I have to do it."

If we look at English in a comparative perspective, two things stand out most: the large number of causative auxiliaries (and an even larger number of grammatical constructions associated with them) and the presence of an auxiliary verb, *let*, specialized in, roughly speaking, noninterference. These features of English are culturally revealing, as they both reflect a concern with personal autonomy. In addition, this concern is reflected in the plethora of more specialized constructions and expressions based on *let* that encode cultural meanings such as "tolerance," "sharing information," "offering to perform a service," "suggesting a joint action," "cooperative dialogue," "cooperative interaction," and "cooperative thinking."

Arguably, *let*, which as mentioned earlier has been described as "the central causative verb" of Middle English, is also the central causative verb of modern English. But the meaning of this central causative verb has changed—roughly speaking, from "causing someone to do something" to "not causing someone not to do something." This shift is symptomatic, as it suggests the same concern that (as discussed in Wierzbicka 1997) is reflected in the changes in the meaning of the word *freedom* itself—roughly, from "freedom to" to "freedom from."

Chapter 7

I THINK

*The Rise of Epistemic Phrases
in Modern English*

7.1. Introduction

As discussed in chapter 2, one of the most remarkable phenomena in the history of the English language is the rise of what can be called epistemic phrases, that is, phrases clarifying the speaker's stance in relation to what is being said. A major question addressed through such phrases is whether or to what extent the speaker is claiming knowledge ("I know").

A declarative sentence without any epistemic qualification can be interpreted as implying knowledge. For example, factual sentences like "Bill is in Sydney now" imply an unqualified claim to knowledge: "I know." By contrast, sentences with epistemic phrases like *I think, I guess,* or *I suppose* ("I think Bill is in Sydney now," "I guess Bill is in Sydney now," "I suppose Bill is in Sydney now") do not imply any such claim.

When one looks at English in a comparative perspective, one is struck by the abundance of phrases like *I think, I guess,* and *I suppose.* Phrases of this kind can be used parenthetically and can appear in different positions in the sentence: at the beginning, the end, or somewhere in between.

In the philosophical literature, verbs like *think, guess,* or *suppose* are often referred to (following Urmson 1956) as "parenthetical verbs." Strictly speaking, however, it is not verbs as such that can be used "parenthetically," but phrases—first-person-singular, present-tense phrases, such as *I think, I guess,* and *I suppose.* Phrases of this kind can be likened to so-called "performative" ones (see Austin 1962) like *I suggest, I confirm,* and *I object* in that they identify the intended status of what the speaker is saying; for example *I suggest* identifies the accompanying sentences as a suggestion. But the term "performative" is usually restricted to phrases with "verbs of speaking," whereas epistemic phrases discussed here are in most cases based on verbs of thinking.

Speaking of verbs such as *know, believe, guess, suppose, suspect, estimate,* and in a metaphorical use, *feel,* Urmson (1956) comments:

> This . . . group . . . is used to indicate the evidential situation in which the state-
> ment is made (though not to describe that situation), and hence to signal what
> degree of reliability is claimed for, and should be accorded to, the statement to
> which they are conjoined. (p. 199)

> When these verbs are used in the first person of the present tense . . . they . . . func-
> tion with regard to a statement made rather as "READ WITH CARE" functions in rela-
> tion to a subjoined notice. (p. 211)

Although linguists must appreciate the subtlety and originality of Urmson's observations, from the point of view of contemporary linguistic semantics, one is struck by the
absence of any cross-linguistic perspective in the consideration of the English data.
When Urmson says that "parenthetical verbs" are important (p. 212) and that they "are
frequently misconstrued by philosophers" (p. 192), he means that they are *philosophically* important. He does not ask whether such philosophically important verbs occur
also (on a similar scale) in other languages and, if not, why not. He thinks of them, as
philosophers writing in English often do, as an "important part of *language*," not an
important part of the *English* language. He does not ask when and in what historical
context they emerged in English and what cultural needs led to their emergence. Nor
does he ask what exactly each of these verbs means and how their meanings may be
related to the historical and cultural context in which they appeared in English.

In the half century since the publication of Urmson's classic paper, linguistic
literature has not addressed these questions either. But they are important and fascinating, and I want to address them in this chapter. First of all, however, it should
again be stressed that what is at issue here is not a particular class of verbs, but a
particular class of first-person, present-tense verbal phrases. I argue that the meaning
of phrases like *I suppose* cannot be deduced from the meanings of the pronoun *I* and
the verb *suppose* and that to explicate the meaning of a phrase like *I suppose*, we
have to treat it as a whole. One linguist who has reflected deeply on the unique status of such first-person epistemic phrases is Emile Benveniste:

> In a general way, when I use the present of a verb with three persons, it seems that
> the difference in person does not lead to any change of meaning in the conjugated
> verb form. *I eat, you eat,* and *he eats* have in common and as a constant that the
> verb form presents a description of an action, attributed respectively and in an
> identical fashion to "I," "you," and "he." . . .
>   Now a number of verbs do not have this permanence of meaning in the chang-
> ing of persons, such as those verbs with which we denote dispositions or mental
> operations. In saying *I suffer,* I describe my present condition. . . . But what hap-
> pens if . . . I say *I believe (that the weather is going to change)?* . . . Can I consider
> *I believe* to be description of myself . . . ? Am I describing myself believing when I
> say *I believe (that . . .)?* Surely not. The operation of thought is not at all the ob-
> ject of the utterance; *I believe (that . . .)* is equivalent to a mitigated assertion. By
> saying *I believe (that . . .),* I convert into a subjective utterance the fact asserted
> impersonally, namely, *the weather is going to change,* which is the true proposi-
> tion. (Benveniste 1971, 228)

As Benveniste notes, this asymmetry between different persons of the verb does not
apply to *all* mental verbs. For example, *I reflect* is no more different from *he reflects*

than *I eat* is from *he eats*. But, for example, *I suppose* and *I presume* are not like *I reflect* in this respect:

> I do not represent myself as being in the process of supposing and presuming when I say *I suppose* and *I presume*. . . . In *I suppose* and *I presume*, there is an indication of attitude, not a description of an operation. By including *I suppose* and *I presume* in my discourse, I imply that I am taking a certain attitude with regard to the utterance that follows. . . . [T]hat personal form is, one might say, the indicator of subjectivity. It gives the assertion that follows the subjective context—doubt, presumption, inference—suited to characterize the attitude of the speaker with respect to the statement he is making. This manifestation of subjectivity does not stand out except in the first person. (Benveniste 1971, 228)

Benveniste's notion of 'subjectivity' has been fruitfully applied in a number of recent works on grammar and discourse (see, e.g., Traugott 1989, 1995; Verhagen 1995; Scheibman 2001). My own focus, however, is on the *meaning* of the relevant expressions, which I will try to elucidate by decomposing each into a number of semantic components, formulated in the natural semantic metalanguage and including no technical terms (like, for example, *subjectivity*). The resulting explications can be regarded as hypotheses about the meanings in the speakers' minds. I will call the expressions under discussion "epistemic verbal phrases." In keeping with Benveniste's discussion, I will explicate each phrase as a whole, in order to show that, for example, *I believe* and *he believes* differ in more than just being in the first or third person, and that *I believe* (in the relevant sense) has a meaning of its own.[1]

The large class of epistemic verbal phrases we find in contemporary English is a peculiarity of modern English. A list like the following one, which is by no means complete, is probably without parallel in other languages of the world: *I expect, I believe, I suppose, I assume, I imagine, I gather, I presume, I guess, I suspect, I take it, I understand, I trust, I wonder, I feel*. Moreover, these simple verbal expressions can be further expanded in various ways, as, for example, *I should think, I should've thought, I'm inclined to think, I tend to think, I don't think, I don't suppose, I would guess, my guess is, my understanding is, I would argue*, and *I would suggest*.

In most other European languages, there are only a few verbal expressions comparable with those on this list. For example, in colloquial German one can say *ich glaube, ich meine, ich denke, ich nehme an, ich schätze*, and *ich finde*; in colloquial French, *je crois, je pense, je suppose*, and *je trouve*; and in colloquial Italian, *credo, penso, suppongo*. In all these languages, it would be difficult to extend these lists significantly. Furthermore, in none of these languages could one use, colloquially, verbal expressions comparable to *I should think, I would've thought*, or *I'm inclined to think*.[2]

It is true that many other languages, for example, German, Russian, and Japanese, have numerous interactional particles—a linguistic resource not similarly rich in English (see Wierzbicka 1976, 1986b; see also chapter 8). But English appears to be unique in its wealth of verbs analyzing in great detail the *speaker's* own attitude to the proposition, in particular, of first-person "epistemic" verbal expressions such as those previously listed. In addition, some of these expressions (above all, *I think*, but also *I don't think, I suppose*, and, in American English, *I guess*) also have remarkably high frequencies (see, e.g., Thompson and Mulac 1991; Aijmer 1997; Scheibman 2001).

It seems that epistemic phrases of the kind discussed here started to be used in English on a large scale in the first half of the eighteenth century, that is, some time after the publication of Locke's *Essay Concerning Human Understanding*. My hypothesis is that this dramatic increase in their use was due to some extent to the influence of Locke's work.

I do not mean to imply that these epistemic phrases all sprang into being within a short time after the publication of Locke's *Essay*. Although the matter requires a detailed historical investigation, it seems more likely that the impact of the *Essay* started a trend and led to the emergence of certain "cultural scripts," which in turn led, over the next two or three centuries, to the cultural elaboration of this area of English lexicon and grammar. I do, however, want to suggest that the publication, and the impact, of Locke's *Essay* constituted an important turning point.

As discussed in chapter 2, the popularity of Locke's *Essay* in both Britain and America was unprecedented. It was so widely read that by 1710, as many as eleven editions had been produced (Jackson 1991, 268) and by 1805, twenty-one (Aarsleff 1991, 280), and sections of it were frequently published in *The Spectator*. It is widely recognized that Locke's writings in general and the *Essay* in particular "exercised a tremendous influence upon . . . the cultural consciousness of individuals several centuries after his death in 1704" (Ashcraft 1991, xiii). The influence of Locke's emphasis on the need for epistemic caution is a good case in point.

The need to specify, in rational discourse, the epistemic status of our utterances is one of the leitmotifs of Locke's *Essay*. According to Locke, our knowledge is extremely limited ("very short and scanty," Locke 1959, 360). In most things that we say, therefore, we rely not on knowledge but on "judgment," and judgment involves, in his view, many different degrees of assent.

> Our knowledge, as has been shown, being very narrow and we not happy enough to find certain truth in everything that we have an occasion to consider; most of the propositions we think, reason, discourse—nay, act upon, are such as we cannot have undoubted knowledge of their truth. . . . But there being degrees herein, from the very neighbourhood of certainty and demonstration, quite down to improbability and unlikeliness, even to the confines of impossibility; and also degrees of assent from full assurance and confidence, quite down to conjecture, doubt and distrust. (Locke 1959, 364)

Locke's ideas concerning degrees of probability and degrees of assent, and the need to always distinguish between "knowledge" and "judgment," that is, between knowing and thinking, have exercised an enormous influence on modern English discourse and indeed on the English language. I have discussed some aspects of this influence in chapters 2, 3, and 4. Here, I want to undertake a detailed discussion of the meaning and cultural underpinnings of a number of selected epistemic phrases· *I believe, I suppose, I gather, I presume, I find, I expect, I guess, I take it, I understand, I imagine, I bet, I suspect,* and *I assume*.

In what follows, I analyze the meaning of these phrases in the natural semantic metalanguage. The key primes in terms of which most, if not all, epistemic phrases can be explicated are *think, know,* and *say*. The key semantic molecules in this area are I THINK, I KNOW, I SAY, I DON'T THINK, I DON'T KNOW, and I DON'T SAY, as well as I CAN (or CAN'T) THINK, I CAN (or CAN'T) KNOW, and I CAN (or CAN'T) SAY.[3]

7.2. *I Think*

The most important epistemic phrase in English is *I think*, without a following *that*: not *I think that* but *I think*. The extraordinarily high frequency of this phrase in contemporary English has been discussed in chapter 2, where I have also discussed its meaning. The present discussion of *I think* is therefore very brief.

Compare the following two sentences:

a. It is raining.
b. I think it is raining.

The first sentence implies: "I know." The second sentence does not imply that, and in fact, it emphatically denies such an implication: "I don't say I know." But the difference between sentences like (a) and (b) is not simply that between two different stances on the part of the speaker ("I know" versus "I don't say I know"). As Benveniste (1971, 10) put it, by preceding a sentence like *it is raining* with a personal frame like *I think*, "I convert into a subjective utterance the fact asserted impersonally . . . which is the true proposition." In my terms, this key difference between an "impersonal" sentence like (a) and a "subjective" one like (b) can be represented as follows:

a. I say: it is raining
b. I say: I think like this: it is raining

This brings us to the following overall explications:

It is raining =
a. I say: it is raining
b. I know

I think it is raining =
a. I say: I think like this: it is raining
b. I don't say I know

As I try to show throughout this chapter, the components "I say I think" and either "I don't know" or "I don't say I know" constitute the semantic core of the class of verbal epistemic phrases that is so prominent in modern English.

7.3. *I Suppose*

The epistemic phrase *I suppose* is often combined with tag questions (examples from Cobuild):[4]

I suppose times change don't they?

I suppose it's up to the public isn't it.

I suppose that's what you'll have to do isn't it.

It also often combines with the phrase *I don't know*:

I don't know I mean being ambidextrous *I suppose* I do use my right hand
for *I suppose* when I think about it. . . .

Furthermore, *I suppose* tends to co-occur with various hesitation markers, such as
well, really, mm, or what is transcribed in Cobuild as *er* or *erm*:

Mm. *I suppose.*

Well it doesn't really, *I suppose.*

Er well it's all right *I suppose.*

Erm *I suppose.* Yeah. Yeah.

Well *I suppose* I've known him all my life really.

The speaker's hesitation and lack of certainty is also reflected in the frequent use of
various approximative expressions such as *about, around,* or *thereabouts*:

I don't remember how long it must have been about a year ago I suppose.

However I did get involved I suppose around nineteen-fifty-four thereabouts.

What all these facts suggest is that *I suppose* includes not only the component *I don't
know* but also a component reflecting the thinking process: "I'm thinking about it
now." The content of what one supposes can be seen as the provisional result of that
thinking process: "I think like this now." This brings us to the following overall
explication:

I suppose it is up to the public =
a. I say: I think like this now: it's up to the public
b. I don't know
c. I'm thinking about it now

Consider, for example, the following sentence:

Well I suppose you know you could just show your face couldn't you.

The discourse marker *well,* the tag question, the use of the phrase *you know* to appeal for the addressee's conversational cooperation, and the use of the modal *could*
all highlight the speaker's hesitation, lack of knowledge, a current thinking process,
and a tentative provisional conclusion. All these features are highly consistent with
the components proposed here: "I think like this now," "I don't know," "I'm thinking about it now."

7.4. *I Guess*

The "epistemic" force of the phrase *I guess* appears to be very close to that of *I suppose,* and many dictionaries treat it as a regional (American) version of *I suppose.*
For example, the *Oxford Advanced Learner's Dictionary* (2005) glosses *I guess* as "informal, especially N.Am.E) to suppose that something is true or likely"; *The Collins
Cobuild English Language Dictionary* (1987) says that "*I guess* is an important ex-

pression used especially in American English to indicate that you suppose, think, or suspect that something is true or likely"; and the *Longman Dictionary of the English Language* (1984) states: "*chiefly N. Am. Informal* to believe, suppose." Certainly, the frequency of *I guess* in conversational American English is extremely high (Thompson and Mulac 1991; Scheibman 2001).

Arguably, what *I guess* shares with *I suppose* are the following two components:

I think like this now

I don't know

I guess is very much an *ex promptu* thought, conceived on the spur of the moment, and the component "I think like this now" accounts for this. At the same time, *I guess* sounds brusquer, more decisive than *I suppose* — not because the speakers feel they have more evidence but because they feel prepared to take a risk, to hazard an opinion, even though there is not a sufficient basis for it. What this feel of *I guess* suggests is that this phrase does not include the "reflective" component "I'm thinking about it now," which I have posited for *I suppose*. Arguably, instead of such a reflective component, *I guess* includes a component linking it with the lexical verb *to guess* and implying an act of hazarding an opinion for which one knows one doesn't have a sufficient basis. This component can be phrased as follows: "if I have to say something about it now I want to say this." This brings us to the following overall explication:

I guess I'll go. =
a. I say: I think like this now: I'll go
b. I don't know
c. if I have to say something about it now I want to say this

For example, if someone asks me if I will do something (say, go to a party) and I reply, "I guess so," I would be implying that I don't really know, but that at the moment I think I will go, and moreover, that if I have to say something about it right now, then I choose to say this ("I will go"). Clearly, *I guess* does not indicate a considered opinion or an intention to which one is committed. One is not certain, but one is not going to reflect on the matter long before replying.

The willingness to say something for which one doesn't have evidence may seem to go against the grain of the caution and scrupulousness characteristic of the set of English epistemic phrases as a whole. In fact, however, the epistemic phrase *I guess* is also cautious and scrupulous, in its own way. Although the speaker is willing to say something without a basis in knowledge, this act is not really rash or overconfident because the phrase *I guess* includes in its very meaning the admission "I don't know."

7.5. *I Gather*

The meaning of the epistemic phrase *I gather* can be said to come close to the meaning of *gather* described by the OED as follows: "to collect (knowledge) by observation and reasoning; to infer, deduce, conclude." The examples cited by the OED in support of this definition are by no means restricted to the first person. For example:

> Pliny supposed amber to be a resin, which he gathered from its smell. (1744)

Sentences of this kind diverge, both in their syntax and their meaning, from those in the present-day usage, as in the following examples from Cobuild:

> Which I gather is what it really means.

> I gather that there was considerable upheaval about this.

> I gather he's taking sort of everybody out for meals and things.

> . . . and that mattered I gather quite crucially for [name]. Yeah. It does.

The restriction of *gather* to the phrase *I gather*; its parenthetical character (in Urmson's sense); its position alternating freely between the beginning, middle, or end of a sentence; and its frequent use in dialogue, in combination with responses like *yeah, sure,* and *it does,* all suggest a shift in meaning as well as in grammatical status. Above all, the epistemic phrase *I gather* appears to suggest a subjective uncertainty or caution, "I don't say I know," which is absent from older sentences with *gather,* like the one about Pliny quoted earlier.

Like the lexical verb *to gather,* the epistemic phrase combines with the syntactic frame "from" ("I gather from"), broadly consistent with the OED definition "to collect (knowledge) by observation and reasoning." But given the uncertainty and caution implied by the phrase *I gather* ("I don't say: I know") what is "collected" by observation and reasoning should probably be interpreted as *hypothetical* knowledge rather than genuine (reliable) knowledge. Reliable knowledge is the *source* of what one gathers rather than its outcome; from knowing some other things, one "collects" bits of hypothetical new knowledge. These considerations lead us to the following explication:

> *I gather there is going to be a further inquiry.* =
> a. I say: I think now that it is like this: people can know that there is going to be a further inquiry
> b. I don't say I know
> c. I think like this because I know some other things now

As the first component of this explication indicates, the speaker's attitude appears to be neither one of "I think" nor one of "I know" but an intermediate and at the same time more objective one of "I think now that it is like this: people can know."[5] The last component of *I gather* refers to some knowledge (evidential basis) that appears to be current: "I know some other things *now.*" Typically, this current evidential basis consists in what one sees or hears: "from what I see/hear, I gather that. . . ."

All in all, the epistemic phrase *I gather* illustrates the post-Lockean emphasis on the limitations of one's knowledge, on the scrupulous acknowledgment of those limitations, and on the importance of evidence for whatever claims to knowledge one may be making.

7.6. *I Presume*

The epistemic phrase *I presume* is often used for making statements about the addressee, as in the following examples from Cobuild:

> I presume you work for the council.

> You're not referring to Funnel I presume.

> You coming from your background you weren't a scholarship boy at school I presume.

Not surprisingly, statements of this kind tend to seek confirmation from the addressee and are often accompanied by tag questions and followed by a confirmatory response such as "yes," "yeah," or "that's right." For example:

> Your going home time will be related to when the counter closes I presume is it?—Yes, that's right.

> I presume this was the preliminary notes you got back from SCPR.—Yes.

At first sight, this common conversational pattern seems to suggest the following combination of components:

> I think now that it is like this
> I don't know
> I know that you (or: someone else) can know

However, if we consider a wider range of examples, we will find some that are not compatible with this hypothesis. For example:

> I presume that any left-handed people like myself who knit just adapt you know.

> There were in the early eighteenth century so I presume also in the seventeenth century ladies whose profession was known as posture girls.

Nobody can know for sure that "any left-handed people who knit adapt." In this case, then, the speaker's recognition that his or her own knowledge is inadequate cannot be linked with a recognition that somebody else's knowledge is superior. What is it, then, that makes the speaker's statement—in her or his own estimation—a "presumption"?

I would like to propose the following interpretation. The person who says "I presume" assumes a more confident stand than someone who merely says "I think." They seem to be saying not only "I think (that it is like this)" but also, more strongly, "I think I can know it." Since at the same time the speaker is acknowledging his or her lack of knowledge ("I don't say I know"), the component "I think I can know it" can indeed make the utterance sound, as it were, "presumptuous," especially given that no reference is being made to some evidence ("I know some other things"), as in the case of *I gather*. This brings us to the following explication:

> *I presume you work for the council.* =
> a. I say: I think now that it is like this: you work for the council

b. I don't say I know
c. I think about it like this: I can know it

Let us consider, for example, the following sentence from a recent article by the anthropologist Naomi Quinn (2002):

What is relevant to my argument is a previously unrecognised pattern of child rearing . . . a pattern that I presume to be universal.

To say "I think that this pattern is universal" would not be "presumptuous" in any way because a person can think what they want, but to say "I think I can know it" *could* be regarded as "presumptuous" because obviously the author doesn't have the evidence from all the languages and cultures. At the same time, the component "I don't say I know it" acknowledges the lack of an adequate basis, and this protects the speaker from being regarded as "presumptuous" (as claiming more than one has evidence for).

As one final example, let us consider the celebrated sentence "Dr. Livingstone, I presume," addressed to the great African explorer, lost in central Africa, by Sir H. M. Stanley, the head of a special search expedition sent to Africa to discover whether Livingstone was still alive. Stanley found Livingstone in the village of Ujiji on the eastern shores of the lake Tanganyika under circumstances that left no doubt as to his identity; he could have been absolutely certain that the white man in front of him was indeed Livingstone—so much so that a mere "I think" would have been blatantly inappropriate. Yet the scrupulous Briton does not permit himself an act of open recognition: "Dr. Livingstone!," which would have implied "I know" ("I know that you are Dr. Livingstone"). Instead, he chooses the formula "I presume"—more confident than "I think" but less so than "I know." With this carefully chosen formula, Stanley is saying: "I think now that it is like this: you are Dr. Livingstone" and "I think about it like this: I can know it," while scrupulously acknowledging at the same time: "I don't say I know it." It is this scrupulous care in acknowledging the limitations of one's knowledge that makes the sentence amusing, in its perceived quintessential Britishness—arguably, Britishness shaped, to a large extent, by the intellectual climate created in Britain by the British Enlightenment.

7.7. *I Believe*

7.7.1. *"I believe" versus "to believe (that, something, someone, it)"*

In what follows I am going to argue that the epistemic phrase *I believe* (without the word *that*) has to be distinguished from the phrase *I believe that*, which does not differ semantically (except in person or tense) from *he believes that* or from *I believed that*. In other words, *to believe that* has a full paradigm (as does also *to believe in*), whereas the phrase *I believe*, which can be used parenthetically, has a meaning of its own, restricted to the first-person present tense.

Let us start by considering some examples of the epistemic phrase *I believe* (without a following *that*: *I believe* rather than *I believe that*) from Cobuild:

I believe you can get low fat custard these days by Ambrosia in a tin so that's even better for you.

—The number of people killed on the roads. Five thousand a year in this country.
—Six thousand it is I believe.
—Six thousand is it, yeah, you may well be right.

He does have, I believe, the club's interests at heart.

And then one of the professors, Professor MX I believe, he lived in there afterwards.

As these examples illustrate, the epistemic phrase *I believe* suggests something like a considered but cautiously expressed opinion. If we compare it with *I suppose*, *I believe* sounds more confident. If we compare it with *I think*, *I believe* also sounds more confident, although the difference is not as sharp as in the case of *I suppose*. For example, if the library recalls a book that I have borrowed, and if I am fairly confident that I have already returned it, I could say to the librarian with calm and self-assurance, "I believe I have already returned it." If, on the other hand, I am not sure at all, I would be more likely to say, "I think I have already returned it." Furthermore (as pointed out to me by Brigid Maher, personal communication), if one is really unsure, one can stress this further by emphasizing the word *think*, and pronouncing it with an intonation that indicates hesitation (often with a frown); one can't do this with *I believe*.

In addition to sounding more confident than *I think*, *I believe* sounds more thoughtful, considered, and cautious—perhaps more intellectual, more controlled, less spontaneous, as well as more formal. It can also sound a little standoffish: although it doesn't claim knowledge, it doesn't give the impression that the speaker might like to engage the addressee in a discussion, let alone an argument.

Both *I believe* (without *that*) and *I think* (without *that*) imply "I don't say I know." But *I believe* implies also *some* grounds, *some* evidence for thinking what one does. This suggests the component "I can say why I think like this," which is absent from *I think*. At the same time, the speaker does not expect that his or her own reasons for thinking this would be sufficient to convince others: "I know that someone else can think not like this."

It is also worth noting that phrases like *I'm not sure* or *I may be wrong* are more compatible with *I think* than *I believe*:

I'm not sure but I think you can get it in a tin.

I may be wrong but I think I have already returned it.

I don't know for sure, but I think you can get it in a tin.

?I'm not sure but I believe you can get it in a tin.

?I may be wrong but I believe I have already returned it.

?I don't know for sure, but I believe you can get it in a tin.

This incompatibility of *I believe* with phrases like *I'm not sure* can be linked with the reference to some objective evidence, or at least some specifiable grounds: "I can say why I think like this." (See Aijmer's [1997, 17] comment: "*I believe* does not only express a subjective attitude. It also conveys that the speaker has some evidence for what he says.") The phrase *I think* lays no such claims to specifiable grounds, and so it is more felicitous in combination with expressions of subjective uncertainty such as *I'm not sure*.

Up till now I have been talking only about the expression *I believe*, without an accompanying *that*, on the assumption that *I believe* and *I believe that* differ in meaning. This assumption may seem arbitrary to the reader. In fact, however, there are good reasons to think that there is a semantic difference between the two. For example, a sentence like the following one:

I believe that having been given a vote it should be compulsory to use it.

states a view that the speaker is committed to, and it could be expanded by phrases like *that's what I believe* or *my belief is*. . . . By contrast, a sentence like *I believe you can get it in a tin* cannot be expanded by such phrases; it does not present "the speaker's belief"—a belief that the speaker is committed to—but merely something that the speaker personally thinks, a kind of personal opinion. I will return to *I believe that* shortly. For the moment, let me propose a full explication for *I believe* (without *that*)— an explication that would account for all the intuitions discussed so far:

I believe (e.g., I believe you can get it in a tin) =
a. I say: I think now that it is like this: you can get it in a tin
b. I don't say I know
c. I can say why I think like this
d. I know that someone else can think not like this

The component *I think that* is clearly there. For example, *I believe you can get low-fat custard in a tin* clearly implies that "I think that you can get low-fat custard in a tin." The component "I don't say I know" explains why *I believe* sounds more confident than *I suppose*: *I suppose* implies "I don't know," whereas *I believe* implies only "I don't say I know." The component "I know that someone else can think not like this" accounts for the "tone" of *I believe*. The speaker does not want to sound dogmatic and wishes to acknowledge the possibility of other opinions and other statements. At the same time, by presenting the thought in question as a personal opinion, *I believe* acts as a distancing device and discourages argument: if one presents what one thinks as a purely personal opinion (that doesn't have to be shared by others), one signals that one is not going to engage in an argument.

The components "I can say why I think like this" and "I know that someone else can think not like this" posited here for *I believe* can derive additional support from the fact that normally one wouldn't use *I believe* in sentences referring to the speaker's own inner states (feelings, intentions, and so on). For example:

a. I think I'll go to bed now.
b. ?I believe I'll go to bed now.

Sentence (b) sounds odd because it implies that the speaker is looking at himself or herself from an external perspective, as if having no privileged access to the subject-matter. The phrase *I think* makes no reference to any grounds or to other people's possible thoughts on the same matter, and so it is compatible with a much wider range of propositions, including those to whose content the speaker has privileged access.

If one reads pages upon pages of sentences with the epistemic phrase *I believe* (from Cobuild), one is struck by the relative absence of tag questions and also of confirming or disconfirming responses from the addressee (*Yeah, Yes, That's right, No,* etc.). This is consistent with the monological and somewhat standoffish tone of *I believe.* It is not like *I reckon,* which tends to combine with a question addressed to the addressee ("What do *you* reckon?"), and it is not like *I suppose,* which is often combined with a tag question and with an interest in the addressee's point of view. Thus, the speaker is expressing a thought, while acknowledging that other people can have different thoughts on the subject and not wishing to engage the addressee or anyone else.

7.7.2. "I believe that"

Let us now consider the meaning of the verb *to believe* used in combination with the word *that* and, in particular, the relation between the phrases *I believe* and *I believe that.* I will start again with some more examples from Cobuild:

I believe that we don't need to go to full integration to obtain the majority.

I believe that it is not inaccurate to say that the sum of human misery created by homelessness and housing problems in our country is probably greater even than that created by unemployment.

I believe that they shouldn't have the votes, expats I mean.

I believe that as little as a hundred and hundred and fifty votes might have swung some marginal seats.

I believe that ultimately we're going to have to get ourselves into a position where we. . . .

I believe that there is a real need. . . .

I believe that we could give encouragement to it.

I believe that that is the key factor to being successful in this particular H.E.O. role.

I believe that it's extremely important that you catch the vision.

As these examples illustrate, typically, *I believe that* conveys a conviction, and it tends to introduce evaluative personal judgments: "I believe that this is good/bad . . ," "I believe that they should . . ," and the like, rather than purely factual statements. Thus, it would be a little odd to use *I believe that* in the sentence about custard:

I believe you can get custard in a tin.

?I believe that you can get custard in a tin.

Because *I believe that* implies something like a conviction or commitment, like taking a stand on some matter of importance, it is inappropriate in a factual-sounding sentence, especially on a trivial matter.

The "commitment" implied by *I believe that* is reflected in the ability of this phrase to collocate with adverbs like *strongly*, as in the following examples:

I believe strongly that education does counter disadvantage. . . .

I believe quite strongly that officers should produce supposed solutions. . . .

The phrase *I believe* without *that* doesn't combine with adverbs like *strongly* (?six thousand, I strongly believe). This fact in itself provides strong evidence for the semantic difference between *I believe* and *I believe that*.

As mentioned earlier, *I believe* is a quasi-performative phrase (in Austin's sense, Austin 1962), restricted—in the meaning under discussion—to the first person (present tense). By contrast, *I believe that* is no different semantically from *he believes that* or *they believe that* (except for the obvious difference in the pronoun). A phrase like *he believes* can also be used without a following *that*, but even when used like that it does not carry all the semantic components postulated here for *I believe* ("I don't say I know," "I can say why I think like this," "I know that other people can think not like this"). Thus, a sentence like:

He believes it's okay to smack children.

sounds natural, whereas a sentence like:

?He believes one can get custard in a tin.

sounds a little odd. The reason, I believe, is that in the first of these sentences *he believes* is a variant of *he believes that*, with *that* conversationally deleted, and so it is perfectly suitable for describing somebody's conviction. The second sentence, however, is purely factual, and so it doesn't easily lend itself to such an interpretation and as a result sounds odd. On the other hand, *I believe one can get custard in a tin* sounds natural, because it is not a variant of *I believe that one can get custard in a tin* but an instance of a distinct, quasi-performative epistemic phrase, which does not imply commitment or conviction.

The distinct, quasi-performative status of the phrase *I believe* is reflected in its parenthetical syntax, that is, in its ability to occur midclause, or clause-finally. Such syntax is not possible with second or third person, as the following contrasts show:

He does have, I believe, the club's interests at heart.

He does have the club's interests at heart, I believe.

?He does have, she believes, the club's interests at heart.

?He does have the club's interests at heart, she believes.

The parenthetical syntax of *I believe* reflects iconically some aspects of its meaning: intuitively speaking, it is "weaker" than *I believe that*. Speaking more precisely, this "weakness" can be linked with the presence of an additional semantic component: "I don't say I know." At the same time, it can be linked with the absence of the element of "conviction," inherent in *believe that*.

To account for the element of conviction implied by *believe that*, we can propose the following explication:

I believe that there is a real need . . . =
a. when I think about it, I think that there is a real need
b. I know that someone else can think not like this
c. I can say why I think I like this
d. I think that it is good if someone thinks like this

Being essentially nonfactual, *believe that* does not include the component "I don't say I know," which has been assigned to *I believe*. At the same time, it conveys the speaker's commitment and conviction, accounted for in the component "I can say why it is good if someone thinks like this."

In contrast to *I believe* without *that*, the version with *that* is not restricted to first person (present tense), and a parallel explication can apply to second- and third-person sentences. For example:

She believes that there is a real need. . . . =
a. when she thinks about it, she thinks that there is a real need
b. she thinks like this:
c. "I know that someone else can think not like this
d. I can say why I think I like this
e. I think that it is good if someone thinks like this"

7.7.3. "To believe what someone says"

"To believe someone" means, essentially, to think that what this person says is true— even though one cannot know that it is true. In addition, the frame "to believe someone" links a person's thinking about the subject matter with his or her thinking about the person who says it. For example, in the following sentence from Cobuild, the speaker thinks that what the psychiatrist says is true not only because of the content of what is said but also because the psychiatrist is a doctor (and thus a competent and trustworthy person):

. . . and a psychiatrist takes out a stethoscope and takes out his blood pressure equipment puts it on and tells me I'm all right . . . I'm not in the middle of a heart attack. I believe him because he's a doctor.

This can be explicated as follows:

I believe him. =
a. [he says something]
b. I say: when he says it I think that it is true
c. I know that I can't know at this time

The "new" element here is the reference to the "truth" of some statement, absent both from the epistemic phrase *I believe* and from the verb *believe* used in the frame *to believe that*. In addition, there is the assumption that the person who believes something cannot know that this something is true.

Since *I believe him*, in contrast to *I believe*, is not a quasi-performative epistemic phrase, the meaning of *believe* exhibited in sentences like *I believe him* is not restricted to first person (present tense), and a similar explication should also be applicable to second- and third-person sentences. This can be tested as follows:

> *She believes him.* =
> a. [he says something]
> b. I say: when he says it she thinks that it is true
> c. I know that she can't know at this time

When the complement of *believe* represents another person's words, the sentence can be explicated along similar lines:

> *I believe it.* =
> a. I say: when someone says it I think that it is true
> b. I know that I can't know at this time

Again there is no difference here between first person and second or third person:

> *She believes it.* =
> a. I say: when someone says it she thinks that it is true
> b. I know that she can't know

7.7.4. *"To believe in someone or something"*

Turning now to the syntactic frame *to believe in*, we will note that it can be used in three different ways, with three different semantic interpretations. Roughly speaking, if one *believes in* something that people say, one thinks that what people say is true. If one *believes in* an ideal—for example, in freedom or democracy—one thinks that, roughly speaking, living according to this ideal is good. Finally, if one *believes in* a person ("I believe in you"), one thinks that this person can and will do good things.

The first sense (*to believe in* something that people say) can be explicated along the following lines:

> *He believes in life after death (in Santa Claus).* =
> a. [some people say: there is life after death (a Santa Claus)]
> b. I say: when he thinks about it he thinks that it is true
> c. I know that he can't know it at this time

The second sense (*to believe in* an ideal) implies, in addition, an evaluation: the "believer" thinks that it is good to do what the complement clause specifies. Let us consider some further examples from Cobuild.

> I believe in treating people that are ill as often and as best as possible.

> I believe in freedom and democracy and wish to join the Conservatives. . . .

> If I believe in elections I believe in democracy and I believe in giving people the right to vote.

> I believe quite strongly in cutting down car usage.

> I believe in negotiation in life.

I believe in the power of positive thought.

I believe in herbal things you know like for colds. . . .

In sentences of this kind, which are not factual, "good" appears to take the place of "true." For example, the sentence *I believe in talking things through* implies that the speaker thinks that it is good to talk things through. *I believe in the power of positive thought* implies that I think that it is good to think positively. If I believe in freedom and democracy, then I am in favor of social and political actions leading to freedom and democracy (the Cobuild example just cited is in fact very telling in this regard: "I believe in freedom and democracy and wish to join the Conservatives"). We can propose, therefore, the following explication:

> *I believe in talking things through.* =
> a. I say: I think like this: it is good if people talk things through
> b. I know that someone else can think not like this
> c. I think like this
> d. I think that it is good to think like this

Finally, sentences like *I believe in you* (or *she believes in him*) can be explicated as follows:

> *I believe in you.* =
> a. I say: I think like this: you can do good things, you will do good things
> b. I know that someone else can think not like this
> c. I think like this
> d. I think that it is good to think like this

I have looked briefly at the different meanings and different syntactic frames of the verb *to believe* with the purpose of isolating, and then seeing in context, the first-person verbal phrase *I believe*. We have seen that the phrase has a unique configuration of semantic components and that it is in some ways closer to the other epistemic phrases than to the other meanings of the verb *believe*, but we have also seen that it shares some components with those other meanings as well. In the last section of this chapter, we will take a quick look at the semantic history of the verb *believe* and at the emergence of the phrase *I believe* in the context of that history. Here, I conclude by noting that *I believe* represents a uniquely English/Anglo concept and conversational tool, with no parallels in other European languages, let alone in languages of other cultural areas. Expressions like *je crois* in French or *ich glaube* in German may seem to be identical in meaning to *I believe*, but in fact they are not. The topic cannot be pursued here in any detail, so I will simply note that, according to native speakers, neither *je crois* nor *ich glaube* could always be used in sentences like those with *I believe* quoted in this chapter.

7.8. *I Find*

Although the OED does not assign a distinct meaning to the epistemic phrase *I find*, it posits two meanings for *find* that are obviously related semantically to that phrase:

"to discover or perceive on inspection or consideration" (with the comment "sometimes approximating to the sense of the French *trouver*") and "to discover, come to the knowledge of (a fact or state of affairs) by experience or trial." The first of these meanings is illustrated, inter alia, with the following sentence:

> Nor did the world find anything ludicrous in the pomp which . . . surrounded him. (1848)

and the second, with the following one:

> Deer forests have been found to pay better than sheep grazing. (1886)

When one examines the examples of the phrase *I find* in the Cobuild corpus, one finds a great many parallels (both syntactic and semantic) to "finding something ludicrous." As evidence for the semantic nature of this category, here are a large number of examples.

> I find it ridiculous.
>
> I just find the practice of singing so tedious. . . .
>
> I find that incredible actually.
>
> I find it quite frustrating.
>
> I find it absolutely amazing that John Major is going . . . to privatise British Rail very shortly.
>
> I find it really difficult to meet people who I really resonate with.
>
> I find it very hard to accept.
>
> I find Stilton too strong.
>
> I find them [Good Morning programs] an intrusion really.
>
> I find that very hard to believe.
>
> I'm just trying to decide whether I find it offensive or not.
>
> I find it depressing too.
>
> They're ideas which on the whole I find rather stimulating.

The syntactic structure of this category of examples can be represented as "I find it/ that ADJ" (a so-called subject-raised construction). Do these examples fit, to some extent, the first OED definition, "to discover or perceive on inspection or consideration"? Or do they come closer to the second definition, "to discover, come to the knowledge of, by experience or trial"? As usual, these definitions are not sufficiently precise to test against the examples, but the elements of thinking ("consideration"), knowing ("coming to the knowledge of"), and experience (knowing something because of what happened to me) are clearly discernible in all these examples.

At the same time, all these examples convey an element of purely personal opinion ("I know that other people can think not like this"), which is not hinted at in either of the OED definitions. It is true that an opinion based on one's own experience is likely to be purely personal, but it doesn't have to be presented as such by the speaker. In fact, neither of the OED examples cited earlier ("Nor did the world find anything ludicrous in the pomp which . . . surrounded him," and "Deer forests have been found to pay better than sheep grazing") implies such a guarded, restrained, purely individual perspective. By contrast, sentences like "I find Stilton too strong" or "I find it ridiculous" clearly restrict the validity of the claim to the speaker's personal opinion; in fact, in all the examples cited here, *I find* can be readily combined with the "delimiter" *personally*: "Personally, I find Stilton too strong," "Personally, I find it ridiculous," and so forth.

In sentences of this kind, it would not be justified to present the speaker's thought in the form of a *that*-clause, such as *I find that Stilton is too strong*. The implication is that it is too strong *for me* (to my taste) rather than, generally speaking, too strong. *Personally*, I think about Stilton cheese like this: "it is too strong"; I do not say that I think that it is (objectively) too strong.

These considerations bring us to the following explication:

I find Stilton too strong =
a. I say: I think about it (Stilton cheese) like this: it is too strong
b. I know that other people can think not like this
c. I think like this because I know what happens to me (what I feel) [when I eat it]
d. I can't say I know what happens to other people (what they feel) [when they eat it]

In sentences like *I find Stilton too strong*, the element of personal experience (eating this kind of cheese) is unmistakable, but does the same apply to *all* the sentences with *I find* cited earlier? Does it necessarily apply to, for example, "I find it ridiculous (amazing, depressing, etc.)"? I would argue that sentences of this kind, which may appear to simply express a personal opinion not necessarily rooted in personal experience, do in fact imply such an experience. If we compare, for example, the sentence *I find it depressing* with *I think it's depressing*, we will note that the latter can combine with the modal *must*, whereas the former cannot:

I think it must be depressing.

?I find it must be depressing.

The modal *must* indicates an inference, and this is compatible with *I think* but not with *I find*. The sentence *I find it depressing* refers to the speaker's own experience of feeling depressed, and so it cannot be based on inference.

Turning now to sentences in which *I find* is used parenthetically (typically, sentence-finally), we will find that the element of personal experience is also present. For example, the sentence (about peanut butter):

It is too dry on bread, I find.

clearly implies that the speaker has come to this particular judgment ("it is too dry on bread") by eating bread with peanut butter. This is not to say that the sentence with a parenthetical *I find* phrase always refers *overtly* to the speaker's experience, as in the case of the texture of peanut butter on bread. But even when this is not the case and when the sentence describes, say, other people's actions, the very presence of the parenthetical phrase *I find* indicates that the speaker has encountered such people, or such cases, in his or her own personal experience. For example:

> A lot of young people are choosing German as the main language to
> learn rather than French nowadays, I find.

The "finding" expressed in this sentence cannot be based on newspaper reports but must be anchored in the speaker's personal experience (probably as a teacher). Generally speaking, sentences with a parenthetical *I find* are very close semantically to sentences like *I find it too strong*, but they are not identical. As their form suggests, the speaker is making a statement (qualified by the parenthetical phrase) rather than expressing a "running thought," and thus they can sound more factual and objectively valid. Schematically (partial explication):

> *I find it (Stilton cheese) too strong.* =
> I say: I think about it like this: it is too strong

> *A lot of young people are choosing German . . . , I find.* =
> I say: a lot of young people are choosing German
> I say this because I think like this

To some extent, this distinction corresponds to that drawn by the OED between "consideration" and "knowledge (of a fact or a state of affairs)," but it is not the case that only one of the two refers to knowledge based on personal experience—they both do. Here is a full explication of sentences with a parenthetical *I find*:

> *A lot of young people are choosing German . . . , I find.* =
> a. I say: a lot of young people are choosing German
> b. I say this because I think like this
> c. I know that other people can think not like this
> d. I think like this because I know what happens to me
> e. I can't say I know what happens to other people

In this case, though, there is no reference to what the speaker feels, only to what has happened to him or her.

Let us consider in turn sentences with *I find* introducing a *that*-clause, as in the following examples from Cobuild:

> I find that there is a kind of merging between memories of the past and a dream.

> I find constantly that kids need reinforcing on what is an economic issue what is a social issue.

> I find that they're much more open with me now asking me things than what they were when I first started teaching.

> I find that it's the younger element that's really struggling.

> I find that it bothers people. . . .

All these sentences clearly imply that the speaker has experienced something him-self or herself—in the first case, the merging of memories and dreams, and in the other four, encounters with certain categories of people.

Thus, the element of personal experience links all the three types of *I find*-sentences, and so does the element of personal opinion derived from that personal experience. In one respect, however, "I find that . . ."-sentences do differ semanti-cally from the "I find it ADJ" ones and from those with a parenthetical *I find*-phrase, and in fact they can be said to occupy an intermediate position between the two. As the surface structure suggests, "I find that . . ."-sentences express the speaker's opin-ion (possibly, on a general topic): "I think that . . ." Schematically (again, partial ex-plications only):

1. *I find it too strong.* =
   I say: "I think about it like this: it is too strong"
2. *A lot of young people are choosing German, I find.* =
   I say: "a lot of young people are choosing German"
   I say this because I think like this
3. *I find that it bothers people. . . .* =
   I say: "(when I think about it) I think that it bothers people. . . ."

In addition, all three types carry almost identical further components:

I know that other people can think not like this
I think like this because I know what happens to me (what I feel)

Thus, by saying *I find*, the speaker is, on the one hand, claiming that some knowl-edge can be derived from personal experience, and on the other, acknowledging that knowledge obtained through personal experience is limited; it is reliable as far as it goes but it doesn't go all that far: "I know what happens to me," but "I can't say I know what happens to other people."

The development and expansion of the epistemic modality expressed by the phrase *I find* is another characteristic feature of modern Anglo culture, with its empha-sis on empiricism, personal opinion, and antidogmaticism. In most other European languages, not to mention languages further afield, there are usually no phrases cor-responding in both meaning and scope to the English *I find* (for example, there are no corresponding phrases in Russian, Polish, Italian, or Spanish). Although in French and German there *are* phrases comparable to *I find* (*je trouve* and *ich finde*), in both cases, their scope is more limited.

Thus, in German the verb *finden* is used typically in questions inquiring about the addressee's subjective judgment, and in answers to such questions, for example:

Wie findest du das Buch (mein neues Kleid)?

lit., How do you find the book (my new dress)?

"Did you like this book / Did you find it good?"

Ich finde das Buch überhaupt nicht gut.

lit., I find the book not good at all

"I don't like the book at all / I don't find it good."

Unlike the English *I find*, *ich finde* cannot be used in factual sentences based on the speaker's experience, such as the one from Cobuild:

> A lot of young people are choosing German as the main language to learn rather than French, nowadays, I find (**ich finde*).

Similarly, in French, the verb *trouver*, "to find," can be used in subjective-evaluative sentences, but not in factual ones. For example, *The Collins Robert French Dictionary* (1990) cites the following sentences:

> *comment avez-vous trouvé le bifteck?* "how did you find the steak?"
>
> *vous la trouvez sympathique?* "do you find her a nice person?"
>
> *je trouve cela trop sucré/lourd* "I find it too sweet/heavy"
>
> *tu ne trouves pas que j'ai raison?* "don't you think (find) I'm right?"
>
> *trouvez-vous cela normal?* "do you think (find) that's normal?"

At the same time, the *Collins Robert* suggests that in some contexts *to find* should be rendered in French as *s'apercevoir*, *voir*, or *constater* rather than *trouver*, and consultations with native speakers confirm this:

> You will find that I am right. =
> *Vous verrez* or *vous constaterez* or *vous vous apercevrez que j'ai raison.*
> "you'll see/discover/ realize that I'm right"

> I find that I have plenty of time. =
> *Je m'aperçois* or *je constate que j'ai tout le temps qu'il faut*
> "I notice/discover that I have plenty of time"

In fact, the French verb *constater*, which has no equivalent in English, can be seen as a French cultural counterpart of the broadly used English verb *to find*. Unlike *to find*, *constater* implies objective knowledge, based on analytical thinking as well as evidence, and not limited to one person's subjective experience. The verb *trouver* can be used in contexts referring to a person's subjective evaluation of an experience, situation, or opinion but not to objective knowledge derived from personal experience, as in the case of *to find*. (It is worth recalling in this connection the OED comment on the French *trouver* quoted earlier, linking *trouver* with only the more subjective of the two meanings of *find* distinguished by the OED.) Objective knowledge implied by *constater* is based partly on analytical thinking, and as such it is presented as intersubjectively valid. It is only the English *find* that combines a claim to empirical knowledge about the world based on personal experience with a recognition of the limitations of that empirical knowledge and with a reference to personal opinion that doesn't have to be shared by other people. Again, the English sentence:

> A lot of young people are choosing German as the main language to learn rather than French nowadays, I find.

cannot be translated into French with the verb *trouver*, because *trouver* sounds subjective and is not compatible with the factual character of the sentence. It can be translated with *constater*, but such a translation would not have the personal, empirical, and limited character of *I find*, which implies, all at once, "in my opinion," "in my experience" and "to my knowledge"—a quintessentially Anglo cultural construct. The expression *in my experience* doesn't have colloquial equivalents in either German or French. The ways of speaking enshrined in this and other related expressions reflect the same cultural tradition that has found its expression in the epistemic phrase *I find* itself—especially *I find* as a frame for factual sentences (such as "a lot of young people are choosing German as the main language to learn rather than French nowadays, I find"). It is the tradition of British empiricism, of the emphasis on personal experience, on the limitations of one's knowledge, and on tolerance for diverse points of view and respect for everyone's "personal opinion."

Finally, it is worth noting that in its reference to personal experience as a source of some (limited) knowledge, the verb *to find* has a parallel in another language-specific English verb—*to sense*, also without exact semantic equivalents in other European languages. For example, the *Collins Robert French Dictionary* (1990) glosses *to sense* (as in "to sense that one is unwelcome") as "*sentir (intuitivement), deviner, pressentir, rendre compte*," that is, "to feel (intuitively), to guess, to have a premonition, to realize," but none of these French glosses captures the characteristic combination of components that makes up the meaning of the English verb *to sense*. Tentatively, I would explicate this meaning as follows:

> *I sense that I'm unwelcome / I sense danger.* =
> a. I say: I think like this now: I am unwelcome/in danger (in this place)
> b. I can't say I know it
> c. at the same time, I know something about it because I feel something in my body now
> d. I know that I feel something like this in my body when something like this happens to me (e.g., when I am unwelcome in a place, when I'm in danger)

What is characteristic about this semantic configuration is a link between knowledge and personal experience (especially sensory experience), as well as a recognition of the limitations of such knowledge.

7.9. *I Expect*

The epistemic phrase *I expect* is closely related to the lexical verb *to expect*, and in many sentences the two can be almost interchangeable. Consider, for example, the following fragment from Cobuild:

> . . . so I expect this one to be really crap.

Here, the last sentence could be paraphrased as "so I expect this one will be really crap." Generally speaking, when the speaker is talking about his or her current expectations, the lexical verb *to expect* used with a direct object can be replaced with the epistemic phrase including the future auxiliary *will*.

This apparent interchangeability of *to expect* as a lexical verb and the epistemic phrase *I expect* seems to suggest that not only the former but also the latter have an inherently future orientation.

I expect this one to be really crap. =

I expect that this one will be really crap.

Following this lead, we can try to explicate the meaning of the epistemic phrase as follows:

I expect it's got to the bottom of the washing basket. =
a. I say: I think now that it is like this: it's got to the bottom of the washing basket
b. I don't know
c. I think that I will know (later)

There are numerous examples of *I expect* in the Cobuild corpus that appear to be consistent with such an explication. For example:

(If anybody has any questions I'll try and answer them)

I expect they'll be difficult ones and I may not be able to. . . . =
a. I say: I think now that it is like this: they will be difficult
b. I don't know
c. I think that I will know (later)

The future tense of the complement clause appears to support such an explication, but the epistemic phrase *I expect* can of course also be used with complement clauses with the present, present perfect, or past tense. For example:

The Chorus of Hebrew Slaves in the opera by Verdi. I expect it's probably Tosca.

She was brilliant—you've heard of her I expect.

I expect you have talked to MX? Yes I have.

It was a rather good bobble hat and I was going to wash it but I've mislaid it. But I expect it's got to the bottom of the washing basket.

The simplest hypothesis seems to be that the complement clause states what the speaker expects to find out (in the near future). Numerous examples referring to the addressee and seeking confirmation from the addressee seem to support this hypothesis. For example:

I expect you have talked to MX? =
a. I say: I think now that it is like this: you have talked to MX
b. I don't know
c. I think that I will know later (i.e., when you tell me)

If one studies all the examples in the corpus, however, one might come to the conclusion that some of them do not seem to fit this formula very well. Here is an example from Winnie the Pooh:

> Don't you know what Tiggers like to eat? asked Pooh. I expect if I
> thought very hard about it I should, said Christopher Robin.

It could be argued that what Christopher Robin is saying is not "I don't know—I
think that I will know" but rather "I don't know—I think that I can know." There are
other examples in the Cobuild corpus where "I can know" seems to fit better than "I
will know." Here is one referring to jogging outfits:

> That one's very popular. Is it? Mm. I expect it's not very comfy though.

If the second speaker doesn't buy the outfit in question, then probably they will not
know whether it is "comfy." What this speaker seems to be implying is that they *can*
find out that the outfit is not comfortable. Another example:

> Just continue over the river and through the city walls and it's just there.
> Oh yes. I expect I could walk that far couldn't I.

Is the speaker saying, roughly speaking, "I think that I will find out" or "I think that
I can find out"? Since the decision to walk as suggested has not been taken yet, here,
too, "I can" appears to fit the situation better than "I will." And one last example:

> . . . and the Secretary of State set up a committee of enquiry . . . which of
> course came out with the expected conclusions. I expect I've got them
> somewhere.

The speaker who doesn't search for the papers in question will not know whether he
or she has them; the speaker *can* know it, however—if he or she can be bothered to
have a look.

On the other hand, all the examples in which "I can" appears to be more appropriate than "I will" can be interpreted as including an understood *if*-clause.

> I think that if I think very hard about it I will know.

> I think that if I jog in this outfit I will know that it's not very comfy.

> I think that if I have a look I will know that I've got them.

Given this possibility of interpreting all the examples in terms of either "I will know"
or "I will know if," the hypothesis that *I expect* is always linked with the future tense
("I will") can be sustained.

The analysis of the epistemic phrase *I expect* proposed here comes close to one
of the meanings postulated for *expect* in the OED: "to anticipate that it will turn out
to be the case that; hence, to suspect, suppose, surmise." This meaning is illustrated
by the OED with the following sentences (inter alia):

> It is expected that the Duke of Guiese's horse was shot under him. (1592)

> I expect they [the forces] are much stronger than I am made believe. (1645)

The OED states that this meaning is "now rare in literary use," adding: "the misuse
of the word as a synonym of *suppose*, without any notion of 'anticipating' or 'looking
for,' is often cited as an Americanism, but it is very common in dialectal, vulgar or
carelessly colloquial speech in England."

One can wonder, however, whether the use of *I expect* as an epistemic marker in twentieth- and twenty-first-century English (and its growing use in the nineteenth century) doesn't actually show that the meaning described by OED as "now rare" has in fact expanded in some ways rather than shrunk in modern English. It is, of course, true that sentences like *it is expected that his horse was shot under him* are now archaic, but if framed by the first-person phrase *I expect*, they would be more acceptable:

I expect that his horse was shot under him.

Furthermore, analogous sentences with *I expect* and without *that*, referring to the addressee, are well attested in modern English. Consider, first, the following nineteenth-century quote (from the writings of Thomas Jefferson):

How many children have you? You beat me, I expect, on that count.
(1812)

As is common in modern English, the speaker is using here the phrase *I expect* to say something about the addressee and is clearly expecting confirmation from the addressee: the speaker expects to hear something that will confirm what she or he now thinks but doesn't know.

The modern wide use of the epistemic phrase *I expect* in dialogue (especially in British English), seeking immediate confirmation from the addressee, may well create the impression that speakers are now using it (OED says: "misusing") "as a synonym of *suppose*, without any notion of 'anticipating.'" In fact, however, we have seen that the quote from Jefferson does lend itself to an interpretation involving anticipation, and the same applies to numerous analogous instances of the phrase *I expect* in Cobuild (typically, with the present perfect rather than past). For example:

I expect you've come across. . . . Yes.

She was brilliant you've heard of her I expect. Yes. I've heard of her yes.

I expect you've talked to MX? Yes I have.

I expect you have enough of the countryside don't you. Yeah.

Examples of this kind are so common in the Cobuild corpus that they point to a well-established modern conversational routine. This routine does not have to be seen as a "misuse of *expect*" and as the speakers' failure to distinguish, intuitively, between *expect* and *suppose*; in fact, it can be seen as building on a meaning of *expect* that OED itself has documented as going back to the sixteenth century.

At the same time, we must note that in contemporary usage, the relevant meaning of *expect* cannot be extracted from the meaning of the epistemic phrase *I expect* as a whole. The emergence of this phrase, with its particular quasi-performative status and its characteristic semantic combination of components "I think" and "I don't know," is clearly part of a more general phenomenon: the development of an elaborate system of epistemic phrases reflecting the intellectual and social legacy of the British Enlightenment. In particular, the expectation that one will "find out" highlights the emphasis on the need for evidence (for *finding out*, empirically, how things are) and also on the need for caution in making statements until the necessary evidence is found.

7.10. *I Take It*

The epistemic phrase *I take it* is typically used in response to something that some-one else has just said to us; at the same time, it is a response that itself is seeking a response. For example:

—[He] was a pop journalist—I wrote him a private letter—he used bits of
it in a review which got published in a music paper.
—You dumped him I take it.
—I've never spoken to him since.
—I take it the natives are friendly?—Yeah.

In broad outline, the role of the phrase *I take it* in sentences like these can be repre-sented as follows:

I take it the natives are friendly. =
a. I say: I can think now that it is like this: the natives are friendly
b. I can think that it is like this because you said something to me now
c. I don't know
d. I want to know
e. I can know if you say something more about it now
f. I want you to say it

The image of "taking something" provides a useful clue here. *I take it* applies to a thought formed on the basis of what the interlocutor has just said: one "takes" that thought from what they have said. But "taking" something from what has been said does not amount to extracting information and therefore obtaining new knowledge: the thought "taken" from somebody else's words is only a thought and, as such, may be mistaken. Conse-quently, the speaker seeks confirmation, or disconfirmation, from the other person. As a result, *I take it* functions somewhat like a yes-or-no question and is typically followed by a *yes* or a *no* (or by something that amounts to a *yes* or a *no*).

Thus, looking in the OED advanced search for the phrase *I take it*, one finds that the vast majority of twentieth-century examples take the form of a question. Some examples:

'Someone crowned me, I take it'? The sergeant nodded. 'With the poker from our own hearth.' (1959)

The Oxford law would know about this, I take it? (1973)

You'd like the Sanction, I take it? (1980)

—The police tried to trace the handkerchief, I take it?
—They did, but no soap. (1972)
—Miss Blandish—I take it you can keep a secret?
—Try me, Mr Stone. (1971)

But even in those sentences where *I take it* is not accompanied by a question mark, it is usually clear from the context that the speaker is asking for confirmation. For example:

> When shall I start? In the spit and sawdust? I take it you'll do the saloon
> bar yourself. (1969)

Typically, the sentence in the *I take it* frame refers—directly or indirectly—to the addressee, who is understandably seen as someone who would know and thus be in a position to confirm.

Although the phrase *I take it* is well attested in English from the end of the sixteenth century, such an interrogatory use of *I take it* (asking for confirmation) is a relatively recent phenomenon in English. Thus, in the OED's advanced search, we find only one nineteenth-century example of it (among numerous examples of other uses), whereas in the twentieth-century material it is the vastly predominant pattern. In older (roughly, pre-twentieth-century) usage, the phrase *I take it* does not imply seeking confirmation. It often occurs in the syntactic frame *as I take it* and as part of the expression *I take it for granted*, both of which indicate the speaker's confidence rather than lack of knowledge.

> I take it for granted, he will come to the moderates (and by thus reuniting
> the party . . .). (1794)

> I take it for granted, this whole affair will end in smoke. (1709)

> Some have been true sportsmen—and as I take it, the phrase true sports-
> man includes everything that is manly and gentlemanly. (1894)

Furthermore, even in those cases where *I take it* occurs on its own (without "as" or "for granted"), it is often clear from the content of the sentence that the speaker is expressing a judgment and is not seeking confirmation. One example from Shakespeare:

> I take it he is somewhat a weakly man: and he has as it were a whay
> coloured beard. (1602)

This character of *I take it* as the speaker's own judgment is also clearly visible in sentences where *I take* is used with a direct object, as in the following example, also from Shakespeare:

> Come, wife, I take it be almost dinner time.

Thus, it is only in the modern use (from the nineteenth century onward) that *I take it* has developed into a distinct conversational routine, with the components "I don't know," "I want to know," "I can know if you say something," and "I want you to say it."

In fact, *I take it* has two variants that are interrogative in structure as well as meaning: *do I take it . . . ?* and *can I take it . . . ?* The first one (though not the second one) can be illustrated with examples from Cobuild:

> He said do I take it that they disobeyed you? And she said of course not.

> Do I take it that you can write Lem? Yeah.

There is a difference of register between the two, *can I take it* being more informal than *do I take it*, and there is also a difference in meaning: *can I take it* implies that the speaker wants to hear confirmation rather than disconfirmation, whereas *do I take it* is neutral in this regard. In the advanced search, there are no examples of *can I take it*, but there is one late-nineteenth-century example of *may I take it*:

May I take it that you will sign the document? (1881)

Clearly, *may I take it* implies here that the speaker would like to hear the question confirmed.

When the sentence with *I take it* does not have an interrogative structure, it can still have an interrogative intonation and be marked in writing with a question mark. Or it can be followed by a pause, indicating that the speaker is waiting for a response. Some examples (from Cobuild):

—So I take it then you're kind of asking my attitude?
—Yeah.
—And I take it you've not used it?
—No.
—I take it then it's ten o'clock and some sort of bell has gone? Has it?
—No. Five past ten the bell's going to go off.
—You mentioned [in] one of your opening phrases that thirty million pounds over the next five years was going to be expended against the arts. That excludes the cost of Symphony Hall I take it.
—Yeah.
—You've see them around I take it.
—Oh yes.

As these examples make clear, what the speaker "takes" to be the case does not have to be a conclusion drawn from the preceding utterance (as in the case of "you dumped him I take it"). Rather, it can be a detail filling in or clarifying some aspects of the picture emerging from that preceding utterance.

All these examples are consistent with the phrasing of the component "I think now that it is like this" but would not necessarily be compatible with an added "because of this." For example, the statement "that excludes the cost of Symphony Hall" is not a conclusion drawn from what the interlocutor has said but rather a kind of lateral comment—a corollary rather than an implication of that earlier utterance.

Finally, we should note the continuity as well as the change in the history of the phrase *I take it*. The confidence that it initially showed through its link with *I take it for granted* gave way to a conversational reserve ("I don't know") and the seeking of confirmation from the addressee. At the same time, the speaker's attitude is one of cautious confidence: he or she is willing to form a judgment, at least a provisional one ("I can think now that it is like this").

As with other epistemic phrases, the OED does not acknowledge that the phrase *I take it* has developed a meaning of its own in modern English. It does posit for the verb *take* a meaning "denoting intellectual action," which it glosses as "to apprehend mentally, to conceive, understand, consider," but this "definition" is so vague and imprecise that it could cover both the older meanings of the verb *to take* and the meaning of the modern phrase *I take it*. Here as elsewhere, it is clear that to be able to understand the semantic change (including its cultural underpinnings), we need a rigorous and effective semantic methodology.

7.11. *I Understand*

Used as a lexical verb, *understand* implies thinking and knowledge. For example, "I understand that it's their problem" implies that "I know that it's their problem" and "I've thought about it." It also implies a causal link between the thinking and the knowing: "I know it *because* I've thought about it" (not because someone told me so).

Used as an epistemic phrase, *I understand* retains its links with both thinking and knowing, but the overall configuration is different. Consider, for example, the following fragment:

. . . so anyway so he left his card and I rang up this morning and said "I understand you called at my home yesterday" and he said "yes"

It is obvious that in colloquial language *understand* can be used in this sense only in quasi-performative first-person (present-tense) sentences. For example, it would not normally be possible to say:

*John understands that you called at his house yesterday.[6]

The speaker's attitude, expressed in the epistemic phrase *I understand*, presents a subtle combination of confidence and reserve, which can be portrayed as follows:

I understand that you called at my home yesterday. =
a. I say: I think now that it is like this: you called at my home yesterday
b. I don't say I know
c. I think that it is like this because someone else said something like this
d. I think that this someone can know

The speaker's attitude is more confident than in the case of *I think*, but it stops short of a fully confident "I know." It is not just "I think that," but it is not quite "I know" either. This midway position between "I think" and "I know" can be captured by means of the component "I think" with a reference to someone else saying something like this—someone who "can know." The widely used syntactic frame "as I understand (it)" highlights this fairly confident and at the same time noncommittal attitude: "as I understand" implies some evidence but also leaves some room for being wrong.

I understand appears to be the only epistemic phrase that allows such a frame: one cannot say *as I gather, *as I assume, *as I presume, *as I suppose, *as I expect, *as I guess, and so on. This tentativeness of *I understand* is highlighted by examples like the following ones:

That's the way I understand it anyway.

Now that is how I understand it. If I'm wrong Martin Deaner can ring up and tell us.

These examples, which feature the introducers *how* and *the way*, are not exactly examples of *I understand* as an epistemic phrase, but the tentativeness implied by *how* (or *the way*) *I understand it* carries over to *as I understand it*, as the following example illustrates:

> I remember reading a book by Gareth Lloyd Davis who as I understand in the past was a lecturer here is that right?

An acknowledgment of the limitations of one's knowledge is also clearly conveyed by another common frame—*as far as I understand.* For example:

> . . . as far as I understand from the let's say first part of your reports all the republics in the former Soviet Union are very closely interdependent.

> . . . as far as I understand what Michael Heseltine's saying he's keeping an element of the people there anyway isn't he?

The pointed tentativeness of the epistemic phrase *I understand* is linked with its implication of being based on what someone else has said (whether orally or in writing). The other person's words can serve both as evidence and as a distancing device.

The frames "as (I understand)" and "as far as (I understand)" reflect the distance and the possibility of error. The reference to evidence provided by somebody else's words is reflected in the syntactic frame "from . . .":

> I think as I understand from conversations last week that is something that we're using both of us.

> I understand from what I've been told that MX did not feel deeply defensive of the Cow Green site.

> As far as I understand from let's say first part of your reports. . . .

> I understand from reading the financial papers that it's fifty percent of the domestic appliance company.

> I understand from the commissioners that they see [house name] as a teeth-cutting exercise on how to get [hospice name]. . . .

Curiously, the phrase *I understand* is also often linked with the preposition *from* in a different way: not as "I understand from" but as "from what I understand." In this latter frame, the understanding itself is presented as the source of the speaker's tentative knowledge:

> . . . from what I understand I think that Princess Diana was addicted to peppermint after tennis.

> from what I understand you know some ecological theories maintain that assemblage might just be by chance rather than actually having any particular internal relationships.

> Most of them are from what I understand they tend to be school-based.

> From what I understand of it they are not allowed to counsel or advise are they.

The first "from" frame is also characteristic of the epistemic phrase *I gather (I gather from).* The second one, seldom used in combinations with *I gather,* has its parallels in expressions like *from what I hear* and *from what I can see.* These parallels suggest that in the expression *from what I understand* the thinking-interpreting process is seen as a potential source of evidence. All these expressions—*from what I understand, from what*

I hear, and *from what I can see*—appear to imply a judgment as well as some basis for making this judgment: judging from (i.e., on the basis of) what I hear/see/understand. . . . This is consistent with the proposed combination of components "I don't say I know," "someone else said something like this," and "I think that this someone can know."

7.12. *I Imagine*

I imagine differs from all the other epistemic phrases in its tendency to co-occur with the irrealis modal auxiliary *would*. Some examples from Cobuild:

> I imagine that would be really interesting.

> I imagine that they would freak out a bit about it.

> Well I imagine a tree would go right through an MR Two. I mean they are not exactly substantial cars.

> I imagine Hull would be a place where there are more scrap Ladas around.

In addition to *would*, *I imagine* often combines with two other modals: *must* and *will*. For example:

> A yearly diary and it listed all the societies. I imagine there must be some still extant.

> Must be very different now I imagine.

> I imagine they'll have a lot of books in common.

> I imagine when this hall opens that Roman Catholics will be using it at least occasionally for worship.

The "irrealis" character of sentences introduced by *I imagine*, often signaled by *would*, can be linked with (though not fully explained by) the speaker's lack of knowledge, which is often expressed overtly. For example:

> I don't actually know how much it is but I would imagine that it would have been too expensive for me to do that.

> I don't know if anyone's actually said it but this is the sort of thing I imagine they would say.

> They do seem to know a lot about drugs, but crime generally I don't know. I imagine that there is but I have got no firm evidence.

As a first approximation, then, we could consider positing for *I imagine* two semantic components: "I think" and "I don't know," bringing it thus very close to *I suppose*. As a final analysis, however, this would not be very satisfactory, because *I imagine* has a more "imaginary" ("unreal") quality than *I suppose*. Consider for example the following sentence:

> I imagine it's very easy to get lost here.

If I say this, am I saying (inter alia) that I think it's very easy to get lost in that place? Not necessarily. I may not actually think so (hold such a view); however, I can *imagine* myself thinking that this is the case. More simply, I can think that this is so if I give free rein to my imagination, that is, if I allow myself briefly to think what I want. Arguably, the combination of an *if*-component with an *I can think*-component would account best for the "irrealis" character of the phrase *I imagine*, reflected in the element *would*. This leads us to the following explication:

> *I imagine it's very easy to get lost here.* =
> a. I say: I can think like this now: it is very easy to get lost here
> b. I don't want to say: I think that it is like this
> c. I don't know
> d. if I want to think something about it now I can think that it is like this

The component "I don't know" links *I imagine* with *I suppose*. The component "I can think" accounts for the more "imaginary," more evocative character of *I imagine* (often associated with mental pictures of imagined states of affairs). By contrast, *I suppose* (a supposition) implies a more or less momentary thought—actual, not potential, and unrelated to fancy, images, or mental pictures: "I think like this now." In addition, *I suppose* implies a moment of reflection, and it is often combined with an intonation indicating indecision and a process of forming a thought: "I'm thinking about it now." There are no such implications in *I imagine*.

7.13. *I Bet*

Let us start by considering a few examples from Cobuild:

> They're very pretty glasses. They're from Snips, I bet.
>
> I bet I win the horrible basket of fruit with one banana in.
>
> I bet the kids don't know what guineas are nowadays, I bet they've never even heard of guineas.
>
> I bet that happens a lot.
>
> He didn't like that at all.—I bet he didn't.

As these examples illustrate, the epistemic phrase *I bet* is related to the lexical verb *to bet* in conveying a paradoxical combination of mental states: on the one hand, they lay no claim to knowledge, and on the other, they express a subjective certainty. If one bets, one knows that one doesn't really know what is going to happen, and yet one feels as confident about the outcome as if one did know—so much so that one is willing to put one's money on it. Similarly, if one says *I bet*, this implies something like "I feel absolutely certain" and at the same time something like an admission that one doesn't really know: "I don't say I know." This leads us to the following formula:

> *I bet that happens a lot.* =
> a. I say: I think now that it is like this: that happens a lot
> b. I can't say I know
> c. I think like this because I know some other things
> d. I say this because I want to say something about it now

I bet you won't get the cash. =
  a. I say: I think now that it is like this: you won't get the cash
  b. I can't say I know
  c. I think like this because I know some other things
  d. I say this because I want to say something about it now

The epistemic phrase *I bet* combines a virtual admission that one doesn't know with a great subjective certainty that something is the case—a certainty reflected in the image of putting one's money on a certain thought (as one would put money on a horse). As in the case of *I guess*, it may seem that the speaker is throwing caution to the winds, expressing a confident opinion without sufficient objective evidence. In the case of *I bet*, however, the speaker has at least some relevant knowledge, which is not the case with *I guess*. At the same time, the very use of the phrase *I bet* indicates that the speaker is aware of the uncertain epistemic status of the utterance and is also drawing the addressee's attention to it. While expressing a subjective certainty, the speaker is scrupulously stressing at the same time: "I can't say I know."

7.14. *I Suspect*

The epistemic phrase *I suspect* is obviously closely related to the lexical verb *suspect*, to the noun *suspicion*, and to the adjective *suspicious*. The OED posits several meanings for the verb *suspect*, beginning with the following two definitions: "1. To imagine something evil, wrong or undesirable in (person or thing) on slight or no evidence; to believe or fancy to be guilty or faulty, with insufficient proof or knowledge. . . . 2. To imagine or fancy something, esp. something wrong, about (a person or thing) with slight or no proof. . . . " What these definitions clearly—and rightly—imply is that the meaning of *suspect* includes, roughly speaking, "thinking something bad" about someone or something, as well as "not knowing." Clues from these related words suggest that in the case of the epistemic phrase, too, there is something one doesn't know that one thinks could be bad. But does this suspected "badness" carry over to *all* the instances of the epistemic phrase *I suspect*?

If one looks through pages upon pages of this phrase in the Cobuild corpus, one can see many examples that clearly do imply something bad. For example:

We're going to have to live with it, I suspect.

Don't you think it's going to backfire on him?—Well I suspect it may.

It would take too long to do it here David I suspect.

It's very time consuming in any case I suspect.

I suspect they'd run into all sorts of trouble.

I suspect he's quite hung up about it.

If one focuses on such examples, one can be tempted to posit for *I suspect* a component along the lines of "I think about it like this: it is something bad." On the other hand, there are also examples in the Cobuild corpus that seem not to be compatible with such a component. For example:

It's all very complicated politics I suspect.

I suspect this citation of "akespeare" is the Bard with his "Sh" missed off.

Examples of this kind suggest that the evaluative component of *I suspect* (if there is one) should be given a weaker form — "I think about it like this: it is not something good," rather than the one derived from the lexical verb *suspect*: "I think about it like this: it is something bad."

In fact, some uses of the phrase *I suspect* may seem to be lacking any evaluative implications whatsoever. For instance, what could be seen as "not good" in the following example from Cobuild?

Now you were obviously quite a bright young person I suspect.

The OED, which doesn't distinguish the epistemic phrase *I suspect* from other uses of the verb *suspect*, is clearly ambivalent about the presence (or otherwise) of an evaluative component in this verb's meaning(s). This indecision is reflected in the sequence of putative meanings, starting with a definitely "bad" one ("1. To imagine something evil, wrong or undesirable"), then moving to a predominantly "bad" one ("2. To imagine or fancy something, esp. something wrong"), and then moving to one without any "bad" connotations ("3. To imagine or fancy something to be possible or likely").

If any uses of *suspect* can be suspected of having no evaluative component at all, the epistemic phrase *I suspect* would be the prime suspect in this respect. The OED (1849) example "The late Alexander Knox . . . learned, I suspect, much of his theological system from Fowler's writings" may seem a good case in point. On the other hand, without context, the following sentences sound rather odd:

?I suspect it's all right.

?I suspect he's okay.

certainly odder than their counterparts with *suppose*:

I suppose it's all right.

I suppose he's okay.

What contrasts like these suggest is that *I suspect* does have some evaluative implications. I suggest that to reconcile our two conclusions, which appear to be in conflict, we need to consider the broader context of those sentences whose propositional content refers to something neutral or "good" rather than something "not good." If, for example, the speaker has been arguing that something must be defective and now begins to think that he or she may have been wrong, then the sentence *I suspect it's all right* does not sound odd any longer. In such a context, "I suspect it's all right" could be seen as a compressed version of "I suspect that I was wrong." Similarly, in my own sentence "if any uses of *suspect* can be suspected of having no evaluative component at all . . ." I have used the word *suspected* because if some uses of *suspect* had no evaluative component at all, this would mean that my initial hypothesis was wrong.

A good example of such a use of *I suspect* is provided by one of the citations in the OED's advanced search—a quote from Richard Dawkins's chapter in *Evolution from Molecules to Men* (1983):

> In the modern context I do not think Darwin should be labelled a strong gradualist. In the modern context I suspect that he would be rather open-minded.

At first sight, the statement that in the modern context Darwin "would be rather open-minded" appears to be saying "something good" about Darwin, rather than "something not good," let alone "something bad." Yet if we follow this citation to its source and consider it in the broader context in which it occurs, we will see that what the author is saying with it can indeed be seen as something "not good." In the passage in question, Dawkins is arguing forcefully against scholars (especially Gould) who see Darwin as a "strong gradualist." Inter alia, he writes: "Why on earth should Darwin have committed himself to such an arbitrarily restrictive version of evolution, a version that positively invites falsification?" (p. 418). Whereas Gould describes the key statement by Darwin on this point as "clearly invalid," Dawkins argues that it is "valid and very wise." In this context, the remark that Darwin would now be seen as "rather open-minded" functions as a polemical shot—understated ("I suspect" rather than "I maintain" or "I believe") but clearly implying something "not good" about Gould's argument.

Before proposing a full explication of *I suspect*, we need to consider one other aspect of its meaning, separating it from most other epistemic phrases: its "detective" connotations. *I suspect* implies that "I don't know" but that someone *can* know—if they do something (investigate, ask questions, follow the clues, etc.). This combination of "I don't know" and "someone can know" links *I suspect* with *I expect*, and indeed in most examples the two appear to be interchangeable. Nonetheless, in native speakers' estimation, *I suspect* has "a different flavor." This perceived "different flavor" can be explained in terms of the evaluative component, discussed earlier ("I think about it like this: it is not something good") and also of a "detective" attitude (an inclination to do something to find out). This brings us to the following overall explication:

> *I suspect he's quite hung up about it.* =
> a. I say: I think now that it can be like this: he's quite hung up about it
> b. I don't know
> c. I think that someone can know if this someone does some things
> d. I think about it like this: if it is true it is not something good

For example, if it is true that in the modern context Darwin would be rather open-minded, this is not something good for Dawkins's argument (although it would of course be something good about Darwin).

7.15. *I Assume*

The epistemic phrase *I assume*, which judging by the OED's advanced search appears to have spread in the twentieth century and originated not much before, clearly has its source in an older meaning of the verb *to assume*, described in the OED as follows: "to take for granted as the basis of argument or action; to suppose." The earliest example of this meaning cited by the OED reads:

> Plotinus always assumeth that beatitude and eternity goeth ever together. (1598)

I argue that the epistemic phrase *I assume* also refers to a thought taken as a basis for "a further argument or action." It would not be accurate to say, however, that *I assume* also implies "I take it for granted." As in the case of several other epistemic phrases, the meaning of the verb on which they are based has "weakened" in those phrases and has developed ignorative components like "I don't know," "I don't say I know," and "I can't say I know."

In the case of *I assume*, this ignorative component cannot take the form "I don't know" because the speaker sounds too confident for that. At the same time, it does not have the overconfidence of phrases like *I presume* and *I bet*, which warrant the component of, as it were, reluctant admission: "I can't say I know." The phrasing that appears to fit *I assume* best is a free, rather than reluctant, admission: "I know that I don't know."

The thought inherent in an "assumption" is often short-lived rather than enduring: "I think now that it is like this." This temporary character of an assumption can be illustrated with the following example:

> are you able to give another description. . . . I assume at this point in time that the gentleman that you are with is perhaps not very tall clean-shaven with dark hair . . . [from a police inquiry]

At the same time, this provisional thought is not a fleeting one, without any consequences, but on the contrary, it is one intentionally taken as a basis for doing something, including speaking or further thinking (e.g., for developing an argument or for proceeding with a hypothesis). Expressions like *I'm working on the assumption that* and *I'll proceed on the assumption that* are particularly revealing in this respect. Thus, we arrive at the following explication:

> *I assume that I will be attacked.* =
> a. I say: I think now that it is like this: I will be attacked
> b. I know that I don't know
> c. I want to think for some time that I know that it is like this
> d. because if I think like this I can do some other things because of this

Let's test this explication against some examples. First, a few examples from the OED:

> *Hansard Commons* I assume that my hon. Friend has in mind what are sometimes called billeting surveys. (1938)

> *Mag. Fantasy & SF* (N.Y.) I assume that I will be attacked, and decide to file a situation report. (1960)

> A.HALL I'd left my things in Room 29 as . . . routine procedure for a skip, to let them assume I was simply out for the evening. (1981)

It seems clear that in all these examples the speaker wants, as the OED puts it, "to take something for granted as the basis of action." The proposed action can be either physical or intellectual: the speaker may want to know something—or to think that they know it—in order to proceed, to build a picture, to continue an investigation. This can be further illustrated with some examples from Cobuild:

> You were born in Minehead.—Right.—I assume your parents for occupational reasons moved to London is that right? (Implied: so that I can proceed)

> Well I was standing at the top and I remember sitting at the bottom so I assume I fell down them. (Implied: so that I can continue my story)

> You mentioned two friends in particular who I assume are about the same age as you. (Implied: I want to build a picture)

> I assume that'll be available. (Implied: I want to base my further planning, etc., on this assumption)

> I assume that if you're called Girls Against Smoking that none of you smoke is that right? (Implied: I want to work on this assumption)

> I assume you've got a good idea of where it is. (Again: I want to work on this assumption)

> So if somebody took your mum's washing machine away I assume it's your Mum's it could be your Dad's how would she feel about that? (I assume it's your Mum's—I want to base my further questions on this assumption)

In all these cases, one wants to proceed to do something, and to do so, one needs to think—if only for a moment—that one knows something that in fact one doesn't know. One is willing to do so, as it were, experimentally—either to have one's thought confirmed by someone who does know or simply to take an intellectual stab and live with the consequences.

There is something counterfactual about an "assumption" and something creative. One is taking a risk, but this risk is well calculated. Above all, one is conscious of what one is doing, and the addressee is warned, too. Thus, in making assumptions one is not acting counter to the Lockean doctrine that the degree of assent must be commensurate with the scope of our knowledge (and our ignorance). Rather, one is acting in accordance with this doctrine, insofar as one is carefully paying attention to, and making clear for the addressee, the exact epistemic status of what one is thinking and saying.

7.16. Conclusion

The set of epistemic phrases discussed here is by no means exhaustive. To mention just a few, the following have not been discussed: *I estimate, I surmise, I conjecture, I speculate, I feel, I foresee, I hear.* The group explored here, however, is sufficient to give us a good insight into the main themes in the semantics of the English epistemic phrases and to throw light on their cultural underpinnings.

The leitmotif of these phrases is the acknowledgment of the limitations of one's knowledge and of the tentative status of most of the things that we say. The recurrent semantic components are "I don't know," "I don't say I know," and "I can't say I know."

This brings us back to Locke's discussion of the limitations of human knowledge and the value of being cautious and tentative in one's statements. In most cases, Locke tells us, our judgments have more or less shaky grounds:

> . . . it is unavoidable to the greatest part of men, if not all, to have several *opinions*, without certain and indubitable proof of their truth. (Locke 1959, 371)

> For where is the man that has incontestable evidence of the truth of all that he holds, or of the falsehood of all he condemns; or can say that he has examined to the bottom all his own, or other men's opinions? The necessity of believing without knowledge, nay often upon very slight grounds, in this fleeting state of action and blindness we are in, should make us more busy and careful to inform ourselves than constrain others. (Locke 1959, 373)

The idea of not imposing our own opinions on others, expressed in the last sentence of this quote, is another great theme in Locke's *Essay* and in modern Anglo culture as a whole, and it is closely related to the Lockean emphasis on the distinction between thinking and knowing and on the importance of acknowledging the limitations of one's knowledge.

Of course, it is one thing to demonstrate the correlation between the semantics of English epistemic phrases and the great themes of the British Enlightenment, and another, to establish a causal link between the two, as I have hypothesized here. To verify this hypothesis, one would need to study in considerable detail the history of English epistemic phrases. This is a task for the future. In this chapter, I can only make some preliminary observations, derived from a partial examination of a limited set of historical sources. In particular, I want to invite the reader to first take a look at the overall epistemic scene in one classic sixteenth-century work, Thomas More's *A Dialogue of Comfort against Tribulation* (1965 [1557]), and second, to briefly consider the history of the epistemic phrase *I believe*.

To begin with More, I suggest that even a cursory reading of his work shows that the epistemic scene in it is quite different from the modern one. First of all, the range of epistemic verbal phrases used by More is very narrow, and those he does use exude certainty and conviction. They include *I doubt not, I nothing doubt, methinks verily, I think verily, I verily suppose, I suppose surely, I suppose very surely, I ween, I verily ween, I trust, I wot,* and *I know.*

It is particularly striking that the phrase *I suppose,* which in modern English implies lack of confidence ("I don't know"), in More's language is confident and combines readily with the expression *very true,* as in the following example:

> This is, I suppose, uncle, very true.

It also combines readily with the adverb *surely,* which has now also changed its meaning but which for More implied certainty. For example:

> For I suppose surely that any man that hath reason in his head shall hold himself satisfied with this. (p. 217)

> For I suppose very surely, cousin, that many a man and woman too . . . of whom there now sit some (and many shall hereafter sit) full gloriously crowned in heaven, had they not first been afraid of hell, would toward heaven never have set foot forward. (p. 227)

The combinations of *I suppose* and other epistemic verbal phrases with the adverb *verily* are also revealing. For example:

> I verily suppose that the consideration of this incomparable kindness could not fail . . . to influence our key-cold hearts. . . . (p. 234)
>
> Me thinketh verily, cousin, that you say the truth. (p. 183)
>
> I verily ween that the thing is thus of very plain truth in very deed. (p. 202)
>
> For I think verily that so much of your tale is true. (p. 211)

In addition to the combinations with the emphatically assertive adverbs *surely* and *verily*, collocations with the adverb *well*, such as the following ones, are also striking: *I perceive well, I see well,* and *I believe well* (not to mention *I wot well*). For example:

> I perceive well . . . that you would esteem Death so much the less if she should come alone without either shame or pain. (p. 210)
>
> That I believe well, cousin. (p. 210)
>
> I see well that you reckon that who so dieth a natural death dieth like a wanton even at his ease. (p. 223)

The frequent use of such expressions implying strong confidence and conviction is, of course, all the more remarkable, given that epistemic expressions implying caution and lack of confidence such as *I expect, I suspect, I gather, I understand, I imagine,* or *I presume* are totally absent. Equally remarkable is the fact that of the large class of cautious epistemic adverbs that we find in modern English (e.g., *presumably, apparently, allegedly, evidently*) the only one that can be found in More's prose is *undoubtedly,* which is the least cautious of them all.

From a modern point of view, it is also striking how frequently the speaker vouches emphatically for the truth of what he is saying, using phrases like *very sure* (*I am very sure*), *very true, very true indeed, plainly true, this is very truth, very truth it is, of very truth, open truth,* and *plain and open evidential truth,* as well as adverbial and exclamatory expressions like *verily, forsooth, by troth, by my troth,* and *in good faith* (not to mention *by our Lady* and the like). There are also various combinations of such expressions, such as, for example, "This is, good uncle, in good faith very true," "forsooth, uncle, this is very truth," and "verily that is truth."

In the semantic universe reflected in this kind of discourse, truth and faith reign supreme, and there is little concern indeed with the limitations of human knowledge or the need for modulating one's assent in accordance with the strength of the available evidence. It is definitely a pre-Enlightenment type of discourse.

Turning now to the history of the epistemic phrase *I believe,* I will point out that this phrase emerged in the history of English in the Age of Reason, not in the Age of Faith. The OED defines the verb *to believe* with a complement clause as "to hold it as true that . . . , be of the opinion, think," but this formula covers different senses of the word and obscures significant semantic and cultural changes.

In Shakespeare's language, *believe* is indeed related to truth: *to believe* someone or something means, essentially, to think that what someone says is true. It is also a matter of choice: one chooses to believe someone or something voluntarily, and although one can do so only "in part," one can also do so "well," even "potently," and "surely." To illustrate:

> The complaints I have heard of you I do not all believe. (*All's Well That Ends Well*)

> DUKES Dost thou believe, Orlando, that the boy / Can do all that that he hath promised?

> ORLANDO I sometimes do believe and sometimes do not (*As You Like It*)

> I will upon all hazards well believe / Thou art my friend. (*King John*)

> I do well believe you. (*Cymbeline*)

> So have I heard and do in part believe it. (*Hamlet*)

> . . . all which, sir, / Though I most powerfully and potently believe, yet. . . . (*Hamlet*)

> MESSALA Believe not so. For we will hear, note and believe in heart. (*King Henry V*)

Furthermore, *believe* is used predominantly in combination with a direct object referring to a person, for instance, "who will believe thee, Isobel?" "you are now bound to believe him," "I do constantly believe you," "do not believe him," "I must believe you," "he will not believe a fool," "would they believe me," and "widow I should believe you," and the most common collocation is the imperative with the first-person object: "believe me, sir," "not I, believe me," "believe me, lord," "believe me, sister," "believe me, I cannot." What all these supplications and pleas appear to mean is not only "I want you to think that it is true" but also "I don't want you to think: maybe this is not true." Although *believe* occurs also in other frames and in other senses, including what may seem to be an epistemic sense, it appears that in Shakespeare, as in More, it is never compatible with doubt; indeed, it is, as it were, an opposite of doubt. Although we do find in Shakespeare's works the phrase "I believe in part" and the sentence "I sometimes do believe and sometimes do not," this is not incompatible with the suggestion that by itself, *believe*, including I *believe*, implies in Shakespeare's language a strong conviction.

Since it is impossible to undertake a fuller discussion of this matter here, I will comment more fully on just one key example: the sentence cited by the OED in support of the claim that the current epistemic meaning of *believe* can be attested in Shakespeare's language. This key example reads: "I believe I know the cause" (*Measure for Measure*). This sounds indeed just like the present-day usage, and this particular instance of I *believe* seems indistinguishable from the epistemic verbal phrase I *believe* discussed in this chapter.

And yet when we consider this example in context, we will see that this impression is deceptive. In this scene, in which Lucio is speaking to the duke, who is disguised as a friar, Lucio has full knowledge of the situation and is constantly making hints to this effect, but he does not want to state overtly what he knows. In particular, he speaks of the duke to the same (disguised) duke like this:

LUCIO: He would be drunk too; that let me inform you.

DUKE: You do him wrong surely.

LUCIO: Sir, I was an inward of his. A shy fellow was the duke: and I believe I know the cause of his withdrawing.

DUKE: What, I prithee, might be the cause?

LUCIO: No, pardon; 'tis a secret must be locked within the teeth and lips: but this I can let you understand. . . .

DUKE: You speak unskilfully; or, if your knowledge be more, it is much darkened in your malice. . . .

LUCIO: Come, sir, I know what I know.

Thus, when the duke responds to Lucio's sentence "I believe I know the cause" with the question "what . . . might be the cause?" Lucio replies that it is a secret; and when the duke tries to question Lucio's knowledge, Lucio replies, "sir, I know what I know." Clearly, then, Lucio's initial *I believe* does not have the present meaning of "I think, I don't say I know." Lucio does know, and he says so. Far from implying "I don't say I know," his "I believe" implies something like "I have no doubt at all, I am certain." This is not the present-day meaning.

Thus, in Shakespeare's times, *I believe* was associated with truth and implied strong conviction (an absence of doubt). By the end of the eighteenth century, however, *believe* had developed a strong association with reasons and, in particular, with the phrase "I have reason to believe" (see Hahn 2002), and in this new use it had lost its association with "truth." For example, when Swift says in *Gulliver's Travels*:

The continent of which this kingdom is a part, extends itself, as I have reason to believe, eastward.

believe is not referring to somebody else's words that the speaker may or may not "hold as true" but rather to what one thinks, and why. It is clearly in this context of "having good reason to believe something" that the epistemic phrase *I believe* is born—a phrase that implies caution and lack of full knowledge and that does not refer to truth. Three early examples from the writings of Daniel Defoe:

In which drawer there was a great deal of money in gold, I believe near two hundred guineas, but I knew not how much.

As covetousness is the root of all evil, so poverty is, I believe, the worst of all snares. But I waive that discourse till I come to an experiment.

"I believe they are dead, for I have heard nothing of them for above two days; and I was afraid to inquire after them," said he, "for I had nothing to relieve them with."

In her highly acclaimed *Bible and Sword*, historian Barbara Tuchman (2001 [1956], 148) characterizes the eighteenth century in Britain as follows: "It was the age of reason and free thought. . . . The awful logic of John Locke opened new realms of uncertainty. . . . Security of faith gave way to the insecurity of knowledge." The chapter from which this quote comes is entitled "The Reign of Mr. Worldly Wiseman," and this title captures a great deal about the new post-Lockean consciousness that developed in Britain at that time. Mr. Worldly Wiseman is a "reasonable man" in the new, post-Lockean sense of the word *reasonable* (see chapter 4), and he is someone sufficiently confident in his reason to be able to form and express an opinion ("I think") but also wise enough to express it very cautiously and "unimposingly": "I don't say I know." Phrases like *I believe* and *I suppose* (in the new, "weakened" sense of these words) were perfect tools for conveying such an attitude.

I said at the outset that the emergence of a large class of epistemic phrases is a striking innovation of modern English, quite remarkable in both a historical and cross-linguistic perspective. I also said that I wanted to investigate not only the semantics of these phrases but also their cultural underpinnings. We can see now that the two tasks are in fact inseparable.

First of all, it is only through a rigorous semantic analysis of the individual epistemic phrases that we can establish the existence of these phrases as a major grammatical and semantic class in modern English—a class that is not recognized either in authoritative English grammars (e.g., Quirk et al. 1985) or in the *Oxford English Dictionary*. As we have seen, the OED makes no distinction between the meaning of verbs like *believe, guess, gather,* or *suspect* when used in the first-person singular present tense and in other grammatical contexts, and English grammars do not make such a distinction either—and so fail to recognize the epistemic phrases as a distinct grammatical class.

Second, it is only through rigorous semantic analysis that we can discover the deep correspondence between the meanings of epistemic phrases and the ideas of the British Enlightenment, epitomized by Locke's *Essay Concerning Human Understanding*, and thus establish a historical link between the two.

A rigorous semantic analysis, valid in both a cross-linguistic and a historical perspective, is not possible without a suitable methodological framework. The natural semantic metalanguage provides such a framework and so opens new perspectives on meaning, grammar, history, and culture.

Chapter 8

PROBABLY

*English Epistemic Adverbs and
Their Cultural Significance*

8.1. Introduction

8.1.1. Epistemic adverbs as a striking category of modern English

As mentioned in chapter 2, English has a much larger repertoire of epistemic (sentential) adverbs than other European languages, possibly indeed without parallel in other languages of the world. The set of these adverbs includes the following: *probably, possibly, clearly, obviously, presumably, evidently, apparently, supposedly, conceivably, undoubtedly, allegedly, reportedly, arguably, unquestionably, seemingly, certainly*, and, in American English, *likely*.

As I will discuss in more detail, this rich repertoire of epistemic adverbs developed in English gradually. Undoubtedly, the rise of this semanticogrammatical category in English was related to the rise of verbal epistemic phrases, such as *I presume, I assume, I gather, I understand*, and *I suppose*. The cultural concerns reflected in the two categories are essentially the same, and in both cases they can be linked with the post-Lockean emphasis on the limitations of human knowledge, on the need to distinguish knowledge from judgment, and on differentiating between different "degrees of assent."

The fact that the existence of a large class of epistemic adverbs constitutes a peculiar feature of modern English appears to have gone unnoticed in the relevant literature. In fact, Nuyts (2001), who has discussed what he calls "epistemic adverbs and adjectives" in English, Dutch, and German in considerable detail, comments that "the classes are actually remarkably comparable across the three languages considered here" (p. 56).

But to compare the class of "epistemic adverbs" in different languages, one must first identify this class in each language, and for this, one needs some explicit semantic criteria. In the absence of a detailed semantic analysis of the individual words, it is impossible to rigorously delimit the class in question; without delimiting it, it is impossible to compare its size across language boundaries.

For example, Nuyts matches the English words *undoubtedly* and *surely* with the German words *zweifelsohne* (lit., "without doubt"), *zweifellos* (lit., "doubtless"), and *bestimmt* (roughly, "definitely"), as well as matching the English *maybe* and *perhaps* with the German word *vielleicht*. He doesn't explain, however, on what basis he places *undoubtedly*, *surely*, and *perhaps* in one class ("epistemic adverbs"), nor does he explain on what basis he matches these English words with what he sees as their German counterparts. In fact, as I will argue in detail in this chapter, the English words *undoubtedly*, *surely*, and *perhaps* belong to different semantic and, indeed, syntactic classes. Furthermore, although the English words *maybe* and *perhaps* (which I am assuming mean exactly the same)[1] do correspond semantically to the German word *vielleicht*, the other correspondences claimed by Nuyts are not in fact correct—not just because the meanings of the individual adverbs do not match exactly but, above all, because epistemic adverbs are not separated from modal particles. Blurring the boundary between epistemic adverbs like *undoubtedly* and *evidently* and words like *surely* or *perhaps* obscures the existence of an extended class of epistemic adverbs in modern English. Contrary to what Nuyts suggests, most of these adverbs do not have corresponding adverbs in either German or Dutch or, indeed, in other European languages. This is illustrated in Table 8.1. (The meanings of the adverbs in one row of the table are not necessarily exactly the same, but this is beside the point; what matters here is the number of epistemic adverbs.)

Although the German repertoire of epistemic adverbs is larger than the Dutch or the French, it is still considerably smaller than the English one. This fact is consistent with Kasper's (1979) observations about German learners of English, who apparently have great difficulty in mastering English epistemic expressions and who

TABLE 8.1 Common epistemic adverbs in English, German, Dutch, and French

English	German	Dutch	French
probably	wahrscheinlich	waarschijnlijk	probablement
possibly	möglicherweise		
clearly		duidelijk (?)	
evidently	offensichtlich (offenbar)	klaarblijkelijk	evidemment
obviously		blijkbaar	
apparently₁	anscheinend	kennelijk	apparemment
apparently₂			
supposedly	vermutlich		prétendument
seemingly		schijnbaar	
conceivably			
undoubtedly	zweifellos	ongetwijfeld	
allegedly	angeblich		
reportedly		vermoedelijk	
arguably			
unquestionably			
likely			
certainly			certainement
presumably		vermoedelijk	
18	8	9	5

demonstrate "a generally low awareness of modality as a pragmatic category" (see also Robberecht and Peteghem 1982).

As I will try to show, the existence of such an extended class of epistemic adverbs in modern English is a fact of great cultural significance. But that cultural significance cannot be explored without first identifying the existence of such a class of words, this cannot be done without a detailed semantic analysis that enables us to identify the semantic components shared by all the members of this class, and such a detailed semantic analysis in turn is not possible without a rigorous semantic framework.

For a long time, the literature discussing epistemic adverbs was focused on their syntax rather than either meaning or use. One syntactic property that frequently attracted scholars' attention was the inability of these adverbs to occur in questions. For example, Jackendoff (1972, 84) noted the infelicity of sentences like:

*Did Frank probably beat all his opponents?

(See also Bellert 1977; Lang 1979; Foley and van Valin 1984; Nuyts 2001.) The inability of adverbs like *probably* and *evidently* to occur in questions is all the more remarkable given that the corresponding epistemic adjectives do not share this restriction, for example:

Is it probable that Frank beat his opponents?

Clearly, the inability of epistemic adverbs to occur in questions is an important clue to their meaning. At the same time, I would argue, it is only their meaning that can explain their inability to occur in questions. Some words that various writers on the subject include in the class of "epistemic adverbs"—for example, *perhaps* and *surely*—do not share the restrictions on their use in questions. For example, it is perfectly acceptable to say:

Perhaps he did it himself?

Surely he did it himself?

Thus, under further scrutiny, even the generalization about the nonuse of epistemic adverbs in questions seemingly evaporates—unless words like *perhaps* and *surely* do not belong in the same class as *probably* and *evidently*.

In what follows, I will try to show that if the class of epistemic adverbs is properly delimited, the generalization about their nonuse in questions can be maintained. And once the class of epistemic adverbs is properly delimited, we can see clearly that it is indeed exceptionally large in modern English, as compared with other European languages and also with earlier stages of English itself. Having established this fact, we can look for its causes and ask how it is related to other striking semantic features of modern English, such as, for example, the great profusion of epistemic verbal phrases. Above all, having asked questions about the meaning of English epistemic adverbs, we can explore their role in Anglo culture, and in doing so, we can link meaning, history, and culture—as well as grammar—in a way that will illuminate them all.

To investigate the meaning of individual words, we need to have a set of indefinables—semantic primes—in terms of which all the other words can be defined. If our definitions are to explain the meaning of the individual words and to do so in a way that would allow us to meaningfully compare them with one another, as well as with the closest words in other languages, they have to be formulated in simple and universal concepts. The key concept relevant to the area under discussion is, I believe, that of 'knowing'—in natural semantic metalanguage (NSM) semantics, KNOW—as argued by Danielewiczowa (2002) with reference to Bogusławski (1981, 2002). In contrast to Danielewiczowa, however, I believe that another equally important building block in the area in question is that of 'thinking'—in NSM semantics, THINK. As I will try to show, all the differences, as well as similarities, between the individual epistemic adverbs can be explained clearly, intelligibly, and in a way that can be tested against the intuitions of native speakers, in semantic explications based essentially on the concepts KNOW and THINK and, more particularly, I KNOW and I THINK. The other concepts recurring in these explications are negation (NOT), CAN, SAY, PEOPLE, OTHER, and a few others. What I will posit as a semantic core defining the class of epistemic adverbs will consist of a specific configuration of these concepts—including, in each case, KNOW, NOT, THINK, and I.

I said earlier that *perhaps* and *maybe* have an exact semantic equivalent in the German word *vielleicht*. In fact, as cross-linguistic investigations show, they have exact semantic equivalents in *all* languages, and all these semantically equivalent words represent an indefinable semantic prime MAYBE (= PERHAPS). If we identify the class of epistemic adverbs in terms of specific configurations of primes including KNOW and THINK, it becomes clear that semantically elementary (nondecomposable) words like *perhaps*, *maybe*, and *vielleicht* do not belong to that class. This is, I think, a good illustration of the general thesis that to make a valid generalization about epistemic adverbs—whether syntactic, typological, or cultural—we need first to delimit this class in a precise way.

In the literature, it is often assumed that speakers can, as Lyons puts it, "qualify their epistemic commitment" (1981, 238) to their statements in various ways and that although languages may differ in their preferred means for doing so, from a semantic point of view, these are only different means to the same goal. To quote Lyons:

> As far as making statements is concerned, there are various ways in which a locutionary agent can qualify his epistemic commitment. He can indicate that his evidence for what he asserts is less good than it might be; that his commitment is tentative, provisional or conditional, rather than absolute; and so on. Subjective epistemic modality is nothing other than this: the locutionary agent's qualification of his epistemic commitment. All natural spoken languages provide their users with the prosodic resources—stress and intonation—with which to express these several distinguishable kinds of qualified epistemic commitment. Some, but by no means all, grammaticalize them in the category of mood; and some languages, like English, lexicalize or semi-lexicalize them by means of modal verbs ('may', 'must', etc), modal adjectives ('possible', etc), modal adverbs ('possibly', etc) and modal particles ('perhaps', etc). (Lyons 1981, 238)

Lyons is right to distinguish "modal adverbs" like *possibly* from "modal particles" like *perhaps*, but I believe that statements of this kind obscure an important semantic and cultural feature of modern English, namely, its extraordinary elaboration of the area of what Lyons calls "subjective epistemic modality." To recognize and explain this phenomenon, we must go beyond abstract linguistic typology, with its assumption of "different means, the same expressive needs and goals," and look at English in its unique historical and cultural context.[2]

Given the role of English in the contemporary world, we must also recognize the needs of learners of English all over the world, who, to be proficient in English, have to learn not only new words and grammatical constructions but also new meanings and new ways of speaking. They have to learn that the need to qualify one's statements and differentiate one's degree of "epistemic commitment" is greater in English than in most other languages and that "speaking English with the appropriate degree of conviction" (Holmes 1983) can present a great difficulty for students of English as a second language (see, e.g., Robbrecht and Peteghem 1982: Kasper 1979: Scarcella and Brunak 1981).

Holmes writes:

> Many language learners report that they have found it difficult to master the expression of degrees of certainty and conviction in English. Without a command of such skills speakers tend to sound abrupt, rude or didactic in different situations. Asserting facts as if they were irrefutable or unchallengeable is appropriate only in very specific contexts such as when providing a factual report or describing an observed event, where the subject matter is uncontentious or the speaker an acknowledged authority on the topic. (Holmes 1982, 24)

Acquiring the means of qualifying one's statements is a matter of great importance for the learner of English. To quote Holmes (1982, 24), "it is more often a speaker's social survival than his or her integrity which is at stake in the skilful use and interpretation of such forms." The need to master this area of English to function in an Anglo society can be compared with the need to master honorifics in Japanese to be able to survive socially in Japan. Consequently, an adequate semantic analysis of epistemic adverbs, which could really explain their meaning to students and teachers of English, is essential for the teaching of English across the world, as well as for understanding modern Anglo culture. To be taught effectively, English cannot be totally separated from its cultural traditions, and its areas of cultural elaboration and special cultural emphasis need to be recognized, elucidated, and examined in their historical and social context.

8.1.2. Epistemic adverbs: A question of truth or a question of knowledge?

In the literature on English, epistemic adverbs have been discussed predominantly from a syntactic point of view. Two important semantic observations have been made, however: first, that epistemic adverbs are "speaker-oriented" rather than "subject-oriented" (Jackendoff 1972, Cinque 1999; see also Lyons's 1977 notion of "subjective modality") and, second, that they express "a lack of confidence on the part of the speaker" (Cinque 1999, 86). Cinque discusses this "lack of confidence" in the context of a comparison between epistemic adverbs and epistemic modals such as *must* and *should*. The focus of his analysis is syntactic, but he also makes some semantic observations:

In English, for example, the epistemic uses of *must* express a confidence stronger than that expressed by the epistemic uses of *should* (but still less than absolute):

a. John must be home, now.
b. John should be home, now.

As many people have observed, the same lack of confidence on the part of the speaker can also be expressed by such "speaker-oriented" or "epistemic" adverbs as *probably, likely, presumably, supposedly,* and so on. . . . For example, Jackendoff (1972: 84, 102ff.) notes that neither "feel[s] comfortable in questions" **Must it be five o'clock?* and **Did Frank probably beat all his opponents?*, concluding that if epistemic modals are treated like "speaker-oriented" adverbs . . . this restriction will follow automatically. (Cinque 1999, 86.)

As this quote illustrates, the generative syntactician's interest in epistemic adverbs focuses mainly on "how they should be treated" or "in what position they are generated" (Jackendoff 1972, 105). By contrast, my concern here is what these adverbs mean. From this point of view, the observations that they are "speaker-oriented" and that they express a lack of confidence on the part of the speaker are relevant and useful but clearly insufficient. In what way exactly are these adverbs speaker-oriented, and how exactly do they differ from other speaker-oriented elements? In particular, how do they differ from speaker-oriented verbal expressions such as *I presume* or *I suppose*? And, above all, how do they differ from one another?

Quirk et al. (1985, 620), in their *A Comprehensive Grammar of the English Language*, put epistemic adverbs in a category they call "content disjuncts," in the subcategory labeled "degree of truth." They define this category as follows: "These disjuncts present a comment on the truth value of what is said, expressing the extent to which, and the conditions under which, the speaker believes that what he is saying is true." Other writers on the subject who have claimed that epistemic adverbs are concerned with the "truth" of what the speaker is saying include Bellert (1977) and Foley and van Valin (1984). To quote the latter work, with its endorsement of the former:

> Bellert (1977) points out an important distinction between modal adjectives and modal adverbs . . . She points out that while modal adjectives modify a proposition by expressing its reality status, modal adverbs modify the *truth* of the proposition, not the proposition. . . . She points out that sentences like . . .
>
> a. Probably, John will come.
> b. Certainly, John can do it.
>
> are paraphrasable as:
>
> a. It is probably true that John will come.
> b. It is certainly true that John can do it. (Foley and van Valin 1984, 219)

I would argue, however, that the semantic characterization linking epistemic adverbs with truth is misleading: from the speaker's point of view, adverbs of this kind refer to thinking and knowledge (or lack of knowledge) rather than to truth. A sentence like *Probably, John will come* does not mean the same as *It is probably true that John will come*, because the latter is concerned with the truth of somebody's (normally somebody else's) words, whereas the former is concerned with the speaker's own current thought. The question whether, or to what degree, a sentence like *Probably, John will come* is true reflects concerns of logicians, not those of ordinary speakers or hearers. From an ordinary person's point of view, the use of *probably* signals opinion ("I think") and lack of knowledge ("I don't know") rather than truth.

"Truth" may be relevant to the meaning of one or two epistemic adverbs (*supposedly, allegedly*) but not all or even most of them. To characterize the class as a whole, Cinque's term *confidence* is more apposite, although the phrase *lack of confidence* is too restrictive in the case of adverbs like *clearly* and *obviously*. The real key to the semantics of epistemic phrases, however, lies in the concepts of 'thinking' and 'knowing' and, more specifically, in the semantic components "I think" and "I don't say I know." The great expansion of epistemic adverbs in English took place at a time when (as discussed in other chapters of this book) the focus of attention shifted, conspicuously, from truth to knowledge and, in particular, to the limitations of human knowledge. As I will try to show, the semantics of the new class of epistemic adverbs (together with the semantics of a new class of epistemic verbal phrases) reflected and epitomized that shift.

The introduction to the well-known typological survey of evidentiality edited by Wallace Chafe and Johanna Nichols opens with the following paragraph:

> This book is about human awareness that truth is relative, and particularly about the ways in which such awareness is expressed in language. . . . Often enough, speakers present things as unquestionably true; for example, "it's raining." On other occasions, English speakers, for example, may use an adverb to show something about the reliability of what they say, the probability of its truth: "It's probably raining," or "Maybe it's raining." (Chafe and Nichols 1986, vii)

It is important to note, however, that "evidential" and "epistemic" systems of the world's languages are typically concerned not with the truth of sentences but the knowledge of the speakers. In fact, later on in their introduction, Chafe and Nichols themselves switch from "truth" to "knowledge," as if it didn't matter which of the two tends to be grammatically and lexically elaborated in the world's languages. The truth of the matter is that while all languages have a word for TRUE as well as a word for KNOW, it is the latter and not the former that tends to be so elaborated. What specific semantic configurations involving *know* are elaborated in a particular language is a matter of great cultural importance. As I will try to show in this chapter (see also chapter 2), in modern English the key configuration elaborated in the language's semantic system is "I think, I don't say I know."

8.1.3. Why can one say "indubitably" but not "dubitably"?

The fact that one can say "indubitably" but not "dubitably" may be shrugged off as a quirk of the English lexicon, and the question posed in the heading of this section may seem gratuitous ("one can't explain everything"). But this question is harder to dismiss when one notices that this supposed quirk has several parallels among other epistemic adverbs. Thus, one can also say "undoubtedly" but not "doubtedly," "unquestionably" but not "questionably," "conceivably" but not "inconceivably," "clearly" but not "unclearly" (in the epistemic sense), "probably" but not (unless in jest) "improbably," and "certainly" but not (in the epistemic sense) "uncertainly." These asymmetries are all the more intriguing, given that the corresponding epistemic verbal phrases often do have their polar opposites. For example:

a. I think he did it himself.
b. I don't think he did it himself.
a. Conceivably, he did it himself.
b. *Inconceivably, he did it himself.
a. I doubt that he did it himself.
b. I don't doubt that he did it himself.
a. Undoubtedly, he did it himself.
b. *Doubtedly, he did it himself.
a. Indubitably, he did it himself
b. *Dubitably, he did it himself.

What is even more intriguing is that the epistemic adjectives corresponding to the "unpaired" epistemic adverbs are often "paired" (see Nuyts 2001). For example:

a. It is clear that he did it himself.
b. Clearly, he did it himself.
c. It is unclear that he did it himself.
d. *Unclearly, he did it himself.
a. It is conceivable that he did it himself.
b. Conceivably, he did it himself.
c. It is inconceivable that he did it himself.
d. * Inconceivably, he did it himself.
a. It is unquestionable that he did it himself.
b. Unquestionably, he did it himself.
c. It is questionable that he did it himself.
d. *Questionably, he did it himself.
a. It is probable that he did it himself.
b. Probably, he did it himself.
c. It is improbable that he did it himself.
d. ?Improbably, he did it himself.
a. It is possible that he did it himself.
b. Possibly, he did it himself.
c. It is impossible that he did it himself.
d. *Impossibly, he did it himself.

What these contrasts suggest is that an epistemic adverb cannot be used to dissociate the speaker from the proposition that is being pronounced: syntactically, this proposition is the main clause, and semantically, it represents what the speaker "says." Thus, the epistemic adverb can *qualify* what the speaker is saying but cannot completely undermine it (see Lang 1979). A verbal epistemic phrase is different because if it is used sentence-initially, it can represent the main clause and be, as it were, the main assertion, and so the speaker doesn't have to be committed in any way to the validity of the complement (one can always say that one thinks that something is not the case).

The semantic restrictions on epistemic adverbs discussed here are similar to those noted by Rardin (1968) with respect to parenthetical verbs. As reported by Jackendoff (1972, 97), Rardin pointed out that "the parenthetical must be of 'positive' import":

John is, I think, a vegetarian.

John is, *I don't think, a vegetarian.

John is, *I doubt, a vegetarian.

John is, I don't doubt, a vegetarian.

Evidently, a parenthetical epistemic verbal phrase (used in a noninitial position) can qualify the speaker's commitment to the statement in some way but cannot cancel this commitment altogether. (For this reason, when the complement clause contains negation, the parenthetical verbal phrase can in fact contain negation, too: a sentence like "John isn't, I don't think, a vegetarian" is not self-contradictory.) A sentence-initial epistemic verbal phrase can have a "negative import" (e.g., "I don't think," "I doubt"), because such a sentence-initial phrase can be interpreted as the main clause, that is, as what the speaker actually "says" (asserts), on a par with a verbal phrase of a positive import, such as "I think."

In the literature discussing the use of *I think* in modern English, it has been suggested that *I think* has now become a discourse marker and that it is no longer a main clause (Thompson and Mulac 1991). But if one were to judge by the "polarity test" (i.e., one based on negation), a sentence-initial *I think* could still be regarded as the main clause (see Aijmer 1997, 40), because in the sentence-initial position *I think* can be replaced with *I don't think*:

I think / I don't think that John is a vegetarian.

When used parenthetically, however, *I think* could no longer be replaced with *I don't think*, and so it has to be regarded as a qualifier of the main clause and not as in any sense itself a main clause. In the NSM system, this can be portrayed as follows:

I think John is a vegetarian =
I say: I think that John is a vegetarian
I don't say I know

I don't think John is a vegetarian =
I say: I don't think that John is a vegetarian
I don't say I know

John is, I think, a vegetarian =
I say: John is a vegetarian
I say I think, I don't say I know

Thus in a parenthetical clause, what the speaker actually "says" (asserts) is the proposition introduced by the epistemic phrase (*John is a vegetarian*, not *I think John is a vegetarian*).

An epistemic adverb functions similarly to a parenthetical clause in that it, too, only qualifies what the speaker "says" (asserts) rather than contributing an assertion of its own: what occurs in the "assertive" frame "I say" is the proposition introduced by the epistemic adverb rather than any attitudinal component of the epistemic adverb itself. For example, the sentence

Undoubtedly, John is a vegetarian.

includes in its meaning an assertion: "I say: John is a vegetarian," qualified by various attitudinal components of the adverb *undoubtedly* (to be spelled out shortly). These components have to be consistent with the assertion. They can include, therefore, the component "I think that it is like this" but not "I think that it is not like this," because the latter would involve the speaker in a contradiction. I can assert that John is a vegetarian, or I can assert that John is not a vegetarian — in neither case would I be contradicting myself in any way — but if I said that "doubtedly (or "dubitably"), John is a vegetarian," I would be asserting something in the main body of the sentence while the sentence-initial adverb would be sending a contradictory message. Schematically:

*doubtedly/*dubitably/*questionably it is like this* =
I say it is like this
I think that it is not like this

This is then, I suggest, the explanation for the absence of epistemic adverbs with a fully "negative import." The same explanation applies to the absence of parentheticals verbal phrases with a "negative import." (such as "*John is, I doubt, a vegetarian"). One feature that distinguishes the two categories is the absence versus presence of a reference to "other people" and of an expectation that they could share the speaker's attitude. I will return to this feature shortly. Another feature that distinguishes the two is the relative emphasis on the speaker's nonassertive attitude, reflected iconically in the word order: parenthetical phrases (of the kind discussed here) do not occur at the beginning of the sentence, whereas epistemic adverbs not only can but also in modern English very frequently do. In fact, Leech and Svartvik (1975, 202) comment: "the normal position for most sentence adverbials is front-position. They are usually separated from what follows by a tone unit boundary in speech or a comma in writing."

The sentence-initial position of epistemic adverbs, which gradually became more and more prominent in modern English, is significant because it serves as a kind of advance warning for the hearers. The prosodic independence of such as an opening gambit (reflected in Quirk et al.'s 1985 term *disjunct*) highlights this initial warning, without which the hearer can expect a declarative sentence to carry the component "I know." Of course, such an expectation can be corrected later on — with a modal verb (*must, can, should,* etc.), a sentence-internal epistemic adverb (e.g., "it was probably/ apparently, etc., like this"), or a parenthetical (sentence-internal or sentence-final) verbal phrase (e.g., "I think," "I presume"). But a sentence-initial, semi-independent disjunct can serve as an advance warning, and thus it places a special emphasis on the component "I don't say I know" — contrary to what Quirk et al. (1985), Bellert (1977), and Foley and van Valin (1984) say, not one qualifying the truth of what is being said but one signaling an abstention from a claim to knowledge. I further explore the historical significance of the component "I don't say I know" in epistemic adverbs in section 8.3.1, focused on the adverb *probably*. For the purposes of exposition, however, it will be helpful to first consider two other epistemic adverbs, *presumably* and *undoubtedly*, in order to develop my general scheme for explicating the words of this category.

Having done this, I will be in a better position to tackle the most important of all epistemic adverbs, *probably*, followed by its close relative *likely*. After this, I will discuss and compare most of the other epistemic adverbs, arranging them in groups: first, the most confident ones, *evidently*, *clearly*, and *obviously*; then the less confident *possibly* and *conceivably*; and then those based on hearsay, *apparently*, *supposedly*, *allegedly*, and *reportedly*. The last adverb to discuss will be *certainly*, which I will argue is only a marginal member of the class (if it belongs to it at all). After that, I will compare and contrast epistemic adverbs with modal particles, and finally I will present a tentative outline of the history of English epistemic adverbs as a lexicogrammatical class and discuss its cultural underpinnings.

8.2. Developing a Format for the Semantic Analysis of Epistemic Adverbs

8.2.1. "Presumably": A personal stance plus an appeal to other people

Let us start with some sentences from the Cobuild corpus.

> Presumably both those aspects of the company's work play a part in its high efficiency.
>
> Presumably, it was the latter type of young man whom the navy was after.
>
> Presumably, blood from sores in the baby's mouth entered the mother's body through the crack in the mother's nipples.
>
> Why should human beings have evolved into intelligent creatures? Presumably we have done so because such a feature is adaptive: it fits us better for our environment.
>
> Tom, Arakny and Abasio were gone. Presumably they were busy.
> —Presumably that means you make sure the customer is satisfied from the minute the car goes out the show room.
> —Correct.
> —Presumably while you were working you also had the opportunity to look at the films.
> —Well you had to.

As these examples illustrate, *presumably*—rather like *I presume*—signals a conclusion that goes beyond what the speaker can know. The first question to ask, therefore, is how the two (the adverb and the verbal phrase) are related.

In their *A Comprehensive Grammar of the English Language*, Quirk et al. (1985, 614) describe sentences like (a) and (b):

    a. Presumably, Alison has bought a new car.
    b. I presume that Alison has bought a new car.

as "plausible paraphrases." But if *presumably* did indeed mean the same as *I presume*, then we would expect that in the following pair of sentences, (b) is as acceptable as (a):

    a. Dr. Livingstone, I presume.
    b. Presumably, you are Dr. Livingstone.

In fact, sentence (b), in contrast to (a), sounds odd. I suggest that the main reason for this contrast in acceptability lies in the fact that *presumably* projects the speaker's own attitude onto other people. Like the phrase *it can be presumed*, *presumably* makes a claim that goes beyond the view of the present speaker and includes other people as well. *It can be presumed* implies not only that "it can be presumed by me" but also that "it can be presumed by other people" or, rather, that it can be presumed by people in general. *Presumably* is not identical in meaning with *it can be presumed* any more than it is with *I presume*, but it, too, refers to "people" and not only to the speaker. It is "speaker-oriented" in the sense that it does refer to the speaker, but unlike *I presume*, it is not exclusively speaker oriented. Roughly:

Presumably, he did it himself. =
a. I presume he did it himself
b. I think that other people can think the same

To be more precise, we need to decompose the meaning of *I presume* into semantic primes. The explication proposed for this phrase earlier (in chapter 7) reads:

I presume he did it himself. =
a. I say: I think that he did it himself
b. I don't say I know
c. I think that I can know it

Apart from the difference in what is the main clause (that is, what occurs in the frame "I say"), the explication of *presumably* should differ from the explication of *I presume* in adding to the speaker's own "I presume" his or her expectation that other people could think the same ("I think that other people can think the same"). Furthermore, if the adverb *presumably* occurs sentence-initially, it sends from the outset a signal that what is being said expresses the speaker's thought: "I want to say what I think" (a point that I will discuss more fully in the next section). This brings us to the following overall explication:

Presumably, he did it himself. =
a. I want to say how I think when I think about it
b. I say: he did it himself
c. I don't say I know
d. I think that I can know it
e. I think that other people can think the same

If this explication of *presumably* is correct, then an epistemic adverb like *presumably* is indeed speaker-oriented, insofar as it refers to what the speaker thinks, but it is not focused exclusively on the speaker; it refers also to what other people can think. The sentence *Presumably you are Dr. Livingstone* sounds strange because, under the circumstances, it would make no sense for the speaker to speculate about any other people's possible thoughts about the identity of the figure in front of him; what matters is who *he* thinks this person is.

The place of "other people" in the meaning of epistemic adverbs is an important clue to their cultural significance. Epistemic verbal phrases like *I presume* or *I believe* present the speaker's own personal attitude, and so by using them, the speaker purports not to be trying to influence other people's ways of thinking. As I discuss in more detail later, the stance they project is therefore quite different from that conveyed by various interactive "particles" or other expressions that do not similarly fence off the speaker's position from that of the addressee. For example, German words like *doch* and *gewiss* or French words like *hein* and *voilá*, which have no counterparts in English, are inherently interactive and, as it were, addressee-oriented (as are also English words like *surely*, *sure*, or the dialectal British *innit*).

The English epistemic adverbs are not like that: they are indeed "speaker-oriented." Of course, they, too, can be used in sentences eliciting a response from the addressee, and in spoken English, *presumably* often does. But they can also be used in sentences that are not seeking to directly engage the addressee. The epistemic verbal phrase *I presume* can also be used in a sentence eliciting a response from an addressee, as the sentence *Dr. Livingstone, I presume* illustrates, and yet the phrase *I presume* can legitimately be regarded as speaker-oriented.

But while epistemic adverbs like *presumably* can also be regarded as speaker-oriented, they are not "personal" and "subjective" like the epistemic verbal phrases. For example, if I say *I presume*, I am presenting my own personal stance and nobody else's, but if I say *presumably*, I am, as it were, supporting my stance with an appeal to some expected general consensus. The difference between the two expressions can be compared in this respect with that between, on the one hand, *it is obvious* or *it seems* and, on the other, *it is obvious to me* or *it seems to me*. *I presume* is personal in the way *it is obvious to me* or *it seems to me* is personal. *Presumably*, on the other hand, implies that other people can think the same as I do, and so it is closer in this respect to impersonal expressions like *it is obvious* or *it seems*. To anticipate the discussion in the next section, to write in a reference that "Undoubtedly Joe Bloggs is the best candidate" is stronger support than "I don't doubt that Joe Bloggs is the best candidate," because it implies that other people can be expected to agree with me.

The rich set of epistemic verbal phrases like *I presume* gives English speakers the means to mark and differentiate their personal stand. The rich set of epistemic adverbs allows them to partly "objectify" their stand, to hint at some valid grounds for it, to convey an expectation that their stance would be seen by other people as reasonable. The two sets can be said to complement each other in that they both allow the speakers to say what they think and to delineate their stance accurately, carefully, responsibly, and unimposingly. They can both be said to reflect the cultural concerns that first arose in Britain at the time of the Enlightenment and that, as I have been arguing all along, have shaped aspects of Anglo discourse in the subsequent centuries as well.

8.2.2. *"Undoubtedly": The significance of the sentence-initial position of the adverb*

In his article "Refocusing the Burden of Proof in Criminal Cases: Some Doubts about Reasonable Doubt," the legal scholar Lawrence Solan writes:

> The verb "to doubt" is what linguists and philosophers call a verb of propositional attitude. It describes the speaker's attitude toward a proposition. Loosely, it means something like, "to think a proposition is not true," as in: "Do you think it will rain tomorrow?" "I doubt it." Justice Scalia's recent characterization of the cognate noun, "an uncertain, tentative or provisional disbelief," gleaned from various dictionaries, describes this sense of the concept well. The word is a label for a cognitive process that occurs innately. (Solan 1999, 132)

But does this definition "gleaned from various dictionaries" really explicate *doubt* well? I believe not, if only because all the words used in the definition (*uncertain, tentative, provisional,* and *disbelief*) are at least as complex as *doubt* itself.

Let us start again with a set of examples from Cobuild:

> He is undoubtedly one of the best players in the world in that position.

> Undoubtedly the problem was that the banking system wasn't geared up to the increase in the number of projected appraisals.

> Undoubtedly there have been wrangles over policy wordings.

> It has undoubtedly affected the Council.

> So undoubtedly the house was overcrowded.

Clearly, just as *presumably* is closely related to *I presume, undoubtedly* is closely related to *I don't doubt,* so it will be useful to begin our analysis of the adverb by comparing it with the verbal phrase:

> a. I don't doubt that he did it himself.
> b. Undoubtedly, he did it himself.

To explicate the phrase *I don't doubt,* we may need to start with its counterpart without negation, that is, *I doubt.* If we rely on simple and universal human concepts like KNOW and THINK, we can explicate *doubt* (and the phrase *I doubt*) clearly and precisely (see the explication later). We can also show that the word *doubt* is not really "a label for a cognitive process that occurs innately" but rather a language-specific configuration of semantic components constructed out of concepts like THINK and KNOW that do indeed "occur innately."

> *I doubt that he did it himself.*
> a. I say: I think that he did not do it himself
> b. I don't say I know
> c. I say this because I want to say what I think when I think about it
> d. I think that it can be like this

For *I don't doubt,* we can then propose a symmetrical explication:

> *I don't doubt that he did it himself =*
> a. I say: I think that he did it himself

b. I don't say I know
c. I say this because I want to say what I think when I think about it
d. I don't think that it can be not like this

For *undoubtedly*, we can now propose an explication extending the attitude of "I don't doubt" to other people (while preserving the reference to the speaker himself or herself):

Undoubtedly, he did it himself =
a. I want to say how I think when I think about it
b. I say: he did it himself
c. I don't say I know
d. I think that it cannot be not like this
e. I think that other people can think the same

I have said earlier that a sentence-initial epistemic adverb emphasizes the non-fully assertive nature of what is being said more than a sentence-internal one, and I have suggested that the explication of a sentence-initial epistemic adverb should include, at the very outset, the "warning" component "I want to say what I think" (by implication, "not what I know"). I have not yet addressed, however, the question of how we can capture in explications the difference between sentence-initial and sentence-internal epistemic adverbs. What I want to propose is that the explication of a sentence-internal adverb should not start with such an initial warning signal ("I want to say what I think") but rather should start, as the sentence itself does, with the main proposition itself and only later add to it a component clarifying the status of this proposition as something that the speaker thinks rather than knows ("I say this because I want to say what I think"). Formulaically:

He undoubtedly did it himself =
a. I say: he did it himself
b. I don't say I know
c. I say this because I want to say what I think when I think about it
d. I think that it cannot be not like this
e. I think that other people can think the same

In what follows, I will be explicating only epistemic adverbs occurring in the initial position. I will do so for reasons of space, on the assumption that in each case the difference between the two versions is exactly the same as that shown here between the two versions of *undoubtedly*.

8.3. "Probably" and "Likely": The Heart of the Category of Epistemic Adverbs

8.3.1. Probably

Probably is the most important of all English epistemic adverbs, insofar as it is the most frequent and the most widely used one (across a wide range of registers and types of discourse). The differences between *probably* and other epistemic adverbs are quite spectacular, as Table 8.2 demonstrates. (I have not included in this table those adverbs whose polysemy would make it impossible to easily find out their frequencies in an epistemic sense. The figures for *likely* include its use as an adjective as well as an adverb. Except for the last one, which has not been discussed in this chapter in any detail, the order of the adverbs in this table corresponds to the order in which they are discussed here.)

The differences in frequency between *probably* and its counterparts in other European languages, though of a different order, are also quite remarkable.

> English: according to the data in the Cobuild UK spoken corpus, the frequency of *probably* in spoken English is 28 tokens per 50,000 words, in Holmes (1988, 35) it is 32 tokens per 50,000 words, and in the Lund corpus of 320,000 words, 44 tokens per 50,000 words (compare Holmes 1988, 35)

> Swedish: in *The English-Swedish Parallel Corpus* (of circa 300,000 words), the joint frequency of its two counterparts *förmodligen* and *antagligen* is 12 tokens per 50,000 words (information courtesy of Karin Aijmer).

> German: in the Mannheim corpus of spoken language (of circa 1.6 million words), the word *wahrscheinlich* has 14 tokens per 50,000 words, and in the Mannheim corpus of written language (of circa 2.5 million words), 9 tokens per 50,000 words.

> French: in the Cobuild corpus of French Books (of circa 3 million words), the word *probablement* has 3.5 tokens per 50,000 words.

The wide use of *probably* across all registers can be illustrated with the following interview with a 14-year-old British schoolboy (note the last sentence):

TABLE 8.2 Frequency (per million words) in the Cobuild corpus

	UK Spoken	UK Books	US Books
presumably	67	26	24
undoubtedly	3	39	22
probably	561	312	219
likely (adv.)	2	5	11
evidently	1.8	15	20
clearly	57	158	143
obviously	346	107	75
possibly	83	74	47
conceivably	0.8	3	2
apparently	62	80	81
supposedly	7	17	10
allegedly	0.8	16	9
reportedly	0.3	1.5	5
seemingly	2	16	23
arguably	0.9	4	2
unquestionably	0.3	4	3

RP: Do you think of yourself as being English, or white?

BEN: Um, I do fink of myself as a British person, a British citizen but I, I don't fink of myself as any other race because I was born in England which makes me English so I'm not nofing else, I wouldn't try and be nofing else.

RP: Right. Do you think some boys do they try and be something else?

BEN: Yeah. Yeah, try and act hard or try and talk in a, like some people like try talkin' like a Jamaican accent or=

RP: =Do they?

BEN: Yeah and like kiss their teeth like Africans, like Afro-Caribbean do, try and copy them.

RP: This is English boys tryin' to be like that. White English boys?

BEN: Yeah. Some do. Yeah.

RP: So why is that then? Why do they try and be like that?

BEN: Dunno because they look as . . . quite hard people and if they try and, if they act like that then they're gonna, people are gonna fink "oh look they look hard. Don't look at them else they're gonna start trouble." So that's **probably** why. (Frosh, Phoenix, and Pattman 2000, 53)

One can doubt whether the German word *wahrscheinlich* or the French word *probablement* would be used in the register spoken by this interviewee, as they appear to belong to a more educated and formal stratum of language. The extremely high frequency of *probably* in spoken English is no doubt linked with its wide socio-cultural range of use.

When and why did the word *probably* (in its modern epistemic meaning) come to occupy such an important place in English Anglo discourse?

To begin with the question "when," we will note that although the word itself was already used in the sixteenth century, its meaning was then different, as the following sentence cited by the OED shows: "You wrote so probably that it put me in fear of dangers to come" (1535). The first fully convincing example of the epistemic use of *probably* recorded by the OED is dated 1774: "The present stones were probably substituted in place of these." My own database derived from the *Literature Online* Web site also suggests that the epistemic *probably* emerged in English in the eighteenth century and that its use has gradually expanded.

In *The Emergence of Probability*, Ian Hacking (1975) has written:

> Until the end of the Renaissance, one of our concepts of evidence was lacking:
> that by which one thing can indicate, contingently, the state of something else . . .
> [A] probable opinion [in the Renaissance] was not one supported by evidence, but
> one which was approved by some authority, or by the testimony of respected judges.
> (Quoted in Franklin 2001, 203)

In quoting this passage, Franklin (2001, 203) remarks, ironically, that "to reach these conclusions, it was necessary to ignore everything written about evidence in law and almost all medieval and early modern writing in Latin," and he cites a long list of other scholars who have tried to refute Hacking's claim. But the controversy between

Hacking and his critics cannot be settled without a meticulous semantic analysis of the relevant words in the Latin documents, as well as in various early sources in modern European languages. In fact, in a section entitled "Probability in Ordinary Language," Franklin himself points out that while "the first known occurrence of the word *probable* in English is in Trevisa's translation of Higden's *Polychronicon*, of about 1385" (2001, 127), it must be borne in mind that "the early uses of *probable* and *likely* in English are nothing like 'It will probably rain tomorrow'" (p. 127).

According to the available linguistic evidence, *probably* as an epistemic adverb first emerged in ordinary English in the eighteenth century, and its use spread gradually, reaching in the twentieth century a position of prominence unrivaled by its counterparts in other European languages or by other English epistemic adverbs.[3]

To the best of my knowledge, the current epistemic sense of the adjective *probable* is not incontrovertibly attested before the eighteenth century either. It is true that the OED includes in its entry on the current meaning of *probable* some examples from the seventeenth century, but the meaning of *probable* in these examples is either obscure or clearly different from the current one. For example:

1. The birds neither sow, reape, &c. as you doe, *Ergo* tis less probable that they should be fed. (1620)
2. This were a probable opinion, though not warranted by holy writ. (1736)

Clearly, in 1, *probable* means something like "justifiable," and in 2, something like "tenable."

The OED distinguishes the meaning of *probable* illustrated in sentences 1 and 2 from that of *probable* used in the frame *probable by* (analogous to *provable by*), as in some other seventeenth-century examples, such as the following two:

3. No man in religion is properly a heretic . . . but he who maintains traditions or opinions not probable by scripture. (1659)
4. Executions by a Barrons Officer are valid, though not given in Writ, and that the same are probable by Witnesses. (1678)

Although the meaning of *probable* in 3 and 4 may indeed be different from that in 1 and 2, its meaning in 1 and 2 is still different from the contemporary one. Examples of this kind, and their treatment by the OED, should alert us to the dangers facing anyone who wants to study the history of "the concept of probability" without careful semantic analysis of the relevant words, at different stages of their history.

The question of why *probably* has become so prominent in modern English leads us, first, to the changes in seventeenth-century European thinking in general and, second, to the ideas and the influence of British thinkers of the Enlightenment, especially to John Locke.

As for the European roots of the modern "probabilistic" outlook, let me quote from a recent book entitled *The Empire of Chance: How Probability Changed Science and Everyday Life*, which "tells how quantitative ideas of chance transformed the natural and social sciences, as well as daily life, over the past three centuries":

> The ultimate result of the Reformation and Counter-Reformation clashes over the fundamental principles of faith and their justification, and of the radical scepticism of Michel de Montaigne and other sixteenth-century thinkers was vastly to

erode the domain of the demonstrative proof and to expand that of probable reasoning. . . . Confronted with a choice between fideist dogmatism on the one hand and the most corrosive scepticism on the other, an increasing number of seventeenth-century writers attempted to carve out an intermediate position that abandoned all hope of certainty except in mathematics and perhaps metaphysics, and yet still insisted that men could attain probable knowledge. (Gigerenzer et al. 1989, cover)

It is widely held that, next to the Reformation, a key influence in the modern prominence of 'probabilistic' thinking must be attributed to the Enlightenment. In a book entitled *Classical Probability in the Enlightenment*, Daston writes:

> The sixteenth-century revival of Greek scepticism, combined with the blistering polemics of the Reformation and Counter-Reformation, had subverted traditional criteria for belief in religion, philosophy, and the sciences. To counter this erosion of belief, a group of seventeenth-century thinkers, including Marin Mersenne, Pierre Gassendi, Hugo Grotius, John Tillotson, Robert Boyle, and John Locke, advanced a new philosophy of rational belief which Richard Popkin has called "constructive scepticism." (Daston 1988, xi)

So far, so good. But tracing the origins of the modern "probabilistic thinking" to the Reformation and the Enlightenment does not explain why the word *probably* is used so widely, and so frequently, in English — more so than its counterparts in other European languages. To explain this, another key historical factor must be taken into account: the influence of John Locke on the everyday ways of thinking, speaking, and writing in Britain and America — an influence far greater than Mersenne or Gassendi could possibly have had in France, or Grotius, in Holland, given that Gassendi and Grotius wrote in Latin, and Mersenne was influential through his correspondence with other philosophers and through his activities as a publisher rather than through his own writings, whereas Locke wrote in English, was endlessly reprinted, and was read by the entire educated public. To quote Yolton:

> Locke's influence on eighteenth-century thought in Britain is extensive. . . . One can find, in the tracts and pamphlets of the eighteenth century, frequent usage of Lockean terminology and concepts. . . . The quick absorption of Locke's language and concepts by his contemporaries is another indication of the impact his ideas had on his own and the following centuries. (Yolton 1977, 8)

As emphasized by Roy Porter (2000, 62), among many others, Locke's ideas on "probable knowledge" in particular "proved enormously influential in staking out an enlightened epistemology":

> Knowledge — as distinct from faith and sham syllogizing — was of two kinds. One was intuitive. This, the more certain but restricted in scope, consisted of truths requiring no proof: for instance, a semicircle is less than a whole circle. The other type arose from the acquisition and assimilation of sense data, and would generate "probable" knowledge. While inevitably lacking the certitude of revelation or intuition, this formed the main stock of truth available to mortals. (Porter 2000, 63)

It is true that (as pointed out to me by James Franklin, personal communication), while Gassendi, Mersenne, and Grotius were not read much compared with Locke, Pascal was. At the same time, however (as Franklin notes), while Locke was *for* probability, Pascal was *against* it—a fact that (as Franklin also notes) could well have been significant.[4]

Turning now to the semantic analysis of the adverb *probably* as it is currently used, I note, first of all, that its meaning should not be uncritically equated with that of the adjective *probable*, because the two cannot always be used interchangeably. In particular, *probably* can be used with personal opinions and moral judgments, whereas *probable* cannot. For example:

a. It's probably not worth it.
b. ?It is probable that it is not worth it.
a. I probably should (do it).
b. ?It is probable that I should (do it).
a. You probably ought to (try harder).
b. ?It is probable that you ought to (try harder).

It is also significant that *probable* can be modified by the adverb *highly*, whereas *probably* cannot (*highly probable* vs. **highly probably*). A collocation like *highly probable* can be compared with *highly paid*: it suggests something that is somehow measurably quantifiable. It is related to the fact that one can ask "how probable" something is, and "what is the probability that. . . ." No such question can, of course, arise with respect to *probably*, which is not an estimate but a hedge. These contrasts in acceptability are consistent with the fact that *probably* has a reduced variant in spoken English (*prob'ly*) and that its frequency is incomparably higher than that of *probable*. Table 8.3 shows the relative frequencies of *probably* and *probable* in the Cobuild corpus.

All these facts suggest that *probably* is less "scientific" and "intellectual" than *probable* and that it is well and truly entrenched in English colloquial speech. While it is epistemically cautious and does imply a certain amount of conscious reflection (perhaps some mental weighing of the evidence), it can also be relatively casual. It does not imply that one can prove the validity of what one is saying or demonstrate how one has arrived at one's judgment.

On the basis of all these considerations, I would propose the following explication:

Probably he did it himself =
a. I want to say how I think when I think about it
b. I say: he did it himself
c. I don't say I know
d. I think that it can be like this
e. I think like this because I have thought about it for some time
f. I think that other people can think the same

TABLE 8.3 Frequency of *probably* and *probable* per million words

	UK Spoken	UK Books	US Books
probably	561	312	219
probable	1	9	12

Thus, like the other epistemic adverbs, *probably* indicates that one thinks something and also that one abstains from claiming knowledge ("I don't say I know"). By itself, the phrasing of the *I say*-component ("I say he did it himself") would sound too confident for a sentence with *probably*, but this seemingly excessive confidence is counterbalanced by the great caution of the *I think*-component: not "I think that it is like this" but "I think that it can be like this." At the same time, the speaker gives some extra weight to the cautiously expressed thought by implying that it is based on reflection: "I think like this because I have thought about it for some time." The speaker's confidence is also reflected in the seemingly self-assured assertion: "I say: he did it himself." Presumably, it is this component of assertion (however qualified by the other components) that gives the adverb *probably* a certain casual confidence, which is absent from the more "scientific-sounding" adjective *probable*.

A detailed study of epistemic adjectives is beyond the scope of this chapter, but I will sketch here an explication of the first component of the phrase *it is probable* to indicate how it may differ from that of the adverb *probably*,

> *It is probable that he did it himself* =
> I say: I think that if someone thinks about it they can think that he did it himself

By itself, this difference in the first component would not be sufficient to account for the more impersonal, more objective, and more intellectual ring of the adjective than of the adverb, but it could be part of the answer.

Given the prominent place that "probability" occupies not only in the literature on the history of science but also in the literature on modern ways of thinking (see, e.g., Hacking 1975; Gigerenzer et al. 1989; Franklin 2001), it is important to take note of these differences between *probable* and *probably*. For example, when Franklin (2001) discusses, in a separate section, "probability in ordinary language," it would be useful to distinguish not only older meanings of these words from the current ones but also the meaning of the adverb from that of the adjective. Given that (according to Cobuild) the ratio of *probably* to *probable* in contemporary spoken English is 560 to 1 (and that even in written English, it is of the order 35 to 1 in Cobuild's U.K. books and 18 to 1 in U.S. books), it is probably *probably* rather than *probable* that can lead us into the heart of modern Anglo cultural attitudes and illuminate the nature of the changes in everyday thinking that are linked in the literature with the "emergence of probability."

Reportedly, Bertrand Russell once said in a public lecture that "probability is the most important concept in modern science," adding, "especially as nobody has the slightest notion what it means" (Stevens 1951). We could complement Russell's statement by saying that *probably* is the most important qualifier in modern English/ Anglo discourse. The two concepts—the scientific concept of 'probability' and the everyday concept encapsulated in the word *probably*—are by no means identical, but they can be traced, in some measure, to the same origins. In English, an awareness of 'probability' as an important philosophical concept appears to have spread relatively early and relatively widely through the titles of books like *The Doctrine of Chances: or, a Method of Calculating the Probability of Events in Play* (1718, De Moivre) and through the *Philosophical Transactions of the Royal Society*.

This new philosophical concept of 'probability' appears to have started early on to influence English speakers' thinking on matters lying outside the province of philosophy or science, as reflected in Bishop Butler 's (1736) statement "Probability is the very Guide of Life" (OED).[5] Arguably, then, the ascent of *probably* in English/Anglo discourse has its starting point in seventeenth-century philosophical analysis and in the dissemination of philosophical ideas through works published in English and widely read. Once again, a special role must be attributed here to John Locke's *Essay on Human Understanding*, both as a source of philosophical ideas and as a vehicle for their dissemination.

8.3.2. *Likely*

According to the OED, *likely* is frequently used as an adverb in American English and only rarely in British English, mainly in the collocations *most likely* and *very likely*. (In Australian English it is hardly used as an adverb at all, although *The Macquarie Dictionary* (1981) does list it as such, with the gloss "probably.")

The OED glosses *likely* (in its current adverbial usage) as "probably, in all probability" and illustrates it with examples like the following one:

> The American public never has understood, and likely never will, the chaotic and complex character of the Indian problem during the 19th century. (1964)

But is it true that when used as an adverb, *likely* means exactly the same as *probably* (or, for that matter, that when used as an adjective, *likely* means exactly the same thing as *probable*)? I do not think this is the case, although undoubtedly both the two adverbs and the two adjectives are very close.

To begin with, there are some phraseological differences between *likely* and *probable* or *probably*. For example, *likely* combines much more readily with *very*. One example (from an American memoir):

> The doctors knew then that Marilee very likely was going to die. (Hermann 1990, 46)

One can, of course, say that something is *highly probable*, but first, this sounds more "scientific" than *very likely*, and second, as noted earlier, a combination of *highly* with *probably* is not possible (**highly probably*).

There are also some syntactic differences between *likely* and *probable*, as the following contrasts illustrate:

> She is likely (unlikely) to do it.
>
> *She is probable (improbable) to do it.
>
> This chair is likely (unlikely) to break.
>
> *This chair is probable (improbable) to break.

What these contrasts suggest is that *likely* can be seen as referring to a person's propensity to behave in a certain way or to an object's invisible individual characteristics (and reflecting the speaker's conjecture based on personal experience), whereas *probable* always refers to a fact or a state of affairs ("it is probable *that*"), never to a person or an object. To put it differently, *probable* is more factual than *likely*, as it were, more objective, whereas *likely* is more subjective, more impressionistic, and more applicable to possible events that are unpredictable and unknowable.

Thus, typically, *likely* is used in relation to the future, which can be regarded as unknowable rather than simply "unknown to me." For example, in the OED sentence about the American public who "likely never will understand the chaotic and complex character of the Indian problem," *likely* does not indicate a prediction that may or may not turn out to be accurate but rather an impression, a subjective assessment, a thought that is not meant to be verifiable, perhaps a lament.

Consider also the following passage from the American memoir quoted earlier, in which *probably* and *likely* are used side by side (in a sermon preached in a hospital by a woman chaplain):

> Somehow I felt like I was preaching at a drive-in movie. The patients
> probably felt the same way. "Most of you likely have heard God defined
> as 'love.'" (Hermann 1990, 56)

In the first sentence, *probably* refers to the patients' current feeling, that is, to something that the speaker doesn't know but that some other people (the patients) can know and that the speaker could perhaps find out. In the second, with its loose reference to "most of you" and an indefinite time frame, *likely* refers to something that probably could not be verified (the patients may not even remember whether they have heard this).

Consider also the combinations of the adjectives *probable* and *likely*, and their opposites, with the nouns *scenario* and *story*:

a. likely/unlikely scenario
b. probable/improbable scenario
a. likely/unlikely story
b. probable/improbable story

According to the intuitions of all the native speakers I have consulted, *likely* and *unlikely* go better with *scenario*, and *probable* or *improbable* with *story*, than the other way around (although the sarcastic use of the expression "A likely story!" is quite common). The expression a *likely scenario* is almost a cliché, whereas a *probable scenario* is not. Consider, for example, the following sentence from Cobuild:

> It was true . . . that the coalition of France and Russia was the maximum
> combination of powers that Germany could hope to defeat, but this was
> no longer the most likely scenario, for, in all probability, Britain would
> enter any war against the Reich.

The expression *the most likely scenario* refers here to a purely hypothetical course of events, whereas *in all probability*, to something real and verifiable that is expected to happen.

The hypothetical and unverifiable character of some sentences with *likely* can also be illustrated with the following example (also from Cobuild) concerning occupancy arrangements between sellers and buyers:

> A more likely scenario works like this: You don't want to move in but
> you would like to paint and fix up. If the property is empty, why not?
> In this situation, sellers are likely to want a pre-settlement decorator
> agreement. . . .

The sellers mentioned here are hypothetical sellers, sellers in general, so their future actions can hardly be described as "probable" (any statements about them are not even *potentially* verifiable). Evidently, however, both the sellers and the scenario can be described as "likely." These contrasts are consistent with the fact that a story can be factual and thus knowable, whereas a scenario is fictitious.

All these considerations lead us to the conclusion that first, the adjective *likely* does not mean the same as the adjective *probable*, and second, the adverb *likely* should not be explicated in exactly the same way as the adverb *probably*. Above all, I would assign to *likely* the component "I don't say I can know" instead of the component "I don't say I know," which has been assigned to *probably*. Since *likely* often refers to things that are not knowable or not verifiable, "I don't say I can know" fits it better than "I don't say I know." *Probably*, on the other hand, implies that what is being said is, in principle, verifiable (if not by me, then by someone else, and if not now, then at some other time, and if not verifiable, then at least justifiable).

Furthermore, since *probably* implies some reflection or consideration, whereas *likely* can be more off the top of one's head, the component "I think like this because I have thought about it for some time," which has been included in the explication of *probably*, has not been included in that of *likely*. This leads us to the following explication:

> *Likely he did it himself.* =
> a. I want to say how I think when I think about it
> b. I say: he did it himself
> c. I don't say I can know
> d. I know that I can't know
> e. I think that it can be like this
> f. I think that other people can think the same

Since many linguists, and not only linguists, like to think about linguistic phenomena in terms of scales, it could be suggested that *probably* occupies, in some respects, an intermediate position between *probable* and *likely*, with *probable* being the most "objective" and "calculable" of the three, and *likely*, the least. However, helpful as such a generalization might be, it cannot replace careful semantic analysis that would identify, in each case, the exact configuration of components that can account best for a given word's range of use.

8.4. "Confident" Adverbs: *Evidently, Clearly, Obviously*

8.4.1. *Evidently*

The epistemic adverb *evidently* doesn't have a corresponding verbal phrase (although there is, of course, the adjectival phrase *it is evident that*), but its semantic structure is analogous to that of *presumably* and *undoubtedly*, insofar as it, too, expresses both the speaker's own attitude and the expected attitude of other people. The speaker's attitude expressed by the use of *evidently* can be clearly seen in the following examples from Cobuild (UK books):

> Cuddly woman—the kind one would least expect to find working as a barmaid. She looked too soft and innocent to handle rowdy drunks, but according to Artie she could gentle the roughest. Evidently Julie approached her job at the Doghouse Bar in the same manner she approached life in general, trusting and carefree.

> There's an airstrip in Edisonville, but I don't think you'll be using it. It belongs to Douglas Osborne. About five years ago, he had it put in and bought a Cessna. Evidently the Cessna was too slow because he had the strip enlarged and bought a small Lear, complete with private pilot.

> Then, as quickly as it had been lost, the truck turned up again. The wind seemed to have blown off some of its makeshift camouflage. Evidently the guerrillas had not yet been able to move it to a better hideout.

> Adam and Zelikov crawled on their bellies through the scrub towards the brick wall of the ablutions block. Evidently the pipe discharged from there. Flares of every size, colour and power, were shooting up into the sky, some bursting randomly like a fireworks display that had got out of hand.

As these examples show, the speaker is making a conclusion on the basis of some evidence and is quite confident that although this conclusion represents thinking rather than knowledge, if other people thought about this evidence, they would have to come to the same conclusion.

> *Evidently, he did it himself* =
> a. I want to say how I think when I think about it
> b. I say: he did it himself
> c. I don't say I know
> d. I think that it is like this because I know some other things
> e. I think that if someone knows these other things they cannot not think like this
> f. I think that other people can think the same

Note here the "semantic weakening" in the history of *evidently*, which can be summed up as a transition from "know" to "not know." The earlier meaning can be illustrated with the following example:

> Things which men by the light of their natural understanding evidently know. (1611, OED).

Collocations like *evidently know*, *evidently prove*, *evidently disclose*, or *evidently show* are common in older English, and the meaning reflected in them was still in use in the nineteenth century (as in A), alongside the "weakened" epistemic one (as in B):

    A. And this is evidently proved to have been fulfilled. (1833, OED)
    B. The spirit and the muscles were evidently at war. (1860, OED)

It is also worth noting that early examples of the epistemic *evidently* co-occur with the intensifier *so*, as in the following example from the OED:

    Reason was so evidently on their side. (1761)

Arguably, when it was used with *so*, *evidently* did not yet include the component "I don't say I know" and was close in meaning to *manifestly*, which also tended to co-occur with *so*, for example:

    The treaty was still so manifestly of advantage to England. (1759, OED)

When used sentence-initially, *evidently* can never be combined with *so* (used as an intensifier; obviously, it can be introduced by the causal *so*, in the sense of *thus*), and even when it is used sentence-initially, in current usage it doesn't present the fact referred to as "manifest" or "plain" but rather as something that can be inferred from what is observed and known.

8.4.2. *Clearly*

To begin again with some examples from Cobuild:

    I think there is clearly a clear evidence [*sic*] that . . . there is much more cooperation, there is much more rapport between them.

    I think CCM Two clearly has a superior climate.

    When I was in my first two years and I was a fag the discipline was imposed by the older boys and so that made life much more pleasant when you became an older boy yourself. . . . Clearly it was better to be an older boy.

    But you're more independent than they think you are . . . you're clearly able to go out alone.

    Clearly the smaller the unit of the loan or the financial asset the higher the transactions cost.
    —Clearly if you look back MX was a tremendous influence in the building programme, the expansion and making the residential provision et cetera.
    —Yes.

The epistemic adverb *clearly* doesn't have a corresponding verbal phrase either, although it can be seen as related to the phrase *I see* (as well as the adjectival phrase *it is clear that*). In addition to its epistemic role, *clearly* is used very widely as a manner adverb, as in *to speak clearly* or *to write clearly*. In fact, *clearly* is such a common and colloquial word that its role as an epistemic sentential adverbial can easily be overlooked. It is important to note, therefore, that in many other languages the counterparts of *clearly* as a manner adverb cannot be used to provide an epistemic frame for a sentence, as *clearly* can in English.[6] Compare, for example:

English: Clearly he did it himself.

French: *Clairement il l'a fait lui-même.

German: *Klar hat er es selbst getan.

Russian: *Jasno on sdelal èto sam.

The attitude conveyed by the English epistemic adverb *clearly* can be compared with that expressed by *evidently*, which in older usage could also be a manner adverb (especially in the collocation *to show evidently*, analogous to *to show clearly*, and also *to show manifestly*). But *clearly* conveys even more confidence than *evidently*. If *evidently* implies inferences drawn from some evidence, *clearly* (like *plainly*) implies knowledge potentially available to anyone. This does not mean that the speaker already knows what he or she sees as "clearly" open to people to know. As the first two examples show overtly, *clearly* implies "I think" rather than "I know," and the "clear evidence" mentioned in the first example does not indicate that the speaker already "knows" but rather that in his or her view, a moment's thought can make a person (anybody) "see," that is, know: no inference from the knowledge of other things is necessary for that. This can be represented as follows:

> *Clearly, he did it himself.* =
> a. I want to say how I think when I think about it
> b. I say: he did it himself
> c. I don't say I know
> d. I think that if someone thinks about it for a short time this someone will know it
> e. I think that other people can think the same

Finally, a few words on the history of *clearly* as an epistemic or quasi-epistemic adverb. Although the details are at this stage anything but clear, it *is* clear that its meaning has changed and that, as the following examples illustrate, its link with knowledge has weakened (that is, it once implied a greater confidence on the part of the speaker than it does now):

> a. There be many other places that clearly prove the same (1651, Hobbes, OED)
> b. They, who have been so clearly detected in ignorance or imposture. (1752, OED)
> c. Sigurd clearly seems to have believed the man to be speaking truth; and indeed nobody to have doubted but he was. (1875, Carlyle, Literature Online)

The collocation *clearly prove*, as in (a), is evidently incompatible with the component "I don't say I know," and so is the collocation *clearly detected* (as in b). On the other hand, the combination of *clearly* with *seems* (as in c) is not only compatible with such a component but in fact clearly implies its presence.

8.4.3. Obviously

The word *obviously* can be used in contemporary English in two different ways. In one sense, it is close to the expression *of course*. For example:

Obviously I don't want to overcook it [the stirfry].

Used in this way, *obviously* is an interactive expression that has nothing to do with the limitations of the speaker's knowledge or with the use of evidence. The epistemic sense of *obviously*, which concerns us here, can be illustrated with the following examples from Cobuild (UK spoken):

It's obviously a brief written by a public servant I would guess.

—Where did you get the lady gnome from?
—She came actually free with the first book. So you know it was obviously a sort of a thing to get you to buy the books I think.

—All mine break in recording. . . .
—Oh well you've obviously never done it properly.

Tell me a bit about your mother then, she's obviously a very important person.

. . . obviously they're going to bring more business to the area.

I saw a different doctor and he turned round and said to me erm You can have the baby at home if you want. And I thought to myself well obviously he's not read my records.

A motorist had pulled up to see to his windscreen wipers into this lay-by but he obviously wanted a tinkle and probably walked into the trees and found her body.

If *clearly* conveys more confidence than *evidently*, *obviously* is even more confident than *clearly*. Roughly (and metaphorically) speaking, what is clear everyone can see, but what is obvious, no one can not see: what is clear *is* visible to everyone, *whereas* what is obvious *has to* be visible to everyone. More precisely, we can represent the meaning of *obviously* as follows:

Obviously, he did it himself =
a. I want to say how I think when I think about it
b. I say: he did it himself
c. I don't say I know
d. I think that if someone thinks about it for a short time they cannot not know it
e. I think that other people can think the same

As the first Cobuild example illustrates, in saying *obviously* one is not implying that one knows, and in fact one is indicating that no claim to knowledge is being made. At the same time, the speakers are extremely confident of the validity of their statement: in their assessment, a moment's thought would be sufficient to reveal to anyone that what they say is really the case, and they expect this assessment to be shared by other people. Thus, in the subgroup of epistemic adverbs that I have called here "confident adverbs" and that includes *evidently, clearly,* and *obviously, obviously* is the most confident one. Yet even *obviously* includes in its meaning the caution component "I don't say I know."

Lyons has observed that, generally speaking, epistemic qualifiers weaken the speaker's commitment to the "factuality" of a sentence:

> Although it might appear that a statement is strengthened by putting the proposition that it expresses within the scope of the operator of epistemic necessity, this is not so, as far as the everyday use of language is concerned. It would be generally agreed that the speaker is more strongly committed to the factuality of "It be raining" by saying *It is raining* than he is by saying *It must be raining.* It is a general principle, to which we are expected to conform, that we should always make the strongest commitment for which we have epistemic warrant. If there is no explicit mention of the source of our information and no explicit qualification of our commitment to its factuality, it will be assumed that we have full epistemic warrant for what we say. But the very fact of introducing "must," "necessarily," "certainly," etc., into the utterance has the effect of making our commitment to the factuality of the proposition explicitly dependent upon our perhaps limited knowledge. There is no epistemically stronger statement than a categorical assertion, symbolized here as *p.* (Lyons 1977, vol. 2, 809)

Lyons's "general principle," to which "we" are allegedly expected to conform, is questionable because expectations may differ from culture to culture, with some cultures favoring hyperbole and others, understatement. Furthermore, even in English, a "categorical assertion" such as *it is raining* can be "strengthened" with words like *definitely* or *indeed.* Nonetheless, Lyons's comment is insightful insofar as the semantics of English epistemic adverbs is concerned: by virtue of their meaning, even "confident epistemic adverbs" like *evidently, clearly,* and even *obviously* can be said to weaken the assertion, because they include in their meaning the semantic component "I don't say I know."

The presence of this component in present-day use of *obviously* (in an epistemic sense) is not reflected in the OED entry, which defines it as follows: "in a clearly perceptible manner, evidently, plainly, manifestly." The examples offered by the OED include the following:

Texts of holy Writ obviously writ or painted. (1638)

Arthur . . . was obviously in a bad temper. (1872)

Clearly, the first of these examples does not include the component "I don't say I know," and it is possible that the second one does not include it either. However, if *obviously* were used at the beginning of that last sentence, then (in current usage) it would clearly imply this component:

Obviously, Arthur was in a bad temper.

In current usage, this sentence would imply inference rather than saying something that one knows.

8.5. "Nonconfident" Adverbs: *Possibly* and *Conceivably*

8.5.1. Possibly

At first sight, *possibly* may seem to mean the same as *perhaps*, and examples like the following one from Cobuild's corpus of spoken English appear to support this:

> I'm seventy-one, and possibly the person who took it perhaps thought they needed the money more than I did.

The speaker seems to be choosing at random between *possibly* and *perhaps*, and the unedited text ends up with both. But the same example that seems to identify the two can also be used to illustrate the difference between them. Most notably, *perhaps*, in contrast to *possibly*, can be used in a question:

> a.Perhaps they thought they needed the money more?
> b.?Possibly they thought they needed the money more?

As this contrast illustrates, *possibly* is "speaker-oriented," whereas *perhaps* is not. It expresses the speaker's assessment of what is possible, what can, or cannot, be the case. It is cautious, reflective, careful, and intellectually responsible. It reflects the speaker's desire not to say more than what one has grounds for saying—grounds that could also be seen as such by other people.

The cautious and reflective attitude indicated by *possibly* is particularly clear in the following sentences (Cobuild, UK books):

> Solomon's fleet of ships . . . brought gold and precious woods from Ophir (probably in South Arabia, but possibly in India).

> Responding to the last sentence, Haig scribbled in the margins: "possibly correct as to the Cabinet, but absolute rubbish as regards the people."

Not surprisingly, scientific and legal language appears to favor *possibly* over *perhaps*. For example:

> The dog did not know anything about thermometers. Possibly in its brain there was no sharp consciousness of a condition of very cold such as was in the man's brain.

> After eight o'clock she would have gone and got dressed . . . and she would be collected by her boyfriend in the car and they were out for the night. So where was MX? Where was the young lad? Possibly with a friend. Possibly at home by himself. And this little lad also has got pretty severe asthma and he uses a bronchial dilator inhaler. So that young lad could have an asthma attack and he's by himself. He could easily die.

In colloquial language, *possibly* occurs more commonly as a kind of intensifier in the collocation *could possibly*, rather than in the epistemic sense. When it is used in an epistemic sense, it implies a cautious, detached, quasi-scientific attitude, as in the following example:

> Possibly the worst attack I ever had was from a cat and that wasn't from a dog.

If we substituted *perhaps* for *possibly* in this last example, or indeed in any other examples, it would suggest a spontaneous thought for which the speaker does not take full responsibility. By contrast, *possibly* implies caution and responsibility.

Finally, as illustrated earlier, *possibly* can be used concurrently with two different possibilities, as in "possibly with a friend, possibly at home by himself." *Perhaps* would normally not be used like that but rather would require an *or*: "Perhaps with a friend, or perhaps at home by himself." But a repetition of *possibly* does not require or even allow an *or*: "?Possibly with a friend. Or possibly at home by himself."

If *possibly he was with a friend* included in its meaning the component "I say: he was with a friend," and *possibly, he was at home by himself*, the component "I say: he was at home by himself," the two sentences would be mutually incompatible, and so a combination of the two would require an *or*. The fact that it does not require or even allow an *or* suggests that the assertion introduced by *possibly* includes the semantic element *can*: "I say: he could have been with a friend, he could have been at home by himself."

All these observations bring us to the following explication:

Possibly, he did it himself. =
a. I want to say how I think when I think about it
b. I say: maybe he did it himself
c. I don't say I know
d. I think that it can be like this
e. I think that other people can think the same

8.5.2. Conceivably

The epistemic adverb *conceivably* implies very little confidence in the validity of the statement that one is making. Indeed, it nearly always co-occurs with the words *might*, *may*, or *could*, as the following examples from Cobuild illustrate:

William thanked him, put it into his desk and forgot about it. Months later, when tidying up, he examined the paper for the first time and, seeing that it was a prescription in Sanskrit, had it made up. It might, conceivably, be efficacious.

Even if spontaneous reincarnation experiences prove to be evidentially valueless, they still . . . could contribute conceivably to the sociological understanding of reincarnation.

Enterprise autonomy means inter alia giving the enterprises the right to set the prices. So that's something else that has to come at the same time as price liberalization. Then the social safety net. Well conceivably that could come before.

"Conceivably, Kritik might also be a paradigm for intellectual activity that is spiritual, i.e. the 'intense contemplation' of spirit, James Joyce's 'epiphany' and Benjamin's 'aura,'" as Steiner observed.

Results like this may represent a real breakthrough, not only in helping us to understand the origins of hyperactivity, but conceivably in devising better treatments.

I believe that to account for this regular co-occurrence of *conceivably* with *might*, *may*, and *could*, we need to include in the "I say" component of its explication too (as in the case of *possibly*), the word *maybe*: not "I say: he did it himself" but "I say: maybe he did it himself." To distinguish *conceivably* from *possibly*, we can replace the component "I think that it can be like this" with an even weaker one: "I can think that maybe it can be like this." This double weakening—"I can think" instead of "I think" and "maybe it can" instead of "it can"—accounts, I believe, for the highly skeptical tone of *conceivably*.

> *Conceivably, he did it himself* =
> a. I want to say how I think when I think about it
> b. I say: maybe he did it himself
> c. I don't say I know
> d. I can think that maybe it can be like this
> e. I think that other people can think the same

8.6. Hearsay Adverbs: *Apparently, Supposedly, Allegedly,* and *Reportedly*

8.6.1. Apparently

The epistemic adverb *apparently* is obviously related to the impersonal verbal phrase *it appears*, as well as to the noun *appearances*. For example, the following sentence from Jane Austen, "Captain Wentworth, however, came from his window, apparently not ill-disposed for conversation," could be paraphrased approximately as "Captain Wentworth, however, came from his window, and he appeared to be not ill-disposed for conversation."

I will call this sense of *apparently*, closely related to the impersonal phrase *it appears*, *apparently₁*. However, in current usage, and especially when it is used in sentence-initial position, *apparently* is usually interpreted as referring to hearsay. Thus, a sentence like *Apparently, he did it himself* is no longer understood as meaning something close to *It appears that he did it himself*, but rather, as the following examples (from Cobuild) make clear, as referring to something that someone else has said:

> I was talking to the Youth Chamber of Denmark this week and apparently they've sent a fax out this week. **So they tell me.**

> This was an article in one of the national papers earlier this week it said er it was talking about er accents it said er Glasgow apparently erm is the pits. The Glaswegian accent is the pits. **They say** it's the verbal equivalent of an arm tattooed with snakes.

> **I was listening to** Derek Jamieson earlier this morning. . . . Apparently . . . before we took Saint George as our Patron Saint . . . we recognised Edward the Confessor as Patron Saint. He was apparently made Patron of the

Order of the Garter in thirteen forty eight and then some time after that declared Patron Saint of England.

When you're on about roads **did you hear the news about** that chap on the motorway today? . . . Apparently a bloke had a heart attack driving down and he was bearing towards the central reservation and a lorry went and pushed him onto the hard shoulder.

I was reading in the paper the other day apparently they [the Germans] have more industrial disputes than we do at the moment.

. . . these have bite pressures of hundreds of pounds per square inch these days. Apparently eighteen hundred pounds pressure they're — Is it really? Apparently — **that's what I read**.

But apparently **so I hear it** [the women's club] was not as well appointed as the Men's Club, apparently.

Apparently there's eight times more sheep than there are people in New Zealand.

This last example does not refer to speech overtly, but it is obvious that the speaker must have heard or read this information somewhere.

The speaker's attitude to what this other person has said is neither one of trust nor one of skepticism. Rather, it is noncommittal: the speaker is not casting doubt on the other person's words but doesn't accept responsibility for their validity either. At the most, it is implied that that person "can think that they know" — they can think that because they have some evidence, some grounds for thinking so, but this evidence may be insufficient or unreliable.

> *Apparently, he did it himself.* =
> a. I want to say what someone else says
> b. I say: he did it himself
> c. I don't say I know
> d. I think that this person can know
> e. I think that other people can think the same

The combination of components "I want to say what someone else says" and "I think that this person can know" implies more trust than skepticism. *Apparently* differs in this respect from *supposedly* and *allegedly*, both of which suggest, in different ways, more skepticism than trust — *supposedly* by means of the component "I think that it is not true" and *allegedly* by means of the component "I think that it can be not true." It is not as positive, however, as *reportedly*, which implies that the original source of information is someone who "can know" not only "this" but things of this kind in general (an expert, a professional reporter, an official).

8.6.2. Supposedly

Let us start again with some examples from Cobuild.

> I mean when the poll tax was introduced it was supposedly to improve services but in all honesty the services have been cut drastically. . . .

You know in local government and government jobs these days they're so hot or supposedly hot on qualifications to get into the jobs and then they're being lectured by somebody who isn't qualified.

Supposedly called the brew house because the middle class reckoned working-class people brewed beer in the copper that was in the brew house but actually the name goes back centuries.

And when they got to there the bigger ones had to walk to give the horses— 'Cos the horses were quite tired by that time. Or supposedly tired.

But I mean they're redoing all or supposedly redoing all the seafront round there aren't they.

Now if you've been pushed down you were manipulated by the person who was supposedly ministering in love.

We had a teacher who supposedly took guitar lessons. But all he did was play all the different things he knew whilst [laughs] we had to sit and listen to him.

There were delivered to every household in the country or supposedly which is half a million households. Now you know I don't know whether they did get to every household 'cos we heard that there were huge gaps.

It's supposedly the family house [laughter]. You could raise a family here [laughs]. Well quite honestly I'd want a bigger house if I was going to raise a family. I'd want a bigger bathroom.

What is particularly characteristic about these examples is the repeated use of the skeptical phrase *or supposedly*, the combination of *supposedly* with laughter (ironic or sarcastic), and in co-occurrence with discourse markers like *but* and *well* (note also the dismissive phrase *but all he did*).

As all these skeptical devices indicate, the epistemic adverb *supposedly* is not related to the verbal phrase *I suppose* as closely as *presumably* is related to *I presume*. It has a closer relative in one of the two meanings of the past participle *supposed*—not in the one the *Collins Cobuild dictionary* (1987) paraphrases "what should be done" (e.g., "I'm not supposed to talk to you about it") but the one described as follows:

> **Supposed** is used when you are referring to a statement or to a way of describing something and when you want to express doubt about the truth of the statement or about how appropriate it is. E.g. . . . *his supposed ancestor, the pirate Henry Morgan. . . . the supposed benefits of a progressive welfare state.*

It is from this latter meaning, according to the same dictionary, that the adverb *supposedly* is derived: "supposedly. E.g. . . . a robot supposedly capable of understanding spoken commands. . . . It supposedly tied up with her interest in dance. . . . a supposedly inferior form of life such as the reptile."

Let us start, then, with the form *supposed*. What exactly does a phrase like *the supposed benefits* or *his supposed generosity* mean? Clearly, one component is that someone else says this (that there are benefits; that the person in question is generous), and another, that this person wants people to think that it is true. But the speaker who qualifies something as *supposed* dissociates himself or herself from the original statement ("I don't say I know") and in fact expresses some skepticism ("I think that it is not true"). For example, in his polemical book *The Case for Christianity*, C. S. Lewis writes:

> Dualism means the belief that there are two equal and independent
> powers at the back of everything, one of them good and the other
> bad. . . . The two powers, or spirits, or gods—the good one and the bad
> one—are supposed to be quite independent. (Lewis 1989, 37)

The word *supposed* implies here not only that the advocates of dualism say that the two powers are quite independent but also that they want people to think that this is true. The polemical intention behind this use of *supposed* is also clearly visible in the following sentence, from the same book:

> If the whole show [i.e., the universe] was bad and senseless from A to Z,
> so to speak, why did I, who was supposed to be part of the show, find
> myself in such violent reaction against it? (Lewis 1989, 34)

Again, C. S. Lewis is arguing here not only against those people who *say* that the universe is bad and senseless from A to Z but also, and more particularly, against those who want people to think that this is true (that is, by implication, that C. S. Lewis himself is but a part of a totally bad and senseless universe). By using the word *supposed*, Lewis dissociates himself from such a view. The adverb *supposedly* appears to carry all these elements, too, adding to them the familiar expectation that other people can think the same. This brings us to the following explication:

Supposedly, he did it himself. =
a. I want to say what someone else says
b. I say: he did it himself
c. I don't say I know
d. I know that this someone else wants people to think that it is true
e. I think that it is not true
f. I think that other people can think the same

Unlike the other epistemic adverbs, and unlike the verbal phrase *I suppose*, *supposedly* has a somewhat sarcastic ring. This can be accounted for by the combination of the "assertive" component "I say" with the component of disbelief "I think that it is not true." In this one case, then, the speaker is undermining his or her own statement. This would be incoherent were it not for the component "I want to say what someone else says," which explains the apparent contradiction and accounts for the somewhat sarcastic tone of the utterance.

8.6.3. Allegedly

The epistemic adverb *allegedly* is clearly closely related to the adjective *alleged* and the noun *allegations*. It is used more widely, however, and although it, too, typically occurs in contexts that imply "bad things," it does not have the same "criminal" implications (or connotations) as the other two words. To illustrate:

Allegedly, Tyrrell had added lead ballast to the fuel.

They had also been used in military intelligence and allegedly as mine detectors.

They had produced a hand-written diary, allegedly written by a member of the Red Army.

The manager, allegedly struck by a flying 200–pound music machine, was in hospital with multiple injuries.

You could also have a special dinner for 3 roubles (30 kopecks). This allegedly had meat in one of the courses, but it need a miracle to find it.

During this short-lived "Mormon War," 120 Gentiles were allegedly led into an Indian trap by overzealous Mormons in the Mountain Meadows Massacre.

The General Services people clogged the elevators, heading down into the bowels of the building to revive, allegedly, the dead air-conditioning system.

He (Nikodim) died, allegedly of a heart attack, in the arms of the Pope.

As these examples show, the use of *allegedly* allows one to distance oneself from what one is saying in a number of ways. First, the statement in the *allegedly* frame is attributed to someone else: "I say: someone else says that. . . . " Second, here as elsewhere the speaker disclaims knowledge: "I don't say I know." Third, in addition to disclaiming knowledge, the speaker expresses some doubt as to the truth of the other person's statement: "I think it can be not true." This brings us to the following explication:

Allegedly, he did it himself. =
a. I want to say what someone else says
b. I say: someone says: "he did it himself"
c. I don't say I know
d. I think that people can want to know
e. I think that it can be not true
f. I think that other people can think the same

Note that the "I say" component of the explication differs from that of *supposedly*, *apparently*, and, as we will see in the next section, *reportedly*. All these four adverbs can be said to be based on hearsay, but it is only in the case of *allegedly* that the speaker distances himself or herself totally from the statement that is being attributed to someone else. In the case of *apparently*, the speaker appears to be prepared to "buy" the original statement, and in the case of *reportedly*, even more so, whereas in the case of *supposedly*, the speaker is, as it were, ironically pretending to be "buying" the original statement. In the case of *allegedly*, however, the speaker is emphatically disassociating himself or herself from the original statement—not by saying "I think that it is not true" (as in the case of *supposedly*) but by not lending his or her voice to that statement at all. This is why in this one case I have formulated the "I say" component as "I say: someone says. . . . "

Finally, it needs to be pointed out that in the case of *allegedly*—in contrast to *apparently* and *supposedly*—what the speaker is repeating after someone else is a matter of public interest. Hence the need for the component "I think that people can want to know." Typically, a sentence introduced in the frame *allegedly* refers to "something bad that someone has done," but this is not invariably so. Invariably, however, what is being "alleged" is something that people can want to know.

8.6.4. Reportedly

Reportedly appears to be the latest addition to the class of epistemic adverbs, presumably linked with the role of the media in modern life. Its use can be illustrated with the following sentences from Cobuild:

> During her first interview with the "superteam," Sonia reportedly began to speak in French, a language she had never studied.

> When the Turks had ruled Cyprus, they had a garrison in the square fort on the harbour wall. It was said that on top of the battlements they placed a huge cannon. Reportedly this piece was able to hurl a ball to any part of the town and thus the Greek Cypriots lived under constant threat.

> But poor Tsa Rongba was in a very bad way. He was reportedly being tortured every other day and was frequently interrogated.

> The average age of face-lift patients has reportedly dropped from sixty to fifty, with many forty-year-olds now facing the knife.

> This report, picked up by an Arizona highway patrolman, bore the notation: "Subject reportedly drunk at time."

> The blackout reportedly reduced some Iraqi surgeons to operating by candlelight.

> Although Schwarzkopf had rated the chances of killing Saddam as high, no one in Washington or Riyadh underestimated Saddam's elusiveness. He reportedly had survived five assassination attempts in 1981 alone and countless plots since.

> Geller was reportedly very shaken by this sudden and unexpected glimpse into his capacity to cause harm.

To account for the fine balance between confidence and caution implied by *reportedly*, I would propose for it the following explication:

> *Reportedly, he did it himself.* =
> a. I want to say what someone else says
> b. I say: he did it himself
> c. I don't say I know
> d. I think that people can want to know what this someone else says
> e. I think that this someone else can know things of this kind
> f. I think that other people can think the same

This explication is fairly close to that of *apparently*, but it differs from it in two respects. First, although in both cases the original speaker is presented as someone who "can know," in the case of *reportedly* this person is, as mentioned earlier, an official or professional source of information (someone who "can know things of this kind"). Second, in the case of *reportedly*, as in that of *allegedly*, the matter spoken of must be of some public interest. Whether this is sufficient to account for the semantic difference between the two is a matter for further consideration.

8.7. The "Uncertain" Status of *Certainly*

Certainly is usually included among epistemic adverbs, and indeed it may seem to be close in meaning to *undoubtedly* and *indubitably*. All these words appear to convey certainty, that is, something like an absence of doubt. In fact, however, in some important ways *certainly* breaks the ranks of epistemic adverbs. To show this, I will first consider sentences with *certainly* in the initial position. Since I will argue in this section that in the case of *certainly*, the two variants—the sentence-initial and the sentence-internal one—are further apart than in the case of the other adverbs addressed in this chapter, I will call the sentence-initial one *certainly*₁ and the sentence-internal one *certainly*₂ Consider, then, the following sentence with *certainly*₁:

Certainly, I lied to her.

It would be difficult to replace *certainly* in this sentence with any of the epistemic adverbs discussed earlier (unless the speaker were suffering from amnesia):

?Apparently, I lied to her.

?Evidently, I lied to her.

?Clearly, I lied to her.

?Presumably, I lied to her.

?Supposedly, I lied to her.

?Probably, I lied to her.

?Possibly, I lied to her.

?Conceivably, I lied to her.

Undoubtedly and *obviously* seem less infelicitous in this context than most of the other epistemic adverbs, but even these two can't always be felicitously substituted for a sentence-initial *certainly*. As for *allegedly*, *reportedly*, and *arguably*, they often sound decidedly odd in sentences with a first-person subject, for example:

Certainly, I was ashamed of what I'd done.

??Allegedly, I was ashamed of what I'd done.

??Reportedly, I was ashamed of what I'd done.

??Arguably, I was ashamed of what I'd done.

All these infelicities can be explained if we recall the semantic component "I don't say I know," which has been posited for all the epistemic adverbs discussed here (with a minor variation in the case of *likely*). Normally, one doesn't disclaim knowledge when one speaks of one's own deliberate actions and conscious feelings.[7]

In fact, I would argue that in a sentence-initial position, *certainly* (*certainly*₁) is not an epistemic adverb at all (i.e., a device qualifying one's "commitment" to what one is saying) but rather that its function is conversational; in this position, *certainly* is used to agree, or to partially agree, with what has been said before. This conversational function of a sentence-initial *certainly* can be illustrated with the following examples from Cobuild, UK spoken (*M* stands for a male speaker, and *F* for a female one; and the numbers identify individual male and female speakers):

1. <Fo21> Fifty pounds a year was something in those days. <Mo1> Certainly was. Yes.
2. you were saying <Fo1> That I had a stronger Lancashire accent. <Mo1> that about losing your Lancashire accent and getting a Scottish one in Glasgow <Fo1> Yes. But London I expect that it modified during the three years. But certainly when I first went up I had a strong Lancashire accent but I didn't notice.
3. <Mo1> How do you feel about gimmick weddings You've talked about weddings which are in many ways traditional even if they're at a registry office. I mean certainly a synagogue wedding can be the most gorgeous traditional thing and equally one in a church. How do you feel about people I don't know getting married under water and all that stuff <Fo4> Well the thing is <Mo1> Bit tacky isn't it.
4. <Mo2> we feel we probably need increasingly more of a general manager down there <Mo1> Mm our Yes. Certainly as administrator.

In example 1, speaker Mo1 agrees with speaker Fo21; in example 2, Fo1 agrees with Mo1; in example 3, Mo1 agrees with Fo4; and in example 4, first Mo1 agrees partially with Mo2.

One can also use *certainly* at the beginning of a sentence to indicate an endorsement or a partial endorsement of something that one has said oneself. For example:

5. I was infatuated with *A Clockwork Orange* and in fact at the age of nineteen I adapted *A Clockwork Orange* for the stage which not many people know about. Certainly MX didn't. <laughter>
6. <Mo1> I think he's threatened by me basically but there's no reason why that should be. . . . <Fo1> Mhm <Mo1> so supervisions initially were excellent very very good. Certainly filled some of the gaps that we were developing. <Fo1> Mhm.

In example 5, the speaker indicates that even if the first assertion could not be fully upheld, a modified version of it certainly could. Example 6 is particularly interesting in showing that a modified reassertion may follow some real or imagined skepticism from one's interlocutor (in this case, Fo1's "Mhm").[8]

The conversational character of the sentence-initial *certainly* distances it from epistemic adverbs and links it with interactive "particles," which will be discussed in section 8.8.

Turning now to the sentence-internal use of *certainly* (*certainly*₂), which is closer to epistemic adverbs, let us consider the following sentences from John Bayley's recent memoir, *Widower's House* (2003):

I asked her if she would like to have a look at it, since the book certainly made an impression. (p. 568)

The way in which the repetition made me forget that Iris was dead was certainly remarkable. (p. 573)

To be "a good cry" it must be done on one's own. . . . Tennyson the Victorian certainly knew all about it. (p. 574)

First of all, it is clear that in these sentences *certainly* is not used conversationally: it is not used to agree or partially agree with something that someone else has said, and neither is it used to modify something that one has said oneself, in response to someone else's real or imaginary reaction to it. In this respect, the sentence-internal *certainly* (*certainly*₂) is more like the genuine epistemic adverbs discussed in this chapter. At the same time, however, it differs from those other adverbs, insofar as it expresses the speaker's full (not merely subjective) certainty—a certainty that is expected to be shared by other people. Unlike the genuine epistemic adverbs, then, a sentence-internal *certainly* (*certainly*₂) does not carry with it the component "I don't say I know." To account for both its closeness to epistemic adverbs in its overall semantic structure and for its sui generis semantic status, I would propose the following explication:

> *He certainly did it himself (I saw him do it).* =
> a. I say: he did it himself
> b. I can't think that maybe it is not like this
> c. I know that it is like this
> d. I think that other people can know the same

What distinguishes the sentence-internal *certainly* from bona fide epistemic adverbs is the presence of the component "I know," the concomitant absence of the component "I don't say I know," and also the absence of the component "I think" (apart from the final "I think other people can say the same"): clearly, the component "I know" precludes the presence of a concurrent "I think" (as well as of a concurrent "I don't say I know").

It is worth recalling in this context Cinque's observation that epistemic adverbs express a lack of confidence on the part of the speaker. Slightly rephrased, this observation can be applied even to adverbs like *clearly*, *obviously*, and *undoubtedly*, which imply if not a lack of confidence, then at least a lack of full knowledge. It does not, however, apply to *certainly*, which is compatible with full knowledge, as the following sentence illustrates:

He was certainly there—I know because I was sitting next to him.

Clearly, *evidently*, and *obviously* could not be used in such a context, and even *undoubtedly* would not sound fully felicitous:

?Clearly, he was there—I know because I was sitting next to him.

?Evidently, he was there—I know because I was sitting next to him.

?Obviously, he was there—I know because I was sitting next to him.

(?)Undoubtedly, he was there—I know because I was sitting next to him.

To conclude, *certainly*—usually treated as one of the prime examples of English epistemic adverbs—differs from the genuine members of this class both semantically and syntactically. Unlike those genuine members of the class, it cannot be used in two different positions in essentially the same sense. Furthermore, when it is used sentence-initially, it is not an adverb at all, but a pragmatic or discourse particle like *surely*—a topic to which I now turn.

8.8. Epistemic Adverbs vs. Discourse Particles

In the literature on English grammar, epistemic adverbs are often treated on a par with various discourse (or "modal") particles. For example, Quirk et al. (1985) include in their category of "content disjuncts," along with epistemic adverbs such as *presumably, undoubtedly, unquestionably, apparently, conceivably*, and *supposedly*, various discourse markers such as *indeed, surely, of course, perhaps*, and *maybe*, which, I will argue, have quite a different semantic structure, and Jackendoff (1972) includes among his "speaker-oriented adverbs" expressions like *of course*.

As mentioned earlier, I believe that the distinction between epistemic adverbs and discourse markers is important and that by blurring it one is obliterating a culturally significant peculiarity of modern English: the wealth of epistemic adverbs. "Particles" and other discourse markers are common in many other languages; for example, there is a great wealth of them in German, Russian, and Japanese. Modern English is relatively poor in this respect. Broadly speaking, the difference between the two classes can be characterized as follows: particles can be interactive, as it were, dialogical, whereas epistemic adverbs are monological or, to use Jackendoff's term, "speaker-oriented." To put it differently, particles can include in their meaning both the speaker and the addressee, whereas epistemic adverbs express the speaker's own stand, without any reference to the addressee. It is true that as analyzed here, epistemic adverbs refer also to other people: the speaker thinks that his or her own stand can be shared by other people. But this reference to other people does not build a bridge between "I" and "you," the speaker and the addressee, in the concrete speech situation.

Traugott, to whose comments on the history of epistemic adverbs I will refer later, has suggested that these adverbs are used for "strategic negotiation of speaker-hearer interaction and, in that connection, in modern English for the purposes of politeness, articulation of speaker attitude" (1989, 51). I think that this comment is valid, but it is worth adding that the kind of speaker-hearer interaction involved in the use of epistemic adverbs is different from that realized by means of interactive particles. Particles build bridges between the speaker and the addressee and often exercise more or less subtle pressure on one's interlocutor (as, for example, *surely* does in English). The epistemic adverbs serve a different, "hands-off," kind of interaction. By pointedly emphasizing that "I want to say what I think," they indicate that the speaker has no wish to "impose" his or her point of view on the addressee. This attitude of "nonimposing" is not part of the meaning of epistemic adverbs, but it can well be their pragmatic effect and, indeed, part of the modern Anglo speaker's motivation for using them. Semantically, however, these adverbs are speaker-oriented; as Traugott says, they articulate the speaker's attitude, and they help keep the addressee at arm's length by not referring to the addressee at all and explicitly limiting the utterance to saying what *I* think. The "strategic negotiation of speaker-hearer interaction" (Traugott 1989, 51) is not part of their meaning (as it is in the case of particles) but a pragmatic effect of their semantic focus on the speaker's attitude. Arguably, then, given the modern Anglo cultural scripts of "nonimposition" and "hands off the addressee" (see chapter 2), the relative scarcity of interactive particles in modern English has the same cultural explanation as the abundance of epistemic adverbs.

Comparing the "English modal scene" with the Swedish one, Karin Aijmer notes in relation to the Swedish particle *väl*, which according to her data is by far the most common Swedish "epistemic qualifier," that *väl* refers to the hearer as well as the speaker ("*väl* is associated with an appeal to the hearer to confirm something or to agree, in addition to the epistemic meaning"; 1997, 29). In Aijmer's view, such an inclusion of the addressee (a hearer) distinguishes modal particles like *väl* from verbal epistemic phrases such as *I think* and *I believe*, which focus exclusively on the speaker's own attitude to the utterance. As we have seen, epistemic adverbs, unlike epistemic verbal phrases, "objectify" the speaker's own attitude by extending it, in anticipation, to "other people." They do not, however, engage the addressee either, in the way particles like *väl* usually do.

English expressions like *of course*, *indeed*, and *surely*, included by, for example, Quirk et al. (1985) and Jackendoff (1972) in the same category of "content disjuncts" or "speaker-oriented adverbs" as epistemic adverbs, are also interactive rather than speaker-oriented. The interactive character of such expressions is clearly reflected in the descriptions of their meaning and use offered, for example, by the *Collins Cobuild English Language Dictionary* (1987). To quote:

> **Indeed** 1 You use **indeed** 1.1 to confirm or agree with something that has just been said . . . 1.2 to add a further comment or statement which strengthens the point you have already made.
>
> You say **of course** 1.1 when you are briefly mentioning something that you expect other people already realize or understand, or when you want to indicate that you think they should realize or understand it. . . . 1.2 when you are talking about an event or situation that does not surprise you. . . . 1.3 as a polite way of saying yes, of giving permission, or of agreeing with someone. . . . 1.4 in order to emphasize a statement that you are making, especially when you are agreeing or disagreeing with someone. . . .
>
> 2 **Of course not** is an emphatic way of saying no.
>
> **Surely** 1 You use **surely** 1.1 in order to emphasize that you think something is true and to express surprise that other people do not necessarily agree with you. . . . 1.2 in order to express surprise at something that seems to contradict what you are saying. . . . 1.3 in order to contradict something that someone else has said.

It is important to note that *Collins Cobuild*'s definitions of epistemic adverbs are phrased quite differently, with no reference to the addressee ("you" in these definitions stands for the speaker). For example:

> **Presumably.** You use **presumably** to say that, although you are not certain that what you are saying is true, you think that it is very likely to be true.
>
> **Probably.** You use **probably** to say that you think that something is likely to be the case, although you do not actually know whether it is the case or not.

Evidently is used . . . to indicate that you think something is true but that you are not sure, because you do not have enough information or proof.

Apparently. Apparently is (1) used to indicate that the information that you are giving is something that you have heard but you are not sure that it is true. . . . (2) used to refer to a situation that seems to exist although you are not sure that it exists.

This is not the place to undertake detailed discussion of the meaning of particles, so I will only sketch a few explications to show how their interactive character can be reflected in semantic formulae. Before doing so, however, I must point out that such particles are often polysemous and require slightly different explications, depending on their place in discourse, as reflected in fact in the *Collins Cobuild* dictionary definitions (see also Travis 2005). For example, we need to distinguish an *indeed* occurring in a response to somebody else's words from an *indeed* referring to something within the speaker's own utterance. I suggest that in the first case, the speaker says, in essence, "I want to say: it is true," and in the second, "I want to say more." (The examples are from *Collins Cobuild English Language Dictionary* 1987.)

indeed$_1$ (e.g., "I think you knew him when you were in Pretoria."—
"I did indeed.") =
a. you said something about something to me now
b. because of this I know that you think something about it
c. I want to say: it is true

indeed$_2$ (e.g., I'm very happy, indeed anxious, that students' views should be expressed)=
a. I said something about something to you now
b. I want to say more

Similarly, I will posit two explications for *of course*, linking them with the expression's position in discourse, with *of course*$_1$ being used, essentially, in response to questions, and *of course*$_2$, in an utterance initiated by the speaker himself or herself.

of course$_1$ (e.g., "Dan, do you remember Margaret?"—"Of course.") =
a. you want me to say something about something to you now
b. I say: it is like this
c. I think that it can't be not like this
d. I don't have to say to you why I think like this

of course$_2$ (e.g., there is of course an element of truth in this argument) =
a. I say: it is like this (there is an element of truth in this argument)
b. I think that it can't be not like this
c. I don't have to say to you why I think like this

For *surely*, we can perhaps propose a uniform explication:
surely (e.g., "she was surely one of the rarest women of our time") =
a. I say: I think like this: she was one of the rarest women of our time
b. I can't not think like this
c. I think that you can't not think the same

As pointed out earlier, Jackendoff (1972, 82, 102ff.) observed that "speaker-oriented" adverbs "do not feel comfortable in questions." Yet Jackendoff's category of "speaker-oriented adverbs" includes elements (e.g., *by the way*) that do feel comfortable in questions (as does *surely*), and so do other scholars' categories of epistemic adverbs. This inconsistency can be eliminated if we distinguish epistemic adverbs, which are "speaker-oriented," from interactive particles or discourse markers, which often refer in their meaning to the addressee as well as to the speaker.

Admittedly, some interactive expressions, for example, *of course*, *indeed*, or *sure*, do not feel comfortable in questions either. This can be explained, however, if we recognize that interactive particles can occur in responses as well as in utterances that invite a response. If we analyze expressions like *of course* and *indeed* in the way that has been suggested here—that is, as essentially "response cries" (Goffman 1981)— their inability to occur in questions will be explained. Of course, epistemic adverbs can also occur in response to somebody else's utterance, as in the following example from Jane Austen's *Pride and Prejudice*:

> —". . . But, in my opinion, it is a paltry device, a very mean art."
> —"Undoubtedly," replied Darcy, to whom this remark was chiefly addressed.

But as the explications developed here show, epistemic adverbs do not engage the addressee in their very semantics, as interactive particles and discourse markers do.

Although modern linguistic accounts of parts of speech tend not to include particles, I would suggest that most languages appear to have a class of words (distinct from nouns, verbs, pronouns, adjectives, adverbs, numerals, conjunctions, prepositions or adpositions, and interjections) whose main function is interactive. Sometimes, as in a recent book by Kate Beeching (2002), these words are called "pragmatic particles." Beeching's book focuses on the French words *c'est-à-dire*, *enfin*, *hein*, and *quoi*, which are said to "lubricate reformulation and contribute to both sociability and social indexation" (cover). The "sociability" of such words is clearly linked to the fact that in their very semantics they engage the addressee.

Words of this kind can be distinguished from "interjections," whose function is, prototypically at least, monological; in most cases, they express the speaker's current emotion (see Wierzbicka 1991/2003; Ameka 1992). "Pragmatic particles," on the other hand, can be said to be, prototypically at least, dialogical: they link, in some way, the speaker and the addressee, the "I" and the "you." In form, some pragmatic particles can be indistinguishable from adverbs, but in their semantic structure they are different. For example, the English word *surely* is analogous in form to the epistemic adverbs like *obviously* or *undoubtedly*; nonetheless, semantically, it is quite different. For example, in the following pair of sentences:

(a) Clearly/obviously/undoubtedly, he did it himself.
(b) Surely, he did it himself.

sentence (b) invites a response, whereas none of the variants in sentence (a) do so.

Looking back at the *Collins* (1987) dictionary entries of *surely*, *indeed*, and *of course* quoted earlier, we can say that epistemic adverbs are not used to agree or disagree, to confirm or disconfirm, to elicit agreement or confirmation, to contradict someone, or to express surprise at being contradicted, that is to say, to perform any of the interactive functions attributed in the dictionary to words like *surely, indeed*, and *of course*. They are indeed "speaker-oriented," and while I have argued that they project the speaker's attitude on some "other people," they do not seek to engage the addressee. Thus, the sentences in (a) express the speaker's own view, and although the speaker expects this view to be shared by other people, there is no appeal to the addressee to either agree or disagree, and there is no expectation that the addressee will respond. On the other hand, sentence (b) appeals to the addressee, and in this case, the addressee can indeed be expected to respond.

Once again, this is not to say that all pragmatic particles invite a response. Some, like the English particle *well*, can themselves be linked with a response:

—Well, yes.

—Well, no.

But clearly, such "responsive" particles are also interactive rather than monological. The widely used term *discourse markers* is suggestive in this regard: *discourse* implies stretches of speaking extending beyond a sentence and thus likely to involve an exchange between a speaker and an addressee (or addressees), and even if one person is speaking and another only listening, discourse markers provide some guidance for the hearer. An "epistemic adverb," on the other hand, has to do with *the speaker's* epistemic stance, quite regardless of what the hearer may think or say.

Thus, having considered the difference between, on the one hand, epistemic adverbs and, on the other, particles and discourse markers, I can finally attempt a definition of the class that is the subject of this chapter. Up till now, I have been talking about the class of epistemic adverbs in modern English without attempting to define this class in a precise way. I have now reached a point at which a precise definition can be proposed. Here it is: the class of English epistemic adverbs includes words that meet the following four conditions:

1. They can be used sentence-initially.
2. They can be used sentence-internally (after the auxiliary if there is one, otherwise before the main verb).
3. They cannot be used in questions.
4. They include in their semantic structure the components "I think" and "I don't say I know."

Having this definition at our disposal, we are in a better position to consider the history of this class in modern English.

8.9. The History of Epistemic Adverbs in Modern English

The question of when the class of epistemic adverbs (as understood here) emerged in English, and in what order they appeared on the scene, deserves detailed study. (For valuable earlier studies bearing on this question, see Goossens 1982; Hanson 1987; Traugott 1989.) All I can do here is to sketch a very tentative outline on the basis of a number of concordances and works from *Literature Online*.

To begin with Thomas More (1478–1535), the only epistemic adverb that can be found in his *Dialogue of Comfort against Tribulation* is *undoubtedly*.

The same is true for Shakespeare (1564–1616). Although the words *possibly* and *apparently* (not to mention *clearly*) also appear in Shakespeare's works, they are not used in them in the epistemic sense. For example:

When possibly I can, I will return. (*Two Gentlemen of Verona*)

Arrest him, officer,

I would not spare my brother in this case

If he should scorn me so apparently. (*Comedy of Errors*)

In Milton's (1608–1674) works, too, *undoubtedly* is the only epistemic adverb that I have been able to find (used in an epistemic sense).

In Daniel Defoe's (1661–1731) works, we can find *evidently* and *probably*, for example:

This was evidently my case. (*Moll Flanders*)

. . . that he might very probably, with my assistance, make a remove from this wilderness, and come into his own country again. (*Robinson Crusoe*)

What is noticeable about the use of *probably* in Defoe is not only that it co-occurs with *very* but also that it is invariably accompanied by modal verbs like *might* and *should*. It is possible, therefore, that its meaning is not yet identical with that which it has in contemporary (twentieth- and twenty-first-century) English.

In Jonathan Swift's (1667–1745) *Gulliver's Travels* (1726), we find again *undoubtedly* and *probably*. *Probably* is, once again, nearly always accompanied by a modal verb: *might*, *will*, or *could*.

In Lawrence Sterne's (1713–1768) *Tristram Shandy* (1760), we find *undoubtedly*, *evidently*, *unquestionably*, and *possibly*.

In Thomas Carlyle's (1795–1881) works, we find *evidently*, *unquestionably*, *possibly*, and *presumably*.

In Jane Austen's (1775–1817) works, we find *undoubtedly*, *evidently*, *probably*, *unquestionably*, *possibly*, *obviously*, and *apparently*. Interestingly, in her usage, *probably* is no longer typically accompanied by modal verbs and can refer to specific facts. For example:

You have probably entirely forgotten a conversation. (*Sense and Sensibility*)

In George Eliot's (1819–1880) works, we find *undoubtedly*, *evidently*, *probably*, *unquestionably*, *possibly*, *presumably*, *obviously*, and *apparently*.

In George Bernard Shaw's (1856–1950) works, we find *undoubtedly*, *evidently*, *probably*, *unquestionably*, *possibly*, *presumably*, *obviously*, *apparently*, and *conceivably*.

The picture that emerges from these (admittedly limited) data can be summarized in the form of Table 8.4.[9]

Needless to say, this table does not claim to represent well-established findings but rather preliminary results that would need to be corroborated by further investi-

TABLE 8.4 The historical expansion of the category of epistemic Adverbs

	16th Century	17th Century	18th Century	First half 19th Century	Second half 19th Century	20th Century
undoubtedly	X	X	X	X	X	X
evidently			X	X	X	X
probably			X	X	X	X
unquestionably			X	X	X	X
possibly			X	X	X	X
presumably				X	X	X
obviously				X	X	X
apparently₁				X	X	X
apparently₂						X
arguably					X	X
allegedly					X	X
conceivably					X	X
reportedly						X

gations. In particular, it is impossible to determine without careful semantic analysis of many examples, considered in context, whether at a particular time a particular adverb included in its meaning the component "I don't say I know." Do, for example, the early (sixteenth- and seventeenth-century) uses of *undoubtedly* include this component? For example, when Milton says of God, in *Paradise Lost and Paradise Regained*, that he "undoubtedly will relent and turn from his displeasure" (Book X), he appears to be expressing a deep faith and certainty incompatible with a cautious "I don't say I know." In fact, even in the following early-eighteenth-century sentence (from *Gulliver's Travels*), in which *undoubtedly* appears sentence-initially, the presence of the component "I don't say I know" is highly questionable:

> Undoubtedly philosophers are in the right, when they tell us that nothing is great or little otherwise than by comparison. (1726, 28)

Undoubtedly appears to mean here (rather like *without doubt* does in contemporary speech) that, roughly, "nobody can doubt," without any accompanying disclaimer "I don't say I know." On the other hand, a century later, when in Jane Austen's *Pride and Prejudice* (1813) Darcy replies, "Undoubtedly." to a remark formulated as a personal opinion ("in my opinion"), his response can be plausibly interpreted as including such a component.

In her paper "On Subjectivity and the History of Epistemic Expressions in English," Hanson writes:

> The epistemic adverbs of English include "possibly," "probably," "evidently," "apparently," "obviously," "certainly," "indubitably," "conceivably," "indisputably," "presumably," "allegedly," "unquestionably," "admittedly," and others. These are all what Jackendoff (1972) has called "speaker-oriented adverbs." "Speaker-oriented" adverbs are understood as conveying something about the speaker's attitude toward the proposition expressed in the rest of his sentence; in the case of these epistemic ones, it is something about his knowledge of it. In discussions of the history of

epistemicity in English, it is commonly said that these adverbs were acquired during the Middle English period. But in fact, although it is true that the words entered the language at that time, none of them had their present-day epistemic meanings then. (1987, 137)

It is interesting to note that Hanson's class of "epistemic adverbs" does not include interactive particles, which are often included in this class by other scholars.[10] It is also worth noting Hanson's comment that "only over a long period of time did they become sentence adverbs, capable of characterizing whole propositions, and ultimately to be clearly 'speaker-oriented' ones, expressing subjective epistemic meanings" (p. 137).

Similarly, in her paper "On the Rise of Epistemic Meanings in English: An Example of Subjectification in Semantic Change," Traugott states that "epistemic meanings arise out of nonepistemic ones" and that "stronger epistemic meanings are later than weak epistemic meanings" (1989, 32), and she sees the same general principles as operating in the history of English epistemic adverbs.

> Hanson 1987 has shown that similar kinds of changes are also attested in the history of modal adverbs such as *possibly, probably, evidently, apparently,* and *obviously,* a set which Jackendoff calls "speaker-oriented" (1972: 76). Exactly as would be expected, where manner and epistemic (sentential) adverb meanings coexist, the former is earlier than the latter. To put this in the terms I have used, the meaning based in the sociophysical world precedes that based in the speaker's mental attitude. Indeed in some cases an adverb that is now no longer a manner adverb originally was one. (Traugott 1989, 46)

Thus, in both Hanson's and Traugott's accounts, nonepistemic meanings of adverbs give rise to epistemic meanings, and "weak epistemic meanings," to "strong" ones. What exactly is meant by "weak subjective epistemic" and "strong subjective epistemic" can be illustrated with Traugott's interpretation of two sentences with *evidently,* one from the seventeenth and one from the twentieth century:

> 1690 Locke, Hum. Und. II. Xxix: *No idea, therefore, can be undistinguishable from another . . . for from all other, it is evidently different* ('evident to all', weak subjective epistemic) (*OED*)
>   20th C?: *He is evidently right* (in the meaning 'I conclude that he is right'; strong subjective epistemic inviting the inference of some concession of doubt on speaker's part). (Traugott 1989, 47)

As these examples and their glosses show, a "weak epistemic" is not yet "speaker-oriented" (e.g., "evident to all"), whereas a "strong epistemic" is "speaker-oriented" (e.g., "I conclude").

The analysis presented in this chapter is consistent with Hanson's and Traugott's conclusions. At the same time, the hypothesis about the rise of the semantic component "I don't say I know" allows us to make the claim about the "pragmatic strengthening" (Traugott's term) more specific and more testable in context (see also Hanson's insightful but vague phrase: "something about his [the speaker's] knowledge"). It also allows us to link the "rise of epistemic meanings in English" not only with the "general principles of subjectification" but also with the culture-specific factors that have led to a unique "modal scene" (Aijmer 1997, 39) in modern English.

The rise of epistemic adverbs in modern English (in what Traugott calls a "strong subjective epistemic sense") reflects, I suggest, a rise of epistemological concerns in Anglo culture at a particular time of its development.

It must be emphasized again that the picture outlined here (and summed up in Table 8.4) has to be regarded as very tentative, and the results presented in it, as only preliminary. Such as they are, however, these preliminary results are, I think, suggestive, and they support the overall hypothesis developed here and in the other chapters of this book. Not only is the semantics of the large class of epistemic adverbs in modern English consistent with the ideas developed in Locke's *Essay on Human Understanding* but also the rise of this class appears to be linked in time with the spread of Locke's ideas. The gradual growth of this class is also consistent with the hypothesis that the Lockean concerns, no doubt together with other factors, have led to the emergence of certain cultural scripts that triggered a trend in the English language continuing, apparently, to this day.[11] The extraordinary career of the word *probably* (and *prob'ly*) in its modern, post-Lockean meaning epitomizes this trend, as does, in its own way, the emergence of the discourse marker *I think*, which has already been recognized as a hallmark of modern Anglo discourse (see, e.g., Jucker 1986; Thompson and Mulac 1991; Aijmer 1997; Scheibman 2000, 2001).

It is worth noting in this context the extremely high frequencies of the formulaic expression *I don't know* and its reduced variant *I dunno* in spoken English (Scheibman 2000, 2001) and the fact that both *I think* and *I know* "function epistemically or serve to mitigate assertion" (Scheibman 2001, 70). I would hypothesize that the elaboration and frequent use of epistemic verbal phrases and epistemic adverbs in English Anglo discourse is closely related to the extremely frequent use of both *I think* and *I don't know* in conversational English, given that "I think" and "I don't say I know" are core semantic components for both these classes; also, the high frequency of *probably* is closely related to the high frequencies of *I think* and *I don't know* (and in American English, *I guess*). I believe that to fully understand these phenomena, we need to look at them, first of all, in a contrastive perspective. Without a contrastive perspective, there is always a danger that we will seek to explain language-particular phenomena in terms of universalist explanations, as Grice (1975) and Griceans once did (and as "Neo-Griceans" still do), whereas "a contrastive perspective provides a window on cultural differences between languages" (Aijmer 1997, 39). Thus, a contrastive perspective leads us to a cultural perspective on English (and, of course, on other languages as well). It also leads us to a historical perspective: for example, twentieth-century English needs to be compared and contrasted not only with twentieth-century Norwegian or German but also with sixteenth- and seventeenth-century English, and the cultural values reflected in twentieth-century English need to be compared with those reflected, for example, in Shakespeare's English. Last but not least, we also need to combine grammatical and pragmatic approaches with careful semantic analysis of the relevant linguistic expressions, because it is only by revealing the exact meanings of these expressions that we can fully understand their cultural underpinnings and the reasons for their salience in modern English and Anglo discourse.

Discussing the origins of the concept of "proof beyond reasonable doubt," which continues to play an important role in Anglo systems of criminal justice, the legal scholar Lawrence Solan writes:

In essence, seventeenth century thinkers, influenced heavily by John Locke, developed an epistemology that differentiated among various kinds of evidence. Demonstrative evidence, experienced first hand through sensory experience, was considered the most reliable. Indirect evidence, from the report of witnesses, was called "moral evidence," and was considered less reliable. The expression "moral certainty," which we still hear in some reasonable doubt instructions today, essentially meant "the highest degree of certitude based on such evidence." Proof beyond a reasonable doubt was equated with moral certainty. (Solan 1999, 111)

As I have tried to show, in the English-speaking world, this epistemology differentiating among various kinds and degrees of certainty has had an impact on ordinary ways of speaking, and on the English language itself. This impact continues to this day.

PART IV

CONCLUSION

The "Cultural Baggage" of English and Its Significance in the World at Large

9.1. The Legacy of History

In a passage titled "The Legacy of History," David Graddol (1997, 5) writes: "Britain's colonial expansion established the pre-conditions for the global use of English, taking the language from its island birthplace to settlements around the world. The English language has grown up in contact with many others, making it a hybrid language which can rapidly evolve to meet new cultural and communication needs." As I have tried to show in this book, however, the legacy of history goes well beyond the fact that English is a "hybrid language" with a capacity to evolve rapidly.

David Crystal (2003b, 20) notes that "language is a repository of the history of a people. It is their identity." Crystal is speaking here of the languages of the world currently threatened by the spread of English as a global language. But as I have tried to show in this book, the same point applies to "Anglo English" itself: it, too, is the repository of the history and culture of a people. The fact that English "can rapidly evolve" does not mean that it has no cultural core, no internal legacy of cultural meanings.

As David Malouf writes in *Made in England*:

> It is all very well to regard language as simply "a means of communication." It may be that for poor handlers of a language and for those to whom it is new and unfamiliar, who use it only for the most basic exchanges. But for most of us it is also a machine for thinking, for feeling; and what can be thought and felt in one language—the sensibility it embodies, the range of phenomena it can take in, the activities of mind as well as the objects and sensations it can deal with—is different, both in quality and kind, from one language to the next. The world of Chinese and Arabic is different from the world of German or French or English, as the worlds those European languages embody and refer to differ from one another. (Malouf 2003, 44)

Malouf's reference to the profound differences between English and other European languages is a useful reminder, given that much of the literature on "English and

Englishes" contents itself with a crude distinction between "Western" and "non-Western" languages and ways of thinking. Malouf, who in addition to his part-English, part-Lebanese background has lived his life through Italian as well as English, has no doubt as to the distinctiveness of Anglo culture, which he calls "our culture — I mean the culture that belongs to the language we speak and have our life in, English" (2003, 2). He also has no doubt that this culture and language have been shaped by history: "A language is the history and experience of men and women, who in their complex dealings with the world, made it; but it is itself one of the makers of that history, and the history it makes is determined—limited—by its having developed in one direction rather than another; in one direction to the *exclusion* of others. It is also shaped and changed by what is said in it" (p. 44).

In addition to the enduring legacy of Shakespeare and other classics of English literature, Malouf emphasizes the impact of the discourse of the British Enlightenment and of the social and political institutions related to it on the English language as spoken, in particular, in Britain and Australia. According to Malouf, the American colonies, founded in the early seventeenth century, inherited an English that — in contrast to that transplanted to Australia — was:

> passionately evangelical and utopian, deeply imbued with the religious fanaticism and radical violence of the time. . . . It was far removed from the cool, dispassionate English in which, a hundred and eighty years later, in the 1780s, a Parliamentary committee argued the pros and cons of a new colony in the Pacific. This was the language of the English and Scottish Enlightenment: sober, unemphatic, good-humoured; a very sociable and moderate language, modern in a way that even we would recognize, and supremely rational and down-to-earth. . . . The business of politics became negotiation, and of conflict, compromise. This was the "reasonable" language of the English and Scottish Enlightenment that became the language in which social institutions in Australia argued and resolved their difficulties. (pp. 46, 48)

Yet despite all the differences between American English and American public discourse, with their roots in pre-Enlightenment English, and the post-Enlightenment English transplanted in the late eighteenth century to Australia (not to mention the differences between British English and Australian English, or Canadian and New Zealand English), all of these Englishes can be seen as sharing a common heritage and a common cultural core. As Malouf puts it, they are not "the same language" but they can be seen as a "shared language" (2003, 4); and with that "shared language" go particular "habits of mind" (p. 3). Judging by linguistic evidence, these shared habits of mind have a great deal to do with the heritage of the British Enlightenment, epitomized by words like *reasonable, fair*, and *pros and cons*, by discourse markers like *on the one hand . . . on the other hand* and *as a matter of fact*, by epistemic markers like *presumably, allegedly*, and *arguably*, and by speaking and writing routines associated with all such characteristically English words and phrases.[1]

9.2. Living with Concepts

In philosopher Cora Diamond's memorable words (quoted in Besemeres 2002), we live with concepts, and the more a given concept is central to the life of a community, the more likely people in this community are not to notice it but simply to take it for granted, as they take for granted the air they breathe. It is the immigrants and other crossers of cultural boundaries who are more likely to notice the key concepts that a given speech community lives by.

For example, a few hundred yards from my home there is a preschool, with a sign warning that "any person who trespasses on these premises without a reasonable excuse may be prosecuted." Every time I pass this school, I am struck by how Anglo and how untranslatable its phrasing is, with its reliance on the key Anglo concept "reasonable"—untranslatable into my native Polish, into French, German, and, I believe, any other language of the world (see chapter 4). I was similarly struck recently by a sign in a British bus asking the passengers not to speak to the driver "without reasonable cause." The commonsense flexibility of such signs (as compared, for example, with the German "Verboten" signs; see Wierzbicka 1998b) echoes the pragmatism of British and American law, with their reliance on phrases like *reasonable doubt, reasonable force, reasonable care, reasonable excuse*, and *reasonable cause*. For non-Anglo immigrants to countries like Britain, Australia, and the United States, it is essential to learn how to interpret such phrases and how to live in accordance with the concepts embedded in them.

For international communication, too, concepts like "reasonable" have become essential, as can be illustrated, for example, by official ASEAN documents. Thus in the 2002 Agreement on Economic Cooperation between ASEAN and the People's Republic of China we read: "Compensation and the suspension of concessions or benefits are temporary measures available in the event that the recommendations and rulings are not implemented within a reasonable period of time" (Agreement on Dispute Settlement 2002, 8).

ASEAN Secretary-General Ong Keng Yong (2003), in a speech delivered during his visit to the United States in November 2003, said: "It is not fair to issue a travel advisory against all of Southeast Asia merely because of one or two acts of terrorism in one or two cities in the region." Clearly, any official warnings against travel to Southeast Asia go against the region's vital economic interests. The ASEAN appeal to "fairness" to prevent the issue of such warnings illustrates the transnational use of English as a "cultural lingua franca" (Krasnick 1995) and not just a "culture-neutral" medium of international communication.

9.3. Two Illustrations: International Law and International Aviation

No domain illustrates the significance of English in the world today better than law, in particular, international law. The very idea of a contract is based on the assumption that the parties agree to the same thing, and this implies that they can understand the text of the agreement in the same way. But if a contract is between native speakers of different languages, how can it be ensured that they can understand the agreement in the same way, given that words in general—and words relevant to law in particular—do not match across language boundaries? As John Locke wrote three centuries ago:

> A moderate skill in different languages will easily satisfy one of the truth of this, it being so obvious to observe great store of words in one language which have not any that answer them in another. Which plainly shows that those of one country, by their customs and manner of life, have found occasion to make several complex ideas, and given names to them, which others never collected into specific ideas. (Locke 1959 [1690], 48)

Locke saw the scale of the phenomenon in question more clearly than many language professionals have in more recent times:

> Nay, if we look a little more nearly into this matter, and exactly compare different languages, we shall find that, though they have words which in translations and dictionaries are supposed to answer one another, yet there is scarce one of ten amongst the names of complex ideas . . . that stands for the same precise idea which the word does that in dictionaries it is rendered by. (p. 48)

Locke also appreciated, before anyone else did, the significance of this phenomenon for law, especially in the context of the expansion of the British empire: "The terms of our law, which are not empty sounds, will hardly find words that answer them in the Spanish or Italian, no scanty languages; much less, I think, could any one translate them into the Caribbee or Westoe tongues" (p. 48). As Caffentzis points out, Locke's concerns were far from purely theoretical:

> As a maker of constitutions for the imperial provinces and as a member of the Board of Trade and Plantations, Locke naturally wondered whether the "native" speakers of the "tongues" . . . of the empire could understand, with the best will in the world, the very law that was to govern them. He undoubtedly wondered what legal status contracts with Americans would have if the parties involved did not understand the very terms of the contracts in the same way (or did not have a similar notion of a contract). (Caffentzis 1989, 82–83)

According to Caffentzis, given the "indeterminacy of translation" (due to the semantic incommensurability of languages), one key question for Locke was "How is world trade possible?"

Three centuries later, in a world where the need for accurate international communication (including international agreements) has increased beyond anything that Locke could have envisaged, questions like "how is world trade possible?" are even more pertinent and pressing; and they are inseparable from questions about the use and role of English.

As the legal scholar George Fletcher has stressed, language is not a neutral field for law, and it is naive to think that the content of law can be transferred, intact, from one language to another:

> Language matters more than most observers realize in shaping the contours of the law. The common law and the English language have a strong affinity for each other. The English common law has flourished in countries where English is the language of legal discourse. Some countries influenced by English law, notably Israel, have endeavoured to translate English terms into the native lexicon, but there seems to be as much lost in translation of law as in the translation of Shakespeare. There is no way to convey the connotations of "due process," "reasonable doubt," and "malice aforethought" in any language except English. (Fletcher 1996, 5)

Consider, for example, Article 13 (concerning copyright) of the international "Agreement on Trade-Related Aspects of Intellectual Property Rights" (so-called TRIPS), accepted by the World Trade Organization in 1994. The official languages of this organization are English, French, and Spanish. In English, Article 13 reads: "Members should confine limitations or exceptions to exclusive rights to certain special cases which do not conflict with a normal exploitation of the work and do not unreasonably prejudice the legitimate interests of the right holder." In the French version, the phrase *unreasonably prejudice* has been rendered as *causent un préjudice injustifié* and in Spanish, as *causen un prejuicio injustificado*. Both the French phrase and the Spanish phrase mean "cause an unjustified loss (damage)." But the words *unjustified, injustifié,* and *injustificado* do not mean the same as *unreasonable* (see chapter 4). Thus, although the three versions of Article 13 are supposed to mean the same, in fact they do not—unless the French and Spanish versions are to be understood via the prism of the English version.

An additional complication is the fact that, according to some experts, the current American "fair use doctrine" may be in conflict with international copyright law as formulated in Article 13. The way the debate about this putative conflict is often framed is shown in the title of a specialist article in the *Stanford Law Review* (Newby 1999): "What's Fair Here Is Not Fair Everywhere: Does the American Fair Use Doctrine Violate International Copyright Law?" Framed in this way, the title question implies not only that "standards of fairness" may differ across countries but also that they can be meaningfully compared (using the same conceptual yardstick, "fairness"). In fact, "standards of fairness" cannot even be debated in French or Spanish (not to mention the languages of all the other signatory nations) because "fairness" is an Anglo/English concept, and the word cannot be translated into other languages (see chapter 5).

Problems of this kind, which beset international trade law, apply even more in the area of human rights, where, for example, two of the fundamental notions are the right to a "fair trial" and the right to a "fair hearing." It is impossible to accurately transfer these notions—which have been established in English for more than two hundred years[2]—into languages that have no word corresponding to *fair,* and the same applies to the use of *fair* in many other contexts. For example, Article 14 of the International Covenant on Civil and Political Rights, which was adopted by the United Nations' General Assembly in 1966 and entered into force in 1976, states that "everyone shall be entitled to a fair and public hearing by a competent, independent and impartial tribunal established by law." In the French version of the same document, *fair* had to be replaced by the adverb *équitablement,* "equitably," and in the Spanish one, by the phrase *con las debidas garantías,* "with due guarantees." (In the Universal Declaration of Human Rights, available in 300 languages, the Spanish version renders *fair* in a similar context as *con justicia* [roughly, "with justice"], the Russian one relies on the noun *spravedlivost'* [roughly, "justice"], and the German one uses the adjective *gerechtes* [roughly, "just"]). Quite apart from the semantic differences between *justice, justicia, spravedlivost',* and *Gerechtichkeit,* the English word *fairness,* which refers to procedures, does not mean the same as *justice,* which refers to outcomes (compare, e.g., *a fair hearing* vs. **a just hearing*; see chapter 5).

My second example concerns English as the language of international aviation. Air traffic controllers and pilots need to communicate with each other everywhere in the world, and the effectiveness of their communication is a matter of life and death for the passengers as well as the crew. The principal medium of this communication is English. Often, communication between pilots and controllers fails, resulting in runway incursions, unauthorized takeoffs and landings, and, most dire of all, midair collisions. Often, failures of communication that lead to tragic results involve non-native speakers of English.

For example, a recent paper entitled "Miscommunication between Pilots and Air Traffic Control" noted that "Aeroflot planes have started to land on a city street in Seattle and a highway in Israel. . . . Under a Hindi controller, a Kazakh airplane collided in midair [in 1996] with a Saudi plane. There were 349 deaths. . . . A New York crash in 1990 . . . was the direct consequence of incorrect wording by the Spanish-speaking copilot. . . . In a recent case . . . the last words of a Chinese pilot recorded on the cockpit voice recorder were 'What does *pull up* mean?'" (Jones 2003, 235–236)

One of the most famous aviation disasters of recent times was the runway collision at the Canary Islands in 1977 between a KLM Boeing 747 and a Pan American Airways B-747, which killed 583 people. The disaster was due directly to the non-native use of English by the Dutch pilot, who radioed: "We are now at takeoff," translating this expression literally from Dutch and meaning, "We are now beginning to take off." The controller, however, assumed that the plane was merely *ready* for takeoff and would await further instructions, so he said "OK" (adding: "stand by for takeoff. . . . I will call you"). The pilot heard "OK," so he continued rolling down the runway and collided with the Pan Am plane, which, invisible in the thick fog, was already on the same runway.

As emphasized in a recent report of the U.S. Federal Aviation Administration (FAA), "Effective and accurate communications are crucial to air safety. As aircrafts approach their destination airport, they converge and operate under reduced separation minima. . . . Under these circumstances, there is little margin for error" (Koenig 1997, 8).

Aviation writers who discuss the tragic costs of miscommunication between pilots and controllers sometimes despair of English as a language of international aeronautical communication. For example, Jones (2003, 244) writes: "The standard form of speech of aviation . . . must be superior to any given variety of English in the clarity of its spoken form. . . . Perhaps here there is a practical solution in Esperanto. . . . The inability of English to express specific instructions to pilots without confusion would seem to disqualify it as a language for permanent use by aviation."

The hope that Esperanto could serve international aviation better than English scarcely seems realistic. But the case of aviation highlights the globalized world's need for a standardized international language. Presumably, it is English that for the foreseeable future is going to play this role, and presumably, it is *Anglo* English that will serve as the touchstone and reference point in efforts aimed at both minimizing variation and at increasing the English proficiency of pilots and controllers to the level necessary for dealing effectively with nonroutine and emergency situations (see Uplinger 1997).

Quintessentially Anglo concepts like "reasonable" also play a not insignificant role in the language of international aviation. For example, the word *reasonable* frequently occurs in air traffic control guidelines and other similar documents in phrases like *reasonable grounds for, for a reasonable period, reasonable level of, reasonable precautions, reasonable amount of, to sustain a reasonable level of, reasonable access to, reasonable steps should be taken, reasonable attempts,* and *reasonable accuracy.* A Web search for the word *reasonable* used in conjunction with the phrase *air traffic control* yielded well over 100,000 results. Thus, living with concepts includes flying with concepts and controlling air traffic with concepts, as well as negotiating international agreements, trading, and the like with concepts. Many of these concepts come from historically shaped Anglo English.

9.4. Communication and "Vibes"

According to a recent article in the *Christian Science Monitor* (Baldauf 2004), the fastest growing language in India is Hinglish, spoken by an estimated 350 million people—a language that "may soon claim more native speakers worldwide than English." The article cites as typical a Pepsi advertisement, "Yeh Dil Maange More" ("the heart wants more"), and Coke's "Life ho to aisi" ("life should be like this"), which have replaced earlier English-language advertisements like "Ask for more." The article cites the head of the creative division of Publicis India, an advertising firm, as saying, if you use English, "you may be understood but not vibed with. That's why all the multinational companies now speak Hinglish in their ads."

The importance of "vibes" in human communication is widely recognized in the literature on the world's new Englishes and post-Englishes: Hinglish, Singlish (from "Singapore English" or "Sri Lankan English"), Pringlish (from "Puerto Rican English"), and so on. It is seldom recognized, however, in the literature on "international English" or on "English as a lingua franca." On the contrary, it is often assumed that the main (if not sole) goal of English used as a tool of intercultural communication is to convey information, that the "pragmatics" of language use are not relevant in this case; and that Anglo conversational norms and conventions are (or should be) irrelevant in English-based cross-cultural exchanges.

The people who are least likely to be aware of the importance of Anglo norms in English-based intercultural communication seem to be 'Anglos' themselves. Ron Scollon and Suzanne Wong Scollon's *Intercultural Communication* (2001, 135–136) contains a nicely illustrative vignette in which two businessmen, one American and the other Chinese, meet on a plane from Tokyo to Hong Kong and strike up a conversation:

MR. RICHARDSON: By the way, I'm Andrew Richardson. My friends call me Andy. This is my business card.

MR. CHU: I'm David Chu. Pleased to meet you, Mr. Richardson. This is my card.

MR. RICHARDSON: No, no. Call me Andy. I think we'll be doing a lot of business together.

MR. CHU: Yes, I hope so.

MR. RICHARDSON (reading Mr. Chu's card): "Chu, Hon-fai." Hon-fai, I'll give you a call tomorrow as soon as I get settled at my hotel.

MR. CHU (smiling): Yes. I'll expect your call.

Commenting on this encounter, the Scollons point out that there is in American business a preference for "close, friendly, egalitarian relationships," linked with the use of first names. By contrast, in Chinese culture, new business acquaintances would prefer a mutual use of titles and a certain initial reserve. In particular, a Chinese given name (in this case Hon-fai) would never be used by a stranger. If a given name is to be used at all (in a cross-cultural encounter), it should be Mr. Chu's Western name, David. As a result, Mr. Chu is embarrassed, and he smiles to cover up his embarrassment. His smile is misinterpreted by Mr. Richardson as an indicator that "he will be friendly and easy to do business with" (Scollon and Scollon 2001, 135–136). Thus:

> When these two men separate, they leave each other with very different impressions of the situation. Mr. Richardson is very pleased to have made the acquaintance of Mr. Chu and feels they have gotten off to a very good start. . . . In contrast, Mr. Chu feels quite uncomfortable with Mr. Richardson. He feels it will be difficult to work with him, and that Mr. Richardson might be rather insensitive to cultural differences. (p. 136)

The Scollons explain the cultural differences involved by using expressions like "symmetrical solidarity," "symmetrical deference," "involvement strategies," and "independence strategies." Since, however, these expressions are tied to technical English, and have no equivalents in either Mandarin or Cantonese, their commentary might be said itself to contain an element of Anglo bias (see Goddard 2002a, 2004b, in press, on "terminological ethnocentrism"). Although the authors show the importance of cross-cultural training for both Anglo and non-Anglo speakers of English, their generalizations are themselves culture-bound (as well as language-bound). By contrast, if we rely on simple and universal concepts like "good" and "bad," "know" and "say," or "when" and "if," their insights into cross-cultural differences can be formulated in a universally teachable form. To see how this can be done in relation to Chinese cultural norms, see Ye (2004; see also Yoon 2004).

I first illustrate this with an example drawn from another work by the same authors (Scollon and Scollon 1983), this time concerned with intercultural communication within America itself between Anglo-Americans and Athabascans (in Alaska). The Scollons call the former of the two groups "English speakers," but in fact the table partially reproduced here (Table 9.1) refers to two groups of English speakers: Anglo and Athabascan.

Perceptions like those reproduced in Table 9.1 point to different cultural scripts that the speakers themselves are not fully aware of. Noticing that the Athabascans behave differently, the Anglos judge them in accordance with Anglo scripts, which they take for granted, and vice versa. Not surprisingly, as a result each group forms a negative view of the other (e.g., "they talk too much"; "they talk too little"). To teach effective intercultural communication, it would be helpful to identify the relevant scripts and state them in a neutral cultural notation that could be intelligible to both

Table 9.1 Anglos and Athabaskan: Mutual (Mis)perceptions

What's confusing to English speakers about Athabaskans	What's confusing to Athabaskans about English speakers
They do not speak	They talk too much
They keep silent	They always talk first
They avoid situations of talking	They talk to strangers or people they don't know
They only want to talk to close acquaintances	They think they can predict the future
They deny planning	They always talk about what's going to happen later
They avoid direct questions	They ask too many questions
They never start a conversation	

sides and would allow the outsiders to understand the perspective of the insiders. Using NSM, this can be done as follows (one example):

> *An Anglo cultural script*
> [people think like this:]
> when I am in one place with someone for some time
> it is good if I say something to this someone

> *An Athabaskan cultural script*
> [people think like this:]
> when I am in one place with someone
> if I don't know this someone
> it is good if I don't say anything to this someone

Communication between Anglo Americans and Athabaskans may seem to be an exotic case, far removed from problems arising in communication between, for example, Arabs, Americans, Russians, and Indonesians, but in fact the same issue is involved in all such cases. The differences in the unconscious cultural assumptions that underlie cross-cultural misperceptions and misunderstandings cannot be efficiently explained to all parties without a neutral cultural notation—a culturally neutral lingua franca for comparisons and explanations.

Andy Kirkpatrick (2004) proposes as an auxiliary language of intercultural communication a "Lingua Franca English" (LFE), which speakers with different mother tongues and different cultural backgrounds can all speak according to their own native norms, understanding each other by virtue of goodwill and mutual tolerance, without any "standard monolithic norms" (p. 88. In this way, "Lingua Franca English becomes the property of all and it will be flexible enough to reflect the cultural norms of those who use it" (p. 87). According to Kirkpatrick, the use of various local cultural norms by speakers of LFE need not be a problem: "I think it is inevitable and desirable that speakers will transfer some of the pragmatic norms of their L1 [first language] to lingua franca English" (p. 88).

But what will happen in a case where the "pragmatic" or cultural norms of different speakers are in conflict—for example, where one interlocutor's cultural background encourages him or her to express requests to equals or superiors in the form of a naked imperative ("Do this!" "Go there!" "Bring me that!"), whereas another regards such bare imperatives as an intolerable assault on their personal autonomy (see chapter 2; see also Clyne 1994)? What will happen when, for example, a Russian uses LFE when speaking to a Malay, given the conflicting attitudes of Russian and Malay culture to spontaneous expression of one's current thoughts and feelings (see Wierzbicka 2002c; Goddard 2000a)? The example is not far-fetched, given the reported use of English as a lingua franca in transnational teams, for example, between Ukrainians and Bangladeshis in the UN Peacekeeping Forces in the former Yugoslavia (Wright 2000, 90).

What the NSM-based theory of cultural scripts offers for such situations is the prospect of intercultural training in the form of culture-specific cultural scripts that can be written in the English (as well as any other) version of the natural semantic metalanguage and that can be easily taught to speakers of any background. For example:

A *Russian cultural script*
[people think like this:]
when I feel (think) something
I can say to other people what I feel (think)
it will be good if someone else knows what I feel (think)

A *Malay cultural script*
[people think like this:]
when I feel (think) something
I can't always say to other people what I feel (think)
it will be good if I think about it before I say it

The language in which these scripts are written—the English version of NSM—can serve as an auxiliary language for teaching intercultural communication: being culturally neutral itself, it can be used effectively as a cultural notation for comparing languages and cultures. Crucially, explanations formulated in the English NSM can be readily translated into any other language, for example, into Russian or Malay. They can be taught through the words of any language the rudiments of which the interlocutors share. If interactants share a hundred (or even sixty or so) simple English words, cultural scripts of any other culture can be explained to them through those simple words (provided, of course, that they share the right ones, that is, the minilexicon of NSM).

"Good vibes" cannot always be achieved in intercultural communication, but many bad vibes can be avoided if the participants receive intercultural training. To be effective, this training must help the trainees learn about their own cultural scripts, as well as those of their culturally different interlocutors. Given the realities of the world today, it is particularly important for both the insiders and the outsiders that the cultural scripts of Anglo English be identified in an intelligible and readily translatable form.

9.5 Intercultural Communication and Cross-Cultural Education

There is a widespread view that English can be used worldwide as a culturally neutral medium of communication. To quote, for example, Wardhaugh (1987, 15), "since no cultural requirements are tied to the learning of English, you can learn it without having to subscribe to another set of values." As I have tried to show in this book, this is largely an illusion: there *are* some values, assumptions, and expectations that one has to subscribe to, at least provisionally, to learn English. For example, to learn English, one has to learn to use the words *right* and *wrong*, and to do that one has to subscribe, if only provisionally, to the everyday philosophy of rationalist ethics embedded in these words. This point is vividly illustrated by a recent experience of the American sociologist Douglas Porpora (personal communication). Lecturing in English on the kinds of moral reasoning used in American newspaper editorials either to justify or to oppose the war in Iraq, Porpora wanted to make the point that presidential candidate John Kerry's statement "Wrong war, wrong place, wrong time" was intentionally ambiguous: did Kerry mean wrong in a moral or prudential sense, or was he skating between the two? The point was easy to make in English—but not in Spanish, as Porpora realized when he was called upon to give a lecture in Spanish on the same topic: there is no word in Spanish that could translate *wrong* in "Wrong war, wrong place, wrong time," rolling into one idea "bad deed" and "bad thinking" (see chapter 3).

Thus, Anglo key words like *right* and *wrong* are not culturally neutral, and neither are key Anglo conversational routines, such as addressing everyone with the same word "you," avoiding a bare imperative in requests (see chapter 2), and softening "no" with an explanation rather than avoiding it altogether in refusals and denials.

Emphasizing the role of such "sociocultural factors" (as she calls them) in intercultural communication, the Indian American scholar Yamuna Kachru (1995) illustrates their importance with an observation made a century earlier by nineteenth-century diplomat and author Chester Holcombe: "Much of the falsehood to which the Chinese as a nation are said to be addicted is a result of the demand of etiquette. A plain, frank 'no' is the height of discourtesy. Refusal or denial of any sort must be softened and toned down into an expression of regretted inability. . . . Centuries of practice in this form of evasion have made the Chinese matchlessly fertile in the invention and development of excuses" (Holcombe 1895, 274–275).

A "plain, frank 'no'" as an expression of refusal or denial is, of course, not a "natural" human way of speaking but a norm (or perceived norm) of Anglo culture. As Kachru illustrates with another apt quote, such norms are often invisible to English native speakers, and their infringement by non-native speakers can lead to "an affective reaction unfavourable to the speaker/writer": "These speakers are often viewed as rude or uncooperative or . . . arrogant or insincere. Native speakers are much more likely to attribute grammatical or phonological errors to a lack of knowledge of the target language . . . conversational features are subtle and not easily recognizable; hence their basis is attributed not to the *language* of the speaker but to the *personality* of the speaker" (Gass and Selinker 1983, 12, quoted in Y. Kachru 1995, 189).

Similarly, Krasnick (1995) links effective teaching of English as a foreign language (EFL) with "bicultural competence" and insists that "language cannot be separated from culture." Discussing cross-cultural problems arising in the teaching of English by Anglo teachers in Indonesia, he comments: "Even when one party is employed specifically to meet the needs of the other cross-cultural communication problems still intrude. If intercultural communication problems appear to crop up in situations like these, where an officially agreed upon agenda and cooperation rather than competition is the clear norm, what must be expected of intercultural encounters in government and business where these supportive conditions are not found?" (Krasnick 1995, 91).

Typically, authors who emphasize communicative failure and problems in cross-cultural encounters between Anglo and non-Anglo speakers call for "more research in world Englishes" (Y. Kachru 1995, 190) and stop short of clearly formulating the conclusion that Anglo English, too, is a "linguaculture" whose concepts and norms need to be articulated. Nonetheless, the whole thrust of their examples and discussions point to such a need.

For example, Krasnick (1995) calls (with special reference to ASEAN countries) for "intercultural communication training" (p. 92) and deplores the fact that "the practitioners of second language teaching have relegated culture to the status of an optional extra" (p. 82). By the year 2020, he predicts, "the problem will be less and less English [as a grammatical code], and more and more intercultural communication competence" (p. 85).

What Krasnick does not say explicitly is that the teaching of "intercultural communication competence" cannot be separated from the teaching of Anglo concepts and communicative norms. Such concepts and norms dominate in particular the domains of international diplomacy, science, business, economics, finance, and geopolitics ("perhaps best exemplified by discourse of the United Nations and in affiliates . . . especially the language of treaties and covenants on human rights that depend on a special vocabulary and collocations" [Gonzalez 1995, 59; see also Toolan 2003]). For these areas, Gonzalez envisages the construction of a "cultural dictionary," alongside a cultural encyclopaedia—a suggestion I regard as eminently sound but realizable only with the help of a culturally neutral semantic metalanguage. The natural semantic metalanguage based on universal human concepts provides a tool with the aid of which such a "cultural dictionary" could be effectively compiled. In a sense, the analyses of concepts like "reasonable," "fair," or "right" and "wrong" carried out in this book can be regarded as sections of such a future "Anglo cultural dictionary," readily translatable into any language and explaining, in simple words, the nature of these foundational Anglo concepts and ideas.

9.6. English in the World Today

Those who write about the global spread of English are often accused of "triumphalism." But the global spread is simply a fact. As Barbara Seidlhofer (2001, 157) put it, "people need and want to learn English whatever the ideological baggage that comes with it, a fact acknowledged even in Canagarajah's 1999 *Resisting Linguistic Imperialism in English Teaching*." Tom McArthur concurs, commenting that "it would appear that no amount of post-colonial liberal-humanist anguish will make much difference to this state of affairs" (2001, 13).

As Wright (2000, 102) points out, "globalisation seems to constitute Anglicisation. Transnational corporations, international organizations, peacekeeping forces all exhibit a tendency to use English as an official or *de facto lingua franca*." This applies even to the UN:

A single *lingua franca* is not the actual policy of the UN, which has six official and working languages: Arabic, Chinese, English, French, Russian and Spanish. However, the primacy of English within the organization has been evident for some time. A graphic illustration of the true hierarchy of languages in the organisation was provided by Kurt Waldheim's message from the UN to be carried by the 1977 *Voyager* expedition into outer space. The Secretary-General's message to other galaxies was in English—and only in English! (Wright 2000, 102)

Discussing the implications of the global spread of English for Singapore with references to accusations of "linguistic imperialism" in works like Phillipson (1992) and Pennycook (1994), Singaporean linguist Phyllis Ghim-Lian Chew (1999, 39) argues that "the concept of 'linguistic imperialism' ascribes too much power to the language as opposed to the language policy makers and language users." In Singapore, which she treats as a case study, "the early dominance of English came about not so much as a result of linguistic imperialism, but through a conscious decision on the part of its leaders and populace, after the careful consideration of world trends and local conditions" (p. 40).

Chew does acknowledge some negative consequences of the rise of English in Singapore. For example, "in Singapore, many grandparents have been unable to communicate with their grandchildren due to the loss of the mother tongue" (p. 42), but as she sees it, this has not changed the country's resounding "yes" to English—resounding but qualified: "'yes' to English and 'no' to western cultural values" (Chew 1999, 39).

At this point, however, the question of the cultural underpinnings of English must again be raised. Can a country effectively say "yes" to English and "no" to all the assumptions embedded in it? To some extent, no doubt, it can. But evidence suggests that when this happens, English diversifies, and there emerge "nativized" varieties of it that are no longer culturally 'Anglo' and that are, as David Parker (2003, 13) says about English in South East Asia, "partly constitutive of local culture and identity."

This is very much the case in Singapore (see Wong 2004a, 2004b, 2005). But the English which, as Wong shows, is partly constitutive of local culture and identity in Singapore, is not the same variety of English that Chew is talking about, that is, the English that is "the language of international communication" (Chew 1999, 43).

Chew says lightly: "As is well-known in Singapore, one language can, in fact, be the courier of many cultures and sub-cultures, of myriad values and sets of values" (Chew 1999, 42). Arguably, however, the Singapore case shows something different: Singapore English is the carrier of Singapore culture, and although it can serve its speakers as a bridge to other forms of English, to take part in global communication, its speakers find that they have to move to those other forms. English as the language of international communication is closer to Anglo English than to Singapore English.

Nothing illustrates this better than documents like the keynote speech delivered by the Prime Minister of Singapore Goh Chok Tong at the ASEAN–United States Partnership Conference in New York on September 7, 2000, a speech that crucially depends on Anglo English words like *resources, challenges, commitment, opportunities, relevance, relevant, controversial, fairly,* and *unfairly* and on epistemic phrases like *I think* and *I believe, both sides view, was perceived to be,* and *in the eyes of.* To give the flavor of Goh Chok Tong's language, here are a few sentences from his speech:

> The US committed enormous *resources* and lives to contain aggression in the region.

> Let me now give my assessment of how *I think both sides* today *view* US engagement with ASEAN, and what *I believe* to be some of the *challenges* that will shape US interests in ASEAN.

> *Fairly* or *unfairly*, the US *was perceived* to be not forthcoming enough in helping the Southeast Asian countries.

> ASEAN is *relevant* to the US for strategic reasons.

> ASEAN's *commitment* to free trade has helped reinforce US interest in preserving an open multilateral trading system.

> ASEAN's current difficulties and *perceived* lack of political cohesiveness and vision *risk* diminishing its relevance *in the eyes of* US policy makers.

Examples like these show how unrealistic the slogan "'yes' to English and 'no' to Anglo cultural values" really is.

The appeal to "fairness" is an obvious bow to Anglo cultural values, as is the structuring of the speech in terms of two perspectives ("the ASEAN perspective" and "the US perspective"), the references to how "both sides view" ASEAN-U.S. relations, and also the epistemic hedges like *I believe* and *perceived*. Less obvious perhaps but no less significant is the covert acceptance of Anglo values like "commitment" and "relevance," implied by the very use of these words in the prime minister's speech. It is worth stressing again that the value-laden words highlighted in these sentences (*challenge, fairly, unfairly, relevant, commitment*) are distinctively English words, without equivalents in other European languages. What is at issue here, then, is not "Western values" but, more specifically, "Anglo values."

Chew emphasizes that Singaporeans want modernity, not Westernness (Chew 1999, 42). As Parker (2004, 31) notes, however (with special reference to Hong Kong, but the same applies to Singapore), "Western modernity has been, and continues to be, mediated through the English language to many non-Western cultures" (see also Ndebele 1987). The English that ASEAN has used from the outset as its only language (without any debate or discussion, by implicit mutual agreement; see Okudaira 1999) is, essentially, Anglo English, and it bears the imprint of the cultural history of the English language. This history "continues to operate as a kind of magnetic field of distinctions and values on those who use the language—or, we might say, who get used *by* it" (Parker 2004, 31). As I understand it, those who are used *by* the English language are people who don't recognize the cultural heritage embedded in it and who simply take it for granted.

When (for example) Seidlhofer (2001) writes about "the ideological baggage" that comes with English, it is clear that she means external factors like its history as a language of colonialism and its role in what Wright (2000, 95) calls "the new geography of power." As this book seeks to show, however, there is also an *internal* cultural baggage. (I prefer to call it "cultural" rather than "ideological" because it is usually unconscious.) English as a language of modernity and as a "global language" has inherited much of that "baggage."

Alongside centrifugal forces leading to the ongoing diversification of English, there are also powerful centripetal tendencies, assisted by new technologies such as satellite television and fueled by the need for English to be fully intelligible in international communication. (See Crystal 2003b.) Furthermore, as the speech of Singapore's prime minister illustrates, what matters is not only intelligibility but also a desire for acceptance and for success in achieving one's goals. For example, it is just as important in international communication to be perceived as "reasonable" as to be simply understood.

Thus, rather than denying the existence and continued relevance of the cultural "baggage" embedded in Anglo English, it is important to explore the contents of that baggage — important for practical, as well as intellectual, reasons: for language teaching, "cultural literacy" teaching, cross-cultural training, international communication, and so on. It is also important to "denaturalize" Anglo English and to identify and acknowledge the historically shaped cultural meanings embedded in it, if only so that they are no longer taken for granted as the voice of "reason" itself.

Notes

Chapter 1

1. The term "English" (as a noun) is used in at least two different senses. Most commonly, it is used to refer to what I am calling here "Anglo English." In a more restricted use, "English" stands for a loose conglomerate of language varieties derived historically from the English spoken in England—roughly, the same conglomerate that in the last two or three decades has started to be referred to as "Englishes."

2. A concept closely related to "Anglo culture" is that of "Anglosphere" (see Bennett 2004).

3. Recently, some Australian government departments have started to promote the use of the term *dob in* in a positive sense, encouraging citizens to "dob in" illegal immigrants, tax dodgers, "dole bludgers," insurance fraudsters, and the like.

Chapter 2

1. For earlier attempts to articulate and justify some Anglo cultural scripts, see Wierzbicka 1991/2003a, 1994a, 1994c, 1997, 1999; Goddard 2003. See also Wierzbicka 2002c, 2003b; Goddard and Wierzbicka 2004; and the studies in Goddard and Wierzbicka, eds., 2004.

2. Strauss and Quinn (1997, 209) talk about "the ethnography of the inner life," based largely on ethnographic interviews. The "ethnography of thinking," as I understand it, is not inconsistent with that idea, but it relies primarily on linguistic evidence (interpreted through semantic analysis carried out in terms of universal human concepts).

3. Hopwood notes that this region as of his writing was divided into the states of Jordan, Syria, Lebanon, Israel, and the West Bank of the Jordan under Israeli occupation, but, he says, the term "is still used to signify the whole area—greater Syria—and to underline that, despite political frontiers, there still exists the concept of unity" (Hopwood 1988, 1).

4. From a cross-linguistic perspective, the most striking piece of evidence is the emergence of the discourse particle *well*, which shows a desire to word one's thought "well" (i.e., carefully and cautiously). Frequent use of this "careful" particle is particularly characteristic of the interviews with Anglo politicians, who like to start their responses to questions with a careful and cautious *well*.

5. To compare semantic domains across languages one needs a *tertium comparationis*, that is, a universal semantic grid. The NSM set of primes provides such a grid, and THINK

is one of its elements. In positing THINK as a universal semantic prime, NSM researchers do not assume that all the uses of the English word *think* realize this prime (and nothing else). The complex meaning of the English "discourse marker" *I think* discussed in this chapter is a good example of a language-specific use of a word that in its other uses is an exponent of a universal semantic prime. The universal syntactic frames that have been posited for THINK are the following five (for detailed discussion, see Goddard 2002b and 2003; see also Wierzbicka 1998d):

1. X thinks about Y [topic of thought]
2. X thinks: "—" [quasi-quotational complement]
3. when X thinks about it, X thinks that [—]$_s$ [propositional complement anchored in time]
4. X thinks like this [way of thinking]
5. X thinks something about Y [nonpropositional complement]

These frames are posited as universal, as is the prime THINK itself. The universality of THINK (identified here, for practical reasons, in terms of its English exponent) is often missed or denied because the English verb *think* is used more widely that the exponents of the same prime in many (most) other languages. For example, Aijmer (1998, 283) states that "there is no corresponding verb in Swedish sharing the vagueness and multifunctionality of *think* but the Swedish translations of *I think* require different verbs." If by "corresponding verb" Aijmer means "corresponding in usage," then no doubt she is right; this doesn't mean, however, that there is no verb in Swedish corresponding in meaning to THINK in the relevant sense. Nor does it mean that the English verb *think* "presents a complex pattern of polysemy corresponding to lexical differentiation in other languages" (Aijmer 1998, 277). As NSM researchers have shown in many publications, patterns of polysemy can be identified only with reference to a set of semantic primes (see Wierzbicka 1996b; Goddard 2000b).

6. Linguistic evidence for the importance of "good thinking" in modern Anglo culture is discussed in chapter 4.

7. For further discussion of "control" over one's emotions in modern Anglo (and especially Anglo-American) culture, see, for example, Wierzbicka (1999, 258–266); Hoffman (1989, 269–270); Lutz (1990, 72).

8. Another characteristic Anglo conversational routine, or group of routines, is based on the word *consider*: "Would you consider doing X?" "You might consider doing X," and so on. Not only does one in this way avoid saying, "I want you to do it" but also "I want you to think about it" (not to mention "I think you will do it because of this").

9. In an interview with Mary Catherine Bateson (1989), Johnetta Cole, the first black woman president of Spelman College in Atlanta, Georgia (in the United States), reminisces about her marriage to a white man (also an academic), whose family was at first strongly opposed to his marriage to a Southern black. "But on the other hand, they loved their son and over the years we got pretty close, although getting close to his folk is about 1,500 yards away from what I would call close. From the perspective of someone born in a very loving black household, this is pretty cold stuff" (p. 70). Cross-cultural interviews and memoirs suggest, again and again, that there may be an inverse relationship between, roughly speaking, cultural scripts of personal autonomy and independence and cultural scripts of interpersonal closeness and warmth.

Chapter 3

1. See the table of primes in chapter 1 of this book.
2. It is worth noting that one can "prove someone right" (or "prove someone wrong")

but not "prove someone good" or "prove someone true." Presumably, to "prove some-one right" means inter alia to prove that they "think well" and that other people can know this.

3. Arnold (1870) renders in this way the Greek *prautes*, known to the readers of the King James version of the Bible as "meekness." In this way, the Beatitude "of the meek" becomes, by implication, the Beatitude "of the reasonable."

4. The reluctance to make absolute moral judgments is also reflected in the present-day use of the words *right* and *wrong* in the frames "right for" and "wrong for," as in the following utterance from the Donahue show:

> There's been other living patterns in the history of the world and what is right for some is not right for others. Maybe it's wrong for her, okay. But maybe it's right for other people and we don't have a right to judge others. (Carbaugh 1988, 32)

5. Fernández-Armesto writes that "reason had its moment of highest prestige and widest acceptance in the western world in the seventeenth and eighteenth centuries" (1998, 113) and that "outside western or western-dominated societies reason has never attained the high place in the common scale of values it won for a brief spell in Europe and America" (p. 87). But "the western world" is not a homogeneous entity, and judging by linguis-tic evidence, some effects of the Enlightenment may have lasted longer and reached deeper in England and then America than they did, for example, in Italy, Spain, or even France.

6. It is interesting to compare, for example, the title of a classic Russian book on ethics, Losskij 's (1991) *Uslovija Absoljutnogo Dobra* ("The Conditions of the Absolute Good") with the characteristic titles of many English and American books: *Right and Wrong, The Place of Reason in Ethics, Methods of Ethics, Reason over Conduct, Search for a Rational Ethics, Our Knowledge of Right and Wrong,* and so on.

7. The importance of the word *right* (as an adjective) in modern Anglo culture is high-lighted by the association with the noun *right* (and *rights*). The central place of "rights talk" in modern English-speaking societies is a huge topic (see Fukuyama 2002) that cannot be discussed here. Suffice it to say that in the linguistic consciousness of contemporary speak-ers of English, the two are closely related and that the appeal of notions like "human rights" and "individual rights" may be heightened by the language-based conviction that it is "right" for people to have those "rights." For example, Francis Fukuyama, in his acclaimed *Our Posthuman Future,* writes:

> The language of rights has become, in the modern world, the only shared and widely intelligible vocabulary we have for talking about ultimate human goals or ends, and in particular, those collective goals or ends that are the stuff of politics. . . . The great struggles over rights since the American and French revolutions are tes-timony to the political salience of this concept. The word *right* implies moral judg-ment (as in "What is the right thing to do?") and is our principal gateway into a discussion of the nature of justice and of these ends we regard as essential to our humanity. (Fukuyama 2002, 108)

Fukuyama takes it for granted that the moral force of the language of rights is derived in part from its association with the word *right* used as an adjective in sentences like "What is the right thing to do?" Although Fukuyama refers here to both "the American and the French revolutions," it is likely that the semantic equivalents of *rights* in languages other than En-glish (e.g., *les droits* in French, *prava* in Russian) do not have the same passionate moral connotations as the English word *rights*, associated by the speakers of English with "what is the right thing to do."

Chapter 4

1. Gertrude Himmelfarb (2005) highlights the culture-specific character of the "Anglo" faith in the ordinary "reasonable man" by contrasting the two Enlightenments, British and French:

> For the British philosophers, that social chasm was bridged by the moral sense and common sense that were presumed to be innate in all people, in the lower classes as well as the upper. The *philosophes*, allowing to the common people neither a moral sense nor a common sense that might approximate reason, consigned them, in effect, to a state of nature—a brutalized Hobbesian, not a benign Rousseauean, state of nature . . . (2005, 156)

As she points out, both Voltaire and Diderot were exceedingly contemptuous of the masses. For example, Diderot wrote: "Distrust the judgement of the multitude in matters of reasoning and philosophy; its voice is that of wickedness, stupidity, inhumanity, unreason, and prejudice . . . The multitude is ignorant and stupefied . . ." (Himmelfarb 2005, 154).

2. For example, Wilkins 1969 [1693] spoke of "assent arising from such plain and clear Evidence as doth not admit of any reasonable doubting" (Quoted in Shapiro 1983, 85).

3. John Wilkins distinguishes "moral certainty" from "physical and mathematical certainty" as follows:

> I call that *Moral* Certainty, which hath for its object such Beings as are *less simple*, and do more depend upon mixed circumstances. Which though they are not capable of the same kind of Evidence with the former, so as to necessitate every man's Assent, though his judgment be never so much prejudiced against them; yet may they be so plain, that every man whose judgment is free from prejudice will consent unto them. And though there be no natural necessity, that such things must be so, and that they cannot possibly be otherwise, without implying a contradiction; yet may they be so certain as not to admit of any reasonable doubt concerning them. (Wilkins 1969 [1693], 7–8)

The term "reasonable doubt" is linked here with the notion of "every man whose judgment is free from prejudice." In the same book, Wilkins speaks of "such Evidence as was itself sufficient to convince reasonable and unprejudiced men" (p. 33) and also refers to beliefs that "every sober rational man, who will not offer violence to his own faculties, must submit to" (p. 40).

4. This is not to say that the phrase *reasonable man* has not been frequently linked, from early on, with "reasons." For example, Shapiro (1983, 34) notes that for the seventeenth-century philosopher Walter Charlton "'substantive and satisfying Reasons' . . . were sufficient 'to the full establishment of Truth in the mind of a reasonable man.'" But the question is whether a reference to "reasons" is included in the meaning of the phrase *reasonable man* itself.

5. It is interesting to note that in earlier (seventeenth- and eighteenth-century) usage the word *unreasonable* was not linked, as it is now, with interpersonal interaction. For example, when Sir Charles Wolseley published his book *The Unreasonableness of Atheism Made Manifest* (London 1675), the word *unreasonableness* in the title of his book had no such implications. But for this very reason, today this title sounds archaic.

6. For a discussion of the differences between the English adverb *reasonably* and the French adverb *raisonnablement*, see Wierzbicka, in press d).

7. I am not suggesting by any means that the English *sensible* means the same as the French *raisonnable*. In fact, *sensible* stands for another culture-specific Anglo concept, linking "good

thinking" with practical wisdom (derived from experience). The practical and empirical character of *sensible* contrasts with the intellectual character of the French *raisonnable*. At the same time, as the phrase *sensible shoes* illustrates, *sensible* has nothing to do with accommodating other people (compare **reasonable shoes*).

8. In her book entitled *Reasonable Democracy*, Simone Chamber discusses the dispute between the Anglophone and Francophone communities in Quebec over language legislation. She notes that although they "resolved their dispute largely through the power of reasoned argument, . . . the settlement took a long time" (1996, 278). One wonders how the concept of "reasonable democracy" was identified in French in this debate and whether the discrepancy between *reasonable democracy* and *démocratie raisonnable* was acknowledged and taken into account.

Chapter 5

1. In proposing this explication of *justice*, I am trying to do what Locke called for more than three centuries ago:

> *Justice* is a word in every man's mouth, but most commonly with a very undetermined, loose signification; which will always be so, unless a man has in his mind a distinct comprehension of the component parts that complex idea consists of: and if it be decompounded, must be able to resolve it still on, till he at last comes to the simple ideas that make it up . . . I do not say, a man needs stand to recollect, and make this analysis at large, every time the word justice comes in his way: but this at least is necessary, that he have so examined the signification of that name, and settled the idea of all its parts in his mind, that he can do it when he pleases. (Locke 1959, vol. II 152)

2. In his discussion of Fukuyama's distinction between high-trust and low-trust societies, Bennett (2004, 114) repeatedly uses the word *fair*. For example: "Properly, this distinction should be termed one of societies with, variously, a high and low radius of trust—the size of the circles within which one can expect fair dealing and impartial treatment."

Chapter 6

1. I say "partial" because *make*-causatives do not passivize straightforwardly but require the addition of the word *to*: "he was made *to* pump the tyres every morning." (See note 2.)

2. One can say, "Mary was made *to* do it," with the added word *to*, but this is not a simple passivization of "John made Mary do it," which does not include *to*. For discussion, see Wierzbicka (1988).

3. "We (us)" is not a semantic prime. For present purposes, however, it doesn't need to be analyzed any further.

Chapter 7

1. The fact that first-person epistemic verbal phrases do not include the corresponding mental verbs in their usual sense has numerous consequences for their grammatical and discourse-related behaviour, as discussed in detail in Danielewiczowa (1998). To illustrate:

1. a. Probably she assumes that he did it himself.
   b. *Probably I assume that he did it himself.
2. a. I think she assumes that he did it himself.
   b. *I think I assume that he did it himself.

3. a. She rightly assumes that he did it himself.
   b. *I rightly assume that he did it himself.
4. a. I now think he did it himself.
   b. *I now guess he did it himself.
5. a. —Is she okay?—Yes, I suppose she is.
   b. —Is she okay?—*Yes, Peter supposes she is.

2. Danielewiczowa (1998) discusses a large number of Polish epistemic verbal phrases comparable to those discussed here. Not many of these phrases, however, are widely used in everyday language. Those that are so used include *myślę, sądzę, uważam, przypuszczam*, and *podejrzewam*.

3. The key concept relevant to the area under discussion is that of 'knowing', in NSM semantics, KNOW, as argued in a recent book on Polish epistemic verbs by Danielewiczowa (2002), who is drawing on the work of Bogusławski (1981, 2002). In contrast to Danielewiczowa, however, I believe that another equally important building block in the area in question is that of 'thinking'—in NSM semantics, THINK. As I will try to show, all the differences as well as similarities between the individual epistemic adverbs can be explained clearly, intelligibly, and in a way that can be tested against the intuitions of native speakers, in semantic explications based essentially on the concepts KNOW and THINK and, more particularly, I KNOW and I THINK. The other concepts recurring in my explications of this area are negation (NOT), CAN, SAY, PEOPLE, OTHER, and a few others.

4. I am by no means assuming that a sentence-initial *I suppose* means exactly the same as a sentence-internal or a sentence-final one. I will address the question of the semantic differences between *I suppose* in these different positions in chapter 8. In this chapter, I will use examples of sentences with *I suppose* regardless of the position of this phrase, but in the explications I will focus on sentences with *I suppose* in the initial position. I will proceed in the same way in the sections on the other epistemic verbal phrases.

5. The alert reader will notice that in some explications in this chapter the initial component is phrased as "I say: I think like this (now)," whereas in some others as "I think now that it is like this." The first phrasing suggests a thought currently going through the speaker's mind, the second—something like a provisional opinion about a factual matter. One test that differentiates between the two types of phrases is that of intention: one can say, "I think I'll go," "I guess I'll go," or "I suppose I'll go" but not "I gather I'll go," "I presume I'll go," "I take it I'll go" or "I bet I'll go."

6. As Cliff Goddard points out (personal communication), a lawyer could say, perhaps: "My client understands that . . ." in the sense in question, but this is not normal colloquial English.

Chapter 8

1. Cliff Goddard (personal communication) has suggested that *perhaps* may in fact include an additional component in its meaning: "I have thought about it." This could mean that only *maybe* and not *perhaps* can be matched with *vielleicht*. I will ignore this possibility in the present discussion, in order not to complicate the argument.

2. For example, Holmes writes:

All languages provide strategies for expressing epistemic modality, but the particular devices used differ from one language to another. In some languages, moreover, speakers cannot avoid providing information concerning the precise degree of their commitment to the truth of every proposition they assert (Lyons 1981, p. 239).

This information is obligatorily expressed by means of a device such as a verb affix (cf. Kiparsky and Kiparsky's comments on Hidatsa, for instance, 1971, p. 367). In English, speakers may choose whether or not to explicitly signal the extent of their epistemic commitment to a proposition. (Holmes 1983, 101–102)

The comments by the Kiparskys referred to in this passage read as follows:

There are languages which distinguish factive and non-factive moods in declarative sentences. For example, in Hidatsa (Matthews 1965) there is a factive mood whose use in a sentence implies that the speaker is certain that the sentence is true, and a range of other moods indicating hearsay, doubt, and other judgments of the speaker about the sentence.

But is it true that, for example, in Hidatsa there is a whole range of moods forcing speakers to provide information about, as Holmes put it, "the precise degree of commitment to the truth of every proposition" (1983, 101–102)? A quick check in Matthews's *Hidatsa Syntax* (1965, 99) will show that this is not the case. Leaving aside two moods that can be glossed as "I think that you don't know" and "I think that you know," which clearly have nothing to do with the speaker's "degree of commitment," there are four moods that can be characterized in these terms: "Emphatic" ("I know" or "I do know"), "Period" ("I think"), "Quotative" ("someone says"), and "Report" ("they say"). If one compares these four moods with the lexicogrammatical classes of epistemic phrases and epistemic adverbs in English, one must come to the conclusion that it is English rather than Hidatsa that provides the speakers with the highly differentiated means of indicating "the precise degree of commitment" to the propositions they assert.

3. Both Hanson (1987) and Traugott (1989) appear to assume that *probably* in the modern sense goes back to the seventeenth century, and they both cite, in support of this dating, the same example from the OED:

A source, from whence those waters of bitterness . . . have . . . probably flowed.
(Clarendon, *History of the Rebellion*, 1674)

However, the meaning of *probably* in this sentence is unclear without a larger context, especially because the OED quotes it in an abbreviated form. The full sentence in the original source reads:

And here I cannot but let my self loose to say, that no Man can shew me a Source, from whence those waters of bitterness, we now taste, have more probably flowed, than from these unreasonable, unskilful, and precipitate Dissolutions of Parliaments; In which, by an unjust survey of the Passion, Insolence, and Ambition of particular Persons, the Court measured the Temper and Affection of the Country; and by the same standard the People consider'd the Honour, Justice, and Piety of the Court. . . . (Clarendon, *History of the Rebellion*, 1674)

Read in context, *probably* appears to mean here something closer to *certainly* or *believably* (compare *provably*) than to the cautious and agnostic *probably* of the nineteenth and twentieth centuries. The seventeenth-century speaker is, in effect, saying, with rhetorical passion, something like this: "No one can show me a source from which those waters of bitterness that we now taste could have more certainly/more believably/more obviously flowed than from these unreasonable, unskillful, and precipitate dissolutions of parliaments."

4. Franklin points in this connection to the following wonderful fragment in Pascal's *Provincial Letters* (a fictitious dialogue between a naive Everyman and a Jesuit father, who defends probabilism—in Pascal's view, a source of the Jesuit moral laxism):

"Think you that Father Bauny and Basil Ponce are not able to render their opinion *probable*?"

"Probable won't do for me," said I, "I must have certainty."

"I can easily see," replied the good father, "that you know nothing of the doctrine of *probable* opinions. If you did, you would speak in another strain. Ah! My dear sir, I must really give you some instructions on this point; without knowing this, positively you can understand nothing at all. It is the foundation—the very A, B, C of our whole moral philosophy."

Glad to see him come to the point to which I had been drawing him on, I expressed my satisfaction and requested him to explain what was meant by a probable opinion.

"That," he replied, "our authors will answer better than I can do. The generality of them, and among others the four-and-twenty elders, describe it thus: 'An opinion is called probable, when it is founded upon reasons of some consideration. Hence it may sometimes happen that a single *very grave doctor* may render an opinion probable.' The reason is added: 'For a man particularly given to study would not adhere to an opinion unless he was drawn to it by a good and sufficient reason.'" [The quotation is from Escobar] (quoted in Franklin 2001, 97)

5. To see exactly what Butler has in mind, it will be helpful to read the context for this characteristic statement. (Not surprisingly, this context includes a reference to "Mr Locke's Chapter on Probability."):

Probable evidence is essentially distinguished from demonstrative by this, that it admits of degrees; and of all variety of them, from the highest moral certainty, to the very lowest presumption. . . . That which chiefly constitutes Probability is expressed in the word Likely, i.e. like some truth, or true event . . . Probable evidence, in its very nature, affords but an imperfect kind of information; and is to be considered as relative only to beings of limited capacities. For nothing which is the possible object of knowledge, whether past, present, or future, can be probable to an infinite Intelligence; since it cannot but be discerned absolutely as it is in itself, certainly true, or certainly false. But to Us, probability is the very guide of life. (Butler 1840 [1736], 1, 3)

6. At the same time, it is interesting to note that in many languages, including German, Russian, and Italian, the counterpart of the English manner adverb *clearly* can be used as a predicative word describing the speaker's attitude to what has been said.

7. In this context, it is also useful to note the following contrast in acceptability:

(a) I'm certain that he lied to me.
(b) ? I'm certain that I lied to him.

Both sentences (a) and (b) imply a "subjective certainty," with no claim to knowledge, and this makes sentence (b) odd, unless again the speaker is suffering from amnesia. But the adverb *certainly*—whether it is used sentence-initially or sentence-internally—has no similar restriction on first-person subjects (compare, e.g., the full acceptability of the sentence *I certainly lied to her*).

8. It is interesting to note what Goossens says of Old English adverbs that he glosses as *certainly* and *very certainly*: "they are probably best regarded as reinforcements of an otherwise unqualified assertion" (1982, 82). The same could be said, I suggest, of the present-day sentence-initial word *certainly*.

9. On the basis of the OED, it can be conjectured that this table could be expanded in the following way (the matter requires further investigation):

TABLE 8.5 Some further conjectures on the historical expansion
of Epistemic Adverbs

	16th Century	17th Century	18th Century	First half of 19th Century	Second half of 19th Century	20th Century
seemingly			X?	X	X	X
likely			X?	X	X	X
clearly				X	X	X
supposedly						X

10. This is not to say that my class of "epistemic adverbs" would be exactly coextensive with Hanson's. In particular, I think that *admittedly*, which figures on her list, is not epistemic and that neither is *definitely*, which is mentioned elsewhere in her article. *Definitely* can even appear in questions (e.g., Was he definitely there?), and when it is used in a declarative sentence, it is what Goossens (1982) calls a "reinforcement," not an epistemic qualification of the statement. The function of *admittedly* is different again: it presents the statement as an admission, but it doesn't weaken in any way the force of the assertion. For example, the sentence *Admittedly, I lied to her* does not imply "I don't say I know."

11. Speaking of the "fairly recent acquisitions" such as *allegedly* and *arguably*, Hanson comments: "Perhaps once the class was firmly established additions to it began to be freely made" (1987, 142). I think this is an insightful comment, as is also the note attached to it:

> There is also an interesting point to be made with regard to the syntactic distribution of these adverbs. . . . In all cases, the first instances of the "speaker-oriented" meanings of the epistemic adverbs occur in this [auxiliary] position, co-occurring with either a copula or a modal. Nowadays, most of the ones that the OED gives no epistemic citation for are ones that seem less natural or impossible in initial position. Perhaps these remain in some kind of transitional stage.

Chapter 9

1. I note that in the television program for preschoolers watched avidly by my two-year-old granddaughter, the speech of animal characters abounds with value terms like *unfair* and epistemic phrases like *I suppose* (*I s'pose*) and that the legacy of the British Enlightenment is being passed on in this way to a two-year-old toddler.

2. The earliest record of the expression *fair trial* in the OED is dated 1623. However, in the course of the seventeenth and eighteenth centuries, the meaning of *fair* changed considerably, and consequently, so did that of *fair trial* (see Langford, to appear).

References

Aarsleff, Hans. 1991. Locke's reputation in nineteenth-century England. In Richard Ashcraft, ed. *John Locke: Critical assessments*. London: Routledge. 278–303.

Agreement on dispute settlement mechanism of the framework agreement on comprehensive economic co-operation between the Association of Southeast Asian Nations and the People's Republic of China. 2002. http://www.aseansec.org/16635.htm.

Aijmer, Karin. 1997. *I think*: An English modal particle. In Toril Swan and Olaf Jansen Westvik, eds. *Modality in the Germanic languages. Proceedings of the IXth International Symposium on Language*. Berlin: Mouton de Gruyter. 1–48.

———. 1998. Epistemic predicates in contrast. In. Stig Johansson and Signe Oksefjell, eds. *Corpora and Cross-linguistic Research. Theory, Method, and Case Studies*. Amsterdam: Rodopi. 271–295.

Ameka, Felix. 1987. A comparative analysis of linguistic routines in two languages: English and Ewe. *Journal of Pragmatics* 11 (3): 299–326.

———. 1992. Interjections: The universal yet neglected part of speech. Special issue, *Journal of Pragmatics* 18 (2/3): 101–118.

———. 1994. Areal conversational routines and cross-cultural communication in a multilingual society. In H. Pürschel, ed. *Intercultural communication: Proceedings of the 17th International LAUD symposium*. Bern: Peter Lang. 441–459.

———. 1999. Partir, c'est mourir un peu. Universal and culture specific features of leave taking. In Jacob Mey and Andrzej Bogusławski, eds. *"E pluribus una": The one in the many (RASK, International Journal of Language and Communication* 9/10). Odense, Denmark: Odense University Press. 257–284.

AND. 1988. *The Australian national dictionary. A dictionary of Australianisms on historical principles*. W. S. Ramson, ed. Melbourne: Oxford University Press.

Apresjan, Valentina J. 2000. Nepravda. In *Novyj Ob"jasnitel'nyj Slovar' Sinonimov Russkogo Jazyka*. Moskva: Jazyki Russkoj Kul'tury. 223–229.

Apte, Mahadev L. 1974. "Thank you" and South Asian languages: A comparative sociolinguistic study. *International Journal of the Sociology of Language* 3: 67–89.

Aquinas, Thomas. 1964. *Summa theologiae. English and Latin*. London: Blackfriars in conjunction with Eyre & Spottiswoode.

Archer, Margaret S. 2000. *Being human: The problem of agency*. Cambridge: Cambridge University Press.

Arnold, Matthew. 1870. *St. Paul and Protestantism: With an essay on Puritanism and the Church of England*. London: Smith and Elder.

Arpino, Giovanni. 1973. *La Suora Giovane*. Milan: Mondadori.

Asano, Yuko. 2003. *A semantic analysis of epistemic modality in Japanese*. PhD diss., Australian National University, Canberra.

Ashcraft, Richard, ed. 1991. *John Locke: Critical assessments*. London: Routledge.

Audi, Robert, ed. 1999. *The Cambridge dictionary of philosophy*. Cambridge: Cambridge University Press.

Austin, J. L. 1962. *How to do things with words*. Oxford: Oxford University Press.

Baldauf, Scott. 2004. A Hindi-English jumble, spoken by 350 million. *The Christian Science Monitor*, November 11. http://www.csmonitor.com/2004/1123/p01s03–wosc.html.

Barnstone, Aliki, Michael T. Manson, and Carol J. Singley. 1997. *The Calvinist roots of the modern era*. Hanover, NH: University Press of New England.

Bateson, Mary Catherine. 1989. *Composing a life*. New York: Atlantic Monthly Press.

Bauman, Richard, and Charles L. Briggs. 2003. *Voices of modernity: Language ideologies and the politics of inequality*. Cambridge: Cambridge University Press.

Bayley, John. 2003. Widower's house. In *The Iris trilogy*. London: Abacus.

Beeching, Kate. 2002. *Gender, politeness and pragmatic particles in French*. Amsterdam: John Benjamins.

Belfellah, Abdellatif. 1996. Konfession: Wem gehört die deutsche Sprache? *Frankfurter Rundschau*. March 9., NR 59: 283.

Bellah, Robert N., Richard Masden, William M. Sullivan, Ann Swidler, and Steven M. Tipton. 1985. *Habits of the heart: Individualism and commitment in American life*. Berkeley: University of California Press.

Bellert, Irena. 1977. On semantic and distributional properties of sentential adverbs. *Linguistic Inquiry* 8:337–350.

Bennett, James C. 2004. *The Anglosphere challenge. Why the English-speaking nations will lead the way in the twenty-first century*. Lanham, MD: Rowman and Littlefield.

Benveniste, Emile. 1971. *Problems in general linguistics*. Trans. M. E. Meek. Coral Gables, FL: University of Miami Press.

Berlin, Brent, and Paul Kay. 1969. *Basic colour terms: Their universality and evolution*. Berkeley: University of California Press.

Berlin, Isaiah. 1969. *Four essays on liberty*. Oxford: Clarendon.

Besemeres, Mary. 1998. Language and self in cross-cultural autobiography: Eva Hoffman's "Lost in translation." *Canadian Slavonic Papers* 40:3–4.

———. 2002. *Translating one's self: Language and selfhood in crosscultural autobiography*. Oxford: Peter Lang.

Besemeres, Mary, and Anna Wierzbicka. 2003. Pragmatics and cognition: The meaning of the particle "lah" in Singapore English. *Pragmatics and Cognition* 11 (1): 3–38.

Besemeres, Mary, and Anna Wierzbicka, eds. To appear. *Translated lives: Australian stories of language migration*. St. Lucia: University of Queensland Press.

Betlem, Elisabeth. 2001. *Assessing bullying behaviour of school students through the use of art*. Paper presented at the annual conference of the Australian Association for Research in Education. http://www.aare.edu.au/01pap/bet01229.htm.

Bevan, E. Dean. 1971. *A concordance to the plays and prefaces of Bernard Shaw*. Detroit: Gale.

Binmore, Ken. 2005. *Natural justice*. New York: Oxford University Press.

Blum-Kulka, Shoshana. 1982. Learning to say what you mean in a second language: A study of the speech act performance of learners of Hebrew as a second language. *Applied Linguistics* 3:29–59.

Boas, Franz. 1911. Introduction. *Handbook of American Indian languages*, Vol. 1. *Bureau of American Ethnology Bulletin* 40:5–83.

Bogusławski, Andrzej. 1981. Wissen, Wahrheit, Glauben: zur semantischen Beschaffenheit des kognitiven Vokabulars. In T. Bungarten, ed. *Wissenschaftssprache. Beiträge zur Methodologie, theoretischen Fundierung und Deskription.* München: Fink Verlag. 54–84.

——. 2002. There is no getting around Gettier. *Journal of Pragmatics* 34:921–937.

Bond, Michael Harris, V. Žegarac, and Helen Spencer-Oatley. 2000. Culture as an explanatory variable: Problems and possibilities. In Helen Spencer-Oatley, ed. *Culturally speaking: Managing rapport through talk across cultures.* London: Cassell. 47–74.

Brett, Lily. 2001. *New York.* Picador: Pan Macmillan Australia.

Brown, Donald. 1991. *Human universals.* New York: McGraw-Hill.

Brown, Donald. 1999. Human universals. In *The MIT encyclopedia of the cognitive sciences.* London: MIT Press.

Brown, Penelope, and Stephen Levinson. 1978. Universals in language usage: Politeness phenomena. In Esther Goody, ed. *Questions and politeness: Strategies in social interaction.* Cambridge: Cambridge University Press. 56–310.

——. 1987. *Politeness: Some universals in language usage.* Cambridge: Cambridge University Press.

Brown, Roger, and Albert Gilman. 1989. Politeness theory and Shakespeare's four major tragedies. *Language in Society* 18:159–212.

Buechner, Frederick. 1957. *The return of Ansel Gibbs.* Harmondsworth, England: Penguin.

Bunyan, John. 1965. *The pilgrim's progress*, ed. R. Sharrock. Harmondsworth, England: Penguin.

Butler, Bishop Joseph. [1736] 1840. *The analogy of religion.* Glasgow: Collins.

Butler, Sue. 2003. Dob in a dumper. http://www.abc.net.au/wordmap/rel_stories/dob-in.htm.

Bütow, H. 1961. *Hände über der See: ein Leben mit England.* Frankfurt: Societas Verlag.

Buzo, Alexander. [1970] 1973. *The front room boys.* In *Four Australian plays.* Harmondsworth: Penguin.

Caffentzis, Constantine George. 1989. *Clipped coins, abused words, and civil government: John Locke's philosophy of money.* New York: Automedia.

Carbaugh, Donald. 1988. *Talking American: Cultural discourses on Donahue.* Norwood, NJ: Ablex.

Chafe, Wallace, and Johanna Nichols. 1986. Introduction. In Wallace Chafe and Johanna Nichols, eds. *Evidentiality: The linguistic coding of epistemology.* Norwood, NJ: Ablex.

Chamber, Simone. 1996. *Reasonable democracy.* Ithaca, NY: Cornell University Press.

Chappell, Hilary M. 1978. Semantics of some causatives in Chinese and English. B.A. honours thesis, Australian National University.

Chew, Phyllis Ghim-Lian. 1999. Linguistic imperialism, globalism, and the English language. *AILA Review* 13:37–47.

Chomsky, Noam. 1987. Language in a psychological setting. *Sophia Linguistica* 22:1–73.

Chow, Claire S. 1999. *Leaving deep water: Asian-American women at the crossroads of two cultures.* New York: Penguin.

Cinque, Guglielmo. 1999. *Adverbs and functional heads: A cross-linguistic perspective.* New York: Oxford University Press.

Clyne, Michael. 1994. *Intercultural communication at work: Cultural values in discourse.* Cambridge: Cambridge University Press.

Cobuild. Collins Cobuild Bank of English. http://titania.cobuild.collins.co.uk.

Collins COBUILD English language dictionary. 1987. London: HarperCollins.

Collins Robert French dictionary. 1990. Paris: Dictionnaires Le Robert.

Conklin, Harold. 1957. *Hanunóo agriculture*. Rome: Food and Agriculture Organization of the United Nations.

Crossan, John Dominic. 1980. *Cliffs of fall: Paradox and polyvalence in the parables of Jesus*. New York: Seabury.

Crystal, David. 1992. *Encyclopaedic dictionary of language and languages*. Oxford: Blackwell.

———. 2001. *A dictionary of language*. 2nd ed. Chicago: University of Chicago Press.

———. 2003a. *The Cambridge encyclopedia of the English language*. 2nd ed. New York: Cambridge University Press.

———. 2003b. *English as a global language*. 2nd ed. Cambridge: Cambridge University Press.

Curti, M. 1991. The great Mr. Locke: America's philosopher. In Richard Ashcraft, ed. *John Locke: Critical assessments*. London: Routledge. 304–341.

Danielewiczowa, Magdalena. 1998. O szczególnych właściwościach 1. os. l. poj. czasu teraźniejszego pewnych czasowników mentalnych. *Prace Filologiczne* 43:119–129.

———. 2002. *Wiedza i niewiedza: studium polskich czasowników epistemicznych*. Warsaw: Uniwersytet Warszawski, Katedra Lingwistyki Formalnej.

Danquah, Meri Nana-Ama, ed. 2000. *Becoming American: Personal essays by first generation immigrant women*. New York: Hyperion.

Daston, Lorraine. 1988. *Classical probability in the Enlightenment*. Princeton, NJ: Princeton University Press.

Davis, Wayne A. 1998. *Implicature: Intention, convention, and principle in the failure of Gricean theory*. Cambridge: Cambridge University Press.

Dawkins, Richard. 1983. Universal Darwinism. In D. S. Bendall, ed. *Evolution from molecules to men*. Cambridge: Cambridge University Press. 403–425.

Dench, Alan. 1982. Kin terms and pronouns of the Panyjima language of Northwest Australia. *Anthropological Forum* 1:109–120.

———. 1987. Kinship and collective activity in the Ngayarda languages of Western Australia. *Language in Society* 16 (3): 321–340.

Diamond, Cora. 1998. Losing your concepts. *Ethics*, January, 255–277.

Doi, Takeo. 1981. *The anatomy of dependence*. Tokyo: Kodansha.

Drasdauskiene, M.-L. 1981. On stereotypes in conversation. In F. Coulmas, ed. *Conversational routine: Explorations in standardized communication situations and prepatterned speech*. The Hague: Mouton. 55–68.

Eades, Diana. 1982. You gotta know how to talk . . . : Information seeking in South-East Queensland Aboriginal society. *Australian Journal of Linguistics* 2 (1): 61–82.

Eakin, Paul John. 1999. *How our lives become stories: Making selves*. Ithaca, NY: Cornell University Press.

Emerson, Ralph Waldo. [1869] 1932. *Uncollected lectures*. Ed. C. Gohdes. New York: William Edwin Rudge.

The English-Swedish parallel corpus. http://www.englund.lu.se/content/view/66/127

Fehr, B., and J. A. Russell. 1984. The concept of emotion viewed from a prototype perspective. *Journal of Experimental Psychology: General* 13:464–486.

Fernández-Armesto, Felipe. 1998. *Truth: A history and guide for the perplexed*. London: Black Swan.

Fernando, Chitra. 1989. English as problem and resource in Sri Lankan universities. In Ofelia Garcia and Ricardo Otheguy, eds. *English across cultures, cultures across English*. Berlin: Mouton de Gruyter. 185–204.

Ferreira, M. Jamie. 1986. *Scepticism and reasonable doubt: The British naturalist tradition in Wilkins, Hume, Reid and Newman*. Oxford: Clarendon.

Fischer, Olga. 1992. Syntactic change and borrowing: The case of the accusative and infinitive construction in English. In Marinel Gevitsen and Dieter Stein, eds. *Internal and external factors in syntactic change*. Berlin: Mouton de Gruyter. 17–88.

Fletcher, George. 1996. *Basic concepts of legal thought*. New York: Oxford University Press.

Foley, William A., and Robert D. van Valin Jr. 1984. *Functional syntax and universal grammar*. Cambridge: Cambridge University Press.

Ford, John. [1634] 1968. *The chronicle history of Perkin Warbeck*. Ed. P. Ure. London: Methuen.

Franklin, Benjamin. 1964. *The autobiography of Benjamin Franklin*. Ed. Leonard W. Labaree, Ralph L. Ketcham, Helen C. Boatfield, and Helene H. Fineman. New Haven, CT: Yale University Press.

Franklin, James. 2001. *The science of conjecture*. Baltimore: Johns Hopkins University Press.

Friedman, P. 1990. *Beyond reasonable doubt*. London: Headline.

Friedrich, Paul. 1966. Structural implications of Russian pronominal usage. In William Bright, ed. *Sociolinguistics*. The Hague: Mouton. 214–253.

Frosh, S., A. Phoenix, and R. Pattman. 2000. Cultural contestations in practice: White boys and the racialisation of masculinities. In Corinne Squire, ed. *Culture in psychology*. London: Routledge. 47–58.

Fukuyama, Francis. 1995. *Trust*. London: Penguin.

———. 2002. *Our posthuman future: Consequences of the biotechnology revolution*. New York: Farrar Straus and Giroux.

Gadamer, Hans-Georg. 1975. *Truth and method*. New York: Seabury.

———. 1976. *Philosophical hermeneutics*. Trans. D. E. Binge. Berkeley: University of California Press.

Gass, Susan, and Larry Selinker. 1983. *Language transfer in language learning*. Rowley, MA: Newbury House.

Gigerenzer, Gerd, Zeno Swijtink, Theodore Porter, Lorraine Daston, John Beatty, and Lorenz Krüger. 1989. *The empire of chance: How probability changed science and everyday life*. Cambridge: Cambridge University Press.

Goddard, Cliff. 1997. Cultural values and "cultural scripts" of Malay (Bahasa Melayu). *Journal of Pragmatics* 27 (2): 183–201.

———. 1998. *Semantic analysis: A practical introduction*. Oxford: Oxford University Press.

———. 2000a. "Cultural scripts" and communicative style in Malay (Bahasa Melayu). *Anthropological Linguistics* 42 (1): 81–106.

———. 2000b. Polysemy: Theoretical and computational approaches. In Yael Ravin and Claudia Leacock, eds. *Polysemy: Theoretical and computational approaches*. Oxford: Oxford University Press. 129–151.

———. 2002a. Overcoming terminological ethnocentrism. *HAS Newletter*. Leiden, The Netherlands: International Institute for Asian Studies. 27–28.

———. 2002b. The search for the shared semantic core of all languages. In Cliff Goddard and Anna Wierzbicka, Vol. I, eds. 5–40.

———. 2003. Thinking across languages and cultures: Six dimensions of variation. *Cognitive Linguistics* 14 (2/3): 109–140.

———. 2004a. The ethnopragmatics and semantics of "active metaphors." Special issue on metaphor, ed. Gerard Steen, *Journal of Pragmatics* 36:1211–1230.

———. 2004b. "Cultural scripts": A new medium for ethnopragmatic instruction. In Michel Achard and Susanne Niemeier, eds. *Cognitive Linguistics, Second Language Acquisition, and Foreign Language Teaching*. Berlin: Mouton de Gruyter. 145–165.

———. In press. Ethnopragmatics: A new paradigm. Introduction. In Cliff Goddard, ed. *Ethnopragmatics: Understanding discourse in cultural context*. Berlin: Mouton de Gruyter

Goddard, Cliff, ed. 1997. Studies in the syntax of universal semantic primitives. Special issue. *Language Sciences* 19 (3).

———. In press. *Ethnopragmatics: Understanding discourse in cultural context.* Berlin: Mouton de Gruyter.

Goddard, Cliff, and S. Karlsson. 2004. Re-thinking "think": Contrastive semantics of Swedish and English. In C. Moskovsky, ed. *Proceedings of the 2003 conference of the Australian Linguistic Society.* http://www.newcastle.edu.au/school/lang-media/news/als2003/proceedings.html.

Goddard, Cliff, and Anna Wierzbicka. 2004. Cultural scripts: What are they and what are they good for? Special Issue on Culture Scripts. *Intercultural Pragmatics* 7(2): 153–165.

———. In press. Semantic primes and cultural scripts in language learning and intercultural communication. In Gary Palmer and Farzad Sharifian, eds. *Applied cultural linguistics, second language teaching and intercultural communication.* Amsterdam: John Benjamins.

Goddard, Cliff, and Anna Wierzbicka, eds. 1994. *Semantic and lexical universals: Theory and empirical findings.* Amsterdam: John Benjamins.

———. 2002. *Meaning and universal grammar: Theory and empirical findings.* 2 vols. Amsterdam: John Benjamins.

———. 2004. Special Issue on Culture Scripts. *Intercultural Pragmatics* 1(2).

Goffman, Erving. 1981. *Forms of talk.* Philadelphia: University of Pennsylvania Press.

Gonzalez, Andrew. 1995. The cultural content in English as an international auxiliary language (EIAL): Problems and issues. In Makhan L. Tickoo, ed. *Language and culture in multilingual societies.* Singapore: SEAMEO Regional Language Centre. 54–63.

Goossens, Louis. 1982. On the development of the modals and of the epistemic function in English. In A. Ahlqvist, ed. *Papers from the 5th international conference on historical linguistics.* Vol. 21. Amsterdam: John Benjamins. 74–84.

Graddol, David. 1997. *The future of English?* London: The British Council.

Gray, Simon. 1986. *Plays: One.* London: Methuen.

Grice, Herbert Paul. 1975. Logic and conversation. In Peter Cole and Jerry L. Morgan, eds. *Syntax and semantics 3: Speech acts.* New York: Academic Press. 41–58.

Hacking, Ian. 1975. *The emergence of probability: A philosophical study of early ideas about probability, induction and statistical inference.* London: Cambridge University Press.

Hahn, Anna. 2002. The semantic history of the verb 'believe': Unpublished manuscript (essay submitted for the Seminar on Semantics, Australian National University).

Hale, Kenneth L. 1966. Kinship reflections in syntax: Some Australian languages. *Word* 22:318–324.

Hall, Edward T. 1976. *Beyond culture.* New York: Doubleday.

Hanson, Kristin. 1987. On subjectivity and the history of epistemic expressions in English. *CLS: Papers from the 23rd Annual Regional Meeting of the Chicago Linguistic Society* 23:132–147.

Hargrave, Susanne. 1991. *Whitefella culture.* Darwin: Summer Institute of Linguistics.

Harré, Rom. 1998. *The singular self.* London: Sage.

Harris, Randy Allen. 1993. *The linguistics wars.* New York: Oxford University Press.

Harrison, Jonathan. 1971. *Our knowledge of right and wrong.* London: Allen & Unwin.

Hayhow, Mike, and Stephen Parker. 1994. *Who owns English?* Buckingham: Open University.

Heath, Jeffrey, Francesca Merlan, and Alan Rumsey, eds. 1982. *Languages of kinship in Aboriginal Australia.* Sydney: Sydney University Press.

Hermann, Nina. 1990. *Go out in joy.* New York: Ballantine.

Hibberd, Jack. [1970] 1973 *Who?* In *Four Australian plays.* Harmondsworth, England: Penguin.

Himmelfarb, Gertrude. 2005. *The roads to modernity: The British, French, and American enlightenments*. New York: Alfred A. Knopf.

Hirsch, Eric Donald. 1987. *Cultural literacy: What every American needs to know*. Boston: Houghton Mifflin.

Hoffman, Eva. 1989. *Lost in translation: A life in a new language*. New York: Dutton.

Hofstede, Geert H. 1980. *Culture's consequences: International differences in work-related values*. London: Sage.

Holcombe, Chester. 1895. *The real Chinamen*. New York: Dodd, Mead.

Holmes, Janet. 1982. Expressing doubt and certainty in English. *RELC Journal* 13 (2): 9–28.

———. 1983. Speaking English with the appropriate degree of conviction. In C. Brumfit, ed. *Learning and teaching languages for communication: Applied linguistics perspectives*. London: Centre for Information on Language Teaching and Research. 100–113.

———. 1988. Doubt and certainty in ESL textbooks. *Applied Linguistics* 9 (1): 21–44.

Hopwood, Derek. 1988. *Syria 1945–1986: Politics and society*. London: Unwin Hyman.

Hornby, Nick. 2001. *How to be good*. London: Penguin.

Howell, Wilbur Samuel. 1971. *Eighteenth-century British logic and rhetoric*. Princeton, NJ: Princeton University Press.

Huebler, Axel. 1983. *Understatements and hedges in English*. Amsterdam: John Benjamins.

Humboldt, Wilhelm von. 1988. *On language: The diversity of human language structure and its influence on the mental development of mankind*. Trans. Peter Heath. Cambridge: Cambridge University Press.

Hymes, Dell. 1962. The ethnography of speaking. In T. Gladwin and W. Sturtevant, eds. *Anthropology and human behavior*. Washington, DC: Anthropological Society of Washington. 15–53. Reprinted in J. Fishman, ed. 1968. *Readings in the sociology of language*. The Hague: Mouton. 99–138.

Jackendoff, Ray S. 1972. *Semantic interpretation in generative grammar*. Cambridge, MA: MIT Press.

Jackson, Gabriele Bernhard. 1991. From essence to accident: Locke and the language of poetry. In Ashcraft, ed., 1991, 242–277.

John Paul II. 1993. *Veritatis splendor*. Homebush NSW: St. Paul's Publications.

Johnson, Oliver A. 1959. *Rightness and goodness*. The Hague: Martinus Nijhoff.

Jones, R. Kent. 2003. Miscommunication between pilots and air traffic control. *Language Problems and Language Planning*. 27(3): 233–248.

Jucker, Andreas H. 1986. *News interviews: A pragmalinguistic analysis*. Amsterdam: John Benjamins.

Kachru, Braj. 1985. Standards, codification and sociolinguistic realism: The English language in the outer circle. In R. Quirk and H. G. Widdowson, eds. *English in the world: Teaching and learning the language and literatures*. Cambridge: Cambridge University Press. 11–30.

———. 1995. The speaking tree: A medium of plural canons. In Makhan Tickoo, ed. *Language and culture in multicultural societies: Viewpoints and visions*. Singapore: SEAMEO Regional Language Centre. 1 20.

———. 1997. World Englishes and English-using communities. *Annual Review of Applied Linguistics* 17:66–87.

Kachru, Braj, ed. 1992. *The other tongue: English across cultures*. 2nd ed. Urbana: University of Illinois Press.

Kachru, Yamuna. 1995. Cultural meaning in world Englishes: Speech acts and rhetorical styles. In Makhan L. Tickoo, ed. *Language and culture in multilingual societies: Viewpoints and visions*. Singapore: SEAMEO Regional Language Centre. 176–193.

Kandiah, Thiru. 1995. Centering the periphery of English. Foreword to Arjuna Parakrama, *Dehegemonizing language standards*. London: Macmillan. xv-xxxvii.

Kasper, Gabriele. 1979. Communication strategies: Modality reduction. *Interlanguage Studies Bulletin* 4 (2): 266–283.

Kelly, Erin. 2001. Editor's Foreword to John Rawls's *Justice as fairness*: A restatement. Cambridge, MA: Belknap. xi–xiii.

Kim, Young Yun. 2001. *Becoming intercultural: An integrative theory of communication and cross-cultural adaptation*. Thousand Oaks, CA: Sage.

Kiparsky, Paul, and Carol Kiparsky. 1971. Fact. In L. Jakobovits and D. Steinberg, eds. *Semantics: An interdisciplinary reader*. Cambridge: Cambridge University Press. 345–369.

Kirkpatrick, Andy. 2004. English as an ASEAN lingua franca: Implications for research and language teaching. *Asian Englishes* 6 (2): 82–91.

Kochman, Thomas. 1981. *Black and white styles in conflict*. Chicago: University of Chicago Press.

Koenig, Robert. 1997. Excess words, partial readbacks score high in analysis of pilot-ATC communication errors. *Airport Operations*. 23 (1): 1–8.

Kohlberg, Lawrence. 1981. *The philosophy of moral development*. San Francisco: Harper & Row.

Kramsch, Claire. 1998. The privilege of the intercultural speaker. In Michael Byram and Michael Fleming, eds. *Language learning in intercultural perspective: Approaches through drama and ethnography*. Cambridge: Cambridge University Press. 16–31.

Krasnick, Harry. 1995. The role of linguaculture and intercultural communication in ASEAN in the year 2020: Prospects and predictions. In Makhan L. Tickoo, ed. *Language and culture in multicultural societies: Viewpoints and visions*. Singapore: SEAMEO Regional Language Centre. 81–93.

Kristeva, Julia. 1988. *Étrangers à nous-mêmes*. Paris: Gallimard.

Kuhn, Thomas S. 1962. *The structure of scientific revolutions*. Chicago: University of Chicago Press.

Lakoff, Robin. 1973. The logic of politeness; or, minding your p's and q's. In *Papers from the ninth regional meeting of the Chicago Linguistic Society*. Chicago: University of Chicago Department of Linguistics. 292–305.

Lang, Ewald. 1979. Zum Status der Satzadverbiale. *Slovo a Slovesnost* 40:200–213.

Langenscheidt Standard German Dictionary. 1983. New York: Langenscheidt.

Langford, Ian. To appear. Fair trial: The history of an idea. Submitted to *International Journal of Speech, Language and the Law*: Forensic Linguistics.

Leech, Geoffrey. 1983. *Principles of pragmatics*. London: Longman.

Leech, Geoffrey, and Jan Svartvik. 1975. *A communicative grammar of English*. London: Longman.

Levin, David, ed. 1963. *The Puritan in the Enlightenment: Franklin and Edwards*. Chicago: Rand McNally.

Lewis, C. S. 1989. *The case for Christianity*. New York: Collier.

Lewis, Clarence Irving. 1955. *The ground and nature of the right*. New York: Columbia University Press.

Li, Ming. 2004. The need to integrate language and culture in teaching English as a foreign language in China. In Tam and Weiss, eds. 219–231.

Literature Online. http://lion.chadwyck.com/.

Livingston, D. W., and J. T. King, eds. 1976. *Hume: A re-evaluation*. New York: Fordham University Press.

Locke, John. [1689] 1968. *A letter on toleration*. Ed. Raymond Klibansky and trans. John Wiedofft Gough. Oxford: Clarendon.

———. [1690] 1959. *An essay concerning human understanding*. Oxford: Clarendon.

———. [1690] 1960. *Two treatises of government*. New York: Cambridge University Press.

———. [1696] 1999. *The reasonableness of Christianity*. Oxford: Clarendon.

Longman dictionary of the English language. 1984. London: Longman.

Losskij, N. O. 1991. *Uslovija Absoljutnogo Dobra.* Moskva: Izdatel'stvo političeskoj literatury.

Luntz, Harold, David Hambly, and Robert Hayes, eds. 1985. *Torts: Cases and commentary.* Sydney: Butterworths.

Lutz, Catherine. 1986. Emotion, thought and estrangement: Emotion as a cultural category. *Cultural Anthropology* 1:287–309.

———. 1990. Engendered emotion: Gender, power, and the rhetoric of emotional control in American discourse. In Catherine Lutz and L. Abu-Loghod, eds. *Language and the politics of emotion.* Cambridge: Cambridge University Press. 69–91.

Lynch, Tiffany. 2000. A cross-linguistic study of particular non-physical meanings of *above, below* and *big, small.* BA honours thesis, Australian National University, Canberra.

Lyons, John. 1977. *Semantics.* 2 vols. Cambridge: Cambridge University Press.

———. 1981. *Language, meaning and context.* London: Fontana.

MacIntyre, Alasdair. 1981. *After virtue: A study in moral theory.* Notre Dame, IN: University of Notre Dame Press.

Maclean, Kenneth. 1962. *John Locke and English literature of the eighteenth century.* New York: Russell & Russell.

The Macquarie Dictionary. 1981. St Leonards, Australia: Macquarie Library.

Malouf, David. 1985. *Antipodes: Stories.* London: Chatto & Windus.

———. 2000. *Dream stuff.* London: Chatto and Windus.

———. 2003. Made in England: Australia's British inheritance. *Quarterly Essay* 12:1–66.

———. 2004. LaFontaine-Baldwin Lecture organized by the Domion Institute, University of Toronto. March 12, 2004. http://www.operation-dialogue.com/ lafontaine-baldwin/e/ 2004_speech_1.html.

Marshall, Herbert. 1955. *Mayakovsky and his poetry.* Bombay: Current Book House.

Matsumoto, Yoshiko. 1988. Reexamination of the universality of face: Politeness phenomena in Japanese. *Journal of Pragmatics* 12:403–426.

Matthews, George Hubert. 1965. *Hidatsa syntax.* London: Mouton.

Mautner, Thomas. 1996. *A dictionary of philosophy.* Cambridge: Blackwell.

McArthur, Tom. 1998. *The English languages.* Cambridge: Cambridge University Press.

———. 2001. World English(es), world dictionaries. In Bruce Moore, ed. *Who's centric now?* Oxford: Oxford University Press. 1–22.

Mikes, George. 1946. *How to be an alien.* London: Wingate.

Miller, Laura. 2000. Negative assessments in Japanese-American workplace interaction. In Helen Spencer-Oatey, ed. *Culturally speaking: Managing rapport through talk across cultures.* London: Casell. 240–254.

Milton, John. 1989. *Paradise lost.* Ed. C. Ricks. London: Penguin.

Moivre, Abraham de. [1718]1967. *The doctrine of chances, or, a method of calculating the probabilities of events in play.* London: Cass.

Montano, Josie. 2003. *Snot fair!* Melbourne: Lothian.

Morano, Anthony A. 1975. A reexamination of the reasonable doubt rule. *Boston University Law Review* 55:507–528.

More, Thomas. [1557] 1965. *A dialogue of comfort against tribulation.* Ed. L. Miles Bloomington: Indiana University Press.

Morgan, Edmund. 1958. *The Puritan dilemma: The story of John Winthrop.* Boston: Little, Brown.

Naipaul, Vidiadhar Surajprasad. 1969. *A house for Mr Biswas.* Harmondsworth, England: Penguin.

Ndebele, N S. 1987. The English language and social change in South Africa. *The English Academy Review* 4:1–6.

Newby, T. G. 1999. What's fair here is not fair everywhere: Does the American fair use doctrine violate international copyright law? *Stanford Law Review* 51(6): 1633–1663.

Novak, Michael. 1972. *The rise of the unmeltable ethnics: Politics and culture in the seventies.* New York: Macmillan.

Nuyts, Jan. 2001. *Epistemic modality, language, and conceptualization.* Amsterdam: John Benjamins.

OED. *Oxford English dictionary.* Oxford University Press. http://dictionary.oed.com.

OED. 1989. *Oxford English dictionary.* 2nd ed. Oxford: Clarendon.

Okudaira, Akiko. 1999. A study of international communication in regional organizations: The use of English as the "official" language of ASEAN. *Asian Englishes* 2 (1): 97–107.

Old Bailey proceedings online. www.oldbaileyonline.org.

Oxford advanced learner's dictionary. 2005. New York: Oxford University Press.

Oxford companion to philosophy. 1995. Ed. T. Honderich. Oxford: Oxford University Press.

Paikeday, Thomas M. 1985. *The native speaker is dead!* Toronto: Paikeday.

Parakrama, Arjuna. 1995. *De-hegemonizing language standards: Learning from (post)colonial Englishes about "English."* Basingstoke, England: Macmillan.

Parker, David. 2001. The global banyan tree: English, culture and Western modernity. An inaugural lecture at the Chinese University of Hong Kong. http://www.cuhk.edu.hk/puo/prof/index.htm.

———. 2003. Introduction. Anglophone cultures in South East Asia: Decolonisation and beyond. In Rüdiger Ahrens, David Parker, Klaus Stierstorfer, and Kwok-kan Tam, eds. *Anglophone cultures in Southeast Asia.* Heidelberg: Universitätsverlag. 13–16.

———. 2004. Global English, culture, and Western modernity. (A revised version of Parker 2001). In K.K. Tam and Timothy Weiss, eds. 23–42.

Pavlenko, Aneta. 2001. In the world of the tradition, I was unimagined: Negotiation of identities in cross-cultural autobiographies. *The International Journal of Bilingualism* 5 (3): 317–344.

Paxman, Jeremy. 1999. *The English: A portrait of a people.* London: Penguin.

Pennycook, Alastair. 1994. *The cultural politics of English as an international language.* New York: Longman.

Phillipson, Robert. 1992. *Linguistic imperialism.* Oxford: Oxford University Press.

Piaget, Jean. 1950. *The moral judgement of the child.* London: Routledge and Kegan Paul.

———. 1969. *Le Jugement Moral Chez L'enfant.* Paris: Presses Universitaires de France.

Pinker, Steven. 2002. *The blank slate: The modern denial of human nature.* London: Allen Lane.

Podleskaya, Vera. 2004. Auxiliation of "give" verbs in Russian: Discourse evidence, for grammaticalization. *Sprachtypologie und Universalienforschung.* Fasc 4.

Porpora, Douglas V. 2001. *Landscapes of the soul: The loss of moral meaning in American life.* New York: Oxford University Press.

Porter, Roy. 2000. *Enlightenment: Britain and the creation of the modern world.* London: Penguin.

Preisler, Bent. 1999. Functions and forms of English in a European EFL country. In Tony Bex and Richard J. Watts, eds. *Standard English: The widening debate.* London: Routledge. 239–267.

Prichard, H. A. 1935. The meaning of *Agathon* in the ethics of Aristotle. *Philosophy* 10:27–39.

Queensland Government. 2002. You and the law: Bullying. http://www.justice.qld.gov.au/education/law/bullying.htm.

Quinn, Naomi. 2002. Cultural selves. Paper presented at the New York Academy of Sciences conference "The self: From soul to brain." New York. Revised version published in *The self: from soul to brain,* ed. J. LeDoux, J. Debiec, & H. Moss. *Annals of the New York Academy of Sciences,* Vol. 1001 (October 2003). 145–176.

Quirk, Randolph. 1981. International communication and the concept of nuclear English. In Larry E. Smith, ed. *English for cross-cultural communication*. New York: St. Martin's. 151–165.

Quirk, Randolph, Sydney Greenbaum, Geoffrey Leech, and Jan Svartvik. 1972. *A grammar of contemporary English*. London: Longman.

Quirk, Randolph, Jan Svartvik, Geoffrey Leech, and Sydney Greenbaum. 1985. *A comprehensive grammar of the English language*. London: Longman.

Rardin, R. 1968. Sentence-raising and sentence-shift. Unpublished paper, Massachusetts Institute of Technology.

Rawls, John. 1999. *A theory of justice*. Cambridge, MA: Belknap.

———. 2001. *Justice as fairness*: A restatement. Cambridge, MA: Belknap.

Reid, J. S. C. 1968. The law and the reasonable man. In *The proceedings of the British Academy*. Vol. 54. London: Oxford University Press.

Rihbany, Abraham Mitrie. 1920. *The Syrian Christ*. London: A. Melrose.

Robberecht, P., and M. van Peteghem. 1982. *A functional model for the description of modality*. Paper presented at the Fifth International Conference on Contrastive Projects, Jyväskylä, Finland.

Ross, William David. 1955. *The right and the good*. Oxford: Clarendon.

Russell, Bertrand. [1935] 1948. *Sceptical essays*. London: George Allen and Unwin.

Sackville-West, Vita. 1947. *Devil at Westease: the story as related by Roger Liddiard*. Garden City, NY: Doubleday

Saltman, Michael. 1991. *The demise of the "reasonable man": A cross-cultural study of a legal concept*. New Brunswick, NJ: Transaction.

Sandall, Roger. 2000. The Book of Isaiah. *Quadrant* June, 10–19.

Sapir, Edward. [1924] 1949. Language. In D. G. Mandelbaun, ed. *Selected writings of Edward Sapir in language, culture and personality*. Berkeley: University of California Press. 7–23.

Scarcella, Robin, and Joanna Brunak. 1981. On speaking politely in a second language. *International Journal of the Sociology of Language* 27:59–75.

Scheibman, Joanne. 2000. I dunno: A usage-based account of the phonological reduction of don't in American English conversation. *Journal of Pragmatics* 32:105–124.

———. 2001. Local patterns of subjectivity in person and verb type in American English conversation. In Bybee J. and P. Hopper, eds. *Frequency and the emergence of linguistic structure*. Amsterdam: John Benjamins. 61–89.

Schiffrin, Deborah. 1984. Jewish argument as sociability. *Language in Society* 13:311–335.

Schwartz, S. H. 1994. Studying human values. In A.-M. Bouvy, J. R. Fons, P. B. van de Vijver, and P. Schmitz, eds. *Journeys into cross-cultural psychology*. Amsterdam: Swets and Zeitlinger. 239–254.

Scollon, Ron, and Suzanne Scollon. 1983. *Narrative, literacy and face in interethnic communication*, Norwood, NJ: Ablex.

———. 2001. *Intercultural communication*, 2nd ed. Oxford: Blackwell.

Searle, John R. 1975. Indirect speech acts. In Peter Cole and Jerry L. Morgan, eds. *Syntax and semantics 3: Speech acts*. New York: Academic Press. 59–82.

Seidlhofer, Barbara. 2000. Mind the gap: English as a mother tongue vs. English as a *lingua franca*. *Vienna English Working Papers* 9 (1): 51–68.

———. 2001. Closing a conceptual gap: The case for a description of English as a lingua franca. *International Journal of Applied Linguistics* 11 (2): 133–158.

Shakespeare, William. 1986. *The complete works*. Ed. S. Wells and G. Taylor. Oxford: Oxford University Press.

Shapin, Steven, and Simon Schaffer. 1985. *Leviathan and the air-pump: Hobbes, Boyle, and the experimental life*. Princeton, NJ: Princeton University Press.

Shapiro, Barbara J. 1983. *Probability and certainty in seventeenth-century England: A study of the relationships between natural science, religion, history, law, and literature.* Princeton, NJ: Princeton University Press.

———. 1991. *Beyond reasonable doubt and probable cause.* Berkeley: University of California Press.

———. 2000. *A culture of fact: England, 1550–1720.* Ithaca, NY: Cornell University Press.

Sharrock, Roger. 1965. Introduction. In John Bunyan, *The pilgrim's progress.* Ed. R. Sharrock. Harmondsworth, England: Penguin. 7–26.

Shorter Oxford English dictionary on historical principles. 1964. Oxford: Oxford University Press.

Shweder, Richard, Mahapatra, M., and Miller, J. G. 1990. Culture and moral development. In James W. Stigler, Richard A. Shweder, and Gilbert S. Herdt, eds. *Cultural psychology: Essays on comparative human development.* Cambridge: Cambridge University Press. 130–204.

Sibley, W. M. 1953. The rational versus the reasonable. *Philosophical Review* 62:554–560.

Simon-Vandenbergen, Anne-Marie. 1998. *I think* and its Dutch equivalents in parliamentary debates. In J. Stig and S. Oksefjell, eds. *Corpora and cross-linguistic research: Theory, method and case studies.* Atlanta: Rodopi. 297–317.

Smith, Zadie. 2000. *White teeth.* London: Penguin.

Snell, George Davis. 1988. *Search for a rational ethic.* New York: Springer-Verlag.

Solan, Lawrence M. 1999. Refocusing on the burden of proof in criminal cases: Some doubts about reasonable doubt. *Texas Law Review* 78:105–147.

Solzhenitsyn, Aleksandr. n.d. *Rakovyj Korpus.* Samizdat.

———1969. *Cancer ward.* Trans. N. Bethell and D. Burg. New York: Farrar, Straus and Giroux.

Speer, Albert. 1975. *Spandauer Tagebücher.* Frankfurt: Propyläen.

Spencer, Herbert. 1892. *Social statics.* London: Williams and Norgate.

Spencer-Oatley, Helen. 2000. Rapport management: A framework for analysis. In Helen Spencer-Oatley, ed. *Culturally speaking.* London: Continuum. 11–46.

Spevack, Marvin. 1970. *A complete and systematic concordance to the works of Shakespeare.* Hildesheim, Germany: Georg Olms.

Stearns, Peter, and Carol Z. Stearns. 1986. *Anger: The struggle for emotional control in America's history.* Chicago: University of Chicago Press.

Stearns, Peter N. 1994. *American cool: Constructing a twentieth-century emotional style.* New York: New York University Press.

Stein, Gabriele. 1979. Nuclear English: Reflections on the structure of its vocabulary. *Poetica* (Tokyo: Sanseido International) 10:64–76.

Stevens, S. S. 1951. *Handbook of experimental psychology.* New York: J. Wiley.

Stevenson, Burton. 1958. *Stevenson's book of quotations: Classical and modern.* London: Cassell.

Stoffel, Cornelis. 1901. *Intensives and down-toners: A study in English adverbs.* Heidelberg: Carl Winter.

Strauss, Claudia, and Naomi Quinn. 1997. *A cognitive theory of cultural meaning.* Cambridge: Cambridge University Press.

Talmy, Leonard. 1976. Semantic causative types. In M. Shibatani, ed. *Syntax and semantics 6: The grammar of causative constructions.* New York: Academic Press. 43–116.

Tam, Kwok-kan and Timothy Weiss, eds. 2004. *English and Globalization: Perspectives from Hong Kong and Mainland China.* Hong Kong: The Chinese University Press.

Tannen, Deborah. 1986. *That's not what I meant! How conversational style makes or breaks relationships.* New York: Ballantine.

Taylor, Charles. 1989. *Sources of the self: The making of the modern identity.* Cambridge, MA: Harvard University Press.

Thompson, Sandra A., and Anthony Mulac. 1991. A quantitative perspective on the grammaticization of epistemic parentheticals in English. In Elisabeth Closs Traugott and Bernd Heine, eds. *Approaches to grammaticalization*. Amsterdam: John Benjamins. 313–331.

Tocqueville, Alexis de. 1966. *Democracy in America*. Trans. G. Lawrence. 2 vols. New York: Harper and Row.

Tong, Goh Chok. 2000. ASEAN-US relations: Challenges. Keynote speech at the ASEAN–United States Partnership Conference, New York. http://aseansec.org/2806.htm.

Toolan, Michael. 2003. English as the supranational language of human rights? In C Mair, ed. *The politics f English language: New horizons in postcolonical cultural studies*. Amsterdam: Radopi. 53–65.

Toynbee, Polly. 2002. Religion isn't nice. It kills. *The Guardian*. September 6.

Traugott, Elisabeth Closs. 1989. On the rise of epistemic meanings in English: An example of subjectification in semantic change. *Language* 65:31–55.

———. 1995. Subjectification in grammaticalisation. In Dieter Stein and Susan Wright, eds. *Subjectivity and subjectivication: Linguistic perspectives*. Cambridge: Cambridge University Press.

Travis, Catherine. 2001. *A semantic analysis of discourse markers in Colombian Spanish*. PhD thesis, La Trobe University, Melbourne.

———. 2005. *Discourse markers in Colombian Spanish: A study in polysemy*. Berlin: Mouton de Gruyter.

Tuchman, Barbara W. [1956] 2001. *Bible and sword: England and Palestine from the Bronze Age to Balfour*. London: Phoenix.

Uplinger, S. 1997. English-language training for air traffic controllers must go beyond basic ATC vocabulary. *Airport Operations* (Flight Safety Foundation) 23/5: 1–5.

Urmson, James O. 1956. Parenthetical verbs. In Anthony Flew, ed., *Essays in conceptual analysis*. London: Macmillan.

Usborne Bible Tales. The Prodigal Son. www.usborne.com.

Uspenskij, Boris. 1996. Rol' dual'nyx modelej v dinamike russkoj kul'tury. In his *Izbrannye trudy*, tom I. Moscow: Jazyki Russkoj Kultury. 338–380.

van Leeuwen, Henry G. 1963. *The problem of certainty in English thought, 1630–1690*. The Hague: Martinus Nijhoff.

Verhagen, Arie. 1995. Subjectification, syntax and communication. In Dieter Stein and Susan Wright, eds. *Subjectivity and subjectivisation: Linguistic perspectives*. Cambridge: Cambridge University Press. 103–128.

Visser, Fredericus. 1973. *An historical syntax of the English language*. Leiden: E. J. Brill.

Waal, Frans de. 1996. *Good natured: The origins of right and wrong in humans and other animals*. Cambridge, MA: Harvard University Press.

Wang, Yanyan. 2005. An analysis of 'whinging', 'dobbing' and 'mateship' in Australian contemporary culture. *Language, Society and Culture* 15. http://www.educ.utas.edu.au/users/tle/JOURNAL/ARTICLES/2005/15–4.htm

Wardhaugh, Ronald. 1987. *Languages in competition: Dominance, diversity and decline*. Oxford: Basil Blackwell.

Weber, Max. [1930] 1968. *The Protestant ethic and the spirit of capitalism*. Trans. E. Fischoff. London: Allen and Unwin.

White, Margaret. 1997. *Let's be reasonable: A guide to resolving disputes*. Sydney: Choice.

Widdowson, H. G. 1994. The ownership of English. *TESOL Quarterly* 28 (2): 377–389.

Wierzbicka, Anna. 1972. *Semantic primitives*. Frankfurt am Main: Athenäum.

———1976. Particles and linguistic relativity. *International Review of Slavic Linguistics* 1:327–367.

———. 1984. Diminutives and depreciatives: Semantic representation for derivational categories. *Quaderni di Semantica* 5 (1): 123–130.

———. 1985. Different cultures, different languages, different speech acts: English vs. Polish. *Journal of Pragmatics* 9:145–178.

———. 1986a. Does language reflect culture? Evidence from Australian English. *Language in Society* 15:349 -374.

———. 1986b. Introduction. Special issue on particles. *Journal of Pragmatics* 10 (5): 519–534.

———. 1987. *English speech act verbs: A semantic dictionary.* Sydney: Academic Press.

———. 1988. *The semantics of grammar.* Amsterdam: John Benjamins.

———. 1991. *Cross-cultural pragmatics: The semantics of human interaction.* Berlin: Mouton de Gruyter. Expanded 2nd ed., 2003.

———. 1992. *Semantics, culture, and cognition: Universal human concepts in culture-specific configurations.* New York: Oxford University Press.

———. 1994a. "Cultural scripts": A new approach to the study of cross-cultural communication. In Martin Pütz, ed. *Language contact and language conflict.* Amsterdam: John Benjamins. 69–88.

———. 1994b. "Cultural scripts": A semantic approach to cultural analysis and cross-cultural communication. *Pragmatics and Language Learning, Monograph Series* 5:1–24.

———. 1994c. Emotion, language, and "cultural scripts." In Shinobu Kitayama and Hazel Rose Markus, eds. *Emotion and culture: Empirical studies of mutual influence.* Washington, DC: American Psychological Association. 130–198.

— — —. 1996a. Contrastive sociolinguistics and the theory of "cultural scripts." In M. Hellinger and U. Ammon, eds. *Contrastive sociolinguistics.* Berlin: Mouton de Gruyter. 313–344.

———. 1996b. Japanese cultural scripts: Cultural psychology and "cultural grammar." *Ethos* 24 (3): 527–555.

———. 1996c. *Semantics: Primes and universals.* Oxford: Oxford University Press.

———. 1997. *Understanding cultures through their key words: English, Russian, Polish, German, and Japanese.* New York: Oxford University Press.

———. 1998a. Anchoring linguistic typology in universal semantic primes. *Linguistic Typology* 1998:141–194.

———. 1998b. German cultural scripts: Public signs as a key to social attitudes and cultural values. *Discourse and Society* 9 (2): 241–282.

———. 1998c. The semantics of English causative constructions in a universal-typological perspective. In Michael Tomasello, ed. *The new psychology of language: Cognitive and functional approaches to language structure.* Mahwah, NJ: Erlbaum. 113–153.

———. 1998d. THINK: A universal human concept and a conceptual primitive. In Jacek Jadacki, ed. *In the world of signs: Essays in Honour of Jerzy Pelc* (Poznan Studies in the Philosophy of the Sciences and the Humanities, vol. 62). Warsaw: Państwowe Wydawnictwo Naukowe. 297–308.

———. 1999. *Emotions across languages and cultures: Diversity and universals.* Cambridge: Cambridge University Press.

———. 2001. *What did Jesus mean? Explaining the Sermon on the Mount and the parables in simple and universal human concepts.* New York: Oxford University Press.

———.2002a. Australian cultural scripts: *Bloody* revisited. *Journal of Pragmatics* 34 (9): 1167–1209.

———. 2002b. English causative constructions in an ethnosyntactic perspective: Focusing on LET. In Nick Enfield, ed. *Ethnosyntax.* Oxford: Oxford University Press. 162–203.

———. 2002c. Russian cultural scripts: The theory of cultural scripts and its applications. *Ethos* 30 (4): 401–432.

——. 2002d. Philosophy and discourse: The rise of *really* and the fall of *truly*. In Christine Béal, ed. *Langue, discours, culture* (Special issue of *Les Cahiers de Praxématique* 38: 85–112).

——. 2003a. *Cross-cultural pragmatics: The semantics of human interaction*. 2nd ed. Berlin: Mouton de Gruyter.

——. 2003b. Sexism in grammar: The semantics of gender in Australian English. *Anthropological Linguistics* 44 (2): 143–177.

——. 2003c. Singapore English: A semantic and cultural perspective. *Multilingua* 22:327–366.

——. 2004. The English expressions "good boy" and "good girl" and cultural models of child rearing. *Culture and Psychology* 10 (3): 251–278.

——. 2005a. In defense of 'culture'. *Theory and Psychology*. 15 (4): 575–597.

——. 2005b. Universal human concepts as a tool for exploring bilingual lives. *International Journal of Bilingualism* 9 (1): 7–26.

——. In press a. Anglo scripts against "putting pressure" on other people and their linguistic manifestations. In Cliff Goddard, ed. *Ethnopragmatics*. Berlin: Mouton De Gruyter

——. In press b. There are no 'colour universals', but there are universals of visual semantics. *Anthropological Linguistics*.

——. In press c. The semantics of colour: A new paradigm. *Progress in Colour Studies*. Carole Biggam and Christian Kay, eds. Amsterdam: John Benjamins.

——. In press d. "Reasonably well": NSM as a tool for the study of phraseology and of its cultural underpinnings. In Paul Skandera, ed. *Idiom(s) and culture(s) in English*. Berlin: Mouton de Gruyter.

——. Forthcoming. The concept of *evidence*: Historical semantics as a gateway to the history of ideas and history of culture.

Wilkins, John. [1693] 1969. *Of the principles and duties of natural religion: Two books*. London: R. Chiswall, W. Battersby and C. Brome.

Wilson, James O. 1994. *The moral sense: An essay*. St. Leonards, NSW: The Centre for Independent Studies.

Wolseley, Charles. 1675. *The unreasonableness of atheism made manifest*. London: n.p.

Wong, Jock. 2004a. Cultural scripts, ways of speaking and perceptions of personal autonomy: Anglo English vs. Singapore English. Special issue on cultural scripts, ed. Cliff Goddard and Anna Wierzbicka, *Intercultural Pragmatics* 1 (2): 231–248.

——. 2004b. The particles of Singapore English: A semantic and cultural interpretation. *Journal of Pragmatics* 36:739–793.

——. 2005. Singapore English: A semantic and cultural interpretation. PhD dissertation, Australian National University, Canberra.

Wright, Sue. 2000. *Community and communication: The role of language in nation state building and European integration*. Clevedon, England: Multilingual Matters.

Ye, Zhengdao. 2004. Chinese categorization of interpersonal relationships and the cultural logic of Chinese social interaction: An indigenous perspective Special issue on cultural scripts, ed. Cliff Goddard and Anna Wierzbicka, *Intercultural Pragmatics* 1 (2). 211–230.

Yolton, John W. 1977. *The Locke reader: Selections from the works of John Locke, with a general introduction and commentary*. Cambridge: Cambridge University Press.

Yong, Ong Keng. 2003. *Mobilizing multilateral resources in the war against terrorism: The role of ASEAN inside and outside of Southeast Asia*. Inaugural Asia-Pacific Homeland Security Summit, Honolulu, HI. http://www.aseansec.org/15399.htm.

Yoon, Kyung-Joo. 2004. Not just words: Korean social models and the use of honorifics. Special issue on cultural scripts, ed. Cliff Goddard and Anna Wierzbicka, *Intercultural Pragmatics* 1 (2): 189–210.

Index

Note: In addition to subjects and proper names, this index lists (*in italics*) words from several languages that are discussed in the book. Non-English words are followed by a rough gloss for ease of reference, but this must not be taken as equivalent in meaning to the word discussed in the text. Abbreviations used include Du[tch], Fr[ench], Ge[rman], Gr[eek], It[alian], Ja[panese], La[tin], Po[lish], Ru[ssian], Sw[edish]. Other abbreviations are adj[adjective], n[noun], pl[plural], pp[past participle], vb[verb].